'If Elected...'

UNSUCCESSFUL CANDIDATES FOR THE PRESIDENCY 1796-1968

The Staff of the Historian's Office
National Portrait Gallery

LILLIAN B. MILLER, *Historian*
BEVERLY J. COX, *Assistant Historian*
FREDERICK S. VOSS, *Research Historian*
JEANNETTE M. HUSSEY, *Research Assistant*
JUDITH S. KING, *Secretary and Research Aide*

Published for the National Portrait Gallery, Smithsonian Institution
by the SMITHSONIAN INSTITUTION PRESS
City of Washington, 1972

104324

Exhibition organized by Beverly J. Cox, assistant
historian, and Harold Francis Pfister, curatorial assistant.
Exhibition installation designed by James Shelton, chief of
exhibits, design, and production, and Joseph M. Carrigan,
assistant chief of exhibits, design, and production.

Library of Congress Cataloging in Publication Data
National Portrait Gallery, Washington, D.C.
Historian's Office
"If Elected . . . ." Unsuccessful Candidates for the Presidency, 1796-1968
Bibliography: p.
1. Presidents—U.S.—Election.   2. U.S.—Biography.   I. Miller,
    Lillian B.   II. Title.
E176.N3   973'.00992 [B]   72-1304

First edition, 1972
Second printing, 1973
Third printing, 1975

For sale by the Superintendent of Documents
United States Government Printing Office
Washington, D.C. 20402
Price: $9.50   Stock number 4706-0008

Table of Contents

Foreword

In the contest for the presidency where the only prize is victory, a full-scale study devoted to the candidates who ran and lost might seem little more than curiosity, especially in a world where losing is regarded as something of a stigma. There are, however, many things that this study reveals about this country and its electoral processes, as well as about the presidency itself. Indeed, it is worth noting that fully one-third of the men who occupied the office also lost it: Jefferson, Jackson, William Henry Harrison, and Nixon—before their ultimate victories; and John Adams, John Quincy Adams, Van Buren, Cleveland (who returned to win again four years later), Benjamin Harrison, Taft, Theodore Roosevelt, and Hoover—after they had once been elected. In addition, Pierce was not renominated, and Tyler, Fillmore, Andrew Johnson, and Arthur, who came to office on the deaths of their predecessors, did not win their parties' nominations to succeed themselves.

While the following accounts amply demonstrate that most elections have been decided on major political, economic, and social questions, they also disclose that coupled with these larger issues, more vagrant elements occasionally have played a decisive role, sometimes just tipping the scales, in determining who was to be president and who was not.

The most conspicuous examples of this phenomenon took place during the elections of 1884 and 1916. In the former, after Tammany had instructed its minions not to support New York's Democratic governor and presidential candidate Grover Cleveland, and it consequently appeared that Republican contender James G. Blaine would carry this pivotal state and thereby win the election, two incidents which took place just six days before the voting are believed to have turned the tide. The Reverend S. D. Burchard of the Murray Hill Presbyterian Church, speaking at a rally at the Fifth Avenue Hotel, pledged his support for Blaine, who was on the platform, stating that the Protestant clergy would not vote for his opponent, whose party he characterized as one of "rum, Romanism, and rebellion." The middle word of Burchard's alliteration was particularly damaging for it alienated the state's Irish, whom Blaine had taken pains to cultivate. In addition, that very night Blaine was the guest of honor at an exceptionally opulent fund-raising dinner at Delmonico's, which a New York *World* cartoon devastatingly satirized as "Belshazzar Blaine and the Money Kings," pointing out

Blaine's association with big business interests at a time when the majority of Americans were bearing the brunt of a severe economic depression. On election day, Cleveland took New York from Blaine by 1,149 votes out of a total of 1,125,159, and with it the presidency.

If three words and a lavish fund-raising dinner made (or, more likely, unmade) one president in 1884, the neglect of a simple handshake probably reelected another in 1916. In that campaign, conservative Republican advisors persuaded their candidate Charles Evans Hughes to ignore progressive Republican Governor Hiram W. Johnson of California, who was running for the United States Senate. While Johnson won by a plurality of 300,000 votes, Hughes lost California to Wilson by 3,800. As New York Congressman John W. Dwight observed, "If a man of sense, with a dollar, would have invited Hughes and Johnson to his room when they were both in the same Hotel in California . . . he would have ordered three Scotch whiskies, which would have been seventy-five cents, and that would have left a tip of twenty-five cents for the waiter. . . . That little Scotch would have brought those men together; there would have been mutual understanding and respect and Hughes would have carried California and been elected."

Although none of the third-party candidates, whose careers and campaigns form such a large part of this study, ever won the presidency, sometimes by capturing the consciences of more Americans than those who voted for them, they played important roles in shaping the policies of candidates of the two major parties—and hence ultimately the future of the nation.

In 1892, James B. Weaver, as the first presidential candidate of the Populist Party, garnered a million popular and 22 electoral votes. Weaver's Populist platform forecast things to come by advocating, among other things, a graduated income tax, direct election of United States senators, and the regulation of work hours for laboring groups. Far better known are Socialist candidates Eugene V. Debs, who ran in five elections between 1900 and 1920, and Norman Thomas, in six from 1928 to 1948, both of whom contributed significantly to the formation of future labor and social legislation.

Happily, not all third-party candidates have been so influential. Thomas E. Watson,

Bryan's Populist running mate in 1896, was the Populist presidential nominee in 1904. Subsequently, Watson, who was again his party's candidate in 1908, began to infuse into his politics a highly intolerant view of blacks, Catholics, and Jews. A quarter of a century later, William Lemke, the presidential nominee of the Union Party in 1936, received nearly 900,000 votes running on a Populist platform supported by reactionaries like anti-Semite Father Charles E. Coughlin.

Although no third-party candidate has ever been elected, three have won significantly large popular votes: Theodore Roosevelt on the Progressive ticket in 1921 (4,120,000, 27.5 percent); Robert M. LaFollette, Progressive and Socialist (4,800,000, 16.5 percent); and George Wallace, American Independence Party (9,900,000, 13.5 percent). Short of outright victory, a third-party candidate with enough electoral votes to deprive either of the other two candidates a majority would throw the election into the House of Representatives where each state has one vote, and the representatives casting those votes are free to choose anyone they wish. Under these circumstances, it is conceivable that such a candidate might himself be elected or be a powerful force in the election of a president. The House has decided only two elections, those of 1800 and 1824, in both of which all the candidates were members of the same party. In 1824, Andrew Jackson, who had a popular plurality, had an insufficient number of electoral votes. In this case, Henry Clay, last in the electoral tally, threw his influence behind Adams, who was elected.

This roster of unsuccessful candidates for the presidency contains the names of those who were president, as well as those who never won the prize, including major-party candidates who tried twice (Charles Cotesworth Pinckney, Thomas E. Dewey, and Adlai E. Stevenson) or even three times (Henry Clay and William Jennings Bryan), plus the even larger number of third-party candidates. Here are contenders who were greater than their victorious opponents (and those who were not), as well as losers who were fairly evenly matched against winners in terms of ability (or the lack of it). Here, too, are names which only studies such as this recall from near oblivion, like Winfield Scott Hancock and Alton B. Parker (although Franklin Pierce and Rutherford B. Hayes are scarcely better known, presidents though they were).

Without attempting to pass judgment on the verdicts of our presidential elections—and bearing in mind that the American electorate includes those who don't vote as well as those who do—it probably is fair to observe that the nation usually gets what it wants, sometimes what it deserves, and more rarely what it needs. One of the great glories of the contest for the presidency is that whatever the verdict, it is accepted, and the opposition is free to continue to promote its cause, always culminating in another quadrennial election. As one unsuccessful candidate for the presidency, Adlai Stevenson, put it so eloquently: "There are things more precious than political victory; there is the right to political contest." May it ever be so.

Marvin Sadik, *Director*
National Portrait Gallery

Lenders

American Antiquarian Society, Worcester,
Massachusetts

The children of Mrs. Oakes Ames

Anonymous lenders

Archives of Industrial Society, University of
Pittsburgh Libraries

The Association of the Bar of the City of
New York

Bayly Museum of Art, University of Virginia,
Charlottesville

Mrs. Dion Scott Birney, Washington, D.C.

Carolina Art Association, Gibbes Art Gallery,
Charleston, South Carolina

Chester County Historical Society, West Chester,
Pennsylvania

Chicago Historical Society

Columbia County Historical Society, Kinderhook,
New York

Columbia Museum of Art, Columbia,
South Carolina

The Corcoran Gallery of Art, Washington, D.C.

Cornell University, Collection of Regional History
and University Archives, Ithaca, New York

Cortland County Historical Society, Inc., Cortland,
New York

The Cox family

Robert R. Coxey, Charlotte, North Carolina

Department of State, Washington, D.C.

The Detroit Historical Museum

Thomas E. Dewey, Jr., New York City

The Filson Club, Louisville, Kentucky

Harry Fleischman, New York City

The Free Library of Philadelphia

Georgia State Capitol Collection, Atlanta

Mrs. Barry Goldwater, Washington, D.C.

Mrs. John Hammond, Washington, D.C.

Houghton Library, Harvard University,
Cambridge, Massachusetts

Thomas W. Harvey, Chevy Chase, Maryland

Eric Hass, New York City

Julia Davis Healy, Princeton, New Jersey

Senator Hubert H. Humphrey, Washington, D.C.

Illinois State Capitol Collection, Springfield

Indianapolis Museum of Art

Kansas State Historical Society, Topeka

Dan Kramer, New York City

LaFollette Senior High School, Madison, Wisconsin

Lancaster County Historical Society, Lancaster,
Pennsylvania

Alfred M. Landon, Topeka, Kansas

Robert M. Lemke, Potomac, Maryland

Library of Congress

Madison County Historical Society, Oneida,
New York

Metropolitan Museum of Art

University of Michigan

The Mariners Museum, Newport News, Virginia

Museum of the City of New York

The National Gallery of Art

National Museum of History and Technology,
Division of Political History (Ralph E. Becker
Collection), Smithsonian Institution

The Newberry Library, Chicago, Illinois

New Jersey Historical Society, Newark

The New York Public Library

New York State Historical Association,
Cooperstown

New York State Office of General Services,
Albany

Pennsylvania Academy of the Fine Arts,
Philadelphia

The Historical Society of Pennsylvania,
Philadelphia

Pioneer Hi-Bred International Inc., Des Moines,
Iowa

Mrs. Francis T. P. Plimpton, New York City

Portland Museum of Art, Portland, Maine

Mr. and Mrs. Jackson P. Ravenscroft, Tucson,
Arizona

Peter J. Rizzutto, Peekskill, New York

Franklin Delano Roosevelt Library, Hyde Park,
New York

Mr. and Mrs. Richard C. Sachs, Brooklyn Heights,
New York

Barbara Shickman, Washington, D.C.

Elna M. Smith Foundation, Eureka Springs,
Arkansas

Tennessee Historical Society, Nashville

Senator Strom Thurmond, Washington, D.C.

TIME, The Weekly Newsmagazine

The Union League Club, New York City

United States Capitol

Francis Vigo Chapter, Daughters of the American
Revolution, Vincennes, Indiana

Chauncey Lockhart Waddell, New York City

Mrs. John A. Warner, New York City

Annie E. Woodman Institute, Dover,
New Hampshire

Worcester Art Museum, Worcester, Massachusetts

Acknowledgments

In assembling the portraits and related materials included in this exhibition, we have necessarily relied on the invaluable assistance and encouragement of local historical societies, libraries and biographers, and friends and families of the candidates. Among the descendants, other than those lending portraits, to whom we owe a debt of gratitude are Mrs. Francis T. P. Plimpton (for Benjamin F. Butler), Mrs. Theodore Oxholm (for Alton B. Parker), Tom Watson Brown (for Thomas E. Watson), Frances Gates (for Norman Thomas), Bronson and Mary LaFollette (for Robert LaFollette), Mrs. Henry A. Wallace (for Henry A. Wallace), and Mrs. Emily Smith Warner (for Alfred E. Smith).

We are particularly grateful to Governor Nelson Rockefeller of New York, Governor Jimmy Carter of Georgia, and Illinois' Secretary of State John W. Lewis for permission to borrow portraits from the public collections of their respective states. Other interested and helpful persons have included George Brownell, Professors Betty Fladeland and Edward Blackorby, Dr. Gladys Baker, Father Edward F. McSweeney, Frank Zabrosky, and Peter Munsing. Mrs. Lorethea Hamke, Gerald T. MacDonough, William Pillsbury, R. Wayne Skidmore, and Mrs. Joan Siedenberg have also been very cooperative in our search for portraits.

The associated materials in this exhibition have, for the most part, come from five institutions, the staffs of which have been especially helpful. Herbert Collins of the Division of Political History, National Museum of History and Technology, Smithsonian Institution; Milton Kaplan of the Division of Prints and Photographs, Library of Congress; Joseph Zywicki and Mrs. Mary Frances Rhymer of the Chicago Historical Society; and Dorothy Lapp and Travis Coxe of the Chester County Historical Society have spent much time and effort in showing us through their collections and facilitating the borrowing process. Our particular thanks go to Barbara Shepherd and Herbert Finch of Cornell University's Collection of Regional History and University Archives for their cheerful enthusiasm and selfless exertions on our behalf.

The entire National Portrait Gallery staff has been more than helpful throughout our preparations. For coordination of information and details Suzanne Jenkins, Curatorial Department secretary, deserves our special thanks, as does Jon Freshour, Registrar of the Gallery, who has arranged all details of shipment and loans. We are grateful, also, to the staff of the

NPG/NCFA Library, and especially to William Walker, Librarian, and Joyce Chisley, for their patience and cooperation.

Without the cooperative response from the institutions and individuals who have agreed to share with us their portraits and memorabilia, there would be no exhibition, and we are deeply grateful for their generosity.

Beverly J. Cox
Harold Francis Pfister

Introduction

Every four years, on the first Tuesday following the first Monday in November, according to Constitutional law and custom, the American citizen is called upon to express his private preference for the next president of the United States. The ritual is uniquely American, as is the frequently wide range of candidates, representing all kinds of causes, reform movements, ideologies, or eccentricities. Against a background of campaign rhetoric with which he has been barraged daily, sometimes hourly, for months preceding the set date, the American voter must make a choice; out of the confusion of promises, accusations, articulated aspirations and prophecies, he must select the individual and the party who seem to him most competent to handle the nation's problems, or who represent to him the best that the nation has to offer.

The American presidency has come to carry a meaning of its own. The president is frequently regarded as a symbol of political values as well as ideas, of national character and national morality as well as policies and programs. Sometimes Americans have preferred that their president be aristocratic and dignified in demeanor; at other times, democratic and of common sympathies. In times of confusion, a quiet-spoken conservative offers promise of order; at times of crisis, the masterful, innovative image may seem preferable. Reform groups have viewed the campaign for the presidency as a platform from which a particular reform interest could be brought to public attention. Special interest groups have agitated for the presidency to insure the introduction or continuation of favoring policies. Parties have fought for the presidency for the power it offered as well as for the patronage it provided. And individuals have sought the office for self-aggrandizement as well as for party strength, out of personal commitment to issues as much as commitment to particular social or economic interest. The belief that any American could become president of the country so long as he met the basic requirements of age and nationality has invited all sorts of people into the contest; but for whatever reasons parties or individuals or reform groups have sought the highest office in the land, there is no question that the prize was considered important enough to be pursued, that the race was open to all Americans who dared contend for it, regardless of class or status, and that in the scramble for office, democracy found its ultimate expression.

The ten crucial elections we have chosen to highlight demonstrate this latter point most clearly. All American elections, of course, have a democratic significance in that they present choices to the people that presumably are pertinent to their needs and goals. But the elections singled out for special attention here illustrate best, we believe, the way in which our political practices affect the democratic process. In the extension of the suffrage to all groups in American society through changes in election procedures, and in the presentation of party platforms concerned with the maintenance or encouragement of social and economic equality, we see the forces of democracy at work. Which programs were selected at varying times tell us something about the meaning of democracy historically, as it meant different things to different groups. In the choice of president and platform, blind or wise as it may have been, democracy found release or suppression; its cause was advanced or retarded; and its principles were clarified or obscured.

These elections also illustrate the way in which democratic change occurs in a republic like the United States. In all cases but one—1860—that change has taken place peacefully, despite the repeated lamentations of prophets of disaster that the nation was headed towards ruin. The flexibility of the party system, the knowledge that in four years alternatives to policies as well as to individuals are possible, and the fact that in all cases parties make their appeal to the same vague but nonetheless uniformly endorsed set of principles embodied in the democratic faith have permitted (except for the one aberration) peaceful succession and the effecting of change with a minimum of strain. This has been no mean achievement.

These elections also illustrate the multiplicity of factors that enter into, influence, and sometimes distort, the democratic process. Myths that are consciously or unconsciously propagated by interested parties frequently affect the course of the electoral process. Power plays, partisan concerns, temporary or transient issues, like the currency question in the late nineteenth century, class antagonisms, as in the days of Jackson's popularity, occupational pressures and religious conflicts—all these factors have at one time or another entered into a presidential contest and frequently determined its outcome. Thus, through an examination of these specially chosen elections, we see American history from a particular, but illuminating, perspective.

But why show losers? Why not emphasize successful political bids? It was not only sympathy for the underdog that propelled us to this decision, but the belief that many of the presidential aspirants who lost out in history simply because they could not command enough votes to win have an intrinsic interest of their own that ought to be recognized. Many who lost remained on the political scene long enough to eventually win; others lost after they had once been winners. Others simply disappeared from the scene, leaving behind little influence on the subsequent course of events. But they still are interesting, even if only as symbolic representations of strands in American thought that tend to be obscured by other, perhaps more significant, concerns; and as representations of facets of American life—the good and the bad—that need to be understood. It is as important to recognize, we believe, that along with the great achievements of men of intellectual breadth and humanity there has always existed in American society groups of "antis" to disturb the nation's equilibrium: anti-intellectuals, racists, anti-Semites, nativists—these groups, and the men who led them, are as significant in American political history as are the more formal party organizations and their candidates; their stories deserve serious attention.

Specific criteria were, however, applied in determining the portraits that would appear in the exhibition and the accompanying publication. Candidates of the major political parties, of course, received first consideration. Candidates nominated by permanent or long-lasting third parties also seemed to us to require inclusion. Of the minor party candidates, like those nominated by the various temperance societies, abolitionist groups, or the America First Party, we decided to include those whose position or ideology represented a movement of considerable enough proportions to command public attention during a particular period. Thus, although Eldridge Cleaver in 1968 received but a handful of votes, he is important as a representative of the Black Civil Rights movement. Earlier in the 1940s, Gerald L. K. Smith also was almost entirely ignored by the electorate, but his isolationism represented a significant minority position at the time.

The exhibition, for which this text was written, and from which the pictorial material included in this publication has been selected, was organized by Beverly J. Cox, Assistant Historian, with the assistance of Harold Francis Pfister of the Curatorial Department of the

National Portrait Gallery. The text represents the cooperative effort of the staff of the Historian's Office. Despite varying political beliefs and loyalties, decisions concerning interpretations as well as inclusions and exclusions were reached by discussion and consensus; therefore, the staff as a whole takes complete responsibility for the statements made herein.

Lillian B. Miller
Historian

From the Constitution to the Emergence of Parties 1787-1796

FROM THE OPENING OF THE PHILADELPHIA CONVENTION ON MAY 25, 1787, TO MID-SEP-tember, delegates intent on writing a new American constitution wrestled with the problem of the executive branch of government. Should the executive be a committee or a single individual? Should he hold office for duration, as a monarch, or for the length of party control, as a prime minister, or for seven years, or four? How should he be elected, and could he be reelected? And what should be his powers so that he could maintain sufficient control of policy without being tempted, by an excess of power, into dictatorial paths?

The delegates were not completely at sea. Many of them had studied ancient govern-ments. Most were versed in the law, which was still essentially English, and they were familiar with English precedent. They shared certain eighteenth-century principles, which they believed were fundamental to the political process, and they participated in an intellectual environment that was half-enlightened, half-Calvinistic, but which nevertheless gave them a fundamental language in common and principles which they could knowledgeably debate.

Yet, the sessions were long and wearying, marked by recesses and private meetings, fatigue, dullness, repetitive argumentation, and confused groping for answers to questions that had puzzled political theorists for centuries. Out of these meetings and the confusions, however, emerged a definition of the office of the president of the United States, with his duties and his limitations clearly defined; there also emerged a most confusing electoral machinery that has from 1788 to the present, at times creakingly and at times smoothly, attempted to inter-pret the results of the people's balloting.

Early in the proceedings at Philadelphia, the delegates opted for a single executive. Of the failure of triumvirates or similar multiple governing arrangements they were certain, being thor-oughly versed in Roman and ancient history. But they were still unable to resolve the manner of the president's election, the length of his term, or the nature of his office. Many delegates could not with equanimity face up to the prospect of the president being the people's choice, agreeing with George Mason of Virginia that "it would be as unnatural to refer the choice of a proper character for chief Magistrate to the people, as it would to refer a trial of colours to a blind man. The extent of the Country renders it impossible that the people can have the requisite capacity to judge of the respective pretensions of the Candidates."

But they could not agree to the alternative, either, that the chief magistrate be elected by the state governors. Edmund Randolph of Virginia maintained that since "the Executives of the States [were] . . . little conversant with characters not within their own small spheres," they would not be able to reach a wise decision. Moreover, seeking to avoid the pitfalls of state sov-ereignty that had crippled government under the Articles of Confederation, many delegates feared that election by the states—whether by state legislatures or state executives—would re-sult in candidates maintaining state loyalties rather than national, a situation that would be encouraged by state governors who would "not cherish the great Oak which is to reduce them to paltry shrubs."

Vacillating thus between fears of democracy and a theory of man's reason that invited trust in the people—after all, hadn't the Revolutionary War been waged in the name of the "people" of the various colonies?—and alternating between a fear of national power and dissatisfaction with state sovereignties—weren't the state legislatures unreliable bodies given to the passing of "pernicious measures"?—the delegates wavered between the unsatisfactory known and the theoretical, and therefore fearful, unknown.

Madison and Washington solved the dilemma—for the time, anyway. Madison cut the Gordian Knot by presenting a logically reasoned compromise proposal eliminating the judiciary, state, and national legislatures, and the people from direct participation in the selection of the president, and by compromising between popular choice and indirect election. Although his proposal was not accepted in its entirety, he stimulated the discussion which led to the final decision that the president be elected by a body of presidential electors chosen according to methods prescribed by individual state legislatures, with the number of electors equaling the combined number of federal senators and representatives to which each state was entitled. To ensure the separation of powers, a principle that was accepted by these political theorists as fundamental, the president would not be made subject to legislative interference either on the national or state level. Therefore, four years with no obstacle to reelection seemed the most satisfactory term of office, one most appropriate for rendering the president independent of legislative or congressional influence. And the complicated system of electors was established, through which the delegates hoped that the voice of the people would be expressed while at the same time, by channeling the decision through electors and Congress, the most worthy person would be selected—one acceptable to all sections because of the need for national agreement.

Washington, by his very presence, indirectly contributed to the solution of the delegates' problems, because as Pierce Butler of South Carolina candidly admitted, he did not think the powers vested in the president "would have been so great had not many of the members cast their eyes toward General Washington as President, and shaped their ideas . . . by their opinions of his Virtue." Washington was universally regarded as the logical first president, the only man capable, as Dr. Benjamin Rush of Philadelphia confessed to Timothy Pickering of Massachusetts, of restoring "order and happiness" to strife-torn Pennsylvania, or any of the other areas of contention in the new country.

In that first presidential election of 1788, Washington had no real rival, although Benjamin Franklin was approached—but he was over 80—and some in New England thought of John Adams for the office. When the votes were counted in the electoral college on April 6, 1789, Washington received one of the two votes of every elector, 69 in all. The second votes of the electors were widely scattered among eleven persons, but John Adams with 34 votes was designated vice-president.

When George Washington took office as the first president of the United States, there were no formal party organizations. Indeed, he and his compatriots shared the common eighteenth-century aversion to party spirit, believing it an evil arising only in dissolute and perverted societies and encouraged by privileged orders and defective institutions. In framing the Constitution, they purposely made no reference to political parties. Unity and harmony were paramount to the success of the new government; an opposition party, or any criticism of the management or policy of the government could only disrupt the stability of the nation. "If we mean to support the Liberty and Independence which it has cost us so much blood and treasure to establish," Washington said in 1790, "we must drive far away the daemon of party spirit and local reproach." Those eighteenth-century political theorists who accepted the inevitability of political differences hoped that a well-designed constitutional system, with checks and balances, would minimize the divisive effects of those differences. James Madison, in the tenth paper of *The Federalist,* stressed that one of the most important advantages of "a well constructed Union" was "its tendency to break and control the violence of faction."

It was, ironically, the successful establishment of a constitutional government that made the evolution of national political parties a natural consequence. Differences of opinion over the interpretation of the Constitution, what the nature of society should be, foreign and economic policies, and sectional interests necessitated the formation of political organizations to regulate and focus conflict and to act indirectly as unifying forces in the face of the nation's diversity. Major interest groups were compelled to unite for the purpose of expressing and directing public opinion, and for translating that opinion into government action. Party structures had to be created to bring coherence to the complicated machinery of national elections and to present to the public clear alternatives between policies and leaders within the electoral process. In short, political parties became instruments of democracy which allowed politics to be conducted without destroying national unity. Thus, legitimate opposition, when manifested in organized popular parties, slowly came to be viewed—albeit reluctantly—as indispensable to the maintenance of republican government and paved the way for the modern party system of today. By 1798 Thomas Jefferson, himself hesitant to take party action, wrote, "In every free and deliberating society, there must . . . be opposite parties, and violent dissentions and discords. . . . Perhaps this party division is necessary to induce each to watch and relate to the people the proceeding of the other."

The original impetus to party growth was the fiscal program presented in 1790-91 by Alexander Hamilton, the first secretary of the treasury. Hamilton feared for the safety of the frail republic; especially did he believe it might founder without the support of the men of wealth and business, for in their hesitancy to invest in the nation's future, they would relegate it to a mediocre status among nations. In its economic weakness, the country would become the prey of stronger nations, and men of substance, in losing faith, would be reluctant to defend its independence. Hamilton envisioned the creation of a strong and efficient government, prosperous because of its economic stability, and therefore commanding the respect of the world. "There is something noble and magnificent in the perspective of a great Federal Republic, closely linked in the pursuit of a common interest . . . ," he wrote in 1782. To fulfill this purpose, he determined to build the country's financial structure on a firm foundation approved of and supported by men of wealth, power, and position. His economic program was designed to appeal to the interests of these groups: the funding and assumption of the national debt would ensure credit stability; the chartering of a national bank would centralize and order the financial activities of the country; the levying of excise taxes and governmental promotion and protection of industry through a tariff would provide revenue for the operation of government while developing the industrial resources of the nation.

Each of these measures, with the exception of a protective tariff, was enacted into law and all were dramatically successful in setting the new nation's finances in order. Yet Hamilton's assertion of the principle of federal sovereignty revived the anxiety of those men who had feared the creation of a strong government at the end of the American Revolution. His nationalism was seen by many Americans as a threat to the liberties of the individual and the rights of the states; his emphasis on the necessity for a broad construction of the Constitution and his liberal interpretation of the "necessary and proper" and "general welfare" clauses appeared to his opponents as further magnification of the central power. The Constitution, they felt, meant exactly what it said; to take a single step beyond the limits it established would ultimately lead to the creation of a Leviathan state with "a boundless field of power." Hamilton, it was believed, was attempting "by arbitrary interpretations and insidious precedents, to pervert the limited government of the Union into a government of unlimited discretion, contrary to the will and subversive of the authority of the people."

While Hamilton viewed government as positive, energetic, and expanding, his opponents saw government as a necessary evil which had to be expressly limited and constantly monitored. Hamilton conceived that wisdom lay in organized control; his opponents felt the country would thrive best on liberty—that the rights of man were promoted by less rather than more government. The extension of authority Hamilton proposed was further seen as a means of subverting America's republican structure to the purposes of a monarchy. It did not help any that Hamilton had at various times expressed his preference for this form of government, even delivering a speech at the Constitutional Convention in praise of monarchy. Each of his measures was seen as a "monarchical plot." His attempt to aggrandize the power of the presidency in order to make the executive department the "cement of the union" and a check on demagoguery was seen as further evidence of his monarchical bias.

Hamilton's program was seen, too, as a challenge to a conflicting political economy based primarily on agriculture. America in the 1790s was rural in character; nine-tenths of its population of four million was engaged in agricultural occupations. Hamilton appreciated the importance of agriculture to the United States, but he believed that if the United States remained an agrarian nation and turned its back on other economic activities it would expose itself "to a state of impoverishment, compared with the opulence to which [its] political and natural advantages authorize [it] to aspire." Hamilton envisioned America as a great industrial nation, varied in its enterprises, whose manufacturing output would raise the general living standard and stimulate both commerce and agriculture. Only through the promotion of manufacturing did he believe the United States could acquire the necessary economic strength that would help it maintain true independence from European nations.

Men like Thomas Jefferson and John Taylor of Caroline, the Virginia planter, economist, and politician known as the "philosopher of agrarianism," had a different vision of America. Their ideal was a nation of small independent farmers, whom Jefferson graphically referred to as "God's Chosen People." "The true Republican," it has been said, "was the man with the hoe and a hundred acres besides." These men saw no urgent need for rapid industrialization and, in fact, feared it.

It was upon these opposing principles that the Federalists and the Republicans divided.

In 1792 there was no contest for the presidency. Washington received the unanimous vote of the electors, Federalists and Republicans alike. But the struggle over the vice-presidency hinted at the rekindling of old divisions and antagonisms sparked by Hamilton's system. Southern planters, who in 1789 had been ready, in fact eager, to cooperate with the moneyed men of the North, parted with them when they realized that the policies designed to benefit northern merchants and bankers brought no profit to them as landed aristocrats. Even more, they saw themselves paying for a system that contributed to another section's prosperity. Although in 1792 they were willing to continue with Washington, they were not as willing to go along with Vice-President John Adams, who represented the commerce, shipbuilding, fisheries, and banking institutions of New England and the North. If the Federalists were to have the first office, then the followers of Jefferson—who had already come to call themselves Republicans in contradistinction to the unpopular term anti-Federalists—insisted that they were to command the second office.

Appealing to the shopkeepers, artisans, laboring men, and farmers of the North on the basis of their sympathy with the French Revolution, and to the southern planters with their agrarian bias, the Republicans waged a gallant but losing campaign for the second office. Their candidate George Clinton carried an anti-Constitution stigma as an early anti-Federalist, and their association with the French Revolution—which they emphasized through demonstrations and symbolic feasts—marked them for some as irresponsible anarchists. But the campaign served notice on the overconfident Federalists that when the Republicans became better organized nationally as well as locally, they would have to be more seriously considered.

This did not take long. In 1793 England went to war with republican France over the guillotining of Louis XVI, and in 1794 Jay's treaty, terminating the United States' difficulties with Britain, seemed to suggest a sympathetic policy toward monarchical, conservative England instead of republican, liberty-loving France. The treaty intensified party spirit, and gave the Republicans a sense of mission that legitimatized their existence: to defend the nation against British domination and against those at home who would surrender to such control. The contest was now between the Republicans and "lovers of liberty" and the Federalist Monocrats. The war, Jefferson wrote in 1793, "kindled and brought forward the parties with an ardour which our own interests, merely, could never excite." Both events sorely tested the ability of the reigning party to accept legitimate opposition.

As the country approached the presidential election of 1796 the atmosphere hung heavy with tension and discord. Opposition against administration policy flared daily. Added to the excitement created by Jay's treaty was the issue of the excise tax, which so incensed frontier and southern farmers that they rose in armed rebellion in 1794. Amidst the loud cries of protest and disunity came President Washington's announcement that he would not accept a third term in office. His decision provoked deep fears for the survival of the Union, and Federalists and Republicans alike openly talked of the imminent death of America's experiment in popular government. Hinging on the outcome of the election was the vital question, could the nation survive what Fisher Ames, a prominent Federalist, called the "transmigration" of power?

THOMAS JEFFERSON   *Charles-Balthazar-Julien Fevret de Saint-Mémin, 1804*
Crayon on paper, 23⅞ x 17⅝ inches   Worcester Art Museum, Worcester, Massachusetts

Thomas Jefferson *Democratic–Republican*

1743-1826

"Heartily tired" from the brutal, almost daily conflicts which erupted over questions of national policy between himself and Alexander Hamilton in the cabinet, Thomas Jefferson resigned his position as secretary of state in 1793 to return to the pastoral tranquillity of Monticello, his estate in the highlands of Virginia. Although his Federalist opponents were convinced that this was merely a strategic withdrawal to allow him an opportunity to plan and promote his candidacy for the presidency should Washington step down in 1796, Jefferson insisted that this retirement from public life was to be final. Too long had he worked "without a single gratification in possession or in prospect, in present enjoyment or future wish." It was now time to return to those things he loved: his farm, his family, and his books, he said, were calling to him irresistibly.

But even in retirement the world of politics pursued him. As the election of 1796 drew nearer and it became apparent that Washington would not seek a third term, rumors of Jefferson's presidential ambitions grew in intensity. Reacting to these "continuous insinuations" in a letter to James Madison, Jefferson admitted that while the idea that he coveted the office of chief executive had been originated by his enemies to impugn his political motives, he had been forced to examine his true feelings on the subject for his own peace of mind. In so doing, he had concluded that his reasons for retirement—the desire for privacy and the delight in his family life and agricultural pursuits—coupled with his now failing health and ripening age, were insuperable barriers to further public service. "The little spice of ambition" he had in his younger days "had long since evaporated," and so, to him, the question of the presidency was "forever closed."

Republican leaders chose to ignore Jefferson's declinations, however, for in their minds there was no doubt that he should be their standard bearer in 1796. A conspicuous symbol of Republicanism, he was the only man in the party with sufficient national appeal to stand up against the Federalist "heir apparent," Vice-President John Adams. By February of the election year, plans were being made to "push" Jefferson's candidacy, but, lest he refuse, he was not consulted nor told of this decision.

Jefferson had not sought the candidacy thrust upon him, but neither would he spurn it. Unlike his contemporaries, the Henrys and the Adamses, Jefferson, as his biographer Merrill Peterson has pointed out, was not "born for the public," and was alternately attracted and repelled by political life. Yet, despite his reservations or personal preferences, when marshalled to a public role, he felt obliged to accept the responsibility. Thus, "on principles of public respect," he could neither have refused to allow his name to be brought forward nor, if elected, to serve.

Jefferson did not actively engage in the campaign on his own behalf; his supporters ran the race for him. The Republican party, presaging modern campaign tactics, created a grassroots sentiment for their candidate by directing their efforts toward the general populace. In newspapers, pamphlets, and handbills, Jefferson was presented as the "uniform advocate of equal rights among citizens" while Adams was portrayed as the "champion of rank, titles and hereditary distinctions." Praises were heaped on the Republican candidate; he was a man of enlightened views, pure patriotism, and unsullied integrity. He alone could heal the country's divisions.

In his "remote canton" Jefferson was not reasonably certain of the outcome of the election until the end of December. Under the original electoral system established by the Constitution, each presidential elector cast his ballot for two men without designating between them as to office. The candidate who received the greatest number of votes became president; the second highest became vice-president. Jefferson foresaw on the basis of his own calculations that the electoral vote would be uncomfortably close. On December seventeenth, he wrote to Madison that in the event of a tie, he wished for the choice to be in favor of Adams. The New Englander had always been his senior in public office, he explained, and the expression of public will being equal, he should be preferred for the higher honor.

Jefferson could more easily accept the vice-presidency than Adams, too. In fact, a more "tranquil and unoffending station" could not have been found for him, he said. Since his presence in Philadelphia would be required only one-third of the year, he would still have time for his flowers and trees. The second office would leave him free of weighty responsibilities and safe from political buffeting. A shrewd politician, he realized that the transition of power from the nearly mythical Washington to a lesser luminary in the midst of the deep and bitter political divisions facing the nation could be perilous, and he had no desire to be caught in the storm which had been brewing for four years and was about to break. "This is certainly not a moment to covet the helm," he wrote to Edward Rutledge.

When the electoral vote was tallied, Adams emerged the victor with 71 votes to Jefferson's 68. Jefferson, as the recipient of the second highest vote, was elected vice-president. Rejoicing at his "escape," he seemed completely satisfied with the decision. Despite their obvious and basic political differences, Jefferson genuinely respected John Adams as a friend and compatriot. Although he believed that Adams had deviated from the course set in 1776, Jefferson "never felt a diminution of confidence in his integrity" and was confident that the New Englander would not steer the nation too far off its republican tack. Within two years, Jefferson's views would be drastically altered as measures such as the Alien and Sedition Acts of 1798 convinced him of the need to wrest control of the government from the Federalists.

THOMAS PINCKNEY *Samuel F. B. Morse   Oil on canvas, 48 x 38 inches*
Charles Cotesworth Pinckney, Jr. Collection, Columbia Museum of Art,
Columbia, South Carolina

Thomas Pinckney *Federalist*

1750-1828

To equalize their voting appeal in the presidential election of 1796 the Federalists selected Thomas Pinckney, a leading South Carolinian, as running mate for the New Englander, John Adams. Forty-six year old Pinckney, a Revolutionary War hero, had served as governor of South Carolina and minister to England. In 1795, as special envoy to Spain, he had negotiated a treaty of great advantage to the United States in which the Spanish agreed to recognize the western and southern boundaries of the United States as established in the Anglo-American treaty of 1783 and to allow the vital free navigation of the Mississippi. Promising immense benefits to the frontier, Pinckney's treaty proved as popular with the American people as Jay's treaty had not, and its author was hailed throughout the country for his outstanding service. His name on the party ballot seemingly insured a Federalist victory for both the presidential and vice-presidential offices.

Still abroad when he received word of the nomination, Pinckney responded with hesitation. He wistfully wrote of his desire to retire from public office, but, in the gentlemanly political tradition, would not refuse public office. Little did he realize when he docked at Charleston in December that he had become, in fact, a presidential candidate.

Since under the voting system established by the Constitution, there was no separate vote for vice-president, Pinckney's southern friends chose to ignore their party's intentions and regarded him as a presidential candidate. In this situation, Alexander Hamilton took an active hand.

Hamilton did not like John Adams and had only reluctantly accepted him as George Washington's successor. He had long been wary of the New Englander's stubbornly independent brand of politics and would have preferred to see Pinckney, over whom he could exert more control, seated in the president's chair. Toward this end, he hit upon the notion of diverting a few electoral votes from Adams; if it could be arranged that one more electoral vote was cast for Pinckney than for Adams, while both bested Jefferson, Pinckney would be elected president. Hamilton's plan was deceptively simple—all the Federalists in the North would vote for Adams and Pinckney equally, because the contest with Jefferson would be so close. The hidden stratagem was that Pinckney would be supported solidly in the South while Adams would not, and the Carolinian would thereby carry more electoral votes than Adams.

Various methods were used to persuade the electors to vote as Hamilton wished. In the press, anonymous articles were published attacking Adams for his monarchical tendencies, Jefferson for being too democratic, and pushing Pinckney as the only suitable candidate. In private correspondence with state party leaders the Hamiltonians encouraged the idea that Adams' popularity was slipping, that he could not possibly win the election, and that the Federalists could only defeat Jefferson by supporting Pinckney.

Had sectional pride and loyalty to John Adams not run as high in New England as in the deep South, Pinckney might well have become Washington's successor. New Englanders realized quickly that equal votes for Adams and Pinckney in their states would defeat Adams; therefore, eighteen electors scratched Pinckney's name from their ballots and deliberately threw away their second votes to men who were not even running. It was fortunate for Adams that they acted as they did for the electors from South Carolina completely abandoned him, giving eight votes to Pinckney and eight to Jefferson.

In the end, Hamilton's interference in Pinckney's candidacy lost even the vice-presidency for the South Carolinian. Without New England's support, he received only 59 electoral votes, finishing third to Adams and Jefferson. He might have been president in 1797, or as vice-president a serious contender for the presidency in 1800; instead, stigmatized by a plot he had not devised, he served a brief term in the United States Senate, and then dropped from sight as a national influence.

"A Revolution in Principles" 1800

THE ELECTION OF 1800 WAS PERHAPS THE MOST BITTER POLITICAL CONTEST EXPERI-enced by Americans since the inauguration of the government under the Constitution. To some Americans the virulence of the campaign threatened the very fabric of the nation's political life, for here was an example of that destructive party spirit that George Washington had warned them against when he pleaded for national cooperation and harmony in his Farewell Address.

The contest of 1800 was made even more bitter by the divisiveness and factionalism within the Federalist Party itself, with the Hamiltonians scheming against the followers of Adams and the president's reelection. But the division in the Federalist ranks, as well as the split between the Federalists and the Republicans, was caused by events that went beyond personal animosity or petty jealousy, events transpiring on the other side of the Atlantic Ocean which reached back across the waters to corrupt American opinion and enflame the already smolder-ing embers of partisanship. For, as the European situation grew more intense, American farm-ers and merchants found themselves making use of it to support their own domestic positions, to bolster their own reach for power within their native domain. Thus, the conflict between Eng-land and France that broke out on February 1, 1793, was the catalyst that brought to the surface of American political life the deep-lying antagonisms that existed between the two great sectional interests—the planting-slaveholding interest and the mercantile-shipping-finan-cial interest. These interests had preceded Hamilton, Adams, and Jefferson by a century and continued to be opposed until 1865.

When Louis XVI lost his head under the "bloody knife" of the guillotine early in 1793, a Reign of Terror followed in France that not only aroused the English to arms, but spread fear and anxiety to conservatives everywhere. No group was as alienated as were the Hamil-tonian Federalists, who saw in the new regime the substitution of the tyranny of the unwashed masses for that of their legitimate rulers. The Republican followers of Jefferson were not pleased either by the gory by-products of the French Revolution; but filled with idealism and republican theory, they were not as quick to lament the loss of a few thousand aristocratic heads if the results seemed to justify the sacrifice. Some extremists in the Republican fold were actually delighted over the royal executions, and all through the winter of 1793 and the follow-ing summer at gatherings in American cities, Louis XVI was guillotined in effigy twenty or thirty times a day.

Passions were thus at a height in the United States, with name calling of the most virulent kind. Federalists demanded intervention in the war on the side of Great Britain, while Repub-licans hoarsely cried for military support of France. Washington's Neutrality Proclamation of April 22, 1793, eventually steered Americans through a middle course, but the emotions re-mained—and subsequent developments in the war between the two powers did little to miti-gate them.

The agitation continued into the administration of John Adams. By 1797 when Adams took office, France was ruled by a five-headed executive known as the Directory, which regarded American policy as evidence of an Anglo-American entente, prejudicial to the interests of France. In retaliation for the hated Jay treaty, the French attacked American commerce; their spoliations became even more active than British depredations, giving France the reputation of being a world menace. The Republicans tried to defend French policy as being the logical response to American partiality towards England; but the Federalists feared French expansionism, especially after the Directory began to establish satellite republics on its borders in Europe and thereby divided the world into two camps: those who had made terms with France and those who had not. Federalist fear was directed also against French policy in Canada, Louisiana, and Florida—a policy designed to contain the United States "within peaceful bounds" and to break their exclusive relations with Great Britain.

The insolence of the French Directory toward the United States made imminent a rupture with that country. Adams, seeking to prevent such an event, sent a three-man mission to negotiate with the Directory, but the mission resulted more in offended feelings than in peaceful decisions, for the French response was the so-called XYZ bribery affair, and the American slogan, "Millions for Defense, not one cent for Tribute."

The high Federalists, led by Alexander Hamilton, turned into a war party, leading the movement for a strong navy and an increase in the regular army. As Hamilton marched his recruits around New York City, however, drumming up martial enthusiasm and waiting for a declaration of war, his partisans in Congress passed the Naturalization, Alien, and Sedition Acts of 1798, aimed against the Republicans, whom they characterized as "servile minions of France," and "troublemaking" foreigners sent to this pure land to sow the seeds of "atheism and disaffection." Even John Adams reacted against these laws, believing that the Sedition Act especially proscribed, "under imputations of democracy, some of the ablest, most influential, and best characters in the Union." The acts of 1798 stimulated the first organized states' rights movement under the Constitution—the Virginia and Kentucky Resolves—and in large measure influenced the election of Jefferson to the presidency in 1800.

While Republicans lamented the Federalist Reign of Terror and southern states passed secession resolutions because of the Federalist measures of 1798-1799, Adams, intent upon keeping the peace, sent a second peace mission to France to negotiate the differences between the two countries. His action was not appreciated by the high Federalists, nor was his diatribe against "the fools who were intriguing to plunge us into an alliance with England . . . and wild expeditions to South America." Deprived of their great issue, which had allowed them to associate Republicanism with Jacobinism and anarchy, and which had promised them a highly desired British alliance, the Hamiltonians broke with Adams and systematically began to harass him while he still held office and to block his reelection.

The Federalist war program had necessitated heavy new taxes that Americans bitterly resented. With the removal of the war scare, the Republicans were relieved of the onus of being allied with the enemy; they could now ridicule the Federalist excitement and fear of subversion.

They could insinuate that the Federalists' purpose had been to "arm one half of the people, for the purpose of keeping the other in awe." As proof of "Federalist tyrannical intentions," they could point to the president's use of federal troops in Pennsylvania to arrest John Fries for leading a mob intent upon liberating "tax-dodgers" from jail. By concentrating on such specific issues as "peace and economy;" "the constitutional right of public inquiry" now threatened by the Alien and Sedition Acts; the maintenance of an army in time of peace; the creation of "an expensive and ineffectual navy;" and the "variety of stock-jobbing acts which have given birth to a system of speculation, fraud, and bankruptcy," the Republicans were able to dismiss Federalist accomplishments— which were not mean. They appealed to the common interests of farmers, artisans, and laboring men, and smaller businessmen who were feeling the effects of heavy taxation and a monetary policy that favored wealthy and powerful financiers and merchants.

The Republicans worked quietly and well through conferences with small groups and through a wide range of correspondence to weld together a powerful party capable of overthrowing the Federalists, who were too busy fighting among themselves, issuing highly critical publications concerning their own presidential leader, and repudiating his policies, to launch much of a campaign. Despite all the last-minute efforts of the Federalists to repair the breaches within the party structure and to wave again the bloody flag of Republican atheism, the Republicans emerged the victor, with Jefferson and Burr tied for first place, and Adams, Pinckney, and Jay following in that sequence.

The contest now became one between two Republicans, resolved only after the Federalists worked out an arrangement whereby Jefferson promised to observe certain policies in exchange for Federalist abstention in the voting. Although Jefferson later denied having entered into such an agreement, there is no question that in most ways he was a more acceptable candidate to the conservative group than the enigmatic Burr. In any case, in February of 1801, Jefferson was elected third president of the United States.

Was the election of 1800 a revolution in principles, as Jefferson observed during his first inaugural address? Both Federalists and Republicans truly believed it was. For most Federalists, it was not only the end of the party—as, in fact, it turned out to be—but the end of the world. The Washington *Federalist* reversed the eagle on its masthead, and put under it the motto *Pluria e Unio*—Many out of One—reversing the older sentiment for unity. "The die is cast!" the editor mourned, "Our beloved ADAMS will now close his bright career. . . . Immortal Sage! . . . Retire and receive . . . the blessings of all *good* men. . . . Sons of faction! demagogues and high priests of anarchy! now have you cause to triumph. . . . Calumny, persecution, and banishment are the laurels of the hoary patriot. . . . Our constitution is our last fortress. . . . When this falls, our country is lost forever!" Similarly, amidst much rejoicing and tumultous celebration, the Republicans exulted in what they were convinced was the defeat of tyranny and the

Thomas Jefferson banner   SMITHSONIAN INSTITUTION

victory of "Jefferson and Liberty." For many Americans the election—for good or bad—was another French Revolution, another dawning of liberty, equality, and the rights of man.

The Federalist anxiety was reflected in the drop in the prices of stocks, a sure indication that the financiers expected social disaster and chaos. How much of this anxiety was prompted by rhetoric and propaganda, and how much by a rational analysis of the parties' positions, is difficult to determine. Certainly calmer voices and steadier eyes did not fear a revolution. The astute and witty wife of the president, Abigail Adams, reflected both her husband's and her own optimism when she wrote to her son Thomas advising him not to sell his stocks, but rather to buy in the declining market. "I think they will rise again," she wrote. "I think when the election is over, unless the party are [sic] more mad and wild than I believe they will be permitted to be, things will not suddenly change."

41

Yet there was much that was revolutionary about the election of 1800. As Jefferson said, it was "as real a revolution in the principles of our government as that of 1776 was in its form; not effected indeed by the sword, as that but by the rational and peaceable instrument of reform, the suffrage of the people." The year 1800 witnessed the first transfer of control over both the executive and legislative branches of government that had taken place in the United States since the Revolution. It was a transfer of power that was effected in a peaceful and orderly fashion. Involving not just individuals, but groups with differing attitudes and concerns towards government, classes, and economic organization, it brought an end to aristocratic domination of American political life.

The Federalists, like Adams, had emphasized the need for balance between aristocratic and democratic forces: "In every society where property exists," Adams had written in his *A Defence of the Constitutions of the Government of the United States of America,* "there will ever be a struggle between rich and poor." Either the poor would plunder the rich, or the rich, "by influence, fleece the many who are poor." Thus a system of checks and balances that gave to each class a forum for the expression of its views and implementation of its policies, each with a veto power over the other, was the only way of ensuring "equal justice . . . and equal liberty" for all. But ultimate power, to the Federalists, had to reside in the hands of those deemed most capable of using it wisely—the rich, propertied, and educated. Some arch conservatives among the Federalists were not even content with a checks and balances system, and yearned for a monarchy like Great Britain's as a way of ensuring social order and economic security.

The Jeffersonians, on the other hand, expressed their faith in the people and the "sufficiency of human reason for the care of human affairs." They emphasized the significance of majority rule as "the Natural law of every society" and as "the only sure guardian of the rights of man." If the majority fell into "error of opinion," Jefferson believed that such errors could be tolerated "where reason is left free to combat it." Yet, Jefferson had respect for minority rights, which "equal laws must protect and to violate which would be oppression." Thus, Jefferson would not change the checks and balance system of the Constitution and accepted the idea of balanced government. "It is not by the consolidation, or concentration of powers, but by their distribution that good government is effected," he wrote in his *Autobiography.* "The purpose of establishing different houses of legislation is to introduce the influence of different interests or different principles." In this sense, then, he agreed with the Federalists, but the difference lay in the tone and attitude that lay behind his expression. Where the Federalists would have insisted upon balanced government because they distrusted the people, the Jeffersonians sought balanced government out of respect for the differing nature of people's opinions and out of their commitment to human reason.

Specific policies of both groups followed from their view of the people. Actually, when in office, Jefferson went along with many Federalist practices. Despite his preference for weak government, he found it necessary to wield strong federal power during most of his administration because events forced him to do so. But underneath this exercise of power lay his deep commitment to the welfare of the people and to a belief in human progress based upon the exercise of Man's reason. Federal power, then, was used to benefit the farmer, the artisan, the townsman, not just the few "well-born" and "well-bred."

These were the people actually whom the Federalists overlooked in their vain search for power and influence, an oversight that brought about the destruction of that party—as a party. As Adams mused later, once the heat of dissension and name-calling had cooled: "No party [has ever] understood so ill the causes of its own power, or so wantonly destroyed them."

JOHN ADAMS   *Gilbert and Jane Stuart, 1798 and later   Oil on canvas, 30 x 24 inches*
From the Collection of the National Portrait Gallery   NPG.71.4

John Adams *Federalist*

1 7 3 5 - 1 8 2 6

Early on the morning of March 4, 1801, while the city was still asleep, President John Adams called for his coach and left Washington to return to his home in Quincy, Massachusetts. Angry and bitter at his rejection by the people he had served so long and so well, the proud old Puritan could not endure the humiliation of seeing Thomas Jefferson, his erstwhile friend, inaugurated in his place.

In the solitude of his farm, Adams gave long thought to the reasons for his defeat. Jefferson referred to his election as a "revolution in the principles of government" and to an extent Adams could agree with this. The political philosophy of the Federalists had been self-defeating. "No party that ever existed knew itself so little or so vainly overrated its own influence and popularity as ours," Adams reflected. Too long had the Federalists distrusted the people and ignored public opinion. Confronted by an opposition which extolled the wisdom of the people and appealed to majority interests, the Federalists as a party could not survive.

More fundamentally, however, Adams ascribed his defeat to the rancorous divisions and discord among the Federalists themselves. Had the party been able to unite in action, they may have withstood the Republican onslaught. But behind both his and his party's troubles, Adams believed, stood the sinister figure of Alexander Hamilton, "the greatest intriguant in the world," and a man who would risk all to further his own ambitions.

Adams was convinced that the origin of the Federalists' defeat lay in Hamilton's opposition to his decision in February 1799 to send a second peace mission to France. The militaristic Hamiltonians had spent months in preparing for war with France; the whole structure of their power was based on their expectation that such a war was inevitable and, indeed, necessary. Adams' effort to avoid war provoked a deep schism within Federalist ranks at a time when unity was essential to prevent the triumph of the Jeffersonian Republicans.

Hamiltonian reaction to Adams' policy was intense: "Surprise, indignation, grief and disgust followed each other in quick succession in the breasts of the true friends of our Country," said the sympathetic Federalist chief, George Cabot. Only Adams' threatened resignation, which would have left the government in the hands of Thomas Jefferson, deterred the faction from overriding the negotiations. Men who had been Adams' personal friends for years angrily spurned him, charging that he had thrown away their chances of staying in power.

Yet, Adams believed his decision had been the right one, made at the right moment. "The end of war is peace," he said, "—and peace was offered me." For the first two years of his administration, Adams had compromised with, if not surrendered to, the demands placed on him by the Hamiltonians. He had not wanted nor recommended the creation of the large, professional army which Congress had approved, the subsequent direct taxes needed to finance that army, nor the Alien and Sedition laws. Adams viewed himself as a national president representing national rather than party interests, and renewing negotiations with France was a policy which he deemed essential to the well-being of the nation and one which he believed the people truly wanted. To guard the nation's welfare, he could not encourage Hamilton's dreams of military glory.

Soon after the mission to France had sailed, the Hamiltonian Federalists began to work against Adams' reelection. Because of the popular sentiment in the president's favor, Adams and Charles Cotesworth Pinckney, brother of Thomas, had been chosen as the party's standard-bearers. Unreconciled to another Adams administration, the Hamiltonians tried to draft George Washington for a third term. The former president firmly declined with the advice that principles, not personalities, should be the true concern of the party. Still unresigned, Hamilton then pursued the same tactic that he had used in 1796, attempting to elevate Pinckney to the presidency over Adams by manipulating the vote in the electoral college.

In August 1800, Hamilton's frustrated rage against Adams overwhelmed his political judgment and he lashed out personally at the president. With the collaboration of members of Adams' cabinet, he collected evidence purporting to prove that Adams was unfit for the presidency and incorporated it into a pamphlet entitled, "Letter from Alexander Hamilton Concerning the Public Conduct and Character of John Adams." Intended for private circulation among Federalist leaders, the phillipic fell into the hands of the delighted Republican, Aaron Burr, who generously turned it over to the newspapers for the amusement of the public. The pamphlet had an effect exactly opposite from its intended purpose. The ranks of Adams' supporters tightened, and the machinations of the conspirators failed.

In the end, the election of 1800 was a defeat not so much for Adams as for the Federalist Party. Adams found solace in knowing that he showed greater strength than he had in the previous election and actually ran ahead of his party. While the turnover in Congress was decisive, Adams received only six less electoral votes than he had in 1796.

Adams remained in the eyes of the people a firm patriot devoted to a policy of peace; his integrity was deeply appreciated, his political troubles at least partially understood. In time, his bruised spirits revived, but he never forgave Alexander Hamilton for robbing him of his second term as president. Of Hamilton's intrigues, Adams wrote in 1807: "Like the worm at the root of the peach did he labor for twelve years underground and in darkness to girdle the root while the axes of the Anti-Federalists, Democrats, Jacobins, . . . chopping as they were for the whole time at the trunk, could not fell the tree."

AARON BURR *Gilbert Stuart, circa 1794   Oil on canvas, 29⅜ x 23¼ inches*
New Jersey Historical Society, Newark

Aaron Burr *Democratic–Republican*

1756-1836

The possibility of a tie vote between Thomas Jefferson and Aaron Burr had been discussed by Republican leaders during the campaign of 1800, but no definite stratagem had been devised to prevent such an occurrence. Everyone assumed that somewhere in the electoral process one or two votes would be dropped from Burr's tally to insure Jefferson the position of priority. Instead, in an unprecedented display of party solidarity, each elector upheld his pledge to support both candidates equally, with the result that Jefferson and Burr tied for the presidency with 73 votes each. The duty of choosing between them fell to the lame-duck House of Representatives still controlled by Federalists. The Republicans soon realized that another ordeal faced them before they could enjoy the fruits of their victory.

The tie presented the Federalists with an opportunity to recoup at least part of their shattered fortunes. Having contemplated such an exigency since early August, a group of them had decided to make Burr the president. So great was their detestation and dread of Jefferson that Burr seemed the lesser evil. Even more, to northern Federalist politicians Burr was a more compatible political figure, one who despite certain enigmatic qualities seemed understandable. He was a man, they believed, with whom a bargain could be made; a political realist rather than "a visionary philosopher," "actuated," as Federalist George Cabot pointed out, "by ordinary ambition" for power and property. To satisfy these ambitions, Federalists were certain Burr would be willing to bargain with them and thus include them and their program in the new administration.

Jefferson, on the other hand, was a Jacobin revolutionary, whose ambition was based on democratic idealism; he would, Cabot believed, "see the roots of our society pulled up, and a new course of cultivation substituted." Moreover, he would not make agreements with them. But the Federalists were mistaken, Burr would not listen to their approaches, and their hopes for influence were dashed.

What manner of a man was Aaron Burr whom the Federalists so mistakenly interpreted? Burr was a northerner, a successful lawyer, and an elegant and urbane aristocrat. The son of a scholar and theologian and second president of Princeton College, and a descendent through his mother of the famed Jonathan Edwards, one of the greatest of the New England religious thinkers, he had been brought up by an uncle in the family tradition and tutored by a law student who later became judge of the supreme court of Connecticut, Tapping Reeve. Thus, all the advantages of education, social respectability, and honor in his community were his by inheritance, as much as his keen mind, graceful manners, and intellectual curiosity.

But Burr had what has been described as "a fondness for adventure and intrigue," and this, throughout his life, gave him a strange cast. In college, curiosity frequently took precedence over piety, disturbing his studies of traditional theology. During his service in the Revolutionary army, his disrespect of military decorum and occasional impertinence antagonized General Washington. Although he was later promoted to lieutenant colonel and earned a reputation for bravery and daring in battle, he continued to irritate army personnel by both his amorous and political intrigues. In the practice of law, which followed his army career, he was "more remarkable for dexterity than sound judgment or logic"; although he earned a substantial income, he kept losing it through extensive speculations, ill-considered generosity, carelessness in money matters, and self-indulgence.

Thus, when he entered politics in New York City and the state of New York, he was quite prepared for intrigue as well as leadership, for expedient decision making as well as serious attention to issues. He had enemies, but he also had friends, and for some years before the 1800 election he had been gathering about himself a group of enthusiastic young politicians as intent as he was on breaking the family alliances that dominated politics in the state of New York. With the help of his loyal followers, he built a power base among the urban masses of New York City, from which vantage point he challenged the power of the Clintons and the Livingstons in the Republican Party structure of New York. In 1800 under his leadership the Republicans of New York City defeated Hamilton, assuring the entire vote of New York in the electoral college to the Republicans. Maneuvering at the same time to have himself endorsed for the vice-presidency, Burr later secured from Republican members of Congress a pledge to support him equally with Jefferson.

Here, Burr's expediency and opportunism came to an end. When the Federalists approached him directly and indirectly to complete the bargain they thought so sure, he turned them away. "Had Burr done anything for himself," a Federalist wrote in the midst of the balloting to break the tie, "he would long ere this have been president." And most historians agree that this could have happened despite the bitter hostility of Hamilton. But Burr seemingly did nothing, and, in fact, issued a statement disclaiming all competition with Jefferson and stating that he would never submit to being "instrumental in counteracting the wishes and expectations of the people." Impelled by an almost pathological hatred of his New York rival, Hamilton did all he could to defeat him. Burr, Hamilton raged, was an "embryo Caesar," a man whose "public principles have no spring or aim than his own aggrandisement." But the Federalists, many of them blaming Hamilton for the shipwreck of their party, ignored his exhortations and threw their support to Burr.

The voting that took place in the House of Representatives on February 11, 1801, took six days and thirty-six ballots to complete. Without any overt encouragement from Burr, Federalist support weakened. The more he persevered in disregarding their overtures, the more he alienated them. Fearing that March fourth might come around without a successor to John Adams, the Federalists, following Hamilton's advice, broke the deadlock and cast their votes for Jefferson. Three years later, the twelfth amendment to the Constitution established separate voting procedures for president and vice-president, in order to prevent such an occurrence from happening again.

As for Burr, he was angrily denounced on both sides. The Federalists were bitter for his failure to aid them in securing his election. "The means existed of electing Burr," wrote James A. Bayard, "but this required his cooperation. By deceiving one man (a great blockhead) and tempting two (not incorruptible), he might have secured a majority of the States. He will never have another chance of being President of the United States. . . ."

The Republicans were antagonized by his participation in the Federalist celebration of Washington's birthday and by the rumors that he had intrigued with the Federalists to supplant Jefferson. Abuse continued throughout the years of his vice-presidency, and in 1804 the party caucus replaced him on the Republican ticket with George Clinton.

Defeat after defeat followed. Federalists and Republicans together wrecked his chances for the governorship of the state of New York; his long-running feud with Hamilton erupted in a fatal duel and Hamilton's death; disgrace and exile, and perhaps his propensity for intrigue, drew him to a conspiracy with General James Wilkinson in the west that brought him to the edge of treason. Hanged in effigy, besieged by creditors, Burr finally fled the country hoping to gain support in England for an insane plan to revolutionize Mexico. Unsuccessful there, he traveled throughout Europe writing wild memoranda to heads of state that reflected his delusions of grandeur. Financial reverses followed, and then poverty, return to the United States, the loss of his beloved grandson and only daughter, Theodosia, and a final unhappy marriage. His was a life that presented lessons for moralists and questions for historians. Still among the most enigmatic of American politicians, he is also one of the most fascinating.

CHARLES COTESWORTH PINCKNEY *Henry Benbridge, circa 1773 and 1775*
Oil on canvas, 30 x 25 inches   From the Collection of the National Portrait Gallery
NPG.67.1   Not shown in the exhibition

Charles Cotesworth Pinckney *Federalist*

1746-1825

In the presidential contest of 1804 the reelection of Republican Thomas Jefferson was conceded as a certainty. The crushing defeat of 1800 had left the Federalist party only a remnant of its former self: caught up in the rising democratic movement, party members had deserted by the thousands and those who remained were bitter and disunited. New England was the only section of the country where Federalism retained any vestige of vitality. Suffering, too, from a dearth of national leaders, the Federalists knew the election would be more of a rout than a contest.

Nevertheless, the party went through the motions of naming candidates. Congressional Federalists, meeting in Washington late in February 1804, nominated Charles Cotesworth Pinckney of South Carolina and Rufus King of New York for the presidency and vice-presidency.

Charles Cotesworth Pinckney was selected primarily because he was the perfect "caretaker candidate." Cited as a man of "sterling" character and patriotism, he was one of the few popular leaders to whom the Federalists could turn. He had served the party and the nation long and well and his candidacy would provoke no bitter opposition. As a southerner, Pinckney's candidacy would also afford the Federalists at least a semblance of national appeal.

Pinckney was the son of a wealthy plantation family and, in the best tradition of the planter class, he had accepted early in his life the obligation of the privileged and talented to render public service. Educated in England, he returned to this country in 1769 to begin a distinguished career as a lawyer, but soon found himself embroiled in the politics of the colony. Elected to the provincial assembly, he moved quickly to a position of responsibility and authority. At the same time, he made a name for himself as a philanthropist, musician, and one of the South's most prominent botanists.

With "a passion for glory and a zeal for the cause of his country" Pinckney entered the Revolution wholeheartedly, serving as colonel and aide to General George Washington. He was captured by the British in the fall of Charleston in 1780, was exchanged in 1782, and completed his service as a brigadier general. After the war he found himself drawn more and more into the vortex of national politics. In 1787 he was a delegate to the Federal Convention where he vigorously supported the Constitution. Between 1791 and 1795, he was offered command of the Army and the posts of secretary of war and secretary of state but he declined all three. Finally, in 1796, he accepted the ministry to France and in 1797 took part in the special peace mission to that country, which later was characterized as the XYZ affair. When the French officials demanded in advance of negotiations a public disavowal of anti-French statements by President Adams, a $12 million loan and a bribe of $250,000, Pinckney's obdurate reply (he believed that the amount of the bribe was excessive), "No! No! Not a Sixpence!" transmuted in after-legend to "Millions for defense, but not one cent for tribute," resounded through America and made him the national hero of his day.

In 1800 Pinckney had been nominated for the vice-presidency by the Federalists in the hope that he could seduce South Carolina from its Jeffersonian predisposition. Unwittingly, he became the principle instrument in the Hamiltonian plot to depose John Adams from the presidency. Pinckney, however, was not a politically ambitious man; his ambition was generated more by a strong sense of duty and patriotism than a desire for power and place, and so he refused to lend support to Hamilton's scheme. In so doing, he lost the vice-presidency but preserved his honor and his reputation.

Pinckney's candidacy in 1804 aroused little public attention: he is said to have had "the dubious honor of being the least publicized candidate in the brief history of American presidential elections." Because of the general support for Republican policies and the personal appeal of Jefferson, the Federalists were hard put to find any issues and in some states no compaigns were waged at all. There was little to do but watch the Republicans roll to a sweeping electoral victory: Jefferson received 162 votes to Pinckney's 14.

Accepting the circumstances, Pinckney troubled himself very little with the campaign. In fact, most of his time during the election period was spent leading a crusade against the custom of dueling. Motivated by the fatal duel between his close friend, Alexander Hamilton, and Aaron Burr, as well as personal experience with the dueling custom, having been wounded himself in 1785, Pinckney spent the summer urging the outlawing of the practice. His efforts were unsuccessful, however, a fact which seemingly troubled him a good deal more than losing the presidential election.

CHARLES COTESWORTH PINCKNEY *James Earl Oil on canvas, 45 x 36 inches*
Carolina Art Association, Charleston

Charles Cotesworth Pinckney *Federalist*

1746-1825

After his defeat in the election of 1804, Charles Cotesworth Pinckney retreated into the isolation of his plantation on Pinckney's Island, one hundred miles from Charleston. Although he had paid slight attention to the election and seemingly had been unconcerned about the outcome, he no doubt felt somewhat chagrined by the decisiveness of Jefferson's victory. In the quiet solitude of his island home he drew comfort from his agricultural and scientific pursuits, giving little thought to political matters. The Federalists also slipped from public view after the election. Unable to make an effective bid for a return to power, that party was limited to rear-guard actions. By 1806, however, developments in international affairs gave the Federalist Party a new lease on life and brought Charles Cotesworth Pinckney out of retirement.

War between France and England had broken out again and the United States was finding itself continuously used as a pawn in the belligerents' struggle for world power. America's attempts to maintain its prestige and neutral rights were proving futile as the search and seizure of vessels and British impressment of its sailors, practices which had long been matters of contention, were resumed with fierce intensity. Combined Anglo-French restrictions on American commerce in an attempt of both powers to stop aid from going to either rival were also becoming intolerable.

The final insult came in June 1807. The nearly defenseless American frigate, the *Chesapeake,* refused to allow itself to be searched for British deserters. In retaliation, the British man-of-war HMS *Leopard* insolently turned its guns on her, and before the *Chesapeake* could strike her colors, killed three men and wounded eighteen. As news of this outrage spread throughout the country, the populace began clamoring for war with Britain. Peace was Jefferson's passion, however, and as a substitute for war, he developed a policy of economic coercion: a total embargo on commerce that prohibited American vessels from sailing to foreign ports and foreign vessels from taking on cargo in the United States.

Seldom has an American governmental policy been met with as much resentment and resistance by the public as was the Embargo Act of 1807. Especially in those regions of the country whose total economy depended upon the prosperity of foreign trade—New York and

57

New England—was there a loud outcry of protest. The sacrifice was considered too great: exports fell from $108 million in 1807 to $22 million in 1808, while imports from $138 million to less than $57 million. In short, the remedy was considered more harmful than the disease. While the embargo struck a hard blow to economic and maritime interests within the United States, to the Federalist Party it was a godsend. Immediately, Federalist leaders began to capitalize on the people's discontent, seeing in it an opportunity to reverse the electoral decisions of 1800 and 1804. Jefferson's handling of the crisis provided a major issue for the Federalists to exploit in the presidential election of 1808; now electoral strategy was all-important.

Not all Federalists agreed that this was the right time to return to power, even if victory was possible. The United States, was, after all, in a difficult position and the Federalists might enter office only to be blasted by the tempests of international politics. As an alternative, it was suggested that Federalist support should be thrown to the least evil Republican. If misfortune struck, it would be the Republicans' problem and the Federalists would then be in a better position for victory in 1812.

Since there were so few Federalists in Congress, a caucus merely of their representatives would not be effective. A new device for selecting a standard-bearer was needed. Thus, in the third week of August 1808 at New York City, the Federalists convened the first national nominating convention ever to be held in this country.

By the time the convention met, the scent of a Federalist victory had grown stronger and the tactic of supporting a Republican for the presidency was quickly dropped. Instead, the party turned once again to Charles Cotesworth Pinckney. The old warrior, riled by Jefferson's failure to take positive action to protect the nation's commerce and coastal cities, resolved to wage a vigorous campaign "to shew that federalism is not extinct, and that there is in the Union a formidable party of the old Washington school, alert to detect and expose any weak or visionary plans which may endanger the prosperity or safety of our Country." Pinckney was now prepared to play an active role in the campaign.

As in 1800, the Federalists hoped that Pinckney could win the support of his native state of South Carolina, which was in the clutches of the Republicans. The campaign was heated there, and the emphasis was placed more on Pinckney's personal merit than on the issues. Federalists praised Pinckney's military career; he was "a defender of his country against every enemy." Residents of the state were chastised for allowing Pinckney, a man of "strict honor and incorruptible integrity, of talents and energy" to be defeated in 1804, but were told that they now had an opportunity to redeem themselves by voting for him in the upcoming election. The Republicans, in turn, attempted to discredit Pinckney's claim for the presidency; he was too old, he had been away from government affairs too long, and as a military man he could not be trusted in a civil office.

In the end, Pinckney was not only rejected by the nation, but by his own state as well. The threat of Federalist victory rallied the Republicans to move with at least a semblance of unity behind Madison, Jefferson's choice for his successor. Moreover, Jefferson still commanded the affection of the majority of Americans, despite the economic blockades, and most continued to look to the Republican Party for peace. In the states, especially, Republican organization was strong and frequently state issues were more important to voters than national issues. Thus, the Republicans won a substantial victory. The Federalists did, however, increase the 14 electoral votes received in 1804 to 47, proving they could by no means be entirely dismissed from the political scene.

Pinckney showed no bitterness over his defeat. Politics had never been his first love, and he minded very little relinquishing the role of Republican antagonist. Henry William De Saussure, a former law student and intimate friend of Pinckney's, expressed the old man's feelings: "He is contented in the shade of privacy which he cultivates, and seeks not public favor or employment! but he cannot resist the call of his Country if it be made."

GEORGE CLINTON   *Ezra Ames, circa 1812   Oil on canvas, 30½ x 25 inches*
New York State Historical Association, Cooperstown

George Clinton *Democratic–Republican*

1739-1812

Thomas Jefferson's wish that James Madison should succeed him in the presidency was well-known in Republican circles. He had thought Madison destined for the post of chief executive even before his own election to that office. Accordingly, a caucus of Republican members of Congress meeting in January 1808 named the Virginian as their candidate for president and nominated New Yorker George Clinton, vice-president since 1804, for the second place.

Not all of the Republicans were pleased with the caucus decision. George Clinton was, in fact, exceedingly disappointed. This time, he believed, his nomination should not have been for vice-president. He wanted to be president, and he felt his previous record and present standing entitled him to the privilege. As vice-president, he expected that the presidential mantle would fall to him just as it had to Vice-Presidents Adams and Jefferson. And, not only had he been a major influence in national politics for over twenty years, with a following few men of his generation enjoyed, but he had been a dedicated Republican leader long before Jefferson appeared on the scene. He believed, too, that his elevation would satisfy the disgruntled New Yorkers who accused Virginia of wanting to monopolize the presidency.

From an early age, Clinton had had a compelling desire to play a decisive role in the political life of New York and the nation, but in a state where family connections and property counted for so much in public life Clinton's modest background was a severe handicap. The son of an immigrant surveyor and farmer, he was a man of "common clay" with only a slight education and no social pretensions. In the democratic ferment of the Revolution, however, he had found the way to political prominence. Embracing with sincerity the ideals of liberty and equality, he came to represent the new bourgeoisie—the farmers, laborers, and tradespeople—who sought not only freedom from England but also the establishment of republicanism in America. His simplicity of character and lack of family eminence became political assets enabling him to become a rallying point for the rank and file who accepted him as one of themselves.

Clinton's service as a brigadier general in the war won him an early reputation as a popular leader despite his self-admitted limitations as a military strategist. When in 1777 New

York elected its first governor under the new state constitution, Clinton's popularity, particularly with the soldiers, was so great that he was elected both governor and lieutenant governor at the same time. Once in office, "His Excellency" built a power structure equal to that of the patrician families and which, maintained by a series of alliances, withstood nearly all opposition for the next twenty years. Clinton served eighteen consecutive years as governor (1777-1795) and another three-year term from 1801 to 1804. Thrust onto the national stage during the bitter controversy over ratification of the Constitution, Clinton's stubborn championship of states' rights made him the leader of northern Republicans who opposed the Constitution and the creation of a consolidated central government. He was, consequently, the vice-presidential candidate in 1789 of those anti-Federalists who wished to be certain of the inclusion of a bill of rights in the new Constitution. From that time on, Clinton was a perennial candidate for the vice-presidency, but not until 1804 did he succeed in attaining that office.

Unfortunately for Clinton, election to national office came too late. In his mid-sixties and in failing health, he found even the few duties of a vice-president too arduous. He often complained that just sitting in his chair as president pro tem of the Senate for the few hours required each day was extremely fatiguing to him. His powers were declining and he was clearly approaching senescence. But in 1808 he could still muster enough influence to cast himself in the role of presidential candidate.

The driving force behind Clinton's candidacy was the ambitious and aggressive DeWitt Clinton, the governor's nephew who, by virtue of his uncle's patronage, had been named United States senator and mayor of New York and who may have seen in the elder Clinton's election an opportunity for himself. DeWitt's own ambition, coupled with his uncle's yearning for the honor of the presidency, moved the Clinton candidacy onward even when chances of success were slim.

George Clinton denounced the decision of the caucus to support James Madison and issued a letter to the press disassociating himself from the proceedings. He carefully neglected to reject their vice-presidential nomination, however, a tactic which prevented Madison forces from leveling any outright attack on him. Meanwhile, every effort was made to capitalize on anti-administration sentiment. The vice-president had early shown his displeasure with Jefferson's foreign policies and showed no hesitation in criticizing the president or his administration. "It is in my opinion impossible," he wrote in April 1808, "that the Cause of republicanism can exist much longer under the present visionary Feeble and I might add corrupt Management of our National affairs." Clinton's opposition to the unpopular embargo was indeed his greatest strength; it was said during the campaign that his views were those of the mass of the American yeomanry on this subject.

The only real hope that Clinton had of deposing Madison was the possibility of forming an alliance with the Federalists. That party was badly divided and hesitated in the selection of a candidate. But too many Federalists believed an alliance with the Clintonians would end only in failure, while others feared Clinton would repudiate them once elected. The result was that the Federalists determined to nominate their own candidate, Charles Cotesworth Pinckney.

Thus, the presidency was removed from Clinton's reach. Without the support of the incumbent administration or of the opposition, Clinton's defeat was inevitable. He polled only 6 electoral votes to Madison's 122. Ironically, he made as clean a sweep of the second office as Madison did of the first and despite his genuine difference of opinion over policy and his thwarted ambition, Clinton served as vice-president until his death in April 1812.

DE WITT CLINTON   *John Wesley Jarvis, circa 1816   Oil on canvas, 48¼ x 36⅜ inches*
From the Collection of the National Portrait Gallery   Gift of Andrew Mellon   NPG.65.53

DeWitt Clinton *Federalist*

1769-1828

In June of 1812 the Congress of the United States declared war on Great Britain, a decision which reflected an outraged national pride at repeated maritime injuries and interference with American commerce, as well as the expansionist ambitions of men of the southern and western frontiers. Prodded by congressional war hawks like Henry Clay and John Calhoun, President Madison had become convinced that the British must be stopped. "I flung forward the flag of the country," he said in later years, "sure that the people would press onward and defend it." But Madison had failed to foresee how badly the question of the war would divide the country. Conflict with the mightiest power in the world seemed certain to end in disaster; American land and naval forces were woefully unprepared for such a struggle. Maritime New England was particularly discontented over this new severing of its commercial ties with Britain. The Republican-enforced embargo had already cost merchants and shippers millions of dollars, and the war would surely cost them much more. From the inception of hostilities, talk of disunion was rampant in the Northeast. Justification and prosecution of the war naturally became the major issue of the presidential campaign of 1812.

One month before the declaration of war, a caucus of congressional Republicans unanimously nominated James Madison for a second term as president of the United States. At that time, his reelection seemed certain. The Federalist Party had almost ceased to exist and could come up with no candidate of significant national appeal to defeat Madison. George Clinton, long a rallying point for anti-administration sentiment and a rival of Madison's in the election of 1808, had died in April. But DeWitt Clinton, George's nephew, who had worked hard to secure the presidency for his uncle four years earlier, harbored his own ambitions for the office. Lacking his uncle's honest simplicity and strong ideological commitment, the aristocratic Clinton profited from his inherited political connection. Well-established in New York—he had been state legislator and United States senator and was presently mayor of New York City and lieutenant governor—he now thought the time was ripe to seek fulfillment of his higher aspirations. Antipathy toward the war and widespread economic discontent seemed to him issues which, if capitalized on, might make him president.

Madison supporters tried to stave off Clinton's candidacy by offering him the vice-presidential nomination. But Clinton saw no reason to accept the second place and on May 29, he was nominated for president of the United States by insurgent Republicans in the New York legislature.

Clinton was well-equipped to handle a rough-and-tumble presidential campaign. He had helped his uncle found a political dynasty in New York and together they had ruled the state for over thirty years, surmounting all challenges. George Clinton had built a power structure on his genuine republicanism and appeal to the common man; DeWitt broadened and strengthened that structure with his great skill as a manipulator and organizer. A political Machiavellian, he was not above exploiting any means to gain and keep power. He lived by the doctrine of expediency and cared little for party discipline except when it suited his purposes. Henry Adams wrote in his *History* that while no one could ever predict Clinton's course in a given situation, it was certain that it would be shaped according to what seemed to be the interests of his ambition.

This judgment seems particularly valid in reference to Clinton's campaign tactics. He had been nominated, said the New York *Columbian,* as "a man Whom Heaven has Reared to fit the occasion of the [war] crisis." But how he was prepared to meet that crisis depended largely on the audience to whom he was appealing. Before entering the campaign he had entertained a Jeffersonian abhorrence of war, and he undoubtedly rued the fact that the struggle with Britain had been undertaken. As a candidate, however, he attempted to attract all elements of opposition to his side. He was both a "thunderbolt of war and an angel of peace." To his Republican supporters, he promised a more vigorous prosecution of the war and peace without dishonor. Madison was vilified for plunging the country into a war without preparation and blamed for every military failure, while Clinton, in contrast, was presented as an effective and energetic war leader. To the Federalists, however, without whose support he had no hope of winning, the candidate pledged the immediate cessation of hostilities; throughout New England, he gave assurances "that he would hasten to finish so disastrous a war."

As in 1808, the Federalist Party had to decide whether to nominate their own candidate or support a Clinton. Most Federalists realized that their party could not elect a president without combining with the dissident Republicans. Their prime goal was, they reflected, to prevent Madison's "annihilation of the Nation" and if Clinton was the man who could do this he should be supported. Only Rufus King offered real resistance to the movement to back the New Yorker. Although Clinton promised if elected to run the government in a manner agreeable to the Federalists, King was unconvinced. Denouncing Clinton for his vacillation and intrigue in the past, he declared that the Federalists would merely be replacing a "Caesar Borgia for James Madison." Ultimately, the Federalists decided not to formally endorse Clinton for fear it might weaken his Republican support, but it was agreed that the party would support Clinton's electors.

Clinton's attempts to seduce support from both sides almost brought him success. He won handily in the commercial states where the war caused real economic hardships. All New England, with the exception of Vermont, went to Clinton and he carried New York, New Jersey,

Delaware, and part of Maryland. Had he carried just one more state—Pennsylvania—he would have been elected president. It is significant, however, that he lost in the West and South where commitment to the war was greatest and nationalism as expressed in expansionism more rampant. The final tally was Madison 128, Clinton 89.

For consorting with Federalists, Clinton suffered the contempt of the Republicans and his prestige in his state reached its nadir. He was not renominated for lieutenant governor and in 1815 he was removed from the mayoralty. In this time of political decline came the crowning achievement of Clinton's life: the building of the Erie Canal which joined the Great Lakes to the Atlantic, the greatest engineering project of the day. The success of this project, for which Clinton was largely responsible, opened a new phase in his political life. Elected governor, he rode a new wave of popularity and was being mentioned once again as a presidential candidate when he suddenly died in 1828.

RUFUS KING *Gilbert Stuart Oil on panel, 32 x 25 inches Anonymous lender*

Rufus King *Federalist*

1755-1827

In 1816, the elderly and politically weary Rufus King became the presidential candidate of a dying party. Suffering from the stigma of its opposition to the War of 1812 and the futile secessionist gesture of the New England Federalists who expressed their opposition to "Mr. Madison's War" in the Hartford Convention, the Federalists had for all intents and purposes ceased to exist as a national power. A faithful few still clung to Federalist ideology, but party organization had crumbled and no policies or programs were being formulated. Most party members were resigned to Republican control of the country; any further attempt to regain power would be as King himself said, a "fruitless struggle." There was little else to do but "adhere to the integrity of their principles" and "assist the true interests of Freedom & of Justice by giving their influence to the least wicked Section of the Republicans." "Federalists of our age," King had written despondently, "must be content with the past."

King was himself a figure of the past both in appearance and philosophy. Still clad in the gentlemanly knee breeches, silk stockings, and buckled shoes of Washington's age, he appeared to younger men as a pompous and arrogant aristocrat. A contemporary said of him that he had "something of pride and hauteur in his manner, offensive to the spirit of republicanism, and inconsistent with the nature of equality." King grew up a member of the upper class of colonial society, attended Harvard and studied law under Theophilus Parsons, later chief justice of Massachusetts, whose tutelage inspired a keen interest and understanding of politics. His traditional Federalist values—belief in social distinctions, control of government by the moneyed classes, and favoritism toward property rights—seemed increasingly anachronistic in the eyes of a generation inflamed with democratic ideals.

King's public career spanned forty years and the formation of the Union. He was a delegate from Massachusetts to the Continental Congress and a signer of the Constitution. As United States senator from New York and as ambassador to the Court of St. James, he served during the administrations of the first six presidents, a record matched only by the sixth president, John Quincy Adams. Other than John Marshall, King was the last Federalist to enjoy continuous national prominence. The men with whom he had united to build a nation and a party had either died or retired from public life and a new generation of politicians, borne on the rising tide of democracy, had gradually taken their places.

In a caucus held in Washington on March 16, 1816, the Republicans had nominated James Monroe to be Madison's successor. The Federalists did not bother to hold a nominating caucus or convention: King's candidacy simply evolved out of a general agreement among remaining party members. Because continued Republican monopoly of the presidency seemed so certain, the Federalists made no serious attempt to organize a campaign. Electoral tickets were presented in only three states. Harrison Gray Otis, an ardent Massachusetts Federalist, indicated the utter hopelessness of his party when he urged his colleagues to vote for Monroe instead of throwing away their votes on a candidate who could not possibly win.

King himself suffered no illusions, nor did he entertain presidential ambitions despite the fact that he had been the Federalist nominee for vice-president in 1804 and 1808. "So certain is the Result," he realistically concluded, ". . . that no pains are taken to excite the Community on the subject. It is quite worthy of remark, that in no preceding Election has there been such a Calm respecting it. . . ."

King received only 34 electoral votes to Monroe's 183 and carried only Delaware, Connecticut, and Massachusetts. The defeat marked the end of Federalism as a national force, though the party continued to operate locally for some years. Rufus King, as its last presidential candidate, had become a symbol of the end of an age.

The Era of Good Feelings and the End of an Age 1820

IN 1820, THE AMERICAN PEOPLE WERE BASKING IN THE CONTENTMENT OF AN "ERA OF Good Feelings," a time of political unity and harmony that marked the culmination of the rule of the Virginia dynasty. James Monroe was the last of the succession of Virginian aristocrats who from 1800 to 1824 occupied the president's office. Acquiring their positions as if through heredity, they exercised power with an aristocratic, although genuine, concern for the national well-being and welfare of their countrymen. All three, Jefferson, Madison, and Monroe, held rational views of men and government, but in office they frequently found their theories severely tested by the events through which they were forced to steer a course. To them fell the job of piloting the nation through prosperity and depression, cold and hot war, domestic tranquillity and conflict. They witnessed the country grow from a population of a little over five million in 1800 to almost ten million in 1820, and they could envision future growth with equanimity. For the tranquil nature of politics, despite the factional irritations that cropped up in congressmen's "questions" of administration policies, promised social harmony as well as peaceful expansion and national prosperity.

By 1820, American territory had expanded beyond its old confines as a result of a steady immigration of Europeans and the "American Multiplication Table"—as Benjamin Franklin amusedly termed the phenomenon of population increase in the United States. Pioneering settlers had pushed relentlessly into the old Northwest and the new territory of Louisiana seeking land and opportunity, writing new constitutions, and clamoring to be heard in the seats of power in Washington. At the time of Monroe's second inauguration, the new states of Ohio and Kentucky surpassed Massachusetts in population, while other western states like Tennessee were fast gaining ground.

Five new states participated in the election of 1820, and four of them were from the West. Although quiet in 1820, four years later these western states would begin to feel their strength and make their influence felt in national politics and demand an end to the monopoly of power wielded by eastern aristocrats. One of these western states was the newly admitted Missouri, so new to statehood that a fist fight occurred in Congress over the question of having its votes counted. The Compromise that had made possible its admission into the Union as a slave state was already being hotly contested in southern legislatures, and the issues it provoked, quiescent in 1820, would erupt during the next election campaign.

In the new western states, state constitutions providing for universal white-manhood suffrage had been written, following the example of four of the older states, which had substantially dropped property qualifications for voters between 1810 and 1821. With the ballot came demands from the poorer farmers and workers that they be allowed to participate more in the formation of public policy and the choice of leaders. New political techniques were seen as necessary to meet the demands and interests of these newly enfranchised groups. Some of these were tried out in 1824, but it was not until 1840 that the full influence of the broadened suffrage was felt. Between 1820 and 1840, however, parties and political leaders wrestled with the problems created by changes in the political life of the country; they evolved new theories of government, and new political institutions and practices, all of which would take time to work out and put in functional order. In 1820, however, these problems were still embryonic, and the "Era of Good Feelings" could continue without having to take full account of them.

With the extension of the country's borders to northern, western, and southern frontiers, speculation in lands and banks increased enormously. Reckless investments led to over-extension of credit facilities and consequent bankruptcies and foreclosures. The Panic of 1819 was a direct result of the over-enthusiasm of a debtor economy for economic development, pointing the need for new economic institutions that would adjust more flexibly to the needs of American farmers, landowners, and manufacturers.

Population and territorial growth also created new sectional problems and renewed old sectional controversies that the "Era of Good Feelings" could only attempt to stifle. But if Monroe was successful in sweeping both the old and new problems under the rug of party unity for a time, his successors were not, and eventually all the questions that would plague the country—the tariff, land policy, banks, slavery, and the economy—would emerge in larger and more virulent form. In 1820, none of the deep-lying problems surfaced to ruffle the political horizon. Actually, the United States was a partyless state—for the last time in its history—and much pride was taken in that fact.

With President Monroe the symbol of national unity, it is not surprising that during his administrations the cause of nationalism secured its most complete articulation. Prominent Republicans like Clay and Adams called for economic nationalism and maintained the necessity for national planning in the economic realm in order to achieve self-sufficiency; cultural nationalists like Noah Webster emphasized the importance of a native cultural life free of foreign influences in language, art, and literature; and political nationalists dwelt on the absence of "discord," as Monroe expressed it in his First Inaugural Address. The diplomatic policies of Monroe and his Secretary of State John Quincy Adams extended the pervasive nationalist psychology beyond the nation's borders in the so-called "Monroe Doctrine," while John Marshall's decisions in the Supreme Court gave the cause of political nationalism even greater support. On the domestic political front, Monroe and his Republican cohorts went about absorbing the weakened Federalist opposition in a display of consensus ideology that reflected the prevailing desire for national unity. By 1819, every former Federalist state except Massachusetts was controlled by the Republicans and Monroe was able to conclude, optimistically but unrealistically, in his Second Inaugural Address that "powerful causes had drawn the people together in a lasting unity of sentiment."

The election of 1820 was virtually uncontested. An attempt was made by a cabal of discontented Republicans to unseat Monroe, but by election time their efforts were frustrated and Monroe received all the electoral votes except the one cast by William Plumer of New Hampshire. History has it that Mr. Plumer cast his vote against Monroe only because he believed that the honor of a unanimous vote should be Washington's alone; but William Plumer also had his eye on 1824, and was serving notice that the candidate of New England would be its favorite son and his, John Quincy Adams.

Thus 1820 marked the culmination of the Era of Good Feelings and the beginning of the end of that Era. From here on, candidates for the presidency would come from all sections of the country and from all walks of life. The office would become increasingly a sectional as well as political prize, and sectional considerations would replace national. And, finally, candidates would come to symbolize specific local and sectional points of view, while party platforms would reflect the necessities of a region more than the aspirations of the nation.

The "Corrupt Bargain" 1824

CHANGES IN THE AMERICAN POLITICAL PROCESS ARE FREQUENTLY SLOW IN COMING, despite all the signposts announcing their inevitable arrival. In 1824, the problems that had quietly made their appearance in 1820 had not become crucial enough to effect marked changes in political behavior. Americans continued to regard presidents as statesmen whose concerns were national in scope, rather than sectional, and who were figures of national respectability rather than symbols of issues. Especially after the War of 1812, the introduction of issues of a sectional nature into a presidential campaign was regarded as divisive; in the movement towards consensus, individual personalities were considered more important than the causes they represented, and issues were separated from candidates. Perhaps this explains the voter apathy in 1824, for only 26.5 percent of the eligible voters went to the polls that year, despite the extension of the suffrage in many states and despite the enthusiasm demonstrated by local crowds for individual candidates. Whatever the desire for a more equitable regional representation in the presidency—in the West especially, where the cry was for "a Western President"—the "roaring flood of the new democracy," that Charles A. Beard saw "foaming perilously near the crest" in 1824 did not overflow the dam of apathy created by the long reign of the Virginia dynasty and the consequent creation of a monolithic Republican Party.

But if a large number of the qualified citizenry of the country neglected to indicate their preferences at the polls, the age was not without its sense of what George Dangerfield has called "democratic urgency." Americans were aware of the issues; more excitement was engendered by this election than by any since 1800, and more questions of democratic import were hotly debated than ever before. The people made a choice, but found their wishes thwarted by a complicated electoral system that forced the decision into the House of Representatives. Acquiescing in 1824, by 1828 the voters would overwhelmingly insist that the most popular candidate, Andrew Jackson, be placed in the White House.

The problem of the congressional caucus nominating system first aroused the democratic sensitivities of the people. In 1824, the Republican caucus gave the official nomination to William Crawford, Monroe's secretary of the treasury. In doing so, it had not taken account of the many factions that restlessly were contained within the one-party structure of the Republican Party and which looked to either John Quincy Adams, Andrew Jackson, John C. Calhoun, or Henry Clay for leadership. These neglected Republicans rallied democratic feeling against the caucus system, accusing it of being an unconstitutional device in which choice by an elite group was substituted for the electors provided by the Constitution. In the Senate, Rufus King assailed "this new, extraordinary, self-created cultural power stronger than that of the Constitution." State conventions ignored the action of the congressional caucus. Reflecting popular choice, they nominated candidates more acceptable to the region involved and assailed the old—and antiquated—party machinery that had served the Republicans well while they were able to maintain party unity.

A two-party system as opposed to one-party consensus was also deemed essential to the democratic process. Followers of Martin Van Buren in the state of New York, who called themselves the Bucktails, were shaping a more modern political ideology emphasizing the

76

importance of opposition. Whereas up to now the idea of national political unity had prevailed, the New Yorkers announced that an opposition party gave voters an alternative, and therefore was more democratic. Moreover, as a corollary, they developed the idea that party loyalty was more democratic than loyalty to an individual leader. They had demonstrated this in New York with their successful opposition to the individual leadership of DeWitt Clinton, and now they were preparing to extend their ideology over the national scene. Eventually, Americans would accept the Bucktails' argument for a two-party system, and would come to believe that majoritarian control of party policy was more appropriate to the nation's political ideals than decision making by aristocrats and autocrats. These changes in the traditional political procedures constituted the democratic thrust of the time. The people, now that they had achieved suffrage rights, were seeking to participate more in the machinery of party organization. If, to some extent, their demands in 1824 were more rhetorical than real and intended as propaganda whereby younger politicians sought to wrest control from their elders, the rhetoric eventually had to express itself in practice and in the creation of new political institutions geared to the changes in ideology. Thus, the seeds of the modern party system were sown and an end written to an era in American political thought and practice.

Beyond democratic political practices, however, were issues that probed even more deeply into the nature of the American Union. The candidates tried to avoid them in order to maintain the semblance of platform unity—after all, they were all Republicans. Smoldering, however, beneath the surface contest of personalities to erupt later into searing flames of violence and war—were the questions posed by federal involvement in the economy through support of internal improvements, a high tariff, and a national bank. Related was the constitutional question of the extension of federal power beyond the letter of the Constitution, a particularly sensitive point to southerners who feared federal involvement in the institution of slavery.

Uneasily, southerners had listened to the decisions of Chief Justice Marshall in 1819 dealing with the power of national law in bankruptcy and contract cases, and the primacy of federal institutions over state taxing power in the famous case of *McCulloch* vs. *Maryland*. If, as John Taylor of Caroline wrote in his classic expression of states' rights philosophy, *Construction Construed and Constitutions Vindicated* (1819), the new aristocracy, of "liquid" (as opposed to propertied) wealth was becoming the "master class" in the United States—a moneyed aristocracy capable of imposing its will on the people and state institutions—then the South had every right, in fact a duty, in defense of its society and traditions, to leave the Union even if that meant civil war.

The Missouri Compromise, following fast on Marshall's nationalistic decisions, strengthened the South's suspicions that—in the words of the Virginia House of Delegates—he had "changed the whole character of the government," and given Congress "unlimited and uncontrolled power." The South, said the Virginia legislative group, must consider forcible resistance

"A Foot-Race" by David Claypoole Johnston, 1824 AMERICAN ANTIQUARIAN
SOCIETY, WORCESTER, MASSACHUSETTS

to national authority if Congress, acting upon the principles by which it had established the Bank
of the United States and imposed restrictions on slavery in United States territories, should
interfere with the institution of slavery within the states.

The tariff was another sectional issue that simmered under the surface of the rhetoric
of 1824. In 1816, the South had supported the desire of the industrializing North for a protective tariff, but only as a temporary expedient to raise much-needed revenues, to encourage
whatever American industry had been established during the War of 1812 in order to be
prepared for another war with England, and to halt the flooding of the American market by
cheap British goods.

By 1819, most of these arguments were no longer serviceable. The country had sufficient
revenue, and whatever new revenues were required could be collected from excise taxes; northern manufacturers were reaping high profits from the Panic of 1819, which had lowered the
price of cotton, rice, and tobacco and other raw materials used in the manufacturing process,

while southern planters were suffering from the low prices of their products and the necessity to pay higher prices for manufactured goods in a tariff-protected market. Meanwhile, the tariff of 1820 extended what had seemed to be a limited tariff in 1816 to other products, and with the addition of new items to the tariff list southerners came to believe that the appeals of northern protectionists were no longer valid. The South, therefore, turned away from the tariff bill of 1820, and in 1824 looked to a candidate who would represent their agrarian interests.

It is not surprising that candidates skirted these issues in their appeal to the voters in 1824. Still inhibited by their membership in the same party, still aiming for national unity and consensus, the candidates remained relatively quiet during the campaign and left the electioneering to partisan newspapers and public speeches by supporters in state legislatures. Here, candidates were attacked because of personal habits and beliefs—either they were aristocrats or barbarians, believers or nonbelievers, spendthrifts or misers, gamesters or snobs. But the electoral and popular votes broken down into regions, states, and counties tell the real story. Clay and Adams, symbolizing national power used efficiently, received the votes of their own sections and of those states that wanted internal improvements and a protective tariff; they lost votes in those counties and cities of the West badly hit by the Panic of 1819 and the restrictive policies of the "monster" Bank, and in the South where states' rights and the protection of slavery interests were uppermost. Crawford's votes were primarily southern, with some from New York and the border states where party loyalty was emphasized. Jackson won all the votes of New Jersey, Pennsylvania, North and South Carolina, Alabama, Mississippi, Tennessee, and Indiana, the majority of Maryland's votes, and more than half of Louisiana's and Illinois'. In his vote, the frontier elements, some working class groups and agrarian interests coalesced, looking to Jackson as a military hero, a westerner with agrarian sympathies, and a defender of the states and of democracy. With such a distribution of votes, there could be no majority, and the choice as expected was given to the House of Representatives according to constitutional dictates.

The House's decision was reached as a result of various factors, not the least of which was Clay's resolve to throw his strength to Adams despite the undoubted preference of his western constituents for Jackson. Clay's acceptance of Adams' offer to become secretary of state earned for him the title of the "Judas of the West" and the unsavory reputation of having sold out for office. The phrase "corrupt bargain" was associated with him and Adams thereafter and to a great extent stimulated Jackson's exertions to win the election in 1828 as well as determining the outcome of the later election.

WILLIAM HARRIS CRAWFORD *John Wesley Jarvis, 1823 Oil on canvas,*
30¼ x 25¼ inches Pennsylvania Academy of the Fine Arts, Philadelphia

William Harris Crawford *Democratic-Republican*

1772-1834

In 1816, William Harris Crawford was James Monroe's chief rival for the presidential nomination of the Republican party, and although he was strong enough politically to have won the nomination if he had pressed, he decided not to oppose such a "venerable figure." Whether he genuinely believed Monroe should have the office, or whether, as some believed, he was induced to withdraw by the promise of support for the succession in 1824, is uncertain. Still young, he could certainly afford to wait for the honor. But one thing was certain: Crawford wanted to be president and having stepped aside in 1816, he would not do so again.

Born in Virginia of impoverished but genteel Scotch-Irish parents, Crawford moved as a child to South Carolina and then across the Savannah into Georgia as his family sought relief from financial strain. When his father died of smallpox in 1783, William, as eldest son, supported his mother and a cluster of sisters and brothers, struggling to gain an education while assuming the responsibility of the family farm. By working as an usher, he managed to attend a local academy run by the Reverend Moses Waddel, known throughout the South as a builder of men. Waddel introduced Crawford to the world of classical literature and philosophy and stimulated his interest in the science and art of government. Determined and ambitious to make something of himself and restore his family to its deserved place in society, Crawford took up the study of law and became a prominent attorney. Through his marriage to Susanna Girardin, daughter of a wealthy planter, he gained entry to the "manor-house nobility." His entrance into politics, which he considered a sure road to prestige, power, and wealth, was inevitable.

Crawford, a gracious and affable giant of a man with a keen mind, first became politically involved while a student. Taking advantage of the scandal aroused by the action of the Georgia legislature making—under shady circumstances—and then canceling a grant of millions of acres along the Mississippi to the Yazoo land companies, Crawford joined the campaign of outraged Republicans to expose the perpetrators of the scheme. The gesture was futile as far as exposing the alleged frauds, but successful in laying the foundation for his future political popularity.

In 1803, he was elected to the Georgia legislature where he managed to champion the Republican interests of the farmer while at the same time building an alliance with the conservative, financially orthodox, businessmen of the state.

Crawford rose steadily in national politics. In 1807, he was chosen to fill a vacancy in the United States Senate and was subsequently reelected in 1811 without opposition. On the death of Vice-President George Clinton in 1812, he was named president pro tempore of the Senate, a manifestation of the members' respect for his ability and leadership. In 1813 he was appointed by James Madison to the post of minister to France; two years later, he was named secretary of war. In 1816 he took another step up in the political hierarchy by becoming secretary of the treasury. Through the influence of his offices and the extensive use of patronage, he strengthened and refined his support to such a degree that by 1817 he was one of the most powerful men in American politics. As such, Crawford, like his northern counterpart DeWitt Clinton, represented a new breed of politician on the American scene. Intensely self-seeking, he was driven by ambition rather than the kind of ideological commitment that moved statesmen like Jefferson and Madison. Men, not ideas, were the bricks of his political structure. More shrewd than profound, he was a superb manipulator and organizer.

With his claim on the presidency established in 1816, Crawford prepared to assert himself in 1824 as the true heir to the "Jeffersonian" tradition and thus to the Republican Party nomination. With support from the "junta of Richmond," the fading remnant of the Virginia dynasty, and the assistance of the well-controlled New York party organization under the direction of Martin Van Buren, Crawford's position seemed impregnable. But in the early fall of 1823 fate dealt Crawford a staggering blow. A paralytic stroke, probably induced by an overdose of a drug prescribed to treat an attack of erysipelas, left him blind, speechless, and paralyzed. As if the stroke had not done enough damage, Crawford's doctor bled him twenty-three times within three weeks.

News of his affliction was closely guarded; only a paragraph indicating he was recovering from a painful illness appeared in the Georgia papers. But rumors abounded, especially in the opposition press. His condition was reported as "pitiable" and "hopeless" by some, while a more hostile newspaper remarked that his death would "be much more of a National Blessing than his election." In time Crawford rallied and by the spring of 1824 had returned to some of his duties at the Treasury Department, but he never fully recovered. Even so, he doggedly refused to quit the struggle. His partisans continued to work in his behalf; too ill to direct his own campaign, he selected Martin Van Buren, a master in the art of political intrigue, as his campaign manager.

Crawford's nomination by a caucus of Republican members in Congress was essential to his election; carrying the weight of tradition behind it, such a nomination would ensure the Georgian of at least a semblance of national support. Consequently, his opponents combined in angry attacks against the caucus primarily on the grounds that such a method of selecting a president was undemocratic and out of step with the times. "Shall Congress or the People elect our President?" they asked bitterly. Despite their efforts, a presidential caucus—the last ever held —met on February 14, 1824, and though attended by only one-third of the eligible members, nominated Crawford. Democratic sentiment against the caucus proved to be stronger than the Georgian realized, however, and he found himself caught in a crossfire of criticism. He was denounced as "an enemy to the rights of the people," and as a man who "wished to ride into power on 'King Caucus'." Andrew Jackson had prophetically written early in the campaign that the feelings of the nation were such "that a congressional caucus would politically damn any name put forth by it," and, indeed, the nomination proved the fatal blow to Crawford's already wavering chances of election.

Obstinately, Crawford held on, and to the very end his candidacy remained a factor to be taken into account. With four candidates in the field, it was unlikely that any one of them would obtain a majority of electoral votes. The election would, therefore, have to be decided in the House of Representatives—and, here, Crawford might still obtain the presidency.

When tallied, the electoral vote in the national election stood, Jackson 99, Adams 84, Crawford 41, and Clay 37. The election would indeed have to be settled in the House, but Crawford, finishing a poor third, realized that the struggle would be between Adams and Jackson. In the final count, he received the electoral votes of only four states. The man who had entered the race with the greatest chance of winning saw his political career come to an end with this election. Crippled in body and mind, he returned to Georgia never again to enter a political contest.

HENRY CLAY *Charles Willson Peale, 1818-1819 Oil on canvas, 24 x 20 inches*
The Historical Society of Pennsylvania, Philadelphia

Henry Clay *Democratic–Republican*

1777–1852

When Albert Gallatin, Jefferson's secretary of the treasury and prominent Swiss-American banker, characterized Henry Clay as "devoured with ambition," he discerned the most important motive in the Kentucky politician's career: his ambition to be president of the United States. An aspirant for the glittering prize five times between 1824 and 1848, he was, as his biographers have pointed out, like a modern Tantalus, "on the never ending quest for a cup that would be forever dashed from his lips."

The first great blow to Clay's political aspirations came during the presidential election of 1824, an intra-party contest in which a galaxy of talented and ambitious men, each commanding a loyal following, vied for the office. Personalities, not principles, were the focal point of the campaign; candidates were judged primarily on their relative personal fitness for the office. For over a decade Clay had been steering a course toward the presidency, and by virtue of his experience and popularity he appeared more than well qualified.

By the 1820s Clay had established himself as the spokesman of the West, which was becoming more and more an important factor in national politics. He was, as John Quincy Adams pointed out in his diary, "the first distinguished man that the Western country has presented as a statesman to the Union [and] they are profoundly proud of him." To his adoring followers, he was "Gallant Harry of the West," ardent patriot, defender of the pioneer peoples, and incarnation of the virile optimism of the frontier.

Virginia born, Clay had made his way at the age of twenty through the Cumberland Gap to Lexington, Kentucky, carrying little more than the law license he had acquired with the aid of George Wythe, friend and mentor of Thomas Jefferson. He found in that bluegrass community an environment well suited to his temperament and abilities. His boastful conviviality, his fondness for gambling and drinking, and his captivating vitality were in harmony with the spirit and life-style of the Kentuckians. Shrewd and facile in argument, he quickly established himself as a brilliant criminal lawyer, so great, says folk-legend, that no person was ever hanged in a trial where Clay appeared for the defense.

His consuming interest, however, was politics. Within one year after his arrival in Kentucky, he ventured into the political scene by taking an active part in the struggle for revision and democratization of the state constitution. In 1803 he was elected to the state legislature; in 1806 and 1810 he served two interim appointments in the United States Senate, identifying himself completely with the interests of his adopted state and the West through his support of internal improvements and encouragement of home markets. In 1811, as the fever of war was beginning to rage across the country, he was elected to the House of Representatives, preferring, he said, the excitement and activity there to the "solemn stillness" of the Senate.

Typifying the intense nationalism of the frontier, Clay entered Congress aflame with determination to uphold national honor against Great Britain whether on the high seas or beyond the Alleghenies. He was almost immediately elected Speaker of the House, a position which grew in power during his long tenure. In this capacity, he quickly assumed leadership of the young "War Hawks," nationalists and expansionists, who steadily pushed Madison toward war in 1812. Clay supported the war vigorously and then in 1814, when Great Britain seemed ready to talk peace, he was appointed by Madison one of the five commissioners to represent the United States in negotiating a peace treaty. During the talks he successfully opposed giving Great Britain the right to navigate the Mississippi River, thereby broadening his influence in the West.

Home from Ghent and back in the speaker's chair, Clay was caught up in the general spirit of national pride and confidence in a future where nothing seemed impossible and turned his energies to empire building. With John C. Calhoun and William Lowndes, he formulated the program that came to be called the American System, a plan for national economic self-sufficiency which he hoped would overcome sectional differences while at the same time build a powerful nation completely free from dependence on Europe. Representing a continuation of the Hamiltonian concept of actively using government to serve the economic needs of the people, his plan included the development through roads and canals of the country's system of transportation to "bind the Republic together," a protective tariff to encourage the growth of American manufacturing, and a national bank to provide uniform currency and regulate the financial activity of the nation.

Clay hoped that his American System, intended to benefit all sections of the country, would also provide him with a key to the White House, and, indeed, it *was* the only clearly recognizable program offered during the campaign of 1824. But each element of the plan aroused strong opposition: the debtor West attributed the Panic of 1819 to the machinations of the Bank of the United States; New England and New York opposed internal improvements at national expense, since they had already invested state funds in such facilities; and the South opposed internal improvements for the power it would give the federal government at the expense of the states, and the protective tariff for the hardship it imposed on an agrarian community. Sectional interests were creating cleavages in spite of Clay's efforts, and inevitably they ate away at his chance of election. Somewhat wistfully he wrote to a friend that he realized he would be opposed "because I think that the interests of all parts of the Union should be taken care of. . . ."

Clay was unanimously nominated for the presidency in November 1822 by a caucus of the members of the Kentucky legislature, and caucuses in Missouri, Louisiana, and Ohio eagerly followed suit. Feeling confident of receiving the support of all the western states, "Gallant Harry" hoped that by appealing to nationalist sentiment elsewhere he could gain enough strength to secure his election. But he failed to recognize the serious threat rising in his own section. Andrew Jackson, who, like himself in earlier days, was being touted as the hero of the common man, was now leading the rising democratic sentiment in the East as well as the West. Busy with his attempt to unite the forces of agriculture and industry under the banner of the American System, Clay lost touch with the thought and spirit of the masses; perhaps more importantly, as his rival John Quincy Adams indicated, Clay's "principles and deportment" had also become "tinged . . . with Aristocracy." He had matured politically and socially, emerging as a dignified gentleman, a statesman, far removed from the popular image aroused by "Old Hickory." Although the Kentuckian never lost the affection of the West, Andrew Jackson came to replace him as representative of its aspirations.

The vote in the national election revealed how deeply Jackson had cut into Clay's support; the latter carried only Kentucky, Missouri, and Ohio, failing even to place among the top three contenders. Eliminated from the electoral college, Clay was now faced with making one of the most important decisions of his life. Because of his influence in the House where the choice of executive would be made, Clay had it in his power to determine the next president. His decision to support John Quincy Adams, who shared his nationalistic views, associated him from that time on with the capitalistic Northeast and alienated his western supporters. Even more serious a blunder careerwise, however, was his acceptance of Adams' offer to become secretary of state, for this decision lent credence to the accusation that he had entered into a "corrupt bargain." Although he remained a powerful political figure, his reputation was never entirely cleansed of this taint.

ANDREW JACKSON *Aaron H. Corwine, 1825 Oil on canvas, 27 x 22 inches*
Mr. and Mrs. Jackson P. Ravenscroft, Tucson, Arizona

Andrew Jackson *Democratic–Republican*

1767-1845

If any candidate was the choice of the people in 1824, it was Andrew Jackson. Although his experience in public affairs was negligible and his politics were vague, men hailed the hero of New Orleans as "the people's friend," a man risen from the masses, who naturally understood their grievances and their aspirations. He was a living legend, equal, in the eyes of the nation, to George Washington; a military hero who had defeated the country's mortal enemies, the British and the Indians, and whom they now hoped would slay the dragons of hard times and economic inequality. Moreover, he symbolized the rising age of egalitarian democracy grounded on the assumption of the political equality of all men, regardless of wealth, rank, or education. His candidacy reflected the determination of the average citizen to share in the government of the nation. Jackson appeared almost heaven-sent to lead the new democracy to the promised land; his charisma inspired a relationship with the people unique in American history, a fact which Martin Van Buren succinctly recognized when he said, "They were his blood relations— the only blood relations he had."

Born in the Carolina back country and early orphaned, Jackson was a self-made man, having forged success from his own exertion and iron will. A "roaring, rollicking, game-cocking, horse-racing, card-playing, mischievous" youth, who cared little for book learning, he neverthe-less found time to study law and was admitted to the North Carolina bar at the age of twenty. In 1788 he emigrated across the Appalachian Mountains to the wilderness which was soon to become the state of Tennessee. There, through shrewd, native intelligence, force of personality, and powers of leadership, he easily acquired wealth and prominence, in the way of extensive lands, slaves, blooded horses, and a fine plantation—The Hermitage—near Nashville.

As a presidential candidate, Jackson's opponents used his wealth and position to prove that he was no democrat. Having identified with the frontier aristocracy, he had, in truth, been any-thing but a consistent friend to the canebreak democracy—supporter more of the "Haves" than the "Have-nots," favoring creditors over debtors and absentee landlords over squatters. Yet, this mattered little to his loyal followers. Perhaps he was rich, perhaps financially and politically conservative, and more country gentleman than common clay, but this only proved the feasibility of the great American dream: that a man born in a log cabin could acquire wealth and become a national figure. Moreover, he was far removed from the aristocracy of the East; he was devoid of snobbishness, disregarded the supposed superiority of birth and breeding, lived according to the honest morality of plain folk that emphasized courage and strength and minimized learning and culture.

Andrew Jackson sewing box   CORNELL UNIVERSITY, DOUGLAS COLLECTION

Although Jackson had served in the House of Representatives and Senate of the United States, his terms were brief and without distinction. It was as a military hero rather than politician that he was thrust into the national limelight. As a major general in the War of 1812, he had crushed the Creek Indians at the battle of Horseshoe Bend in what is now Alabama, and in the Battle of New Orleans had won the greatest victory of the war, routing the British regulars, "the conquerors of the conquerors of Europe," with his hodgepodge force of sailors, regulars, pirates, Frenchmen, and militiamen. His later cruel and even arrogant exploits against the Seminole Indians in Florida, of which territory he was named military governor, only enhanced his appeal to a people insensitive to racial problems. Everywhere, Old Hickory

—as his soldiers had named him because of his toughness—was hailed as America's deliverer and his name became a household word.

The potency of Jackson's popular appeal and his heroic military record gave him presidential stature. Yet, he seemed to have no ambition for the office. Early in the 1820s when friends had hinted that he might be named as a candidate in 1824, he had firmly replied, "No sir, I know what I am fit for. I can command a body of men in a rough way; but I am not fit to be President." The idea took hold in spite of his initial lack of interest; mass meetings and newspapers boomed his candidacy. On July 17, 1822, the Nashville *Whig* reported "GREAT RACING!!! . . . The prize to be run for is the *Presidential Chair*. . . . There have already four states sent their nags in. . . . Why not Tennessee put in her stud? and if so, let it be called

Andrew Jackson frog doorstop CORNELL UNIVERSITY, DOUGLAS COLLECTION

Old Hickory. . . . Within a month after this item appeared, the Tennessee legislature nominated Jackson for the presidency.

As his aversion to presidential politics slowly waned, Jackson was stating by 1823 that although the presidency should not be sought, neither should it be declined, and he was willing to do what the people demanded of him.

His candidacy was carefully guided from its beginning by a corps of able politicians, men like Amos Kendall of Kentucky and William L. Marcy of New York, who saw in Jackson's popularity an opportunity to further their own careers. The primary tactic was to appeal to the patriotism and emotion of the masses, to the instincts not the intellect of the voters. Throughout the country, Jackson partisans engaged in pyrotechnics directed to honor a military conqueror. As John Quincy Adams observed, while the other candidates were discoursing on Jeffersonianism, internal improvements, and the tariff, all the Jackson people had to do was shout "8th of January and the battle of New Orleans" to win votes. "[He] has slain the Indians and flogged the British & . . . therefore is the wisest and greatest man in the nation"—this was the theme of Jackson's campaign.

The feeling of the country was reflected in a resolution passed by a North Carolina grand jury: "He is a favorite of the people; he belongs to them; he has been raised with them, he has served them both in peace and war; they feel grateful." And they showed their gratitude by giving him 153,000 popular votes, nearly twice the combined total for Crawford and Clay. In the electoral college, however, Jackson's 99 votes fell considerably short of the required majority, and the contest was thrown into the House of Representatives. There, Henry Clay, Jackson's bitter western rival, was so placed as to be able to decide the election.

To Clay, the elevation of Jackson to the presidency "would give to the military spirit a stimulus and confidence that might lead to the most pernicious results." Jackson was merely a "military chieftain" in his eyes, with no qualifications for the presidency. "I cannot believe," he observed, "that killing 2,500 Englishmen at New Orleans qualifies [a person] for the various, difficult and complicated duties of the chief magistracy." Adams was surely the better qualified candidate, and Clay delivered his supporters to the Yankee who was thereupon elected.

Though his supporters howled with indignation, Jackson accepted his defeat with gentlemanly good grace until the disclosure that Clay was to be Adams' secretary of state. The news aroused his well-known temper. Transfixed with anger, he wrote, "So you see the Judas of the West has closed the contract and will receive the thirty pieces of silver." Through "bargain and corruption" he had been cheated out of the presidency and the people had been cheated out of their choice! Whether a "deal" had been promulgated or not, appearances were so damning as to render denials unconvincing. Burning for revenge, the general and his lieutenants immediately began an unrelenting campaign to oust Adams which ultimately resulted in Jackson's accession to the presidency in 1828.

JOHN QUINCY ADAMS   *Thomas Sully, 1824   Oil on canvas, 24½ x 20 inches*
The National Gallery of Art, Washington, D.C.

John Quincy Adams *National–Republican*

1767-1848

The defeat of the incumbent President John Quincy Adams and the election of Andrew Jackson in 1828 was a foregone conclusion, even to Adams himself. The President, identified with the elite, aristocratic element which had up to now dominated the federal government, was being challenged by a candidate who represented a new democratic concept rising in the land. No longer were the people satisfied to be governed by their "betters"; they wanted to choose their leaders from among themselves. The architect, Benjamin H. Latrobe, explained: "The extension of the right of suffrage in the States to a majority of all the adult male citizens, planted a germ which had gradually evolved and has spread actual and practical democracy and political equality over the whole union." Thus, Adams, "bred among the aristocracy," had not the remotest chance of winning in a contest with Jackson, "the people's friend." As his enemies said, "His habits and principles are not congenial with the spirit of our institutions and the notions of a democratic people."

This rejection by the people he had served so faithfully for over thirty years was to John Quincy a curious political phenomenon which he never fully understood. As with his father, John Adams, public service was an obligation always to be met; duty must always take precedence over popularity, profession, and personal pleasure. While he had never catered to public whim, he had always responded to national needs. There is almost a religious zeal in his statement: "I never will shrink from any post which . . . my country shall assign me, for any difficulty or danger with which it may be beset." He considered the presidency—the ultimate service to one's country—to be his personal destiny, a rare inheritance from his father and an office for which he was better qualified than any man of his day.

By the age of eighteen, Adams—a precocious youth—had studied in Paris, Amsterdam, and Leyden, spent two years as private secretary and translator for the American minister to Russia, and served as his father's secretary on diplomatic missions in Holland and Paris. At the age of twenty, he was graduated from Harvard College and then studied law under Theophilus Parsons, later chief justice of Massachusetts, being admitted to the bar in 1790. He did not enjoy waiting for legal clients in a state of "useless and disgraceful insignificance," and readily turned in his spare time to political discussion. For writing a series of articles defending the Washington administration he was awarded in 1794 the post of minister to the Netherlands, the beginning of a distinguished career as a diplomat. He later served as minister to Russia and Great Britain and presided over the American Peace Commission which drew up the treaty ending the War of 1812. From 1803 to 1808 he served as a United States senator from Massachusetts where, although elected as a Federalist, he proved as unorthodox and "unmanageable" in party politics as his equally unmanageable father. Acting with militant independence in his rebellious support of the Republican Embargo bill, an "unpardonable sin against *Party*," he was denounced by the majority of his constituents and by party chiefs and forced to resign from his position. He later wrote, "I have been styled a deserter from all parties because I truly never belonged to any party."

In 1817 Adams was invited by the newly elected Monroe to become secretary of state. No more congenial office could have been offered him. Adding strength and brilliance to American foreign policy, he arranged with England for the joint occupation of the Oregon territory, secured from Spain the cession of the Floridas, concluded a treaty with Russia that limited her claims to the Northwest, and capped his eight years in office by helping to formulate the Monroe Doctrine which defined United States interests in the Western Hemisphere.

"Cabinet succession" to the presidency was a political tradition of the early nineteenth century and when Monroe stepped down in 1824, Adams as secretary of state believed himself the natural heir to the office. There were, however, three other ambitious candidates actively seeking the prize and his claim was not easily won. No one of them received a clear majority and the election was decided in the House of Representatives where, with the crucial support of the defeated Henry Clay, Adams was elected despite the fact that Andrew Jackson had received a popular plurality.

Adams' appointment of Clay as secretary of state evoked vehement cries of "corrupt bargain" that were relentlessly repeated throughout his entire administration. The "unholy alliance," conceived by Jackson's supporters as a deliberate thwarting of the popular will, became a rallying point for the opposition. Insisting upon the injury done to the people in 1824, they urged the vindication of their "hero" in the defeat of those who had cheated him of what was rightfully his. The cloud of suspicion engendered by this affair in no small way contributed to Adams' failure to win reelection in 1828.

Believing that the greatest objective of lawful government was the improvement of the condition of all parties to the social compact, Adams worked as president to advance the nation's civilization by proposing a broad system of internal improvements ranging from roads and canals to astronomical observatories. Coming at a time when ideas of sectionalism and states' rights were gaining momentum, his nationalistic programs aroused popular antipathy, and having characteristically ignored partisan politics, Adams could not muster enough support to carry them through. Every administration measure was, in fact, met with a barrage of Jacksonian criticism.

While the Jackson forces were building a strong party welded together by the hero's personal popularity, Adams was a leader without a following. At times totally insensitive to the "ebb and flow" of public feeling, he was never really able to catch the popular imagination. Aware of his own shortcomings, he confided to his diary, "I am a man of reserved, cold, austere, and forbidding manners; my political adversaries say, a gloomy misanthropist, and my personal enemies, an unsocial savage." Yet, he confessed, he had not the "pliability" to reform this "defect." Short, thickset, and balding, he was an unimpressive figure compared with Old Hickory. Even his intellectualism worked in his disfavor as evidenced by a ridiculous but effective campaign slogan: "John Quincy Adams who can write/and Andrew Jackson who can fight."

Like his father before him, John Quincy Adams was denied a second term and was overwhelmingly defeated at the polls. Despondent, he wrote in his diary, "The sun of my political life is in the deepest gloom." Little could he have known that the most fruitful portion of his long career lay ahead. Elected to the House of Representatives from Massachusetts in 1830, he served there until his death in 1848, championing the causes of science and education, and tirelessly leading the resistance to the slave powers.

HENRY CLAY   *William James Hubard, circa 1832   Oil on canvas, 21 x 15⅛ inches*
Bayly Museum of Art, University of Virginia, Charlottesville

Henry Clay *National–Republican*

1777–1852

The overwhelming defeat of John Quincy Adams in 1828 automatically removed the New Englander from leadership of the National Republicans, and, as that faction planned stratagems whereby it could recover its power in 1832, it turned with complete unanimity to Henry Clay, the "Western Star" and the "Nation's only hope" against "King Andrew" Jackson. As though his "imperishable ambition" would not have made the Kentuckian a willing enough candidate, Daniel Webster wrote Clay in 1830, urging him to run. "You cannot be kept back from the contest. The people will bring you out, *nolens volens.* Let them do it." Clay needed little persuasion. Since 1829 when he had left the office of secretary of state, Clay had restlessly remained at Ashland, his Lexington plantation, considering his future course and watching with keen interest the political happenings across the nation. At the same time, he carefully kept himself in the public eye, speaking at banquets and barbecues throughout the state.

In November of 1831, Clay was returned to the United States Senate; admirers flocked around the affable statesman, and he quickly resumed his former political and social influence in Washington. Within a month after his election, the National Republicans, meeting in convention in Baltimore, unanimously nominated him for president. Several months later, his nomination was ratified at a young men's National Republican convention in Washington which also issued the first platform adopted by a national convention.

Centering around Clay's "American System," the platform was essentially conservative and far more appealing to the Northeast than to the West. Its appeal to a single section represented the basic weakness of Clay's campaign, for ultimately the presidential contest became a struggle between Jackson and the people of the South and West on one side, and Clay and the aristocrats and capitalists of the East on the other.

The paramount issue of the campaign was the question of the rechartering of the Second Bank of the United States. Well managed by Nicholas Biddle, the Bank had brought profit to the government, the business community, and the stockholders, but it was still hated in the West. Although the Bank's charter was not to expire until 1836, Jackson, who shared the western prejudice against the Bank, had already expressed his opposition to its renewal. Here,

Clay thought he saw an issue that would defeat Jackson; if the president refused to renew the charter, he would hopefully lose enough votes in the East to cost him the election. Consequently, the Kentuckian came out for immediate action on renewal, and through his efforts, a recharter bill was pushed through Congress. Jackson promptly vetoed the bill in a message that appealed to the democratic instincts of the people. The Bank was designed, said Jackson, "to make the rich richer and the potent more powerful." He denounced it as a monopoly which

Henry Clay clay-bowl pipe   CORNELL UNIVERSITY, DOUGLAS COLLECTION

was draining money from the West to the East, and as "UnAmerican" for much of the stock was held abroad.

The veto delighted National Republicans who believed that thereby Jackson had signed his own death sentence, but they terribly underestimated the popular feeling against the Bank.

Jackson was lauded for saving "the people from becoming enslaved by the corruptions of a moneyed aristocracy and desperate politicians," and the veto was, as Martin Van Buren said, "popular beyond [our] most sanguine expectations." Clay, in turn, was criticized as a tool of the Bank and of the money power; as the leader of an unpopular cause, he inevitably went down to defeat. Once more he had failed to grasp the significance of Jackson's appeal. He won the votes of Kentucky, Maryland, Delaware, Massachusetts, Rhode Island, and Connecticut, but he did not carry a single state of the lower South or of the new West; his electoral vote was only 49 as compared to 219 for Jackson.

Although his Bank tactic had proved counterproductive, Clay remained committed to the principles of the American System, and despite his loss, continued to be, next to the president, the most powerful influence in the federal government. His defeat was bitter, but he could not give up the struggle, and over the next decade he continued to lead the opposition against Jacksonianism in defense of "the Country, . . . its civil liberty, its institutions, its property, its virtue."

WILLIAM WIRT   *Attributed to Samuel Lovett Waldo   Oil on canvas, 22¼ x 18¾ inches*
From the Collection of the National Portrait Gallery, Washington, D.C.
Gift of Wilmarth Sheldon Lewis   NPG.71.47

William Wirt *Anti-Masonic*

1772-1834

William Wirt was the first presidential candidate of the Anti-Masonic Party. The earliest third party in the United States, the Anti-Masons organized in western New York in 1826 when William Morgan, an itinerant bricklayer and Freemason, was kidnapped for attempted exposure of the secrets of Masonry and never seen again. His probable murder at the hands of the Masons aroused an astonishing furor of mass protest against the order. Representing the "select class in the community," the Masons were deemed conspirators against the democracy; not only did they possess undue power and privilege, it was somewhat hysterically believed, but they acted as subversive forces in business, government, and the courts, and would resort to "commissioning murder" if anyone opposed them. The press, churchmen, anti-slavery, and temperance elements, united by what they considered a "democratic" spirit, resolved to rid American society of this "aristocratic" scourge and, gathering momentum and excitement, the Anti-Masonic movement spread quickly across New York into Pennsylvania, New England, and parts of the Midwest.

This flaming agitation culminated in the creation of an Anti-Masonic Party pledged to the extirpation of all secret societies. It was only a matter of time, then, before shrewd politicians took advantage of the hysteria in their pursuit of bigger game. Under the direction of dynamic young men like Thurlow Weed and William H. Seward of New York, the party was used as a galvanizing agent for the various elements of opposition to Andrew Jackson, who conveniently was a high chieftain in the Masonic order.

Encouraged by many local political victories, the Anti-Masons were eager to venture into the national arena. They set their sights on the presidential election of 1832 and began an intensive search for a candidate around whom all the forces opposed to Jackson might rally. They would have liked to support Henry Clay, now the acknowledged leader of the debilitated National Republicans, but he—like Jackson—was a Mason and, although he considered the order "a mere bauble," refused to retract his membership. Other prominent leaders were approached, including Secretary of State Richard Rush and Supreme Court Justice John McLean, but each refused the nomination. Finally, meeting in a national nominating convention in Baltimore in

September 1831, the party chose as their leader William Wirt, also a Mason but "in cordial sympathy with Anti-Masonic principles."

Wirt was a dignified and scholarly Virginia attorney, perhaps one of the finest constitutional lawyers of his day. He came to national attention first as counsel for James Callender in his trial under the Alien and Sedition Acts of 1798, and later, as a member of the prosecution team charged with trying Aaron Burr for treason. He served as attorney general for twelve years, during which time he presented the government's case before the Supreme Court in such famous cases as *McCulloch* vs. *Maryland, Cohens* vs. *Virginia,* and *Gibbons* vs. *Ogden,* defending in each the superior power of the federal government and the Court over the power of the states.

A writer by avocation, Wirt's *The Letters of the British Spy,* which appeared in 1803 in a Richmond newspaper, enjoyed enormous popularity. It was followed by *The Life and Character of Patrick Henry,* the first in a projected but never completed series of biographies of American heroes.

Wirt was sixty years old when he received the nomination, and he believed himself too old to embark on a race for the presidency. Moreover, he was not a "party man—much less a party leader"; he believed he had too much conscience for that. Only once had he been elected to an office—as delegate to the Virginia Assembly—and then had served just one term. Neither were his ambitions of a political nature; he wished only to be respected for his professional competency and to be able to retire to the country to live a life of literary ease. As a friend and admirer of Henry Clay, he would have much preferred to see him nominated, and it was only after Anti-Masonic leaders convinced him that Clay could not win the party's support and that it was his duty as a "patriot" to unite the anti-Jackson men that he relented. In Wirt's view, Jackson was a demagogue and despot, and he was ready to put aside all personal inclinations in order to defeat him.

Doubting that he could strike the people as the "proper person for the office" of president, Wirt admitted that he had "none of the captivating arts and manners of professional seekers of popularity." Nor did he desire them: "I shall not change my manners; they are a part of my nature. If the people choose to take me as I am—well. If not, they will only leave me where I have always preferred to be, enjoying the independence of private life." He took no part in the electioneering, refusing even to write private letters which could be interpreted as canvassing for office.

Wirt's sole purpose for accepting the nomination—to effect the union of the Jacksonian opposition—was thwarted when in December 1831, the National Republicans refused to back him and proceeded to nominate Henry Clay as their candidate, thus splitting the potential vote against Jackson. Wirt tried to withdraw his candidacy, for he believed by remaining in the contest he would only give the appearance of "a sickly vanity and morbid appetite for the office, which is utterly false." "The only sensible or reasonable purpose of nominating a man for an office is, the hope of his election," he wrote, "the only sensible or reasonable purpose of agreeing to be nominated is, that the person may be submitted to the consideration of his fellow-citizens for the office. But after this has been fairly done, and the people have given the most conclusive demonstrations that they do not choose the individual proposed, but prefer another, what dignity, what propriety, what decency, even, is there in continuing to press him?"

Indicating that his "only motive . . . for accepting the nomination" was now gone, he expressed a wish to withdraw for "if I still remain before the public, I exhibit the appearance of counter-acting the very purpose I had in view, & permitting myself to be used as an instrument for disunion."

Wirt finally acquiesced to the urgings of the Anti-Masons that he remain in the contest, but as he foresaw, without the union of the Anti-Masons and the National Republicans to oppose Jackson, the president's popularity carried him to victory. While he remained bitter over the "wilful obstinacy" of the National Republicans, Wirt was obviously relieved that his political experience had come to an end. Writing to a friend he explained: "A culprit pardoned at the gallows could not be more light-hearted."

DANIEL WEBSTER   *Chester Harding, circa 1828   Oil on canvas, 36¼ x 28¼ inches*
From the Collection of the National Portrait Gallery
Gift of Mrs. Gerard B. Lambert   NPG.67.59

Daniel Webster *Whig*

1782-1852

In 1852, shortly after losing the Whig nomination for president to Winfield Scott, Secretary of State Daniel Webster wistfully spoke of the position of chief executive as "the greatest office in the world." As to his own aspiration for the glittering prize, he unabashedly admitted, "I am but a man sir, I want it, I want it"—a confession perhaps unique in American political history. To Webster, a statesman of great stature and talent who had spent many years in public service, the presidential office was the final seal of success, the ultimate honor. He confided to his friend, William Plumer, that he had "glorious dreams" of immortality—through the presidency he could see the dreams "wake into glorious realities." While his chances of attaining the presidency would never be good, in 1836 it did seem almost within his grasp.

Born in the granite hills of New Hampshire, the son of a farmer and political leader, Webster had by the early 1820s established himself as the nation's foremost constitutional lawyer. His famous arguments in 1819 in *Dartmouth College* vs. *Woodward* and *McCulloch* vs. *Maryland* had brought him to the forefront of the federal bar. Yet his strong conservative convictions and interest in public affairs, inherited from his politician father, coupled with his facility in debate, naturally drew him into politics. Reflecting the beliefs of the dominant New England commercial and shipping interests, his opposition to the Republican embargo and the second war with England brought him to Congress in 1812 where he consistently supported the views of his constituency. In 1816, he moved to Boston and in 1823 he was again elected to the House of Representatives, where he quickly assumed a position of leadership. Philip Barbour, Speaker of that body, considered him the most powerful man "ever sent from the North." He was truly a commanding figure, one who projected remarkable strength and confidence. In fact, it has been said that no man was ever so great as Webster looked. A swarthy Olympian with a magnificent head and craggy brows that shadowed deep-set black eyes, to his worshipful followers he was "Godlike Daniel." The minister and author, Theodore Parker, thought there had not been "such a grand figure in Christendom" since Charlemagne.

With his rich, melodic voice and dramatic delivery, Webster was unquestionably the greatest orator in a generation of orators. When stirred by a great occasion or crisis, it was said he could shake the world with his fiery speeches. In the Senate to which he was elected in 1827 he was often, as Emerson remembered him, "the great cannon loaded to the lips" speaking most effectively against those he considered enemies of the Union. His stirring defense of national sovereignty in 1830 in response to South Carolina Senator Robert Y. Hayne's acclamation of the doctrine of nullification, is considered one of the most powerful speeches ever delivered before Congress. The final words—"Liberty and Union, now and forever, one and inseparable" —have become part of America's national literature.

That peroration, which riveted the attention of the nation on Webster, propelled him into the role of one of the leading statesmen of the day and gave him popular credibility as a presidential contender. George Ticknor Curtis, Webster's literary executor, noted in his official biography that the years 1830-1831 marked "the period in Mr. Webster's life when he began to be considered . . . the most suitable person to be brought forward as a candidate for the presidency"; from this time until the end of his life, the hope of reaching the White House was always in the back of Webster's mind.

Anxious as he was, Webster had to wait until 1836 to run for the presidency. After the defeat of John Quincy Adams in 1828, National Republican leaders unanimously accepted Henry Clay as their candidate to oppose Jackson in 1832, and it was only after the Kentuckian's overwhelming defeat in that election that they turned their eyes to Webster.

Weakened by Clay's defeat and the lack of popular support, the National Republicans were obviously ineffective as an opposition group. The crystallization of some new form of political order was essential. Thus, they broke away completely from the Republican Party and in the spring of 1834 created the "Whig" Party, so named because of its opposition to "King Andrew" and his "Tory" followers. Embracing a "mixed multitude of discordant materials"—the debilitated National Republicans, the Anti-Masons, Democratic businessmen disgruntled by Jackson's veto of the Bank bill, states' rights zealots, planters, and professional men—the Whig Party was nevertheless a rallying point for anti-Jackson forces from all sections of the country. Unfortunately for Webster, this new alignment was too young to wage a concerted, well-organized battle; in 1836, it could only produce a somewhat desperate and ineffective electoral strategy.

The most difficult and embarrassing problem faced by the new party was its "plethora of prima donnas," each eager for the presidency and each representing different sectional and economic interests. The selection of a single standard-bearer was thus rendered impossible in 1836, and the decision was made to run several regional candidates in the hope of preventing Martin Van Buren, whom Jackson had dubbed his successor, from obtaining an electoral majority. The election would then devolve upon the House, where conceivably the Whigs might be able to elect one of their own. Accordingly, Hugh Lawson White of Tennessee, a "soured" Jackson supporter, was nominated by southern Whigs; William Henry Harrison was the choice of the West; and Webster, nominated by the Massachusetts legislature, theoretically was the candidate of the North. Unable to put himself at the head of Jackson's opponents, Webster could still hope that his strength in Congress would resolve the election in his favor if the decision came to the House.

The nomination of Harrison, popular Indian-fighting hero of the Battle of Tippecanoe in 1811 and the War of 1812, deprived Webster of his only chance of success. The urbane statesman could not compete with the general's popularity, even in the North. Harrison, like Jackson, was a man "with the bark on." Awe-inspiring though he was, Webster did not "take with the people"; by reputation, he had little concern for the rank and file. As English traveler Harriet Martineau observed, Webster was admired but not trusted by the people. "His ambition for office, and for the good opinion of those who surround him, is seen too often in alternation with his love of ease and luxury. . . ." Allied with the well-to-do and established elements in society, he was at heart an aristocrat who clung to the traditions of the past and had little sympathy for the democratic revolution sweeping the country—a fatal handicap in the presidential politics of the 1830s and 1840s.

Loyal Websterites, though unable to withstand the encroachment of Harrison support in the North, strove to the end to unite the Whig Party behind Massachusetts' favorite son. Circular letters were sent to all sections of the country on his behalf, a two-volume edition of his speeches and a biography were widely distributed, and newspaper editorials supporting him were continued until prospects seemed hopeless. Webster himself was "depressed and gloomy in his feelings." By spring of the election year, his campaign had completely collapsed outside his own state; in March, he sent a letter to the Massachusetts legislature offering to formally withdraw as a candidate if it was thought best. The Whigs would hear naught of this, resolving that Webster, whatever might be his fate in the country at large, should receive at least the support of his own Commonwealth.

In the end, Van Buren, with a "united Democracy" behind him, had little difficulty in defeating the disorganized Whigs. The "Godlike Daniel," whose possible election, according to one impassioned supporter, "should make the heart of every American leap in his bosom," won only the electoral votes of his home state.

Yet, his career was far from ended: he continued for a number of years in the Senate and served two terms as secretary of state. But sadly, his successes would never equal his highest ambition, or his greatest defeat.

WILLIAM HENRY HARRISON   *Rembrandt Peale, circa 1812   Oil on canvas,*
30 x 25 inches   Francis Vigo Chapter, Daughters of the American Revolution,
Vincennes, Indiana

William Henry Harrison   *Anti-Masonic / Whig*

1773-1841

William Henry Harrison was immensely pleased with his nomination for the presidency by the Pennsylvania Whig and Anti-Masonic parties. In a letter to his friend General Van Rensselaer in January 1835, he wrote, "I am the clerk of the Court of Common Pleas of Hamilton County at your service. But I have news still more strange to tell you if you have not already heard it. Some folks are silly enough to have formed a plan to make a President of the United States out of this Clerk and Clod Hopper!"

Harrison was one of three sectional candidates nominated by the young Whig Party in its disorderly but determined effort to prevent the Democrats from winning a majority of the electoral votes in 1836. For the Whigs in the middle and northwestern states "Old Tippecanoe," the Indian fighter from the War of 1812, represented another Jackson-style hero with unmistakable political possibilities as a representative American pioneer, sharing the interests of common men everywhere.

Born on a western Virginia plantation, the son of a founding father, and educated at Hampden-Sidney College, young Harrison joined the army and served for three years in the Northwest Territory. Although he resigned his army commission in 1798, public service activities continued to hold him in the Northwest. During twelve years as governor of the Indiana Territory, he dealt with steadily worsening Indian problems. Eventually, white pressure on Indian lands triggered the uprising of the Indian chief Tecumseh and the Battle of Tippecanoe, a conflict that gained a national military reputation for Harrison, leader of the unequal battle that resulted in a white victory. As supreme military commander of the Northwest in the War of 1812, he won the Battle of the Thames, finally securing the area against the combined forces of the British and Indians. Controversy surrounded General Harrison's victories, however, for his critics believed them to be the results of his enemies' rash blunders rather than his own brilliant strategies.

After resigning from the army in 1814, Harrison settled in North Bend, Ohio, where he tended his land, grappled with personal financial problems, and constantly pursued more lucrative political offices. He served three years in the United States Senate and briefly held the post of American minister to Colombia. But when the Whigs considered his candidacy in 1835, Harrison's career was languishing in the office of the Hamilton County clerk of court; clearly he welcomed Whig endorsement for the presidency, while the party equally appreciated his winning potential at the polls.

At sixty-three, his genial charm and modest simplicity were among "Old Tip's" most admirable qualities. Complementing his engaging manner was the advantage of his freedom

William Henry Harrison mirror medallion CORNELL UNIVERSITY, DOUGLAS COLLECTION

from untoward political entanglements. His was the enviable role of the old hero of the "War of 1812 who had, like Cincinnatus, returned to the bucolic joys of his quiet farm until the voice of the people summoned him to public service."

Harrison enthusiastically embarked on a campaign of Tippecanoe rallies and celebrations of the Battle of the Thames, recalling nostalgic memories of bygone days in a way soothing to voters at a time of change. He successfully completed a three-month campaign tour—and endurance contest—through Virginia, Maryland, New Jersey, New York, Pennsylvania, and Ohio, mainly to dispel rumors of ill health and doubts concerning his age. Adopting the Whig anti-Jackson doctrine, the general left no doubt regarding his sentiments on all topics: he favored a distribution of surplus revenue among the states according to their population, which would help the states develop and improve transportation facilities; he approved of a bill for the like distribution of revenues from land sales; he favored appropriations by the United States to improve navigable streams (if the benefits would be national); he approved of another national bank charter, if necessary, for the public interest; and he did not believe it constitutional to expunge from the records of Congress any of its proceedings. He believed Anti-Masonry to be out of the realm of politics and government, and on slavery—looking to the southern vote—he was for emancipation only by colonization. Regarding the spoils system, Harrison insisted that he would be grateful to those who put him in office, but he would not bestow favors.

The greatest surprise of the campaign was the general's excellent showing everywhere. He won seven states and ran well wherever he appeared on the ticket. Although Van Buren captured 170 votes for the Democrats, Harrison received 73 of the Whig's total of 124 votes—an impressive tally for a "Clerk and Clod Hopper" and, indeed, one to keep in mind in 1840.

Harrison himself conducted a campaign "by continuation" between elections and once again, despite the fearsome rivalry of Whig-leader Henry Clay, managed to win his party's nomination in 1840. The "Log Cabin and Hard Cider" campaign of that year, unequaled in election annals for its rousing emotional appeal to the people, put Harrison in the White House for the shortest term in American history—for in delivering his long inaugural address, hatless, in frigid weather, President Harrison contracted pneumonia, and one month later the nation mourned his death.

HUGH LAWSON WHITE *Unidentified artist Oil on canvas, 29½ x 24½ inches
Courtesy of the Tennessee State Museum, Nashville, Tennessee; from the collection of the
Tennessee Historical Society*

Hugh Lawson White *Whig*

1773-1840

Hugh Lawson White, widely respected Tennessee judge and president for twenty-five years of the Bank of Tennessee, was an able, conscientious public servant of "incorruptible integrity." Although largely self-educated and conditioned in boyhood by the most rugged frontier existence, White became a leading gentleman–statesman of his time. He rose from state affairs to national prominence in 1821 when President Monroe appointed him to serve on the Spanish claims commission under the Florida treaty. In 1825, he entered national politics when he was unanimously elected to fill the Senate seat vacated by Andrew Jackson. The two men were on friendly terms and bore marked similarities in appearance—tall, lean, and impressive figures. Both were emigrants from North Carolina to Tennessee; however, Jackson's high-spirited nature contrasted sharply with the judge's reserve.

White loyally supported and admired "Old Hickory" and from his senatorial vantage point he viewed the White House inner circle with high hopes and, after 1828, distinct hints of his availability for public service. But Jackson had other plans. He tapped Van Buren, whom White disliked, as his successor and generally ignored the mild-mannered senator from his home state. White's resentment of administration tactics grew, while the Whigs became increasingly aware of his political potential in securing for them the vote of those southern dissidents who feared the future of republican principles under a northern president. Bitter towards Jackson, jealous of Van Buren, lured by the Whig Party, and encouraged by an ambitious wife and friends, Hugh White inevitably deserted the Democratic fold to become a Whig candidate for the presidency.

Although the three-pronged Whig campaign was unexciting nationally, it did serve notice on the Democratic Party that it would have to contend eventually with a better organized opposition. Describing the campaign in his diary, John Quincy Adams wrote that "this bolstering up of mediocrity would seem not suited to sustain much enthusiasm." In some southern states like Virginia and North Carolina, White's candidacy was construed as a front for William Henry Harrison; while in others, his defection from the Democratic ranks was seen as a real obstacle to election.

In the state of Tennessee, however, the campaign took on greater significance, for here, in the home state of both Jackson and White, the contest boiled down to personalities more than issues. In this race, Hugh White triumphed. Fighting against a hostile president who campaigned personally and vigorously for Van Buren, the senator won 44 counties to Van Buren's 19. It was a humiliating defeat for Jackson. National results were disappointing to the Whigs and to White who carried only Georgia and Tennessee. Lacking the support of a united party, he had run as well as could be expected. For the Whig Party, the outcome clearly demonstrated the advantages of national party organization.

Hugh White continued to serve in the Senate until 1840 when his resignation was forced by Democrats who had regained power in Tennessee. He returned home a political martyr, and three months later he died. Public reaction to his martyrdom and death strongly contributed to the Tennessee Whig victory in 1840.

Log Cabin and Hard Cider Democracy 1840

WITH THE ELECTION OF 1840 AND THE VICTORY OF THE WHIGS, THE AGE OF JACKSON came to an end; however, Jacksonian democracy and the ideal of egalitarianism it symbolized persisted, and its effects have been felt ever since in American politics.

Many different groups of Americans were caught up in the Jacksonian enthusiasm. "Jackson men" included not only the "men of the Western Waters" who had crossed the Allegheny Mountains into Ohio and Tennessee during the Revolution, but also the frontier settlers in Pennsylvania, the New York dock workers and small, self-made businessmen, the tidewater aristocracy of large plantations and agrarian concerns, and Wall Street bankers who sought relief from the restrictions of the bank monopoly concentrated along Chestnut Street, Philadelphia. Representing disparate economic, ethnic, and social interests, the groups who gave their votes to the Democrats between 1828 and 1840 nevertheless did share some general goals that made it possible for them to identify with Jackson and his party. Especially did they share the sense that through politics they could serve their own economic needs and the knowledge that through actual political participation, they could themselves rise socially and economically.

How such a varying group arrived at similar conclusions at this time derives from a number of developments. The emergence of Jackson as the "Old Hero," symbol of the democratic man, coincided with the larger movement toward political democracy that was developing just prior to his presidency and that we see demonstrated in the extension of the suffrage and the subsequent challenge of egalitarian philosophy to older elitist practices. Jackson's contemporaries, as well as later historians, concluded that the two events were synonymous and that Jacksonianism was actually responsible for the egalitarian revolution rather than simply coincidental with it, or, indeed, a by-product of it. Ralph Waldo Emerson, for instance, commented that of the two parties, the Jacksonians and their opponents, "one has the best cause, and the other contains the best men." Jacksonianism to Emerson represented democratic reform; it facilitated, he believed, "the access of the young and the poor to sources of wealth and power." The Whigs, many of whom were Emerson's friends and patrons, although morally superior in the writer's estimation, were "timid and merely defensive of property."

Jackson's policies and those of the democracy he represented utilized an anti-monopoly and agrarian vocabulary that appealed to the democratic principles of the day. Especially when Jackson defended the little man in his Bank Veto Message and set himself up as the protector of "the farmer, mechanic and laborer" against the potent wealthy, he identified with the aspirations of the people for greater economic achievements, which seemed even more possible in the light of the widening of the suffrage and the seeming extension of the decision-making power. Urging equal protection by government of all classes of people, "the high and the low, the rich and the poor," Jackson preached a philosophy of "negative government" that promised to release economic controls and promote freedom of economic opportunity. In doing so, he attributed to the "monied powers," the aristocracy of "privilege" and "monopoly," the ills of "positive government"—meaning a strong government that directly intervened in the economy presumably for the general welfare. Negative government, or laissez-faire, offered a program that was equally acceptable to such different groups as the extreme Democrats or

Log Cabin sheet music LIBRARY OF CONGRESS

Locofocos who rioted in New York's City Hall Park in 1837 protesting the "monopolists and extortionists" who, they claimed, were artificially maintaining the high prices of bread, meat, rent, and fuel; and the New York bankers who, the following year, enthusiastically welcomed New York's free-banking act that gave them "the legal right to mobilize [the city's] already substantial financial power in banking associations of [their] own choosing." "*Viva la Loco-focoism*—if these be its fruits!" exulted the writer in the New York *Times and Commercial Intelligencer* of April 21, 1838. "Wall Street will soon become the great focus of the money power of the western hemisphere."

The rhetoric developed by the Jacksonians early in the Old Hero's administration separated his supporters from his opponents, and led to the reemergence of the two-party system. Among the Jacksonians responsible for this development, Martin Van Buren was particularly influential. While directing politics in the state of New York, he had developed a philosophy of party solidarity and the importance of a dual party system. Later in Congress, during John Quincy Adams' administration, Van Buren perfected the techniques whereby he could implement his beliefs. He established a tight network of committees filled with supporters and friends of

Old Hickory—a system later copied by his opponents, who came to call themselves Whigs. By reiterating Jeffersonian principles, while at the same time weeding out all who were not sufficiently enthusiastic for the party candidate, Van Buren formed a Jackson Party which remained effectively Jackson's until the leader's death in 1845.

Strong opposition to Van Buren's ingenious organization did not emerge until the formation of the Whig Party in 1834. Led by Henry Clay, the Whigs soon developed strength in all sections, including the South, and were able to mount successful political campaigns on both state and national levels in 1834, 1836, and especially in 1840.

The success of the Whigs was due to other factors, however, as well as to the leadership of Henry Clay. Jackson's tariff policies, his Nullification Proclamation and Force Act, his Bank Veto and withdrawal of government deposits from the national bank for the benefit of "pet" banks, his Specie Circular, and the ensuing Panic of 1837, all played into the hands of the Whigs. All that remained for them was to take advantage of the discontent caused by these various measures, clothe in rough garb their candidate, General William Henry Harrison, a

William Henry Harrison log cabin pin   CORNELL UNIVERSITY, DOUGLAS COLLECTION

popular Indian fighter, adopt the pioneer symbols of a log cabin and hard cider, and ride into power on a circus-wagon campaign filled with hullabaloo, cheers, songs, slogans, and epithets. In other words, although there were real issues facing the country that sent the electorate to the polls in unprecedented numbers, the parties never faced up, or addressed their campaigns, to them. Instead, the Whigs in particular predicated victory on a campaign that drew its inspiration from their opponents' democratic rhetoric, but did them one better.

The issues in 1840 were complicated, but with all their difficulties, they did involve intimately the man in the street, on the farm, even on the plantation. For in their determination lay the answers to the day-to-day questions that plagued them: the amounts of money they would have to spend on manufactured goods and the amount of credit they could expect to receive at a local bank and, therefore, the amount of expansion they could undertake. The resolution of these issues affected the way in which farmers in the West could buy new lands in which to expand—whether through credit or cash. Each of these economic concerns pointed to deeper implications, relating to the role of government in local affairs and institutions, the composition of the American governmental system and the meaning of the Constitution, and the role of the executive in the legislative process. And when the Panic resulted, or seemed to result, from one administration's exercise of power, and when subsequent depression and bankruptcy spread throughout the country, then even more did individuals from all walks of life question governmental policies and given attention to the issues involved.

The tariff problem was the earliest to confront the Jacksonians. It threatened not only to split the party, but the nation as well. In 1828, heated debates between advocates of a protective tariff and its opponents resulted in the alienation of John Calhoun, Jackson's vice-president, from the northern wing of the party. The South Carolinian then began to search for new alliances for the South in order to offset the threat of that section's becoming a permanent minority in national affairs. Calhoun's theory of nullification, which was expressed in South Carolina's Nullification Ordinance of 1832, emphasized the justice of a sectional veto over congressional legislation that was palpably injurious to that section's interests. In this instance, South Carolina refused to pay tariff duties, and justified such a refusal with states' rights doctrine. Jackson's response in the Nullification Proclamation and the Force Bill, fulfilling the promise of his earlier toast, "Our Federal Union—it must be preserved," emphasized the nationalist position that the "Constitution of the United States . . . forms a *government,* not a league" and that it operates "directly on the people individually, not upon the States." Needless to say, such a positive statement of nationalism was not welcomed by Democrats, who thought they had built a bridge between northern and southern interests by their espousal of states' rights doctrine as well as by their defense of slavery. Although Jackson maintained his popular position, his standing in some parts of the South was considerably weakened by his heresy and the Democratic Party faced a serious ideological rift.

It was Jackson's economic policies, however, that most directly led to the rejection of the Democrats by the electorate in 1840. At first, Jackson had convinced the people of the need to destroy the Second Bank of the United States by calling attention to its restrictive policies that prevented full exploitation of the nation's resources. From 1815 on, the states had been involved in a course of economic development that had opened up boundless opportunities in land, farming, and manufacturing. Undertaking extensive internal improvements like the Erie Canal, the states had forged ahead in their efforts to encourage the "enterprise of a free people." But in a capital-short economy, credit became a matter of crucial need; however, an overextension of credit could also lead to disaster. The Second Bank of the United States had on the whole done a good job in maintaining the economy on an even keel, but for a people faced with seemingly unlimited resources of land and aware of the nation's industrial potential, the bank seemed more restrictive than necessary.

To Jackson, who had a crude notion of banks and financial policy, the Bank was a monster that had to be dealt with forcibly. Jackson began by withdrawing government deposits in the Second Bank and placing them in "pet" banks—state institutions many of which were newly chartered and certainly not strong enough to withstand the temptation of speculating with their newly obtained funds. Jackson then compounded the financial situation by issuing his Specie Circular, an executive order forcing payment for lands purchased from the federal government in specie—cash—rather than bills of credit or bank notes. The Specie Circular represented Jackson's attempt to curb the reckless speculation that his removal of the deposits had prompted. The pace of economic development before Jackson's bank war had been rapid enough; with the removal of the deposits, the acceleration of economic activity had become frenzied. The expansion of the economy, reflecting international prosperity and a demand for American cotton and foodstuffs, had resulted in more economic activity than could be handled by the existing mechanisms. By 1836, much of this activity was more speculative than real: land sales skyrocketed, and so did the chartering of new banks to provide the necessary credit. In 1837, the whole edifice collapsed when the Specie Circular forced the overextended banks to provide cash to replace their notes for the purchase of government lands. Unable to do so, banks closed their doors, throwing investors, customers, and related groups into bankruptcy or economic distress.

The depression that followed was a long one, continuing through the administration of Martin Van Buren. Although it affected Americans of all classes and in all regions of the country, it fell most harshly on the lower and lower-middle classes, the groups ironically that Jacksonianism promised to protect. Laborers in the cities went unemployed, while crops rotted in southern fields as southern and southwestern planters found themselves without the means to add laborers to their slave force. To the general public, it was as though the country was submerged in catastrophe. "The conquest of the land by a foreign power," wrote British Minister Henry Fox to his government, "could hardly have produced a more general sense of humiliation and grief."

The Panic of 1837 and the ensuing depression raised doubts everywhere about the wisdom of all Democratic fiscal policy. Van Buren's attempt to establish an Independent Treasury as a fiscal agency for the government was intended to separate bank and state and prevent

William Henry Harrison log cabin whiskey bottle   CORNELL UNIVERSITY, DOUGLAS COLLECTION

public resources from being used for private speculation. The Independent Treasury not only caused further controversy between the parties—which was to be expected—but also set off explosions within Van Buren's own Democratic fold, especially in the key states of New York and Virginia. The difficulties that the Democrats faced were augmented, too, by the inconsistency between their established principle of "negative" government and states' rights, and the necessity for strong federal intervention to solve the problems created by economic distress. If the executive "despotism" practiced by Andrew Jackson had been acceptable to the people as an aspect of Jackson's personality, such a similar "despotism" on Van Buren's part was not; yet, any kind of executive leadership in the situation would have to take on aspects of "tyranny" and add another source of criticism to an already long list accumulated by the Whigs.

The Texas question also troubled Van Buren's administration in 1836, adding to the dissatisfaction of many large groups of Democrats. Texan independence in 1836 had to be acknowledged, and the hopes of the southerners for annexation met, but neither Jackson nor Van Buren was willing to take positive steps that would commit the country to a policy that had international as well as domestic implications. Finally, Van Buren signed a convention with Mexico agreeing to arbitration of the difficulties that had cropped up between the two nations as a result of the Texas–Mexican war. In doing so, he brought an end temporarily to agitation for annexation.

The Panic and depression, the crisis in foreign affairs, and the disunity within the Democratic Party excited interest in national politics as no other issues had done. The Whigs were ready to take advantage of the tremendous excitement generated. Having developed smoothly efficient machines in New York, Pennsylvania, Ohio, Tennessee, Kentucky, and Virginia, they were ready to challenge the incumbent party in 1840.

The Whigs found their campaign issue not in any of the current dilemmas facing the administration, but in the rhetoric of the Democratic attack. When a Baltimore newspaper supporting Van Buren sneered at Harrison's lowly origins, adding the advice that he should be given "a barrel of hard cider and . . . a pension of two thousand a year . . . and my word for it, he will sit the remainder of his days in his log cabin . . . ," the Whigs were quick to take advantage of the democratic sentiments of the age. The log cabin became the symbol of the struggles of the frontiersman and of the simple ways of the common American. Hard cider was distributed free and freely at Whig rallies. The arch-Whig and man-about-New York Philip Hone noted approvingly in his diary that "on all their [the Whig] banners and transparencies the temple of Liberty is transformed into a hovel of unhewn logs; the military garb of the General, into the frock and shirt-sleeves of a laboring man. The American eagle has taken his flight, which is supplied by a hard cider barrel, and the long established emblem of the ship has given way to the plough." Through huge mass meetings, processions, and parades, replete with music, torches, and banners, the Whigs rallied the emotions of the downtrodden and seemingly forgotten man of the streets, hard hit by a depression he could neither understand nor cope with. Transforming Van Buren into an Oriental monarch, with a taste for luxury as well as despotism, they weaned the normal followers of the Democratic Party temporarily away from their old political home, and to the tune of "Van, Van, . . . Van is a used-up man," they put "Tippecanoe, and Tyler, too" into the White House.

MARTIN VAN BUREN *Henry Inman, circa 1840 Oil on canvas, 30¾ x 25½ inches*
Metropolitan Museum of Art, New York Gift of Mrs. Jacob H. Lazarus, 1893

Martin Van Buren *Democrat*

1782-1862

Martin Van Buren was defeated for reelection in 1840 by the very campaign tactics that he had helped introduce to defeat John Quincy Adams in 1828. With what some felt was poetic justice, the "little magician," who as Jackson's campaign manager, had hurrahed Old Hickory into the White House with ballyhoo and clever manipulation, discovered to his dismay that two could play at the same game. For his lessons were easily learned and mastered by the Whigs, especially his understanding of the importance of the press, local political machines, stump oratory, and mass meetings; in other words, all the paraphernalia necessary for popular persuasion and personal appeal. In 1828 Van Buren had seen in Jackson's popularity not only the potential for gaining political power, but also an instrument whereby a viable political structure could be erected around the Jeffersonian principle of government by the choice of the people. By creating a myth around the hero of New Orleans, by concealing or ignoring public issues, and by loudly and often reiterating praise of the common man, Van Buren had led the young Democratic Party to dramatic success.

Now, in 1840, the Whigs came to realize the power of "passion and prejudice, properly aroused and directed," and by elaborating and improving on Van Buren's techniques, they achieved victory. Selecting as their candidate General William Henry Harrison, they transformed him into a super-hero. In doing so, they transmuted a college-educated member of one of the first families of Virginia into a son of the soil, a plain and simple man of the people, living in a log cabin (instead of a mansion on a three-thousand acre farm), where the latchstring was always out and where hard cider, hog jowl, and hominy grits provided the staple diet. And carrying Van Buren's policy of avoiding issues—John Randolph once spoke of the New Yorker's propensity for "rowing to his object with muffled oars"—to its ultimate point, the opposition carefully avoided reference to controversial issues or the formulation of a party platform. Campaign claptrap was everywhere substituted for argument.

Van Buren, meanwhile, had no choice but to run on the record of his administration, and unfortunately, his four years in the White House had been filled with trouble. Within months after his inauguration, the Panic of 1837 and a searing depression gripped the country, and as is always the case with the party in power, the new president and the Democrats were blamed. In the face of such hard times, "Martin Van Ruin," as his opponents called him, was unable to create enthusiasm for his administration or his programs. Though a shrewd politician, he inevitably suffered from comparisons with his decisive and colorful predecessor.

In reality, however, Van Buren came far closer than Harrison to the image of the "self-made man of the people" that Americans of the 1830s and 1840s admired so much. The son of a truck farmer and tavernkeeper, he had risen through his own ambition and motivation to a position of prestige and power. With little formal education but a penchant for law, he had been admitted to the New York bar after six grueling years of determined study during which he was dogged by poverty. Successful in practice and adroit in his dealings with men, he was irresistibly drawn into the factional struggles that characterized New York politics. He assumed an active role in the Republican Party, rose rapidly in its ranks, and won for himself a number of state offices while battling his way into leadership of the "Albany Regency," the party machine that dictated Republican policies in the state. In 1821 he was sent to the United States Senate, remaining there until elected governor of New York in 1828. It was from this office that Jackson summoned him to become secretary of state. Winning the complete confidence of the president, Van Buren replaced John C. Calhoun in 1832 as vice-president, and with Jackson's support, he received the Democratic presidential nomination in 1836. On March 4, 1837, he became the eighth president of the United States. He had not missed a single rung of the political ladder on his way to the top.

The Democrats failed to take advantage of Van Buren's humble background or his struggle to reach the top in order to project a popular image of their candidate, while the efforts of the Whig propagandists to make merry with "Little Matty" went unopposed. The tone of the campaign was sounded by Pennsylvania Congressman Charles Ogle who, during debate on a routine appropriation bill for repairs to the White House, gained the floor of the House of Representatives and for three days delivered a malicious diatribe on the "Regal Splendors of the President's Palace." Just as in 1828 John Quincy Adams had been portrayed as a pompous and profligate patrician, Ogle unsparingly attacked Van Buren from his beginnings in the "cabbage patch at Kinderhook" to his present reign as a "lily-fingered aristocrat" in a sumptuous "Asiatic mansion" and charged him with the waste of thousands of tax dollars on "silly fancies." In the midst of a depression, the picture of a courtly, luxury-loving leader, indifferent to the sufferings of the common man, had a devastating effect.

> Let Van from his coolers of silver drink wine,
> And lounge on his cushioned settee;
> Our man on his buckeye bench can recline,
> Content with hard cider is he!

The voices of the Democrats refuting and denying could scarcely be heard above the rollicking revelry and invective of the Whigs as waves of emotional enthusiasm drowned out reason.

Stimulated by hard cider and hard times, the Whigs eagerly sang and shouted Van Buren out of the presidency:

Farewell, dear Van,
You're not our man;
To guide the ship,
We'll try old Tip!

HENRY CLAY   *George Peter Alexander Healy, circa 1845   Oil on canvas, 30 x 25 inches*
From the Collection of the National Portrait Gallery
Gift of Andrew Mellon   NPG.65.44

Henry Clay *Whig*

1777-1852

The year 1844 brought "Justice to Harry of the West." Having been passed over for the Whig presidential nomination in 1840, when he felt sure of election, in favor of a man whose chief claim to fame was his military record, Henry Clay was vindicated by the receipt of his third and final opportunity for attaining the presidency.

Gallant Harry's disastrous defeat in the presidential election of 1832 had done little damage to his national popularity or his political prestige. Retaining his seat in the Senate, he had maintained his mastery of the anti-Jacksonian forces in Congress and, although unable to control patronage, by the sheer force of his personality embraced a loyal following. Nor had the defeat dampened his presidential ambitions. In 1836, realizing that there were too many obstacles in his path to renomination, he had announced he would not be a candidate, but immediately after that campaign he declared his intention to oppose Van Buren in 1840.

In that election year, however, the Kentuckian was confronted with the emerging concept of "availability"—a realistic appraisal by party leaders of a contender's chance for success at the polls. Liberal Whigs concluded that Clay was too vulnerable to Democratic attacks, had made too many enemies in the course of his long career, was too closely identified with the aristocratic and moneyed interests to mount a viable candidacy. Believing that they should enter the election unencumbered by former issues and leaders, the Whigs instead chose a plain man of the people, innocent of political controversy—General William Henry Harrison.

Convinced that he was the popular choice, Clay naturally felt he had been deprived of the nomination by intrigue. It is said that on hearing the news of Harrison's nomination, a black cloud of fury passed over his face and he burst out wrathfully: "I am the most unfortunate man in the history of parties: always run . . . when sure to be defeated, and now betrayed for a nomination when I or any one, would be sure of election." His so-called friends were "not worth the powder and shot it would take to kill them," he complained. He quickly submerged his anger, however, and although disapproving of the demagogic methods used by the Whigs to capture votes, loyally supported the Harrison ticket.

While Harrison, who died after one month in office, and his successor John Tyler held the nation's highest office, Clay looked on them as mere figureheads whom he undoubtedly planned to control. He saw himself in a role equivalent to that of a British prime minister—the real power behind the administration. But Tyler, who at heart was a states' rights Democrat from Virginia, disagreed with Clay and his group of Whigs over what the party stood for. When he asserted his independence, the Kentuckian led the drive to destroy him. As "His Accidency" fell from grace, the party rallied around Clay, the true "embodiment of Whig principles."

The "Star of the West" had never shone brighter than he did in the early 1840s. Angered by Tyler's politics, he resigned his seat in the Senate on March 31, 1842, but he still dominated the Whig Party with an iron hand. A New York newspaper wrote of him at this time, "Old Hickory himself never lorded it over his followers with authority more undisputed, or more supreme." Gray-haired and elderly, Clay was one of America's most beloved political leaders. Everywhere the ranks of his supporters were clamoring for his nomination to the presidency. By August of 1842 over two-hundred Whig newspapers were advocating his candidacy; between July 1842 and July 1843 he was nominated by Whig conventions in thirteen states. Although some party leaders doubted whether Clay had enough "sympathies in common with the people" to be elected, the Kentuckian entered the Whig national convention of 1844 as its predestined nominee.

His candidacy having begun under such auspicious terms, Clay had little doubt that this time he would reach his long sought-after goal. He decided on a safe and conservative platform, dropping the controversial Bank issue, to advocate reform of executive usurpations and extension of the protective tariff. As with the Bank issue in 1832, however, he failed to judge the depth of popular discontent attached to what would become the real issue of the campaign—the annexation of Texas.

Since winning its independence from Mexico in 1836, Texas had clamored for annexation to the United States, but despite the considerable sentiment in its favor, fear of free state opposition—it was understood that Texas would be slave territory—and of war with Mexico had caused the Van Buren administration to shy away from the proposal. In 1842, however, another request for admission to the Union was made and John Tyler, an expansionist, negotiated a treaty of annexation which was proposed to the Senate on April 22, 1844. Texas immediately became the hottest question of the presidential campaign.

Clay had hoped to avoid the Texas problem, closely tied as it was to the slavery controversy. Convincing himself that the people had no burning desire for annexation, he felt he could treat the question in such a manner "as to reconcile all our friends, and many others to the views which I entertain." His ideas were officially made known in the "Raleigh letter" —so-called because of the city of its origin—written in April 1844 and published in the Whig paper, the *National Intelligencer.* Annexation "at the present time" was, he said, dangerous to national unity, financially inexpedient, and almost certain to provoke war with Mexico. A political straddle, the letter left uncertain what Clay's future attitude toward annexation might be.

The Raleigh letter had no serious effect on Clay's standing with the Whigs, who unani-

Justice to Harry of the West [Henry Clay]   LIBRARY OF CONGRESS

mously nominated him on May 1 with no mention of the Texas issue. The Democrats, however, intoxicated by the expansionist fervor, dropped Van Buren, the leading contender who had opposed annexation, in favor of "dark horse" James Knox Polk, and came out squarely for the "reannexation of Texas." Their strategy forced Clay into an uncomfortably defensive position.

The defeat of the annexation treaty in the Senate did not kill the issue of expansion; in the land-hungry South and West, Clay proved particularly vulnerable to Democratic attacks on his opposition to the acquisition of Texas. In an attempt to soften the impact of his Raleigh letter, he wrote two letters to Alabama friends declaring that he would now accept the admission of Texas if it could be accomplished "without dishonor . . . upon fair and just terms" and that "slavery ought not to affect the question one way or another." This equivocation, while encouraging the South, alienated the anti-slaveryites and was perhaps fatal to Clay's prospects of winning the presidency. In the final tally, which was incredibly close, the balance of power in New York state was held by the abolitionists, and James G. Birney, the candidate of the anti-slavery Liberty Party, cut so deeply into the Whig ranks as to give the state's electors, and thus the election, to the Democrats. If he had not lost New York by a scant 5,000 votes, Clay would have been president.

In his stand on the Texas question, Clay had appealed to nationalist sentiment as he had throughout his entire career. "If anyone desire to know the leading and paramount object of my public life," he had written, "the preservation of the Union will furnish the key." Compromise appeared to him the only way to preserve the Union. Thus, he attempted to conciliate the northern abolitionists and southern annexationists just as earlier, through his American System, he had meant to draw together the "democracy of the West with the conservatism of the East." All through his life, in fact, he worked to maintain the integrity of the nation, acting as moderator in 1820-1821 during the Missouri crisis, and in 1833 during the Nullification arguments, and again as the Great Pacificator of 1850. It is for these efforts that Clay is most remembered, rather than his failure to achieve the presidency.

JAMES GILLESPIE BIRNEY *Attributed to Benjamin Trott Watercolor on ivory,
2⅞ x 2¼ inches, oval Mrs. John Hammond, Washington, D.C.*

James Gillespie Birney *Liberty*

1792-1857

"Who is James Gillespie Birney," rhetorically questioned Elizur Wright, secretary of the American Anti-Slavery Society in 1844. Answering himself, he replied, "The finest specimen of the glorious, erect, reasoning animal." Comparing Birney to George Washington, he went on to add: "Should he die this day, he has achieved more for the liberty and welfare of his country than all the presidents or other candidates for the presidency that have lived since Washington died."

Wright's words echoed the sentiments of many Americans who in the 1840s were beginning to look favorably on the anti-slavery movement. For James G. Birney's life was devoted to arousing his fellow countrymen through political action against what he considered the evil institution of slavery. In 1844, the anti-slavery movement's political instrument, the Liberty Party, unanimously nominated Birney for president.

Kentucky born and Princeton educated, James Birney came from a family of culture and wealth. Leaving Kentucky in 1818, however, he settled on the Alabama frontier as a planter, in which he failed miserably, and lawyer, where he achieved uncommon success. Described as earnest and thoughtful, Birney held the typical southern liberal's attitude toward slavery—that slavery was bad but until it could be restrained by law, all one could do was to take care of the slaves entrusted to him as best he could.

But in 1828 Birney got caught up in Charles Grandison Finney's revival which taught the doctrine of salvation not just by repentance, but by good works. Man's duty as a Christian, Finney preached to ever-increasing crowds, was to see that society moved in the direction of justice and human progress. Finney's revival moved from one Presbyterian church to another, from western New York to the frontier areas of the Midwest and Southwest. Wherever he went, he left behind zealots and converts. One of these was Birney.

"Old things passed away," wrote Birney, talking about his conversion to Finney's message; "all things become new." Life should be measured by the extent of its improvement of other lives, not by worldly prosperity. Beginning his labors in the field of education and civic improvement, Birney moved quickly into the free public-school movement, the temperance movement, and the American Bible Society. It was his involvement in the cause of the Cherokee Indians, however, that brought him into the abolition fold where he remained for the rest of his life.

At first, Birney applied his reforming zeal to work within the American Colonization Society, because in it he saw "a germ of effort capable of expansion adequate to our largest necessities in the extermination of slavery." He saw the colonization movement as offering an opportunity to help free Negroes who were denied the society of both blacks and whites and also denied the legal benefits of being free. After serious study of the works of leading English and American abolitionists, he became convinced that colonization was an inadequate solution to the race problem. In 1834, he announced his withdrawal from the Colonization Society in his *Letter on Colonization* and declared himself an abolitionist. He emancipated his own slaves, and turned his attention to the national anti-slavery movement.

As a southern aristocrat turned abolitionist, James Birney was advanced far beyond the views of his time. Attempting to form an anti-slavery society in the border state of Kentucky, and later to publish an anti-slavery paper—*The Philanthropist*—near Cincinnati, Ohio, he met with abuses, threats of danger, and alienation from friends and relatives. Finally, reasoning that no society based on slavery could be permanent and prosperous, he became the Anti-Slavery Society's strongest advocate for organized political action.

The abolitionist movement split ranks in 1839 and anti-slavery men who favored political action founded the Liberty Party. Loyal to the Constitution, its members did not advocate secession or dissolution of the Union. Meeting in 1840 only as a party of protest, they unanimously nominated James Birney for president, repeating their endorsement of him in 1844 when the name Liberty Party was selected; in 1848 it was changed to the Free Soil Party.

A vigorous campaign followed the nominating convention of 1844. Lively meetings and picnics were held, giving vent to rousing campaign songs, mottos, odes, and a Liberty Call to Battle: "We are coming, we are coming! Freedom's battle is begun!" The Cedar of Lebanon was chosen as the party symbol and articles were printed with inscriptions: "The righteous shall grow like a Cedar in Lebanon," and "The Cedar is the emblem of Constancy, of Protection, of Renown, of Immortality."

In a campaign tour through New England, Birney discussed the issues, stating that he favored a tariff for revenue only—protective tariffs "smacked" of "immunity or privilege conferred on a particular portion of the community." He was opposed to a national bank while slavery still existed in the South, because it favored that "insolvent" region at the expense of the "hard-earned" capital of the North. He was against distributing proceeds from public-land sales to the states, because it deprived future states of their rightful share in the national heritage. And he was also opposed to discrimination against the foreign born once they were naturalized. But to him all issues were subordinate to the main issue of slavery. Candidacy for election was meaningful to him only because its positive results would further his cause, his lifework.

Birney dismissed the opposing candidates, James K. Polk, the Democratic "dark horse," and Whig-nominee Henry Clay, with the observation that they denied "the paramount object

James Gillespie Birney, tinted lithograph   MRS. DION SCOTT BIRNEY

of the UNION, the perpetuation of liberty to all." In a campaign marked by vicious attacks on all candidates, Birney did not escape abuse: just prior to the election the Whigs printed a forged letter containing alleged "proof" that he had bargained with the Democrats for the defeat of Clay. Despite the letter's shattering effects—Birney did not receive even one electoral vote—the Liberty Party received substantial support, particularly in the state of New York where Birney made significant inroads on Henry Clay's popularity. The election marked the transformation of the anti-slavery movement into a political party of major status.

James Birney's last public appearance as a leader of anti-slavery forces was in Cincinnati, Ohio, when he was chairman of the party's convention in 1848. After a fall from his horse in August of that year, he suffered a severe paralytic stroke and never again made a public address. In 1857, his friend Theodore Parker penned a fitting eulogy to a life of self-sacrifice and devotion to the anti-slavery cause: "Posterity will not disregard the memory and services of one of the best and noblest of that band of patriots who freely sacrificed ease and wealth, the applause of their contemporaries, and tempting prospects of political distinction and preferment, for the purpose of redeeming the slave from thralldom, and delivering their native land from its greatest curse."

LEWIS CASS *George Peter Alexander Healy, 1840 Oil on canvas, 45 x 34½ inches*
The Detroit Historical Museum

Lewis Cass *Democrat*

1 7 8 2 - 1 8 6 6

Burdened with dull, old ideas, or plagued by disruptive new ones, the two major parties were in a state of flux in 1848. At the same time, a new third-party movement, spurred by a striking growth of anti-slavery sentiment in the North, began to attract men of all political groups, particularly a faction of the Democratic Party called the Barnburners. This group seceded from the party causing a split severe enough to bring about Democratic defeat despite the appeal of the party's stalwart nominee, Lewis Cass.

"It would have been difficult," remarked Professor George P. Garrison, "for the Democrats to find a stronger man for the first place on their ticket than Cass." Cultured and scholarly, distinguished and popular, sincere and upright in political affairs, Cass possessed an incomparable record in public service. He established a law practice in Ohio in 1802, attained the rank of brigadier general while serving with General Harrison's forces in the War of 1812, and gained an appointment by President Madison to the governorship of the Michigan Territory, a post he held for eighteen years. Cass then served as secretary of war under Jackson and Van Buren, became American minister to France in 1836, and was elected to the Senate by the voters of Michigan in 1845. To all this government service, he brought not only ability, but a deep-rooted patriotism.

Born in Exeter, New Hampshire, Lewis Cass grew up in a heavily saturated Federalist environment. As a small boy in his mother's arms, he remembered watching the bonfires blazing in the streets of Exeter in celebration of New Hampshire's distinction as the ninth state to ratify the Constitution; in later years, Cass liked to tell of that special time in American history when he "saw the Constitution born." He heard accounts of the leading part played by his father in suppressing Shays' rebellion, and he remembered a day when his father, an army captain and a veteran of Valley Forge, introduced him to President Washington who was visiting Exeter on a tour of the country.

Such inspiring beginnings were reinforced by his experiences pioneering with his father in Ohio where "he felt the impulses, generous and strong, which come to the woodsman. The settlers in the west of after years needed to tell him nothing. He knew their needs, he realized their capacities, he sympathized with their longings. . . ."

In Ohio, Cass studied for the law and became the first man in that new state to be admitted to the bar. He regarded his profession as a public trust. The law, Cass believed, was integral to the American democratic ideal, for by its moral force it "ensures the obedience of society."

As the pioneer leader of the Michigan Territory, Cass applied Thomas Jefferson's doctrine that "it is in those New England divisions known as townships that the future of democracy lies." He guided Michigan toward statehood by applying deeply ingrained principles of government far "in advance of any statesman of his time in his ideas of popular interference in the selection of all grades of public officers." Replacing British influence with American democratic ideals, he transformed the territory of Michigan from wilderness into an orderly community to the complete satisfaction of its inhabitants and the federal government. At the same time, he accumulated a fortune in Detroit lands. It was no small wonder, then, that he was called the "Father of the West."

By 1848, however, Cass had lost touch with popular sentiment in the old Northwest. The anti-slavery movement had loomed into national focus and it appealed to northwestern men of Puritan stock, who were among the first to support it. But Cass, the great American statesman of the Northwest whose life was so closely interwoven with the region's growth, failed to realize the trend. The Baltimore Democratic convention, split by disagreement between the "Barnburner" and "Hunker" factions of the New York delegation, fell apart on this issue. The anti-slavery and anti-administration Barnburners, unable to wrest leadership from the party regulars, seceded from the convention. Led by Martin Van Buren, they combined with other anti-slavery men to form the Free Soil Party—a clear demonstration that issues were more important than strict party loyalty. The withdrawal assured the defeat of Lewis Cass.

After nominating Senator Cass, the weakened party approved a brief and weak platform endorsing the war with Mexico and the Polk administration. It ignored the slavery issue. Although Cass regarded slavery as a "great social and political evil," he nevertheless challenged the Wilmot Proviso—which would have prohibited slavery in any of the territories won from Mexico. In a letter to A.O.P. Nicholson, a Tennessee editor, Cass proposed the doctrine of popular sovereignty—that each territory be permitted to decide for itself whether it would be slave or free. Designed to remove the slavery issue from consideration by the federal government, the doctrine also became known as squatter sovereignty; it foreshadowed the stormy political career of young Stephen A. Douglas who would soon command the nation's attention on the same issue. Like Douglas, Cass was an expansionist, fired by the spirit of manifest destiny and eager to claim all of Oregon and the Mexican territory for the Union. With his attention diverted to the growth of the West, as James B. Ranck put it, he "failed to appreciate the fact that the institution of slavery was fundamentally opposed to the ardent individualism of the frontier and that in his day the basic Revolutionary doctrine that 'all men are created equal' must include the Negro."

The Whig nominee, General Zachary Taylor—Old Rough and Ready—having no policies, principles, enemies, political stature, or party, won the election. For the American people, he held the tremendous appeal of the military hero. The results of the bitter three-cornered campaign were close: for Taylor, 163 electoral votes (eight slave states and seven free states); and for Cass, 127 (eight free states and seven slave states); with a very narrow popular margin. The Free-Soil Party won no electoral votes, but it prevented Cass from receiving New York's 36. In 1848, the northern opposition to slavery extension was clear. Cass, disappointed but calm, regretted ". . . our defeat for the sake of the party and of the Country."

In January 1849, still admired and respected by the people of Michigan, Cass was given his former Senate seat which he held until 1857. Although his popularity declined as Free-Soil sentiment increased in the Northwest, he made his greatest—two days—Senate speech in 1850 defending his doctrine of popular sovereignty. He became secretary of state under Buchanan, but resigned the post in December 1860, because the president refused to take a firm stand against secession by strengthening the Charleston forts. To James A. Garfield in 1861, Cass recalled that he "saw the Constitution born, and I fear I may see it die." But fortune favored him: after over fifty years of public service, his career and life came to an end with peace and Union restored to his native land.

MARTIN VAN BUREN   *Daniel Huntington   Oil on canvas, 40 x 30 inches*
New York State Office of General Services, Albany

Martin Van Buren *Free-Soil (Democrat)*

1782-1862

Martin Van Buren, chastised by his opponents in the campaign of 1840 as being a "used up man," left office determined that he would return again to the White House. His defeat by William Henry Harrison, although somewhat subduing, was, he believed, only an interruption in a career intended to be an unqualified success. One more victory was all he wanted before settling down into honorable retirement. Still young at the age of fifty-nine, he considered himself neither too old nor too beaten to seek "restoration of his crown."

With the unexpected death of Harrison one short month after his inauguration and the succession of the unpopular Virginian, John Tyler, Whig strength was severely weakened and there was positive indication that Van Buren could be reelected in 1844. Proving far from used up, the "Little Magician" began honing his political weapons. First, he regained control of the Albany Regency, and he quickly restored his party's strength in New York. Then, he began issuing statements broadly referring to the "apparent success of last year's buffoonery" and expressing his faith in what he called "the sober second-thought of the People." Meanwhile, he suggested that 1844 would not be too late to make amends. As the election year began, his nomination seemed secure, but at the last minute his opposition to the annexation of Texas— then a fiery issue between proponents and opponents of the extension of slavery—cost him the party's nomination. The Democrats turned instead to James K. Polk of Tennessee, the first "dark-horse" candidate in American presidential history. Van Buren was not only passed over for a man whom he had never considered more than a subordinate, but he was quietly read into exile as the nominating convention passed a resolution tendering him "in his honorable retirement the . . . confidence, affection, and respect of the American Democracy."

Still, he could not abandon all hopes of returning to office, and as the election year of 1848 approached, his eagerness grew. Much of his former political strength had been sapped, both by his retirement and by his opposition to slavery expansion which had now become a more important concern of the Democratic Party; it was necessary for him to cast about for a new cause that would provide the momentum necessary to project him into the presidency.

He did not need to look far. By 1848 anxiety over the question of slavery increased. The war with Mexico and the treaty with Great Britain settling the Oregon boundary had increased the country's size by an area larger than France and Germany combined, and whether this new territory would be slave or free was a question hotly debated both in Congress and throughout the country. Adding fuel to the fire was the Wilmot Proviso of 1846 advocating the prohibition of slavery in any newly acquired lands. In New York, argument over the Proviso rent in two the already weakening Democratic Party, with the Van Burenites, known as Barnburners (satirically likened to farmers willing to burn down their barns in order to get rid of the rats in them) supporting the Proviso, and the Hunkers (said to lack principles and simply to "hunker after office"), opposed. Van Buren's necessary "issue" was ready-made.

When the Democratic convention met in Baltimore, delegates from both New York factions attempted to be recognized. The convention finally decided to admit both delegations with the state's votes divided equally between them, but the Barnburners would have none of this and promptly bolted. Soon after they departed, Lewis Cass of Michigan was nominated.

The Barnburners had vigorously opposed the nomination of Cass because of what they considered his imperialistic views and "let the people decide" attitude toward the extension of slavery. Van Buren entertained a particular resentment toward Cass for his role in the "vile intrigue" which had cost him the nomination in 1844. Thus, a "combination of principle and a thirst for revenge" brought about the creation of a third party and the subsequent nomination of Martin Van Buren as a candidate again for the presidency.

Meeting in Buffalo on August 9, 1848, the Barnburners, joined by a heterogeneous group of "Conscience Whigs" and veterans of the anti-slavery Liberty Party, entered wholeheartedly into the amalgam they called the Free-Soil Party. To the convention Van Buren sent an emotion-laden letter in which he forcefully argued that Congress had the undeniable right to exclude slavery from new territories and stated that he could not support any candidate who felt otherwise. In a frenzy of admiration, Van Buren was unanimously chosen standard-bearer of the new party as it marched into the fray with the slogan, "Free Soil, Free speech, Free labor, and Free men."

Van Buren's acceptance of the nomination thrilled the Free-Soilers. One enthusiastic member said, "When I saw this man that I formerly believed to be timid and calculating; this man enjoying the universal confidence and affection of the Great Democratic Party, willingly sacrifice all this public confidence and esteem, and plant himself upon the spot where freedom dwelt ... it was a sublime spectacle—it was the poetry of politics—it was the religion of patriotism!" But to many others the idea of Van Buren defying the Democratic Party, which he had helped organize, was shocking. Master politician that he was, he had revitalized the old Jeffersonian-Republicans and through the imposition of strict party discipline had turned the new structure into an effective, smooth-running machine. Now the "inventor of party regularity" appeared to be throwing discipline to the wind in an effort to harness a cause to his own promotion, and in doing so, inevitably ensured a Democratic defeat in 1848. He had never shown great sympathy for abolitionists and as president had announced that he would veto any bill abolishing slavery in the District of Columbia. For him now to stand at the head of a militant anti-slavery group seemed incomprehensible.

"Little Van's" only hope was to throw the election into the House where, with both major parties vying against each other, he might be preferred to Taylor or Cass. The Democrats and Whigs chose, however, to avoid discussion of the slavery issue, concentrating instead on the military prowess of their candidates, so that personalities, rather than issues, ruled the day. The new party, though unable to carry the election, won a balance of power in several states; and in New York, Van Buren drew enough votes from Cass to throw that state and the election to Taylor. The "Little Magician" polled ten percent of the total presidential vote, but his electoral count was zero.

For abandoning the Democratic Party, Van Buren was branded a traitor, hypocrite, and party apostate. His political career ended with his defeat in 1848, and he played no further role in national politics.

GERRIT SMITH   *Daniel Huntington, 1874   Oil on canvas*
Madison County Historical Society, Oneida, New York

Gerrit Smith *National Liberty/Liberty League*
1797-1874

Gerrit Smith, wealthy New York state businessman and philanthropist, entered the 1848 electoral contest with no less than three nominations for the presidency: from the Liberty League, the National Liberty Party, and the Industrial Congress. Although his candidacy was insignificant in the final election results, Smith epitomized the extremist view—by 1848 standards—on political abolition of slavery in America, for his major aim was the "entire extinction" of that institution.

Smith lived most of his life in the small village of Peterboro, New York, which had been founded by his father, Peter Smith. The elder Smith had accumulated his fortune through fur trading and land speculation, some of it in partnership with John Jacob Astor. Soon after having been graduated with highest honors from Hamilton College, Gerrit began his own business career. Taking up where his father had left off, he continued to make investments in land, and his holdings eventually totaled nearly a million acres in Oswego, New York.

Peterboro, situated in central New York state, was at the heart of the revival movement that swept through the country in 1825 under the leadership of Charles Grandison Finney. Carried on by Finney's young convert to evangelical religion—Theodore Weld—the movement influenced many Americans including Gerrit's father. It was inevitable, therefore, that the elder Smith should pass on his religious enthusiasm as well as his lands to his son. Gerrit's wife also came under the influence of the revival and kept urging her family to care for their spiritual health. Under such pressures, Gerrit Smith became heavily involved in church affairs and in philanthropy.

Committed to a war against the evils of his time from the moment of his conversion, Smith began to devote almost all his energies to reform movements for the betterment of mankind. His philanthropies included anti-slavery, religion and education reforms, international peace, women's rights, the Anti-Masonic movement, diet reform, dress reform, prison reform, causes of oppressed people the world over, the abolition of capital punishment and temperance. Smith enjoyed "the luxury of doing good." He sponsored and supported many of his causes independently, providing for them much of the essential oratory and written propaganda.

According to William Lloyd Garrison's paper, *The Liberator,* Smith was "one of nature's noblemen—an ornament to the Christian religion, and an honor to his age . . . as remarkable for the blandness of his manners, as for generosity and greatness of soul." But a thread of instability ran through his life making it difficult for him to pursue one course of action for a sustained period, and causing frequent outbursts of bad temper, often in the form of published letters to friends, that contradicted to some extent his good works and finer qualities. Still, Edmund Quincy of Massachusetts wrote in 1838: "Gerrit Smith is one of the finest specimens of a Man, physically, morally and intellectually that I ever knew."

As an abolitionist who believed that the great political parties were "pro-slavery and antirepublican—utterly contemptuous of the great foundation doctrine of our Republic 'that all men are created equal,'" Smith became a founder in 1840 of the Liberty Party whose name and motto he proposed: "vote for no slaveholder for civil office—nor for anyone who thinks a slaveholder fit for it." Pledged to only one idea, however, the party remained small and weak. By 1847 it was plagued by a tendency toward factionalism, and in June of that year advocates of a broader program for gaining major party status adopted the name Liberty League and nominated Gerrit Smith for president.

The remaining members of the Liberty Party went in two directions. One small group merged with the new Free-Soil Party in the summer of 1848. The second group attended a political convention at Buffalo that was called by Gerrit Smith at the same time, and this group also nominated Smith for president. Calling themselves the National Liberty Party, they wrote a platform declaring their opposition to slavery and "wars, tariffs, the traffic in intoxicating drinks, land monopolies, and secret societies, and whatever else is opposed to that comprehensive, great and glorious One Idea." The convention also approved the doctrines of "Land Reform" and condemned the war with Mexico.

An "Industrial Congress" representing the various national reform associations also nominated Smith for the presidency in 1848. Now, he had the endorsements of three organizations; but still, when the tally was in, Smith polled only 2,733 votes. Although he had not attended the Free-Soil convention, Smith advised those who would not vote for a total abolitionist— himself—to vote for the Free-Soil candidate, Martin Van Buren.

Through conferences and a "Liberty Party Paper," Smith enthusiastically but futilely attempted to revive the Liberty Party until its final convention in 1854. Controlled by enthusiasts—and sometimes fanatics—who "could neither follow leaders nor lead followers," the party failed to gain power in the nation because it demanded too much of its constituency. Smith appeared on the National Liberty Party ballot in 1852 and on a Land-Reform ticket in 1856, but received few votes.

After the annexation of Texas in 1845, Smith wrote that he had no "great confidence that American slavery would die a peaceful death. . . . The strong probability is that this infatuated nation will go on in its pro-slavery wickedness until her slavery has come to a violent and bloody end." On the conviction that bloodshed could be used effectively in freeing slaves, Smith aided John Brown's raid at Harper's Ferry, a venture which caused him temporary insanity; but he forever denied complicity in the affair.

A Republican by 1864, Smith campaigned for Lincoln and—in 1868—for Grant. His reputation, built upon his extraordinary ability and generosity in reform causes, disappeared with the issues themselves. He was "completely a man of his own time."

WINFIELD SCOTT   *Henry Kirke Brown, cast, 1966, from original plaster of 1858*
Bronze bust, 28¾ inches   From the Collection of the National Portrait Gallery.   NPG.65.38.1

Winfield Scott *Whig*

1786-1866

From the day of its entrance into national politics, the Whig Party's only victories in presidential elections had been won with military heroes as its nominees. General William Henry Harrison, hero of the Battle of Tippecanoe, and General Zachary Taylor, hero of the war with Mexico, had each been successfully projected into the presidency in 1840 and 1848, respectively. Now, in 1852, though they might logically have nominated a better qualified candidate, the Whigs attempted to repeat their triumphs by naming another soldier as their candidate, Winfield Scott, perhaps the ablest American general of his generation.

A Virginian by birth, Scott was a career soldier with forty years' service in the army to his credit when he was nominated. For every president since Jefferson, he had undertaken critical missions aimed at either preventing or winning wars. Publicly acclaimed for his courage at Chippewa and Lundy's Lane in the War of 1812, he emerged from that conflict a major general. He fought in the Black Hawk War in 1832 and led the Creek and Seminole campaigns in Florida in 1835. An energetic and diplomatic peacetime officer, his accomplishments as pacificator in 1838 and 1839 were impressive; in little more than a year, he had transported 16,000 dispossessed and embittered Cherokees peaceably across the Mississippi, eased border tensions with Canada, and brought about concessions which averted war with Great Britain in the Maine boundary dispute.

Named general-in-chief of the army in 1841—an office he held for the next twenty years —Scott was responsible for many reforms in the service, particularly the modernization of military administration and the strengthening of the program for professional training of officers. He conceived of the army almost as his own possession and fashioned and molded it to fit his personal conception of what an army should be. He knew hundreds of his men by name and was well respected as a leader. Intelligent and scholarly, he was also a giant of a man—nearly six and one-half feet tall, weighing 250 pounds—and in his resplendent uniform with its gold epaulets cut an impressive figure. Somewhat punctilious, he loved all the pomp and glitter of military life; "Old Fuss and Feathers," his soldiers called him.

When war with Mexico erupted in 1846 after the annexation of Texas, Scott devised a strategic plan which would, as he put it, "conquer a peace." Hampered by untrained officers, inadequate supplies, mountainous terrain, and political backstabbing in Washington, the general nevertheless marched his troops from Vera Cruz to Mexico City, overwhelming the enemy in one of the most brilliant campaigns in American military annals.

Politicians were quick to seize upon the glamour of Scott's victory. Hailing him as a new Andrew Jackson and "defender of the frontier," the Whigs passed over such notables as incumbent Millard Fillmore and Secretary of State Daniel Webster to select Scott as the most "available" candidate for the presidency in 1852. Scott, like his Democratic opponent Franklin Pierce, was unencumbered by a previous political record or commitments—although during his years in Washington, he had become keenly aware of political machinations. The Whigs accepted him largely because he seemed a "safe" candidate, who would remain discreetly silent on major issues and could be quietly controlled. It was hoped that people would be content to vote for him simply because of his war record.

It is a striking irony that while Scott's victory in the war with Mexico led to his nomination for the presidency, that same victory ultimately stirred up the issue that defeated him, and that a silent strategy meant to win his election actually lost him support.

Through Scott's conquest, an area of inestimable value—larger than the size of the entire nation in 1783—was added to the growing nation. Yet, the acquisition of this territory aroused irreconcilable differences over the question of the extension of slavery and created a furor which did not die until drowned out by the thunderous guns of the Civil War. The Compromise of 1850 was an attempt by moderate men of both the North and South to avoid disunion and resolve peaceably the problems raised by the territory Scott had wrested from Mexico. Though certain of its provisions were bitterly contested—the South particularly resented the admission of California which upset the delicate balance between slave and free states, and northern abolitionists found the enforcement of the Fugitive Slave Law repugnant—the Compromise technically eliminated slavery as an issue in the election of 1852. In reality, it loomed like a dark cloud on the horizon throughout the campaign.

The Whig Party suffered drastically from the divisive slavery issue. Although the platform adopted by the national convention "acquiesced in" the Compromise measures, northern and southern factions within the party were unable to resolve their differences about the institution, and the nomination of Scott did little to help the disintegrating party. While Franklin Pierce and the Democrats came out solidly for the Compromise, Scott was induced by his northern backers to keep silent on the measure, neither favoring nor opposing it. This reticence was taken by a leading body of Southern Whigs as proof of Scott's free-soil tendencies and they promptly bolted the party. Had they known that Scott, an unquestionable Unionist, had supported the Compromise, and, indeed, lobbied for its passage in Congress, they might have acted differently. But that fact was glossed over in an attempt to win the support of northern Whigs who opposed the Fugitive Slave provision of the Compromise. At the same time, Free-Soil radicals and "Conscience" Whigs, militant opponents of the Compromise, spurned Scott, whom they considered the instrument of southern slaveholders, and held their own convention, nominating John Parker Hale.

While the slavery issue rent the Whig Party in two, it remained undeveloped in the electoral contest. The country, enjoying the lull before the storm of 1854, chose to ignore questions of public policy, and the campaign degenerated into a series of scurrilous personal attacks. The Democrats had great fun ridiculing the swashbuckling Scott whose "airs and foibles," as Samuel Eliot Morison has pointed out, were unlikely to win golden opinions from the democracy. With the two candidates virtually indistinguishable, except for Pierce's less conspicuous military record, it is probable that Scott's failure to take a positive stand on the Compromise of 1850 ultimately lost him the election. After the campaign ended, the *National Intelligencer* reported that the people had voted for Pierce, not only because they looked upon the Compromise measure as the final settlement of the slavery issue, but also because they were "tired of the feeble, amicable neutrality of the administration" and were ready for something more positive. Thus, the general who had been so victorious on the battlefield, met defeat at the polls largely because of a point of strategy. His friends facetiously remarked that the general simply was not used to "running."

Although growing old and feeble, Scott continued as general-in-chief of the army after the election. In spite of his affinity for the South, he remained strongly loyal to the Union, and as the Civil War approached, he actively encouraged President Buchanan to prepare to defend federal property in the South; his advice, however, was regarded as the senile ranting of an old man. In 1860, after the appointment of George B. McClellan as commander of the Army of the Potomac, Scott finally requested retirement.

JOHN PARKER HALE   *Unidentified artist   Oil on canvas, 35½ x 28¾ inches*
Annie E. Woodman Institute, Dover, New Hampshire

John Parker Hale *Free-Soil*

1806-1873

The pioneer anti-slavery leader and politically independent senator from New Hampshire, John Parker Hale, headed the Free-Soil Party ticket in 1852. Nationally known for his courage in the fight against slavery, Hale had taken a dramatic stand alone against powerful pro-slavery interests in the Senate until other abolitionists joined him in 1849. Combining skillful eloquence and a genial wit and humor with commonsense and firm resolve, he was uniquely suited for a prominent role in the earliest phase of the abolitionist movement.

Hale inherited the gift of wit and eloquence from his father, a lawyer, who died when John Jr., the eldest of twelve children, was only thirteen. Determined to educate her eldest son, his mother moved the family from Rochester, New Hampshire, to Eastport, Maine, where she managed a boardinghouse. Hale enrolled at Phillips Exeter Academy in 1820 where he studied under the well-known Benjamin Abbott for three years before entering Bowdoin College. Although disposed toward carelessness and indolence, he was a good student with a talent for debate and for amusing others with his quick wit; as one friend noted, he liked "to spout before an awe-struck assembly." Having inherited his father's gift for swaying audiences, it was natural for Hale to choose a legal career.

After establishing a law practice in Dover, New Hampshire, John Hale soon became a master of courtroom rhetoric. His abilities in the art of persuasive techniques prompted him to enter politics, and he began a decade of public service and a rise to political prominence in New Hampshire through his election to the state legislature in 1832; two years later, President Jackson appointed him to the post of attorney of the United States for the district of New Hampshire. Hale was an independent thinker with a propensity toward reform—he had already taken the temperance pledge—and he often attended the sermons of John Parkman, minister of Dover's First Unitarian Society, who preached on the evils of the slavery system. During this period, then, despite his loyalty to the Democratic Party and in a political climate unfavorable to the growth of abolitionism, Hale turned his attention to anti-slavery activity in New Hampshire.

Elected to Congress by the Democrats in 1842, Hale served until February 1845, when he boldly took independent action on the issue of Texas annexation, a measure supported by Democrats; he brought about a breach within his party after writing a letter to his constituents denouncing annexation as "eminently calculated to provoke the scorn of earth and the judgment of heaven." The New Hampshire Democrats read him out of the party at a special convention on February 12, 1845. Hale reacted by conducting single-handedly the "Hale storm" of 1845, a campaign vigorous and effective enough to prevent his replacement from winning election. Hale supporters from all over the state rallied to his cause. John Greenleaf Whittier, the poet laureate of anti-slavery, contributed a poem to "the noblest combat ever waged with Tyranny," and said that he "would rather be the author of that letter than the President of the United States." Theodore Parker noted that in Hale's speeches "the masterly eloquence which broke out from his great human heart, and rolled like the Mississippi in its width, its depth, its beauty, and its continuous and unconquerable strength" captivated all who heard him. Sent again by his hometown to the state legislature, he then won election by that body to represent New Hampshire in the United States Senate, a unique triumph for Hale. Excluded from his own party because of his convictions, he was swept into the Senate on his own merits with the backing of no party.

As one of the first critics of slavery in the Senate—and without party support—John P. Hale was ignored, reproached, denounced, subjected to arguments, and denied appointments to committees, but he was neither intimidated nor diverted from duty. His ready wit and abundant good nature helped avert personal assaults. As George W. Julian wrote, "He kept down the ire of his enemies by compelling them to laugh at the moral grotesqueness of the attitude in which he placed them." His rare gift of satire without cruelty coupled with good manners impressed the entire assemblage and commanded respect. But Hale considered his most outstanding achievements in the Senate to be those he made in behalf of naval seamen; he secured an amendment prohibiting flogging in the navy and worked steadily toward improving conditions for these young men.

By 1848, Hale had gained a national reputation as a champion of the anti-slavery cause, and he easily won the Liberty Party nomination for the presidency. But in that year, when all anti-slavery groups merged into the Free-Soil Party, he withdrew in favor of Martin Van Buren. Between elections, the new party declined as many Free-Soilers drifted back to the major parties. The ominous provisions of the Compromise of 1850, however, again galvanized the Free-Soilers —sometimes called Free Democrats—into action in 1852 for their last rousing convention. Meeting in Pittsburgh with greater zeal than at any time since the foundation of the original Liberty Party, the anti-slavery men unanimously nominated the reluctant John P. Hale for president. With more spirit than hope, the enthusiastic delegates adopted a platform of twenty resolutions reaffirming the 1848 platform against slavery extension, with added clauses denouncing the Compromise of 1850, calling for recognition of Haiti, and favoring arbitration of international disputes.

The lack of activity by Whigs and Democrats for the anti-slavery cause prompted Hale to accept the nomination and to embark on an enthusiastic campaign. Not all Whigs were jubilant over the nomination of General Winfield Scott, and the Democratic candidate, Franklin Pierce, was little known. Both major parties conducted campaigns on "safe" platforms and drew attention to candidates rather than issues. In a dull campaign, Hale and the Free-Soil Party encountered little opposition and as little attention; in the major parties, as a correspondent of the *National Era* noted, "The discussion of the great question, the only vital one, is carefully avoided." Franklin Pierce won overwhelmingly in all but four states; the Whigs met the worst defeat in their history. Although the Free-Soil Party tallied only 155,285 votes, party members were elated by the crushing defeat rendered the Whigs. Their determination to work and grow was evident everywhere, as expressed by the *Racine Advocate*: "We want it perfectly understood that we cannot be conquered; that agitation of our principles cannot be prevented; and that we mean to grow more and more earnest with every assumption of the slave power."

John P. Hale supported the Republican Party in 1856 and served in the Senate until 1865 when he became the United States minister to Spain. But as the anti-slavery crusade triumphed, the great humanitarian crusader was denied a share in the glory; his qualities of nonpartisanship and a disposition geared to opposition tactics had been expressly relevant to the early phase of the anti-slavery movement. After years of involvement in bitter personal feuds with associates, he retired in 1870 to New Hampshire where, according to press reports, Dover welcomed him with "a reception of which kings might have been proud."

JOHN CHARLES FREMONT   *Bass Otis, 1856   Oil on canvas, 48 x 44 inches*
University of Michigan Museum of Art, Henry C. Lewis Collection   L/NPG.67.2

John C. Frémont *Republican*

1813-1890

On January 4, 1854, Stephen Douglas introduced in Congress a bill for the organization of a large part of the Louisiana Purchase—the so-called Nebraska Territory. Ambiguously dealing with the slavery issue, the bill incorporated the principle of popular sovereignty, the right of the people of any new state to decide for or against slavery. Because this territory fell north of the latitude of 36°30', the bill by implication repealed the sacred Missouri Compromise of 1820 which forbade slavery north of that line. Thus, slavery would be allowed to advance into regions from which it had been hitherto excluded. While the great majority of southerners accepted the bill, its passage fanned to a white heat the animosity toward slavery felt by northerners who saw the possibility of a vast slaveholding belt stretching from the Gulf of Mexico to Canada. Emotions in the North were so intense that Douglas said he could travel from Boston to Chicago in the light of his own burning effigies.

Out of this "fanatical excitement," a new and powerful political party arose almost spontaneously. On July 6, a great mass meeting of disgruntled elements, including Conscience Whigs, Independent Democrats, Free-Soilers, and other enemies of the Kansas-Nebraska Act, was held in Jackson, Michigan. Dedicating itself to opposing "by every constitutional means the existence of slavery in any of the territories of the U.S.," the Republican Party came into being.

Aroused by an intense moral fervor, the new organization grew so quickly that virtually overnight it became the second major political party. In the congressional elections of 1854, the Republicans won striking victories; by 1856, its leaders were ready to enter the presidential campaign.

In selecting its first presidential candidate, the young and purposeful party passed over more conspicuous Republican leaders in favor of a man unassociated with the radical slavery issue, a fresh contender, with no political past to speak of—explorer John C. Frémont. He was young—just forty-three—but had already achieved prominence through an adventurous career, his marriage to the daughter of the Senate powerhouse, Thomas Hart Benton, and his role in California history.

To thousands of settlers moving West in the meridian years of the nineteenth century, John C. Frémont was the "Pathfinder"—the man who had blazed wagon trails through the mountains to the rich lands of the Pacific Coast. The detailed maps and scientific reports of his four exploring expeditions into the trans-Mississippi frontier between 1842 and 1853 greatly enhanced public interest in the Far West and lured restless men to make the great American trek.

Frémont was himself a restless man with an intensely "kinetic temperament," perhaps the result of his illegitimate birth—always a nettle pricking at his consciousness—and his subsequent years drifting about the country with his parents. Throughout his life, he displayed an inordinate fondness for the nomadic out-of-doors life and reacted somewhat like a bull in a china shop when hemmed in by civilization. At seventeen, he was expelled from Charleston College largely as a result of his wanderlust, which all too frequently tempted him from the classroom. Through the influence of Joel R. Poinsett, South Carolina congressman and first United States minister to Mexico, who marveled at the youth's "flashing spirit," he secured a position as instructor of mathematics on the navy sloop *Natchez,* only to find shipboard life more confining than the classroom. Again with Poinsett's help, he was commissioned second lieutenant in the United States Topographical Corps through which the joys of surveying the country's forested valleys and hills were first revealed to him. It was then that he decided to make exploration his lifework. It was a career well suited to his nature, for he later wrote that as an explorer he found "the true Greek joy in existence . . . the gladness of living."

Frémont's supreme ambition was "to make known the unknown country of the Far West"; to equal the great exploring feats of Lewis and Clark and Zebulon Pike. Through his marriage to the beautiful and brilliant Jessie Benton, daughter of the senator from Missouri, the means of achieving this end were placed before him. Thomas Hart Benton was the most powerful expansionist voice then in the United States Senate and the most interested in mapping and colonizing the West. Through his sponsorship, Congress appropriated the necessary funds for the expeditions which made Frémont the best known frontiersman of his time.

During his third western expedition, which began as war with Mexico was brewing, the Pathfinder played a major role in the conquest of Mexican-owned California, inspiring discontented Americans there to rise in the "Bear Flag" revolt and establish California as a republic. Though acclaimed a hero by the populace, he unfortunately became engaged in an interservice rivalry over the control of the California government, was court martialed and found guilty of insubordination. The nation almost universally resented the verdict, and Frémont became a cause célèbre. President Polk pardoned him, but the volcanic explorer refused to acknowledge the gesture on the grounds that it implied his guilt.

Frémont returned to California and his newly purchased Mariposa Ranch on which gold was soon discovered, making Frémont one of the few millionaires of his day and one of the best known men in California. In 1850, he was elected the first United States senator from the new state, a position he held only six months. This was the total of his political experience when he was nominated by the Republicans for the presidency in 1856.

Frémont had first been approached by the Democratic Party to be its presidential candidate, but it was said at the time that he refused because the party had been instrumental in passing the Kansas-Nebraska Act. Whether true or not, this strengthened his reputation with the Republicans, many of whom saw the young explorer as the personification of Free-Soil principles.

Frémont was not a radical abolitionist; in fact, he proposed gradual emancipation of slaves with federal compensation to owners. He owned no slaves, however, and had refused to use slave labor in his gold mines, although it would have substantially increased his profits. Moreover, he was publicly and firmly opposed to the extension of slavery into the territories—all of which made him an acceptable candidate for the new party.

The Republicans carried on their campaign with the enthusiasm of a religious crusade. Sentiment for the Pathfinder and the "sacred cause" grew into an emotional frenzy. Frémont rallies sprang up almost spontaneously, particularly in the Midwest, and, as in 1840, "acres of men" gathered to hear an impressive array of stump speakers including William Cullen Bryant, Ralph Waldo Emerson, and Henry Wadsworth Longfellow. Every conceivable campaign trapping was brought into service: biographies, poems, songs, posters, cartoons, and portraits of Frémont abounded—the portrait used here was painted expressly for the campaign. One of the most popular songs, set to the tune of Stephen Foster's "Camptown Races," described Frémont as a strong mustang colt who far outdistanced the lame Buchanan. Everywhere, in speeches and newspapers, rang the slogan, "Free Speech, Free Press, Free-Soil, Free Men, Fremont and Victory!"

To counteract the Republican hoopla, the Democrats made energetic use of the threat of secession in an attempt to induce moderate men to vote for the Buchanan ticket. Many Democratic papers predicted, and southern leaders declared, that Frémont's election would herald an immediate dissolution of the Union and possibly civil war. The threat to some seemed very real, and conservative anti-slavery men, fearful of a future in the hands of the "Black Republicans," refused to support the largely sectional party. One such was Thomas Hart Benton, Frémont's own father-in-law, who published an open letter denouncing the party for accentuating sectional hostilities and questioning if the people believed that the South would submit to such a president as Frémont. "We are treading," he wrote, "upon a volcano that is liable at any moment to burst forth and overwhelm the nation."

Disunionist threats ultimately proved the decisive force in the campaign, though other issues were discussed and the usual amount of personal invective tossed back and forth, but Frémont was ultimately defeated by the nation's fear of war. James Buchanan, an experienced statesman who typified the old order, was the victor.

Although Frémont lived for thirty-four years after the election, the remainder of his life was sadly anticlimactic. He seemed pursued by a nemesis which turned all his successes into failures. Appointed commanding general of the Department of the West during the Civil War, his extravagance and arbitrary handling of confiscated property led Lincoln to remove him. In 1864, he was again nominated for the presidency by a convention of radicals, but his candidacy displeased the administration which struck a bargain with his supporters, leaving him to with-

Frémont ribbon   CORNELL UNIVERSITY, DOUGLAS COLLECTION

164

draw ungracefully. The gold found on his huge Mariposa estate slipped through his fingers, and he was saved from poverty only by his wife's work as an author, and by his appointment as territorial governor of Arizona in 1878. He could be pleased, however, by the memory of his and the Republican Party's impressive showing in 1856, for he had carried all of New England, the western states, and New York. After his campaign, the future success of the young party seemed certain.

> "If months have well-nigh won the field,
> What may not four years do?"

MILLARD FILLMORE   *George Peter Alexander Healy, 1857   Oil on canvas,
30 x 25 inches   The Corcoran Gallery of Art, Washington, D.C.*

Millard Fillmore *American (Know-Nothing)*

1800-1874

While friends at home laid the groundwork for his 1856 nomination and campaign for the presidency, Millard Fillmore traveled around Europe on a grand tour, receiving the attention and honors of ministers, ambassadors, and crowned heads of state. It was from Paris that Fillmore sent his acceptance of the American Party nomination, offering his past experience as president of the country and his efforts for the preservation of the Union as a guarantee for success in 1856.

Industry, commonsense, and devotion to duty marked Millard Fillmore's course of action early in life when he determined to rise above the poverty of the frontier and to overcome the drawbacks of a meager education. His father, Nathaniel, had settled west of the Appalachian Mountains in Cayuga County, New York, where Millard was born. Considering his own hardships and misfortunes in farming, Nathaniel urged his sons to seek other trades; later, he arranged for Millard, who supplemented his intermittent education with extensive reading, to clerk in the law office of the county judge whose land Nathaniel worked as a tenant farmer. When his family moved to East Aurora near Buffalo, Millard continued to work as a law clerk in the city. By 1823, he gained admission to the bar in Erie County and moved to Buffalo to practice law.

To fulfill his ambitions, young Fillmore acquired proper manners, temperate habits, and careful speech. Already active in politics by 1828, he was elected with the help of the powerful Thurlow Weed to the New York state legislature as an Anti-Mason. In 1832, he won election to Congress as a Whig and steadily gained in stature until he became one of the party's leading members. Through the influence of Henry Clay's friends, he was nominated, and subsequently elected, to the vice-presidency on the Zachary Taylor ticket in 1848. After Taylor's death on July 9, 1850, Millard Fillmore became president of the United States.

Fillmore believed that "the man who can look upon a crisis without being willing to offer himself upon the altar of his country is not fit for public trust." During the years that witnessed bitter sectional struggle, he remained a strong Unionist. The Compromise of 1850 was the outstanding measure of his administration. He detested slavery, but wanted to "get rid of it

Fillmore and Donelson lithograph   CORNELL UNIVERSITY, DOUGLAS COLLECTION

Fillmore and Donelson ribbon   SMITHSONIAN INSTITUTION

without destroying the last hope of free government in the world." The Compromise endeared him to the southern Whig group, who chose him—reluctant as he was—to be their candidate at their nominating convention in 1852. The party, however, endorsed Winfield Scott as a more neutral candidate and suffered an overwhelming defeat.

The Whigs, in a state of decline and confusion after 1852, split into an anti-slavery group, which later became Republican, and a conservative faction, the "Silver Greys," whose aim was to maintain the Union by rebuilding the "Know-Nothing" movement. The Know-Nothings, native American groups who opposed the extension of the suffrage to Catholics and foreigners, combined in 1854 to form the American Party. Horace Greeley dubbed it the "Know-Nothing" Party because members always answered "I know nothing about it" when questioned about their secret society. The "Silver Greys," led by Fillmore, converted the American Party from an anti-Catholic and anti-foreign position to anti-sectional. The platform adopted in Philadelphia on February 22, 1856, condemned the repeal of the Missouri Compromise effected by the Compromise of 1850 and demanded a twenty-one-year residence in the United States for all foreigners before naturalization. Millard Fillmore was nominated for president and Andrew Jackson Donelson for vice-president.

A gigantic political demonstration staged by the American Party welcomed Fillmore's arrival in New York from Europe. Followers greeted him with a key to the city and an invitation to return to the White House "to remove," according to the *New York Express,* "the vermin that have gathered there during . . . [his] unfortunate absence from the national helm." In a speech sounding the keynote of the American Party campaign, Fillmore appealed to patriotism and the Union, criticized the sectional interests of the other parties, and reminded enthusiastic listeners of his past success in holding the nation together. Ignoring the usual custom of remaining aloof from the campaign, Fillmore then proceeded on a triumphant campaign journey to his home in Buffalo, making planned impromptu speeches and meeting with delegations along the route. His message was clear: the Union was in danger and its enemies were sectional candidates. The question of "Native Americanism" disappeared as the great issue of slavery in the territories took its place.

The passage of the Kansas–Nebraska Act created a new furor against the extension of slavery. While Republicans tried to focus on the slavery issue by drawing attention to the chaos in Kansas, American Party members and Democrats feared that if the Republicans won, the South would secede, thus endangering the future of the Union. Fillmore's policy, therefore, was one of noninterference with slavery in the territories, while the Republicans would have abolished slavery in the territories altogether. Both Republicans and Democrats fought a vigorous campaign, but the American Party, lacking organization and leadership, was helpless against the emotional appeal that the Kansas disorders held for the North. Fearful of a Republican victory, many Americans sacrificed Fillmore and voted for the Democrat, James Buchanan, who won an easy victory. Fillmore carried only Maryland with eight electoral votes. Ruined by the Kansas issue, the American Party collapsed. The "Silver Grey" remnants of old Whig conservatism joined the Constitutional Union Party in 1860 and voted for John Bell.

After the election Fillmore had no regrets, although he was a "little mortified" at "being so unanimously rejected." Defeat removed him from the political arena. Although he opposed Lincoln's candidacy, he worked tirelessly for the war effort in support of the Union cause. For eighteen years after the war, Fillmore led a full life devoted to civic and philanthropic activities in the Buffalo community.

"A House Divided" 1860

IN 1860, ALL CANDIDATES AND ALL PARTIES AGREED THAT THE COUNTRY FACED IMMI-nent danger, although the Republicans were less worried about the possible length and intensity of its duration. "I believe that this country is in more danger now than at any other moment since I have known anything of public life," warned Stephen A. Douglas, Democratic nominee, and throughout the campaign, Douglas continued to alert his listeners to the impending catastrophe. John Bell's supporters shared Douglas' fears, as did many other farsighted and astute Americans sensitive to the state of sectional opinion. Dr. Francis Lieber, professor of German at Columbia College and formerly professor at the University of South Carolina, who knew both sections intimately, believed that the situation was fraught with peril for the Union, and that southerners were quite sincere in their threat to secede if Abraham Lincoln, the Republican candidate, was elected president. Quoting Thucydides on the Peloponnesian War, he applied the Greek historian's conclusion to the contemporary situation: " 'The Greeks,' he said, 'did not understand each other any longer, though they spoke the same language; words received a different meaning in different parts.' " He advised the country to take more seriously such threats as those made by Alexander Stephens, later to become vice-president of the Confederacy, that the result of Lincoln's election would be "undoubtedly an attempt at secession and revolution."

It is true that the North and the South were sections that no longer spoke a language that conveyed a commonly held meaning. In questions of constitutional interpretation, the northerners and southerners had clearly parted ways by the 1830s; and in their references to the American Constitution, a stranger might wonder if they were discussing the same document. Up to this time, Americans from both sections had alternated between the belief that the states were the sole determinants of local institutions and policies and that in any conflict between state interest and national policy, state interest was supreme; and the contrary belief that the United States was a government that acted directly on the people not on the states, and that in the event of differences, federal law and interest prevailed. Political parties adopted either stance depending upon the current policies of the federal government and upon the advantages or injuries which important economic groups seemed at the moment to derive from these policies.

After the 1830s, however, with industrialism more entrenched in the North, northerners moved toward a more firm nationalism, with exceptions, of course. Secession had been threatened if Texas was admitted as a slave state, if the war with Mexico continued, if slavery was not abolished in the South. The personal liberty laws of the northern states in effect nullified the federal Fugitive Slave Act of 1850. But these were not general expressions of states' rights. Mainly in the North, where population and economic and political power were growing fast, most statesmen identified their interests with the federal government and emphasized the integrity of the nation that could not be destroyed. In the South, where economic development lagged, politicians espoused defensive doctrines of localism. They clung to the idea that the states created the Union, and insisted that any state could dissolve its relationship with the federal government if its interests were threatened. Fearing that a Republican victory would create a northern majority party in Congress hostile to the agrarian South, they also feared that such majoritarianism would destroy the nature of the "compact." The South would lose its position of equality in Congress, and, then, as the southern firebrand William L. Yancey of Alabama pointed out, it would become "the duty of the state to protect its people by interposing its reserved rights between the acts of the general government and its people." Such a step might eventuate in revolution, but revolution, said Yancey, "is the right of humanity, the right of civilization, the right of an intelligent public opinion, the right of freemen. . . ."

Beyond differences of understanding lay different economic and social developments characterizing North and South. This difference in development was most keenly felt by southerners, who believed they were left behind economically because of the exploitation by northern merchants and manufacturers of the South's agrarian resources. The absence in the South of those institutions of learning, culture, and amusement which characterized northern urban society, also depressed those southerners who were aware of the disparities between the two civilizations. Hinton Helper of North Carolina in his 1857 tract *The Impending Crisis of the South,* argued that because of the slaveholders' "villainous institution," the "development of our commercial and manufacturing interests" and the South's "inventive genius," were stifled, while "the heaven-born sweets of literature and religion" were "barred" from the southern experience.

Other questions cropped up as events propelled people and their thoughts forward to the precipice of war. The question of northern civil rights arose, to be tied in with the South's defense of slavery. The gag rule imposed by southerners on petitions coming to Congress seeking the end of the slave trade and slavery itself threatened the much-treasured freedom to petition which Americans believed was their right from birth; while the Fugitive Slave Act of 1850 forced northerners to act against their conscience in returning escaped slaves.

Whether such questions would have made a civil war necessary or inevitable, however, is questionable. What really precipitated the struggle between the two societies and exacerbated the sense of difference that all these issues reflected was the question of the extension of slavery in the western territories of the United States. Thus, explained James Russell Lowell, writing in the *Atlantic Monthly* of October 1860, what made "this election . . . a turning point in our history" was not a question of "policy" but the future of freedom. Slavery, then, was the important issue behind the crisis posed by the election of 1860, and Lowell's explanation was conceded by citizens on both sides of the Mason–Dixon line.

In the North, the arguments against slavery were almost all moral, involving the God-given right of human beings to their freedom. To southerners, slavery was a good institution because it offered protection and civilization to the "inferior" African; moreover, it represented an economic investment which had to be protected as property. Imbued with sectional pride, southerners found it insulting to be called unfit to settle in a land devoted to "freedom," or to have their cultural and social institutions branded as immoral and therefore confined, as a disease, to a quarantined area. If slavery was the good that they believed it to be, then it ought to be permitted wherever the flag of the United States flew. Even more important to southerners than the extension of the area of slavery was the threat posed by Republicans to the permanence of slavery as an institution. To a few southern extremists—who were, however, very articulate—the future of slavery rested upon the necessity to reopen the African slave trade legally in order to make extension of slavery into United States territory possible: "We have no slaves to carry to these territories," lamented the Georgia delegate to the Charleston convention of the Democratic Party; "we can never make another Slave State with our present supply of slaves. . . . I would ask my friends of the South to come up in a proper spirit, ask our Northern friends to give us all our rights, and take off the ruthless restrictions which cut off the supply of slaves from foreign lands. . . . I tell you, fellow-Democrats, that the African slave-trader is the true Union man. . . ."

The Ostend Manifesto, which in 1854 suggested the Pierce administration's interest in Cuba, proved to the North that the Democrats, influenced by southern desires were intent upon leading the country into a policy of national expansion contrary to old principles for the sake of acquiring new slave territory. In addition to Cuba, it appeared that Mexico and possibly Central and South America were part of a grand scheme of acquisition being plotted by the Democrats and the Slave Power—all under the rubric of "Manifest Destiny."

Democratic utterances and policy underscored such a belief. Stephen Douglas proclaimed that the United States was bound to become "one grand ocean-bound Republic." One Mobile, Alabama, newspaper, voicing approval of filibustering expeditions into Central America, saw the "establishing on the Southern frontier of slaveholding Republics, encouraging and legalizing the importation of Africans," as involving no financial expenditure on the part of the South, but as providing "natural allies who may eventually, if deemed proper, be connected to us by close ties." And Senator Albert Gallatin Brown of Mississippi summed up the southern attitude towards expansion when he indicated to his constituents that he wanted all this territory—Cuba, Tamaulipas, Potosí, and "one or two other Mexican states"—"for the planting . . . of slavery." "I would spread the blessings of slavery," he orated, "like the blessings of the Divine Master, to the uttermost ends of the earth; and rebellious and wicked as the Yankees have been, I would even extend it to them."

If the Republicans talked of Manifest Destiny, as did indeed one of its chief spokesmen, William H. Seward, it was in terms of adding free states rather than slave enclaves. Seward looked to continental development, to the addition of British America, Russian America, and Spanish America, to the already existing states and territories, all "united in a land of freedom." Thus, he underscored the distinction between the nothern and southern positions.

As for the question of who should decide the nature of territorial government—the set-

1860 cartoon LIBRARY OF CONGRESS

tlers under popular sovereignty, or Congress—the Douglas Democrats emphasized the right of "self-government inherent in a program of popular sovereignty." The Republicans, aware of the popular response to what was obviously intended as an extension of the democratic principles implicit in the Declaration of Independence, were willing to speak vaguely on the issue, applauding acts that forbade slavery in the territories, bemoaning acts that did not. But if the Republicans showed little attention to means, they knew what end they wished to see effected: the end of slavery in the territories, by any means.

The decision of the Supreme Court in the Dred Scott case in 1857, which in effect abrogated the Missouri Compromise of 1820 and the Compromise of 1850 by declaring that slaves were property and that as property they could be taken by their owners from territory to territory regardless of status, had serious implications for the country. As Lincoln recognized in his 1857 debates with Douglas, if the Constitution because of its protection of property rights guaranteed the right to hold slaves anywhere in United States territory, then in effect it refastened slavery on free states as much as it did on new states being carved out of territories.

Although this possibility was not as strong a campaign issue as the more simple facts of southern slavery and the necessity to keep territories free, it did point up the logical results of a policy of popular sovereignty. As a result, then, of the crucial nature of this issue, neither northerner nor southerner, Republican nor Democrat, would submit to the process of compromise by which previous conflicts had been avoided. Both groups had reached an impasse, and the election of Lincoln, on a sectional platform of no further compromise, posed a real danger to the continued functioning of an undivided nation.

Events preceding the election of 1860 did not promise any relief from the tensions of Lincoln's nomination. The Dred Scott decision, the bloody fighting in Kansas after President James Buchanan tried to force the pro-slavery LeCompton Constitution through Congress, and finally, perhaps one of the most disastrous of all events, John Brown's attack on the small village of Harper's Ferry in Virginia in 1859—each of these, and all the lesser but nevertheless painful happenings that occurred between the passage in 1854 of the Kansas–Nebraska Act and 1859 added to the propaganda exchanged between northern and southern agitators. In no small way, these events contributed to a real enmity between the two sections. In 1860, Senator Alfred Iverson of Georgia spoke to the Senate concerning the hostility between northerners and southerners that was "deep and enduring" and that could never be eradicated. It was, in fact, this sense of continuing hatred that in 1860 prompted Seward to speak of the "irrepressible conflict," and others to think in terms of the perils facing the country if Lincoln should be elected president.

Despite the strong feelings, however, the campaign of 1860 was a relatively quiet one. People listened rather than shouted; thought, rather than yelled. Marching parades of "Wide-Awakes" for Lincoln, the "Ever-Readys" for Douglas, and the "fusionists" for Bell hardly disturbed the contemplative mood of the people or interrupted the everyday activities of the urban worker or rural farmhand. It was as if they had already made up their minds.

The presence of four candidates, however, testified to the hopeless divisions of the major national parties. The northern Whigs divided between the Republicans, represented by the rail-splitter from Illinois, Abraham Lincoln, and the Constitutional–Unionists, represented by John Bell. The Republicans were adamant on the question of slavery extension, while the middle-of-the-road, conservative Unionists deprecated the sectional hatreds and divisiveness caused by that question and preached unity under the Constitution. The Democrats divided between Stephen A. Douglas, who represented the northern wing of the party with a program resting on "squatter sovereignty," and John C. Breckinridge, the candidate of the seceding Democrats who would brook no compromise on the question of slavery in the territories at all.

During the campaign itself, the Republicans, besides pressing the issues contained in the party platform dealing with Union, the national interest, slavery, and slavery in the territories, and the reopening of the slave trade, also hammered at the Democratic administration of President Buchanan, charging it with "systematic plunder of the public treasury." The mud of partisan politics was hurled freely and thickly before the campaign was over, while stories of "Old Buck's" corruption filled the newspapers and furnished colorful material for campaign orators. In comparison, "Honest Old Abe" stood out as a paragon of virtue.

The Democrats devoted their efforts to a defense of the Supreme Court and the Dred Scott decision, the advocacy of a transcontinental railroad, the acquisition of Cuba, and faithful execution of the Fugitive Slave Law. They also indulged in intraparty fighting that did neither group much good. Douglas stumped the country calling upon the people to preserve the Union and hang the traitors "higher than Haman." The Breckinridge Democrats used the spoils systems as a weapon against Douglas by removing his friends and supporters from office. Actually, the intraparty fight between Douglas and Breckinridge supporters took away some of the steam of their conflict with the Republicans. As a result, the campaign seemed exceedingly unexciting, the *New York World* deeming it the "tamest presidential contest since the second election of Monroe." The *New York Evening Post* also spoke of the quiet accompanying the campaign, and Horace Greeley in his *Tribune* considered the campaign of 1856 much noisier, much more enthusiastic. The personalities of the candidates hardly came under attack at all, as compared to former campaigns where each candidate received his proper share of vilification. But the campaign speeches, although not noisy, were long and many. Many orators spoke for days on end, ten-thousand speeches being made for Lincoln in the state of New York alone. Principles were being discussed and these required sober reflection. It was perhaps the most serious election in American history. But the results were seldom in doubt.

The expected victory of the Republicans and their candidate, Abraham Lincoln, stimulated much rejoicing in the North. William Cullen Bryant, poet and editor of the *New York Evening Post* proclaimed the inauguration of "a new era . . . a new order of things" which would "reap the harvest of liberty and peace." Needless to say, it was far more a harvest of blood and war, consuming hatreds, and eventual repression.

STEPHEN ARNOLD DOUGLAS   *Duncan Styles, 1860   Oil on canvas, 49¾ x 35¼ inches*
From the Collection of the National Portrait Gallery   NPG.70.42

Stephen A. Douglas *Northern Democrat*

1813-1861

Stephen A. Douglas, the "Little Giant" from Illinois, was one of the nation's most celebrated orators and senators during the decade before the Civil War. His life story was typically American, from his birth in a New England town, his apprenticeship in cabinetmaking, his emigration West to the "paradise of the world," and his meteoric rise to fame through practice of the law and politics. "A lively five-footer full of brains, bounce and swagger, this . . . senior Senator from Illinois . . . was the idol of the northern Democracy."

Douglas' public career began when he became the state's attorney of Illinois at the age of twenty-one as a result of heated political debates in which his oratorical skills were first manifested. At twenty-seven, he became the youngest supreme court justice in the history of Illinois and was considered the ablest man on the bench in that state. By 1842, he had elevated himself to the House of Representatives, and four years later, to the Senate. He was immediately elected chairman of a new Committee on Territories, the key congressional spot for directing the expansion of the United States and a position which was to dominate his political career from that time on. As Abraham Lincoln expressed it in 1856, reminiscing about his acquaintanceship of twenty-two years with Douglas: "With me the race of ambition has been . . . a flat failure; with him, it has been one of splendid success. His name fills the nation. . . ."

It was from his chairmanship of the Committee on Territories that Douglas propelled himself into the national limelight. Here, he was in a position to act on the welter of bills which Henry Clay was finding so difficult to get passed, but which were intended to settle the controversy arising out of the lands gained as a result of the war with Mexico. By turning these measures into the one omnibus bill that has since come to be called the "Compromise of 1850," Douglas brilliantly brought an end to the stalemate and a temporary halt to the argument over slavery in the territories. The essence of that compromise—emphasizing the right of a people to form and regulate their own internal affairs—was later more clearly defined as "popular sovereignty" in the Kansas–Nebraska Act of 1854. It was on this principle, which Douglas believed was derived from the Declaration of Independence, that the Democratic candidate based his campaign for the presidency in 1860.

179

The Kansas–Nebraska Act, ironically, proved Douglas' undoing. By applying the principle of popular sovereignty directly to these territories, the bill reopened the issue that the Compromise of 1850 seemingly had closed. It led to bitter fighting in Kansas, as both sides, slaveholders from Missouri and northern farmers and abolitionists from the East and West, hastened to Kansas territory to form a government favorable to their individual interests. Popular sovereignty led to bloodshed, and the Kansas debacle ominously presaged bloodier battles to come.

The Kansas–Nebraska bill also led to the famous Lincoln-Douglas debates during the summer of 1858, seven public encounters during which the two great Illinoisans battled for the senatorial seat and established the positions that they were to take two years hence. Although Douglas was ostensibly the winner, Lincoln came away from the debates with heightened prestige and a reputation that made him an immediate front-runner for the Republican nomination.

In these debates, Douglas expressed what came to be known as the "Freeport Doctrine," stating that slavery could not exist unless supported by local police regulations; therefore, its continuation was subject to the sympathy of the community. Douglas believed that the Republic could continue forever divided into free and slave states; only war, or the use of force, could destroy the institution of slavery, and he expressed himself unwilling to go so far. Force would negate the Constitution itself, and "to violate [the Constitution] for one purpose will lead to violating it for other purposes." The "integrity" of the Union was, said Douglas, "worth more to humanity than the whole black race." Lincoln replied that "a House Divided" could not survive; that either "it will become all one thing or all the other. Either the opponents of slavery will arrest the further spread of it, and place it where the public mind shall rest in the belief that it is in the course of ultimate extinction; or its advocates will push it forward till it shall become alike lawful in all the States, old as new, North as well as South." Thus, Lincoln put himself squarely into the anti-slavery camp.

It was Douglas' ill-fortune to appear as a candidate for nomination before a bitterly divided party. From the moment of his nomination in Baltimore, Maryland, which sparked the withdrawal of the southern firebrands, the legitimacy of his nomination was questioned. The so-called "Baltimore Bolters" claimed that they were the rightful retainers of the Democratic name and party machinery, and since they had the support of President James Buchanan, they insisted that Douglas' nomination had proceeded from a mob rather than from duly appointed delegates to a Democratic convention. At a second meeting convened in Baltimore, they nominated John C. Breckinridge of Kentucky.

Whatever the arguments or claims of either side, Douglas and his supporters realized the necessity of organizing an effective machinery to carry on a victorious campaign. With so many Democratic office-holders in Buchanan's camp, this was no mean task. Party committees in the South and border states were also mainly in the hands of Buchanan supporters; thus, the Douglas campaign team had to create new centers of strength in states where the Democrats had always been the victors, especially in the South and on the border. They had to call for new state committees, new state conventions, and new electors. In the North, of course,

Stephen Douglas ribbon SMITHSONIAN INSTITUTION

the Buchanan–Breckinridge alliance had to do the same, for here the Douglas regulars were still in control.

Douglas waged an energetic campaign based upon a platform that sanctioned the popular-sovereignty principle, but looked to the Supreme Court—which had already in the Dred Scott decision declared itself favorably inclined to the southern view of slavery—to settle the issue of its extension in the territories. It was a platform designed to appeal to moderate northerners who were ready to countenance slavery just so long as it stayed put and did not disturb the political equilibrium.

181

Stephen Douglas wood carving NATIONAL PORTRAIT GALLERY, *gift of Mr. Richard Guggenheim* NPG 71.59

Douglas' was, however, a futile campaign. Some southern Democrats may have agreed with his defense of the Constitution and his stand against secession. "I would hang every man higher than Haman who would attempt to resist by force the execution of any provision of the Constitution which our fathers made and bequeathed to us," he had told his audiences in Raleigh, North Carolina; but the force of the secessionists was too great. They denounced his journeying into the South for campaign reasons; his life was threatened, and he was frequently the target of overripe fruit and raw eggs. Still, he continued to make his eloquent pleas against both secession and abolitionism: "I am for burying Southern disunionism and Northern abolitionism in the same grave," he asserted and refused to consider making common cause with the followers of Breckinridge for the sake of victory.

The split in the Democratic ranks placed Lincoln in the White House. Immediately, Douglas rallied his followers around the new administration; and when secession did occur, he expended all his energy to oppose it. Exhausted by his strenuous campaign, and even more strained by a speaking tour designed to rally "the best elements of [the Democratic] Party to the colors" of the Union, Douglas succumbed to ill health while speaking in Chicago and died.

Because Douglas wanted to be president so much, his motives have been questioned and impugned. Called by some "a reckless demogogue," he has been even more maligned because of his moral obtuseness on the slavery issue. His personal economic interest in westward expansion—he had speculated in land along proposed railroad lines—has also contributed to the image of a crass and self-seeking politician.

But Douglas also loved the Union and much of his political effort was expended to that end. Having married a southern woman and managed her inherited estates, including its slaves, he found himself straddling in his sympathies at a time when to straddle meant to fall. Men were taking and calling for extreme positions, and Douglas' kind of compromising was neither welcomed nor desired. Some have said he "would have made a better president than candidate," that he would have avoided conflict and attempted a course of moderation both North and South. But his election would also have preserved the institution of slavery— something which the temper of the times would never have permitted. His defeat, then, reveals the direction of his age which was divided in its loyalties and caught between the past and the future. The majority of Americans opted for the nation, whether they voted for Douglas, Bell, or Lincoln. A large enough group, however, also wanted freedom and were willing to risk the safety of the nation in fighting for it. Douglas' willingness to support an institution fast becoming anachronistic lost him the confidence of the North and the West and, therefore, election to the highest office in the land.

JOHN CABELL BRECKINRIDGE   *Nicola Marschall, 1881, after unidentified artist*
Oil on canvas, 35 x 29 inches   The Filson Club, Louisville, Kentucky

John Cabell Breckinridge *Southern Democrat*
1821-1875

The rise to leadership of John Cabell Breckinridge was unequaled in American political history. At the age of thirty-nine, he held simultaneously the offices of vice-president of the United States and senator-elect from the state of Kentucky, and he was presidential nominee of the Southern Democratic Party. Ironically, Breckinridge was politically unambitious. As the reluctant candidate for one of the seceding factions of the Democratic Party in 1860, his sentiments were poignantly expressed to Mrs. Jefferson Davis when he said: "I trust I have the courage to lead a forlorn hope." John Breckinridge was a man of extraordinary courage; however, the divided party lost the election to the Republicans, and his offices dissolved in the heat of Civil War.

The Breckinridges, one of the great political families of Kentucky, possessed the strong character of their Scottish background; self-reliant, high-spirited, and devoted to principle, its members fought fiercely on both side in the Civil War. John Breckinridge, whose grandfather had been a United States senator and attorney general under Thomas Jefferson, inherited superb qualities of leadership, a rare talent for public affairs, and a reputation as an orator which inspired James Tandy Ellis to write eighteen verses of praise including the following:

> And when he rose, Lor', sech a yell!
> And when he spoke, a magic spell
>   Seem'd droppin' from each cloud;
> And ev'ry feller held his breath,
> The silence was as still as death
>   That settled o'er the crowd.
>
> If there be orators in heaven
> When I git thar and I am given
>   A chance to hear them speak,
> I'm goin' to say to old John C.,
> 'Jest say agin that speech for me
>   You made on Eagle Creek!'

Tall, dashing, and strikingly handsome, educated for the law and disciplined by a brief stint in the army where he served as a major of volunteers in the war with Mexico, Breckinridge was destined for a political career. He became a member of the Kentucky state legislature in 1849 and was elected to Congress in 1851 from the Ashland district, the former Whig Party stronghold of Henry Clay. Political differences notwithstanding, he was destined to succeed Clay in the high regard and affection of Kentuckians. Despite his talents and popularity, Breckinridge intended to retire from public life after two terms in Congress, but his unexpected nomination for vice-president by the Democrats—who needed a southerner to balance the Buchanan ticket in 1856—changed his plans and made him, at thirty-five, the youngest vice-president in the nation's history.

Elected on a platform affirming the Compromise of 1850, Breckinridge supported the Kansas–Nebraska Act as a solution of the slavery question. His own doctrine regarding states' rights was that "the right of the people to regulate in their own way all their domestic institutions [should be] left wholly untouched, except that whatever is done must be in accordance with the Constitution." In this sense, then, Breckinridge supported the Douglas position of popular sovereignty. Elected to the United States Senate in 1860 even before the expiration of his term as vice-president, Breckinridge made his point of view clear. He told a Frankfort, Kentucky, audience that no sensible man wanted slavery in the territories. Some territories would not support slavery, but south of "a certain line," climate, soil, the Constitution, and the courts would support slavery. Therefore, slavery where it existed or was desirable had to be defended. The goal of the Republican Party, however, was emancipation, and he warned against "blazing border war." Closing with an eloquent appeal for the Union, he promised that Kentucky "will cling to the Constitution while a shred of it remains."

It was his fear of disunion that ironically encouraged him to accept the nomination of the extremist wing of the Democratic Party, who, having split from the Douglas majority, reconvened in Baltimore in 1860 to listen to fiery speeches and adopt an extreme pro-slavery platform. Breckinridge vigorously defended himself against charges of inconsistency and disunion, despite the fact that his supporters were breathing secession with every speech and advocating a policy of no compromise any longer on the South's "peculiar" institution. "The man does not live," said Breckinridge, "who has power to couple my name successfully with the slightest taint of disloyalty to the Constitution or the Union. . . ." In a stirring speech at Frankfort, he reiterated, "I am an American citizen, a Kentuckian, who never did an act nor cherished a thought that was not full of devotion to the Constitution and the Union."

How, then, could he lend his name to an extremist ticket, bent on creating such dissidence as to force southern independence? It is probable that Breckinridge did not go as far as his supporters, but campaigned in the hope that no candidate would receive a majority of electoral votes; thus, the election would be thrown into the House of Representatives, where he could hope to bring influence to bear on the Democratic majority. As the secessionists grew more vociferous within his faction, Breckinridge grew more silent, preferring to remain neutral and in the background during much of the campaign. Unable to speak out boldly for Union, while still claiming attachment to it, in fear of offending the secessionists of the lower South, and unable to support secession for fear of offending the border states, he had to stand aside and let events take their course.

Throughout the turbulent campaign of 1860, prospects were grim for both groups of Democrats. The Breckinridge faction found itself without campaign strategy and unable to formulate effective opposition. Despite support from President Buchanan, whose office in the White House provided unofficial headquarters for the Breckinridge forces, the southern extremists were unable to unite. They did place second in the electoral vote, however, winning all of the cotton states and North Carolina, Delaware, and Maryland.

With the election of Lincoln, Breckinridge turned his attention to compromise, hoping thereby to save the Union he loved so much. He pleaded for peace—not secession—and voted against Lincoln's determination to maintain Fort Sumter even if it meant war. With the firing on Fort Sumter, however, Breckinridge felt obliged to join the southern elements in his home state, and accepted a commission of brigadier general in the Confederate Army. Expelled from the Senate, he proudly commented, "I exchange with proud satisfaction a term of six years in the Senate of the United States for the musket of a soldier."

Yet, although he served the "lost cause" brilliantly and courageously, Breckinridge was never sure that he had made the right decision. After the war, and after eight years of hardship and exile abroad, he was convinced that it was "far better that we still live as one people." Upon his return to his native state, he was "more loved by Kentuckians than any living man," but he never again entered public life.

JOHN BELL   *William Cooper—Oil on canvas, 35¼ x 27½ inches   Courtesy of the
Tennessee State Museum, Nashville, Tennessee: from the collection of the
Tennessee Historical Society*

John Bell *Constitutional Unionist*

1796-1869

While sectional bitterness monopolized the platforms of the major parties in the momentous election of 1860, the voice of moderation—however faint and tardy—was heard through the Constitutional Union Party. Representing a patriotic and conservative element with a sincere desire to preserve the Union, these former Whigs and Know-Nothings met at Baltimore on May 9, 1860, and nominated for president the former senator from Tennessee, John Bell, who epitomized the hopes, principles, and campaign of the new party.

The son of a pioneer farmer of moderate circumstances, Bell attended Cumberland College, a frontier institution that later became the University of Nashville. He was a hard worker —although slow in making decisions—deeply earnest, and a good speaker. Looking forward to a career in public life, he was admitted to the bar in 1816 and practiced in Nashville until 1826 when he defeated Felix Grundy, the well-known criminal lawyer who was supported by Andrew Jackson in his first campaign for Congress. Bell never wavered from the promise he made to young Republicans in that campaign: that if elected, he would always be "open, direct and independent."

During fourteen years in the House of Representatives and twelve years in the Senate, Bell courageously maintained his independence. Although a member of Jackson's party, he led a struggle against Jackson in the 1836 campaign on behalf of Hugh Lawson White, the Tennessee Whig candidate for president, and against Martin Van Buren. For the next two decades after White's defeat, Bell continued to be the leading Whig from Tennessee and considered his participation in the Whig Party organization "the proudest circumstance" of his career. In 1852, when the party dissolved, he was among the last of the Whig leaders elected to the Senate. Although a southerner and a slaveholder, Bell had the principles of a conservative nationalist and the courage to act accordingly. He supported the Compromise of 1850, voted against the Kansas–Nebraska bill, and opposed the admission of Kansas under the pro-slavery Lecompton Constitution. Unsympathetic toward extremists from the North or the South, John Bell would have made any sacrifice—personal or political—for the preservation of the Union.

The group of old Whigs who met in Baltimore, Maryland, sincerely hoped to prevent dis-

John Bell medal CORNELL UNIVERSITY, DOUGLAS COLLECTION

union through formation of the Constitutional Union Party. Although some members supported Sam Houston of Texas on the first ballot, on the second Bell won the nomination with Edward Everett of Massachusetts who was the unanimous choice for vice-president. The convention condemned sectional parties and expressed the belief that party platforms were misleading and deceptive. The only political principle they chose to recognize was the Union of the states and the enforcement of the laws according to the Constitution. James Gordon of the *New York Herald* referred to the assembly of delegates in Baltimore as a "great gathering of Fossil Know-Nothings and Southern Americans." Irritated by Bell's refusal to take a stand on the slavery issue, the Nashville *Union and American* declared:

> The 'Constitutional Union' Ticket—
>   John Bell
>   Nóbody's man!
>   Stands on nobody's platform!!
>   Fights nobody!!!
>   Loves nobody!!!!
>   E Pluribus Unum!!!!!

Throughout the campaign Bell promised that if elected all his "ability, strength of will and official influence . . . [would] be employed for the maintenance of the Constitution and the Union against all opposing influence and tendencies." Too weak to counteract the enthusiasm for Lincoln in the North and Breckinridge in the South, the Constitutional Union Party could only hope to throw the election into the House of Representatives, and thereby effect a compromise at a time when no other mechanism was available.

In the final results, Bell carried only the border states of Virginia, Kentucky, and Tennessee with 39 electoral votes. As William Winter described it: "The thin ghosts of the old silver-gray Whig party, led by Bell and Everett, moaned feebly at parting and faded into air."

Bell opposed wholeheartedly the entire doctrine and policy of secession. He held to the idea of a border-state block which might prevent civil war. But after the firing on Fort Sumter, the Tennessee legislature voted to join the Confederacy, and Bell went with his state. Strong in intellect, but deliberate and cautious in action, he was not a forceful leader in times of crisis; under the pressure of the times, he could do nothing. Deeply grieved, he spent the war years in retirement in Georgia and returned to Nashville only when the war was over in 1865.

GEORGE BRINTON MC CLELLAN   *Julian Scott   Oil on canvas, 40 x 30 inches*
From the Collection of the National Portrait Gallery   Bequest of
Georgiana L. McClellan   NPG.65.35

George Brinton McClellan *Democrat*

1826-1885

Fort Sumter had fallen and with it the precarious unity of the States. General-in-chief Winfield Scott and Lincoln's cabinet argued the merits of an immediate march on Richmond or an autumn campaign down the Mississippi. The *Merrimack* lay in the mud of the Elizabeth River of Virginia; but in the Alleghenies of western Virginia, in a theater of war virtually ignored by Washington, the North's first victory was taking shape. George Brinton McClellan, commanding the troops of Ohio, defeated two Confederate detachments of 4,500 men "securing," in Bruce Catton's words, "everything west of the Alleghenies for the Union, and making possible the formation of the state of West Virginia." The North went wild. During the early summer of 1861, three months after he was given command of the Ohio troops, McClellan was called to Washington. By November, when Scott retired, he was general-in-chief. "Who would have thought, when we were first married," he wrote to his wife, "that I should so soon be called upon to save my country."

McClellan was graduated from West Point second in his class, with a degree in engineering. He served in the war with Mexico, and later the War Department sent him to the Crimea to observe the British and French in their war with the Russians. After Crimea, he resigned his commission to work as chief engineer for the Illinois Central Railroad. At the time he accepted Ohio Governor William Dennison's commission to lead that state's troops, McClellan's genius for organization and his influential friends had earned him the presidency of the eastern division of the Ohio and Mississippi Railroad. Now, taking command of an undisciplined rabble, McClellan forced the raw recruits of the Army of the Potomac to think of themselves not as civilians in uniform, but as soldiers of the Republic. He drilled them, marched them, gave them orders and a sense of purpose. In the process, he earned their intense devotion.

But McClellan was not as successful in his relationship with President Lincoln and his cabinet. Embarrassingly outmaneuvered at Manassas and Centerville by the Confederate "Quaker Gun"—logs painted to resemble cannon—and believing implicitly in reports of an overwhelming opposition, McClellan found it increasingly difficult to force an attack. His frequent hesitancy and caution provoked executive irritation and often, anger. "You must act," President Lincoln adjured McClellan in April 1862, for "the present hesitation to move upon an intrenched [sic] enemy is but the story of Manassas repeated." Finally, in September, McClellan engaged Lee's army in the "bloodiest day of the war"—Antietam. Here, the "young Napoleon," numbed by the enormous losses suffered by his army, and reluctant to throw his reserve troops into the deadly conflict, passed up an opportunity to cut Lee's army in two. Instead, he allowed Lee to withdraw up the Shenandoah, and the Army of the Potomac remained to bury its dead and fight for three more years.

On November 7, 1862, McClellan received a deputation carrying a letter relieving him of his command. He was sent to Trenton, New Jersey, to await further orders—which never arrived. On election day, November 8, 1864, McClellan finally resigned his commission.

Consideration of McClellan for the presidency had begun when he first arrived in Washington in 1861. "I receive letter after letter," he wrote to his beloved wife Nelly, "have conversation after conversation, calling on me to save the nation, alluding to the Presidency, dictatorship, etc. . . . I have no such aspirations." By the summer of 1864, however, McClellan appeared to the Democrats as their strongest hope; they regarded him as the one man who could take the soldiers' vote from Lincoln. Reluctant at first, McClellan finally succumbed to the pleadings of his supporters. He saw acceptance of their nomination as his duty: "It is my firm conviction that no man should seek the high office, and that no true man should refuse it." McClellan had changed his mind for other reasons as well. He truly believed that Lincoln had become the tool of vindictive elements within the Republican Party and that his reelection would usher in even harsher policies toward the South. Lincoln's *Emancipation Proclamation,* he believed, in itself was a portent of the administration's increasingly stringent attitude toward the rebellious states.

The Democratic "nest of foul birds," as Gideon Welles, Lincoln's secretary of the navy, characterized the "party of secession," met in Chicago in August of 1864 and drew up a platform which included a strong peace plank. It termed the war a four-year "failure to restore the Union" and demanded "immediate efforts" for a "cessation of hostilities." McClellan, however, had made his feelings clear in a speech at West Point in June of that year: "Rebellion against a government like ours . . . should never be confounded with a revolution against despotic power. . . . Such a rebellion cannot be justified upon ethical grounds, and the only alternatives for our choice are its suppression or the destruction of its nationality." In his letter of acceptance, he adhered to his original purpose and rejected the Democratic peace platform.

The election year 1864 was quickly approaching disaster for Lincoln. Since no president had been reelected since Andrew Jackson, the Democrats were making definite plans to take over the White House. The Republican Party—a conglomeration of old Whigs, Free-Soilers, and dissident Democrats—was breaking down under the strain of war. At the convention, however, the Republicans "laying aside all differences of political opinion," united behind the president. Once renominated, his opponents—one of the most vocal was Horace Greeley, publisher of the New York *Tribune*—only grudgingly backed his candidacy. Attacks on the president lessened, but did not disappear.

McClellan's problems began at the outset of the campaign. Much of the country and, more importantly, the army were incapable of distinguishing between the true feelings of the candidate and the platform under which he ran. No matter what he said, McClellan, who spent most of the campaign "at home in dignified retirement," was unable to dissociate himself from the "follies of Chicago." Charles Davies, the father of a boy who had served under McClellan in two campaigns, wrote to him: "When I heard your address at West Point . . . I felt that you had done the great deed of your life, and that your fame and history were safe. Allow me . . . to suggest, that you stand firmly on the noble platform constructed by your own hands, rather than step off on the one constructed for you at Chicago." A letter from McClellan's friend, William Aspinwall, said: "Many of your warm personal friends say that if you . . . adopt this platform, 'pure & simple,' they cannot vote for you." The soldiers of the Army of the Potomac felt that "to vote against Lincoln would be to consent to the dissolution of the Union."

The election campaign ended in high form, with charges and countercharges of fraud coming from all sides. Horace Greeley's *Tribune* thundered that the Democrats were making up ballot lists by digging up unmarked soldiers' graves to get additional names; ballots came into states from regiments that no longer existed. But through all the irregularities and explosive language, one thing was certain. Lincoln was reelected by an electoral vote of 212–21, although McClellan's popular vote was 45 percent of the total cast. On November 10, two days after the election, McClellan wrote to his friend Samuel L. M. Barlow: "For my country's sake, I deplore the result—but the people have decided with their eyes wide open & I feel that a great weight is removed from my mind."

HORATIO SEYMOUR *Alvah Bradish Oil on canvas, 37½ x 28½ inches*
New York State Office of General Services, Albany

Horatio Seymour *Democrat*

1810-1886

As the Democratic Party's presidential choice in 1868, Horàtio Seymour was undoubtedly one of the most reluctant candidates in American history. Clearly overshadowed within his party by any number of declared White House aspirants, the retiring ex-governor of New York opposed his own nomination practically to the very end. Only after his supporters had literally dragged him from the convention platform to head off his final refusal did the tearful Seymour become reconciled to his ultimate selection as Democratic presidential candidate.

Seymour's nomination was logical. In terms of his devoted service to the Democratic Party, he certainly was a good choice. A lawyer by profession, he had served his party faithfully both as a healer of party wounds and as an articulate spokesman for Democratic policies and principles. Thus, as a New York legislator in the 1840s and later as governor from 1852 to 1854, his ability to conciliate the dissenting factions within his party made him the object of undying respect and affection among New York Democrats.

By 1868 Seymour was also revered by Democrats on a national level. Certainly there were few who could equal his record as Democratic spokesman during the Lincoln and Johnson administrations. In his second term as governor of New York from 1862 to 1864, he consistently supported the Democrats in their opposition to Lincoln's war policies. An advocate of state and local autonomy, he criticized Lincoln's *Emancipation Proclamation* on the grounds that the abolition of slavery did not lie within the powers delegated to the federal government. Believing that enlistment of soldiers was a state rather than a federal responsibility, he requested the war president to suspend the draft. Finally, he took Lincoln to task for his suspension of civil rights in northern states and took up the cause of the "copperhead-critic" Clement Vallandigham when Lincoln ordered him placed under military arrest.

After the war, Seymour continued to speak on behalf of Democratic principles when he opposed the stringent Reconstruction measures placed on the South by the Radical Republican majority in Congress. Personally fearful of Congress' growing authority, he never ceased to question the constitutionality of military rule in the South. Thus, this articulate and eloquent "idol of the Democracy" appeared in many ways eminently fit to lead the Democrats in their

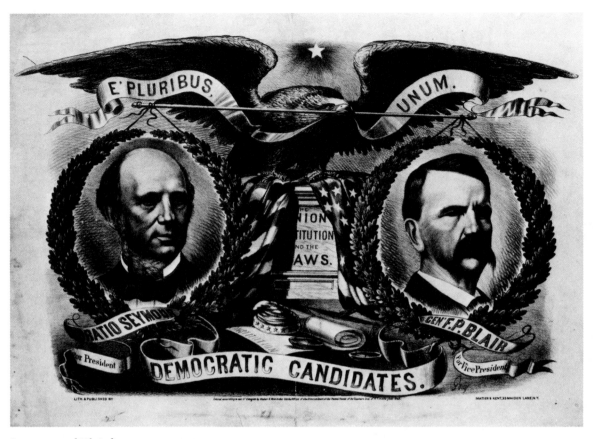

Seymour and Blair banner   SMITHSONIAN INSTITUTION

drive to depose the ascendant Republicans who had been formulating federal policies since 1861.

Seymour, however, possessed some drawbacks. Concerning his national reputation, there was no doubt; but perhaps it was not quite the kind that would make him a suitable presidential candidate after all. Equating his criticisms of Lincoln and Radical Reconstruction with sympathy for slavery and the southern insistence upon the right of secession, many northerners considered Seymour and other dissident war Democrats as national traitors. Aware of this himself, Seymour knew that his name on the Democratic ticket could never attract those voters who, though disenchanted with Radical policies, could not support a Democrat who had so often been identified with "copperhead" treachery.

Both before and during the convention of 1868, Seymour flatly shunned the idea of his own candidacy and instead devoted his efforts to gaining the Democratic nomination for Chief Justice Salmon P. Chase, who had just broken with the Republican Party on the question of its harsh Reconstruction policies. In Seymour's view, this was the man who could wrest the White House away from the Republicans. As a former Republican and cabinet adviser to Lincoln,

Chase carried enough prestige to attract other disgruntled Republicans, who would have otherwise hesitated to cast their lot with the Democrats.

Chase, however, was not the only Democratic possibility. In settling on a nominee, the convention delegates who gathered in New York's Tammany Hall in July 1868 had a wide field of hopefuls from which to choose. Among the more prominent contenders were three Civil War generals, George McClellan, Winfield Scott Hancock, and Francis Blair, as well as President Andrew Johnson; however, the two potential nominees who were to prove crucial in bringing about Seymour's candidacy were George Pendleton of Ohio and Thomas Hendricks of Indiana.

Optimistic during the convention's early balloting, Pendleton supporters became embittered when their candidate began to lose ground to Hendricks. Considering the latter a traitor for withdrawing his promised support for Pendleton, the Ohio delegation determined to block Hendricks' nomination. On the twenty-second ballot, with Hendricks' victory appearing imminent, Ohio took the step that was to prove the Hoosier's deathblow: it announced its wish to nominate Seymour.

Seymour pin   CORNELL UNIVERSITY, DOUGLAS COLLECTION

Although he took the platform in an effort to decline, Seymour was powerless. With his name in nomination, his official candidacy was all but final. The Ohio delegation had calculated well. Having sweltered through three frustrating days of balloting, the tired delegates now viewed the distinguished New York Democrat as the answer to their prayers. Acceptable in every way save for his reluctance, Seymour almost instantaneously became the unanimous choice of the convention.

In the final contest against Republican Ulysses Grant, Seymour was certainly no match. Against Grant's Civil War record, Seymour's consistent criticism of Lincoln's administration was made to appear all the worse in the public mind. In a double cartoon entitled "Matched," Thomas Nast left his readers with little doubt as to the Democrat's traitorous nature: while portraying Grant as the patriotic hero of Vicksburg, he depicted a treacherous Seymour openly consorting with the New York draft rioters of 1863. Finally, Grant's public pleas for moderation and conciliation with relation to the South served to weaken the effect of Democratic attacks on Republican Radical Reconstruction.

By November of 1868, then, there was little question of Grant's victory. To some extent, this came as a relief to Seymour. Although he had taken a conscientious interest in his campaign, he did so only out of a sense of obligation. Preferring less obtrusive roles within his party, the New Yorker could now retire with honor from the political spotlight that he had never sought.

HORACE GREELEY   *Thomas Nast, 1872   Watercolor drawing, 12⅛ x 7¼ inches*
From the Collection of the National Portrait Gallery
Gift of the Trustees, National Portrait Gallery, London   NPG.64.2

Horace Greeley *Liberal Republican/Democrat*

1811-1872

On November 29, 1872, Horace Greeley died a broken and disillusioned man. As founder of the prestigious and influential New York *Tribune,* the reforming journalist had been a significant force in American life. Even his most formidable critics could not dispute his reputation as a molder of public opinion—a reputation so aptly summarized by Ralph Waldo Emerson's observation that "Greeley does the thinking for the whole West at $2 per year for his paper." Nor could they question his influential role in spurring westward settlement. By the end of 1872, however, the great journalist could take little comfort in this knowledge. Crushed emotionally and physically by a presidential campaign in which he had endured innumerable and brutal attacks, the once confident and incurably optimistic Greeley now seemed to welcome death "with open arms."

However tragic the result, there was no doubt that Greeley had wanted to run for president. Never willing to limit himself to the role of a spectator–reporter, political activism and ambition were as much a part of the man as was his flair for journalism.

Greeley's idealism had drawn him to a multitude of causes during the years preceding the Civil War, ranging from utopian Fourierism to feminism, prohibition, vegetarianism, and abolition. With unbounded capacity for reform activity, Greeley also had found time for political involvement, and was an active member of the Whig Party until its final disintegration in the mid-fifties. With the formation of the anti-slavery Republican Party in 1856, he found a welcome political home temporarily; by 1862, he was one of the principal leaders of the party in New York as well as in the nation.

Greeley, however, was too much of an independent gadfly to maintain influence in his newly adopted party. Already distrusted for his frequent criticisms of Lincoln's policies during the Civil War, he continued to lose prestige in Republican councils after 1863 as a result of his vocal opposition to the vindictive Radical policies toward the South. Yet, Greeley was in many ways as much a Radical as the men he criticized. He favored Negro equality and civil rights, but disagreed with the Radicals' severe policy with respect to former Confederates.

In 1872, Greeley and the Republican Party finally parted ways. "Grantism," or corruption in high government circles, offended his moral sense, and his ego was hurt by his diminishing influence among party members. He saw in the Liberal Republican's opposition to Grant and Grantism another moral crusade and also an opportunity for achieving his long-cherished hope of public office. Thus, when allies in the movement spoke increasingly in favor of his nomination, Greeley's identification with the Liberals grew.

Formed in Missouri under the leadership of Carl Schurz and B. Gratz Brown, the Liberal Republicans consisted of disenchanted Republicans who deplored Grant's failure to halt Radical Reconstruction policies and to grant political amnesty to the many southern leaders who still remained disenfranchised. Even a greater source of discontent for the morally sensitive Liberals was the incompetence and corruption that had come to characterize the Civil Service during Grant's first term as a result of the "arbitrary" party favoritism that dictated government appointments.

Many Liberal Republicans also opposed the high tariff, pro-business policy, of the Republican Party. These joined in Greeley's nomination with reluctance, for Greeley was unwilling to accept the Liberals' advocacy of low tariffs. In fact, it was his confused yet staunch defense of high tariffs which branded him as a person of little judgment. "If I had my way," Greeley had said in 1870, "if I were king of this country, I would put a duty of $100 a ton on pig-iron and a proportionate duty on everything else that can be produced in America." The reason: so that "our people would be obliged to supply their own wants, manufactures would spring up, competition would finally reduce prices, and we shall live wholly within ourselves."

Once nominated by the Liberal Republicans, Greeley had to become the reluctant choice of the Democratic convention. For despite the bitter residue left by Greeley's scathing editorial attacks on the Democratic Party during his heady Republican days, the Democrats believed that their opportunity for national leadership lay in an alliance with the Liberals, particularly in light of the similarity of their views toward Grant.

As in 1868, Grant Republicans had more than enough weapons to wield against their political opposition. Now advocating lenient reconstruction policies, Greeley became fair game for Republicans who could portray him as a Confederate sympathizer and foe of black equality. Ironically, the vocal abolitionist who, after the war, had argued so strenuously on behalf of black political equality, now found himself denounced as a "Negro trader" and Ku Klux Klan sympathizer. Having become the Democratic candidate, Greeley was further open to attacks that directly linked him to the corrupt dealings of New York's Tammany leader, Boss Tweed; although as a Liberal Republican, he was presumably fighting corruption. Even his very tenuous connection with free-love advocate Victoria Woodhull was used against him by the press.

His appearance also militated against him, especially his round spectacles perched on a small nose in a round, sparsely bewhiskered face. Already bearing a reputation as a crackpot because of his many "fads," Greeley's eccentricities—his vegetarianism, all-white hat and white homespun suits, high-pitched voice—turned his candidacy into one huge joke. He became the butt of cartoonists, the most scathing of whom was the Grant partisan, Thomas Nast. In one

Horace Greeley eagle pin   CORNELL UNIVERSITY, DOUGLAS COLLECTION

cartoon, Nast represented Greeley's conciliatory attitudes toward the South by picturing the journalist shaking hands with John Wilkes Booth over Lincoln's grave. Finally, to weaken Democratic support for Greeley, Republican newspapers dredged up the many diatribes which Greeley had directed toward the Democrats during the Civil War, especially his 1866 public branding of the party as "the traitorous section of northern politics."

In the face of these attacks, Greeley maintained a valiant front. Indefatigably, he addressed hundreds of groups, speaking eloquently and endlessly on behalf of North-South reconciliation and more lenient Reconstruction policies. Thus, in one speech, he pleaded: "Let us forget that we fought. Let us remember only that we have made peace. Let us say there shall be no degradation, no people over whom we triumph. . . . Our triumph is the uplifting [of] everyone to the common platform of American liberty and American nationalism."

Despite his best efforts, Greeley never gained the support needed to win. On election day, many Democrats stayed away from the polls in preference to voting for their former archenemy of the *Tribune.* More important, the loosely formed coalition of Liberal Republicans never succeeded in forming the tight, united organization so necessary to overcome Grant's "hero" reputation.

Greeley's defeat was not simply political. Wounded deeply by campaign attacks, there seemed nothing left for which to live. His wife's death during the campaign increased his depression. Still a further source of demoralization was the fact that in returning to the *Tribune* in November, which he had neglected during his campaign, he found his influence had been pretty much displaced by his younger co-worker, Whitelaw Reid. By the middle of November, Greeley had given up on life and within a few weeks was dead.

VICTORIA CLAFLIN WOODHULL   *Mathew B. Brady   From the photograph in the*
New-York Historical Society, New York

Victoria Claflin Woodhull *Equal Rights*

1836-1927

By the early 1870s, Victoria Claflin Woodhull had become one of the most notorious and legendary women of her times. A flagrant violator of the staid and genteel prescriptions that nineteenth-century America sought to impose on the gentler sex, the bold Victoria had shocked her contemporaries with her open advocacy of free love as well as her sortie into the male world of New York finance. It was not surprising, then, that the beautiful and controversial "siren" of Wall Street should continue to startle America by becoming in 1872 the first woman candidate for president.

Victoria's disregard for political, moral, and social convention seems natural. Born into a family of free-wheeling mesmerists, spiritualists, and medical eccentrics whose chief characteristic seems to have been their insensitivity to popular opinion, she could hardly have developed otherwise. Moreover, if she had ever entertained the idea of conforming to popular social mores, particularly as they related to the position of women, her early experience with men precluded such a possibility. Dominated in childhood by an irresponsible and profligate father and as a young woman by a weak and chronically alcoholic husband, Victoria required no encouragement in flaunting the constraints placed on her by a male-controlled society.

Victoria began her rise to controversial fame in 1868 in Wall Street. Having charmed the aging Commodore Vanderbilt with their supposed spiritualist powers, she and her sister Tennessee Claflin found the great railroad magnate a most willing investment counselor and, armed with the Commodore's inside tips, proceeded to astound New York's male world of finance with dazzlingly profitable ventures into stock and bonds. Operating first as private investors and later as the proprietors of their own brokerage house, it was not long before they earned the title of "Queens of Wall Street."

Hardly content to rest on the laurels of financial success, Victoria now took to the lecture platform as an advocate of women's rights and in 1870 joined her sister in publishing *Woodhull and Claflin's Weekly*. In both endeavors, Victoria remained true to her unconventional ways. Never one to compromise, she outraged New York and eventually the whole nation by combin-

"GET THEE BEHIND ME, (MRS.) SATAN!"—[SEE PAGE 143.]
WIFE (with *heavy burden*). "I'D RATHER TRAVEL THE HARDEST PATH OF MATRIMONY THAN FOLLOW YOUR FOOTSTEPS."

"Get thee behind me, (Mrs.) Satan!"   THOMAS NAST, *Harper's Weekly,* FEBRUARY 17, 1872

ing her crusades for female emancipation and social justice with a frank adherence to free love as well as frontal attacks on the sanctity of the family.

But public indignation did not keep Victoria from new undertakings. Knowing full well that the leaders of the National Women's Suffrage Association had long sought an opportunity to present their cause to Congress, Victoria skillfully preempted these comparatively staid reformers who had for the most part regarded her with moral disdain. In 1871, she became the first woman to testify before a congressional committee on behalf of female suffrage.

The year 1872 saw the climax to Victoria's career. Prosperous and unquestionably famous, she now unabashedly cast herself as a candidate for president. As she boldly told the readers of her weekly, her name alone had destined her for the nation's highest office. After all, was there not another Victoria already reigning in Britain? What better way could there be, then, to cement the friendship of the two great Anglo-Saxon nations than to have the Queen's American namesake in the White House? In accepting the nomination of the Equal Rights Party, formed from the cadre of spiritualists and fanatics of all stripes who had rallied around her, Victoria remarked on the fortuitous effect her presidential leadership would have on world peace: "It is true that a Victoria rules the great rival nation . . . on the other shore of the Atlantic," she seriously explained to her following, "and it might grace the amity just sealed between the two nations [settling the *Alabama* claims with the Treaty of Washington (1871)] and be a new security of peace, if a twin sisterhood of Victorias were to preside over the two nations."

The public reaction to Victoria's candidacy ranged from mild amusement to moral indignation. Horace Greeley commented rather lightly in verse: "Gibbery, gibbery, gab, the women had a confab, and demanded the rights to wear the tights. Gibbery, gibbery, gab." On the other hand, the governor of Massachusetts refused to allow Victoria to carry her campaign to Boston: "You might as well have the undressed women of North Street on stage there."

Victoria's campaign was short-lived. The presidential candidate had finally become more than New York citizenry could swallow, and a concerted effort was now afoot to drive the siren and her family from the city. Soon after her nomination, she became increasingly preoccupied with the more pressing problem of eviction notices and finding a landlord in New York who would risk his reputation by renting to the notorious "Woodhull."

More diverting, however, was Victoria's and Tennessee's involvement in the famous Beecher-Tilton scandal. Bitter over Henry Ward Beecher's refusal to exert influence in solving their housing problems, the sisters used their weekly to expose the famous Brooklyn minister's affair with the wife of his prominent parishioner, Theodore Tilton. As a result, Victoria became implicated in a series of legal proceedings that were to continue for three years.

Thus, the most colorful part of Victoria's career drew to a close. Although she continued to lecture and publish the weekly, ill health and declining finances removed her gradually from the public eye. Moreover, her speeches were beginning to take on a more restrained aspect. In 1877, she left for England with her sister. It was here that she finally gained some degree of respectability as the reforming wife of a prosperous British banker.

CHARLES O'CONOR   *Benjamin Franklin Reinhart, 1877   Oil on canvas, 50 x 40 inches*
The Association of the Bar of the City of New York

Charles O'Conor *"Straight-Out" Democrat*

1804-1884

A distinguished legal career and frequent service to the Democratic Party would suggest that Charles O'Conor had been destined for political prominence. But the "austere" and "stern" New Yorker was never attracted to such a prospect. A man of principle and "inflexible temper," he was largely repelled by partisan intrigues and machinations. As a result, throughout his public career he remained for the most part on the political periphery. When he became a candidate for the presidency, it was not of his own choosing nor did he make any attempt to rise to the political occasion.

The son of impoverished Irish-immigrant parents, O'Conor somehow made his way through the necessary schooling to be admitted to the New York bar at the early age of twenty. It was not long before his contemporaries became aware of his brilliant reasoning abilities and, if not colorful, extremely cogent courtroom presentations. Of O'Conor's extraordinary skills, one contemporary observed that "his pleadings were beautiful examples of art."

Among the cases contributing to O'Conor's reputation was the Forrest divorce case of the 1840s. As defender of Edwin Forrest's wife, his name became a household word among New Yorkers who had little sympathy for the philandering actor and his drawn-out attempt to avoid, what appeared to be a just financial settlement. Also adding to his fame were several fugitive-slave cases in which he argued brilliantly on behalf of the property rights of slave owners. Even lawyers of abolitionist sympathy begrudgingly admitted the brilliance of his arguments. After the Civil War, O'Conor continued to achieve prominence as one of the prosecutors of the infamous Boss Tweed and again in 1876 as Tilden's counsel in the election dispute of that year.

O'Conor's presidential candidacy resulted from his lifelong admiration for the South. Throughout the 1840s and 1850s, he had consistently voiced sympathy for the slave interests and in the presidential election of 1860 supported southern apologist, John C. Breckinridge. Regarding slavery as the "main pillar of our strength and an indispensable element of our growth and prosperity," he continued to sympathize with the South during the Civil War by arguing the legality of secession. After the war, he again demonstrated his southern affinities by putting up bail for the Confederate president, Jefferson Davis.

213

It was in recognition of these southern loyalties that the "Straight-Out" Democrats nominated O'Conor for president in 1872. Composed partly of adventurers—but chiefly of southern Democrats—the splinter party found the southern partisan from New York considerably more palatable than the one-time abolitionist-Republican Horace Greeley who had been endorsed by the regular Democrats.

O'Conor refused to accept the nomination for the presidency. Nevertheless, his name appeared on the ballot in many states. Although he never campaigned, the prestige of his name and perhaps the response to his party's cause earned him almost 30,000 popular votes.

JAMES BLACK   *B. Frank Saylor   Cabinet photograph, 5¾ x 3⅞ inches   Lancaster
County Historical Society, Lancaster, Pennsylvania*

James Black *National Prohibitionist*

1823-1893

It was teenage experience that committed James Black to his lifelong fight for prohibition. Employed as a mule driver when he was sixteen, the future temperance leader succumbed one night to the proddings of some of the older drivers and joined them in what turned out to be a drinking orgy. Clearly the experience was not a happy one. Shortly afterward, the impressionable youth joined the Pennsylvania temperance movement and ultimately became a primary force in its statewide crusade during the 1850s.

Although a lawyer by profession and a farmer by avocation, the temperance cause occupied much of Black's time throughout his life. In 1865, he founded the National Temperance Society and Publishing House which subsequently became the chief outlet for temperance tracts and propaganda. Two years later, he became the moving spirit in organizing Pennsylvania's first prohibition convention. He also served for four years as chairman of the national committee of the Prohibition Party and, until his death in 1893, devoted much energy both to the collecting and writing of prohibition literature.

Despite the fact that Black's presidential candidacy in 1872 attracted little popular support, it nevertheless represented a turning point in the prohibition movement. Prohibitionists had involved themselves politically before, but for the most part they had worked through the Republican Party, which before the Civil War had been mildly sympathetic to its more temperance-minded members. After the Civil War, however, the situation changed significantly. Formed originally in an effort to fight the war tax on liquor, the Brewers Association of the United States gained considerable influence by the end of the war in both the Republican and Democratic parties. The Prohibitionists could no longer further their cause within the Republican ranks. Consequently, in 1869, Black and others formed the National Prohibition Party in the belief that an independent party was the only political alternative now open to them.

The formation of the party and Black's candidacy marked the beginning of a new chapter in prohibition history. Every roster of presidential aspirants up to 1920 would include a prohibitionist. Although these candidacies had little effect on the outcome of most elections, they played a significant part in gradually winning substantial segments of the population to their cause. For, while few Americans actually voted for them, prohibitionist candidates eventually generated enough public sympathy by 1919 to permit final enactment of a national prohibition amendment.

Ultimately, then, Black's candidacy was not a failure. Although it took longer than he might have wished, his party finally did fulfill what he considered to be its most important objective in placing candidates before the electorate: it "taught" the "people of the land" the need for legally imposed temperance.

Bargains and Compromise 1876

THE CIVIL WAR HAD BEEN OVER FOR MORE THAN A DECADE BY THE TIME THE ELECTION of 1876 came around, but the scars it had inflicted on both southerners and northerners still were not healed. Destroyed and ravaged by invading armies and the fire of battle, the farming lands of the South had been left "a wilderness of ruins"; without roads, railroads, ports, and coastal harbors, goods could not be moved easily from place to place nor economic recovery effected in commerce, industry, or agriculture. Emancipation had disrupted the South's labor system, making the resuscitation of industry and large-scale farming impossible. At the same time, southern political life was so affected by the Fourteenth and Fifteenth Amendments disenfranchising white leaders in the rebellion while giving political power to former slaves, and by the subsequent inroads of northern Reconstructionists that a new political organization had to be built.

The social and political upheaval in the South brought into political power elements that in the ante-bellum period had been ignored by the more dominant planter class. Former southern Whigs, who represented business and industrial interests and who found the Republican economic program more attractive than Democratic economic policies, now emerged as the powerful group within the solidly Democratic South and attempted to transform party politics into a machine receptive to the interests of business. These so-called "Redeemers" by 1876 had reconstituted government in all the southern states except South Carolina, Louisiana, and Florida, ousting northern Reconstructionists and their southern "scalawag" collaborators. They preached a social doctrine of white supremacy and racial segregation, and an economic program of industrialism and cooperation with northern businessmen. These were the southerners who were most clearly involved in the election of 1876 and in the Compromise of 1877 that was necessitated by its entanglements.

The northerners who were caught up in the election crisis did not form as easily an identifiable group as did the southern "Redeemers." Northern Republicans had split very early in Grant's first administration, with the "Liberals" focusing their discontent on the corruption, graft, and incompetence that marked the general's civilian performance. They also opposed the Radical Republicans as much for their stringent program with respect to reconstructing the South as for the fact that the party had been taken over by a group marked by greed and partisanship—Roscoe Conkling of New York, Zachariah Chandler of Michigan, and James G. Blaine of Maine. The main ambition of this group of Radicals was to protect wartime legislation favorable to business and industry, and to use government patronage for their own ends. Although the "Liberal Republican" movement ended in a fiasco with the nomination and tragicomic campaign of Horace Greeley in 1872, the spirit of reform it generated grew stronger as the extent of the corruption became more widely known and as the after effect of the Panic of 1873 became more intimately felt. By 1876, the Republicans had split again into two groups: the "Stalwarts," who were the hard-core politicians anxious to see Grant obtain a third term in order to maintain the party machine and the privileges of receiving bribes from businessmen who wanted favors; and the "Half-Breeds," who, opposing Grant, were still not reformers but, as the Democratic governor of New York, Horatio Seymour, put it, "men in office who will not steal but who will not interfere with those who do."

In 1876, however, it was not a contest between partisan groups representing northern and southern interests, but between two national parties, both of which were economically conservative, but divided on the question of governmental reforms and the position of the South in the congressional structure. The Democratic Party had grown in northern strength even as it continued to represent a solid South, while the Republican Party was weakened by the dissensions within it and the splintering of the various interest groups. Except when they "waved the bloody shirt," the Republicans could not stir the voters, but they did command the loyalty of substantial numbers of businessmen because of the party's stand on high tariffs, liberal aid to railroads, and "sound"—or restricted—money.

These elements of the Republican program appealed to many of the Democrats who joined Samuel Jones Tilden's "crusade"; they differed with the Republicans on details—not the essentials—of economic questions. The similarity between the parties as far as programs were concerned gave politics in the Gilded Age a generally uniform aspect, where money bespoke power and parties were merely "unprincipled patronage machines." Morally, too, there was little difference between the parties, although the Democrats were limited in their activities to local areas of control, while the Republicans enjoyed a larger canvas. But whether in a small or large way, each party was as corrupt as circumstances permitted. Although Tilden came into prominence as a reformer, and the Democratic platform carried a plank criticizing the corruption that characterized higher echelons of government, the Democrats were as hungry for the spoils of office as were the Republicans.

Then what made the election of 1876 such a crucial one, if the course of American life was not to be seriously affected by the choice of one or the other party? It was important for a number of reasons.

In the first place, the Republicans had been in the ascendancy for sixteen years, and it looked as if the propaganda of the "bloody shirt" might continue to maintain for some time to come that party's supremacy in the public halls of Washington. Indeed, the outcome of the election decision did eventuate in Republican rule for the next three decades, with the exception of the two terms served by Grover Cleveland; it rooted even more deeply than before in the American mind Republican attitudes toward laissez-faire business, creation of trusts, high tariffs, stabilization of currency for the benefit of creditors and in disregard of the needs of the producers of commodities and debtors, and other social and economic policies of what could be termed a conservative cast. The election of 1876 was the first challenge to Republican supremacy by a revived Democratic Party, and it was a challenge not to be taken lightly. For some Republicans in the North and West, the possibility of a Democratic administration amounted to returning the nation to a tyranny that would result only in more blood and tears. It threatened repudiation of Republican economic policy and, especially, social policy as embodied in the Thirteenth, Fourteenth, and Fifteenth Amendments to the Constitution. It constituted a threat to the elaborate structure created by tariff policies, banks, railroad subsidies, and monetary arrangements upon which the new economic order of the Republicans was founded. Cartoons showing the Old

South as a poisonous snake winding itself around the Republican oak, spitting out the venom of white supremacy, reminded northern voters of the South's "brutal treatment" of Negroes, of its propensity to violence, and of its lack of sincerity. One cartoon showed Tilden as "Mr. Facing-Both-Ways," with, of course, different messages for the two sections. Whatever the exaggeration, the message to northern voters was quite clear and persuasive, and as the Democratic Party grew in power and influence—especially after the 1874 congressional elections, which gave the Democrats control of the House by a vote of 198 to 94—the fear that the Democrats would drag the country down again to southern programs made this election seem crucial.

For the Democrats, the sense that they were on the rise, and that there was a good possibility that they might regain national power just as they already had gained power in some states like Massachusetts, gave them an enthusiasm that knew no bounds. To southern Democrats, this meant the end of Reconstruction government in the whole South and the resumption of white supremacy in that section; for northern Democrats, it meant renewal of local power through exercise of patronage and distribution of offices. Thus, both parties had a great deal to gain from winning, and much to lose with failure.

Beyond the crass aims and motives of the parties, however, the election of 1876 grew crucial as it neared its climax in that a successful resolution of the problems it presented was necessary to reaffirm the flexibility and adaptability of the American governmental system. Could the country again resort to compromise measures to bridge differences over policy as well as seemingly unresolvable divisions in the electoral process? Could the country reestablish the time-honored mechanism by which presidential elections were decided without resort to force? In 1860 that mechanism had broken down with the South's secession as a result of the election of an unpopular president; during the following years, elections—in the South, at least—had hung upon the employment of military force, or the threat of it; and, in 1876, there were individuals and groups who would resort to force once again if necessary rather than accept defeat. The phrase that was most common in 1876 was "mexicanization"—referring to the anarchy produced in that country for the past decade by election coups. The election of 1876, then, presented a crucial test of the American system: the Compromise of 1877, by meeting that test, gave strength and endurance to that system. As C. Vann Woodward has written, "The compromise laid the political foundation for reunion. It established a new sectional truce that proved more enduring than any previous one. . . ."

The story of the election and the "Bargain of 1877" is well known. The Republicans, aware of the issue of corruption, and wishing to meet the scandals of "Grantism" head on, had nominated General Rutherford B. Hayes, governor of Ohio, as a reform candidate and had written a reform platform. Thus Tilden's promise of reform struck an empty note—for that

"The Electoral Commission of 1877" by Cornelia Fassett UNITED STATES CAPITOL

issue was already decided. But the question of the honesty of Republican "carpetbaggers" in the South, the Republican wooing of the ex-slave, and the facts of Reconstruction itself turned white southerners almost unanimously toward the Democrats; the local machines in the urban centers of the North also influenced the voters in some of the larger eastern states like New York, New Jersey, and Connecticut to the Democratic Party. When all but three still-unreconstructed southern states had reported their returns, it looked as if the Democratic candidate, Samuel J. Tilden, had won, with 184 electoral votes and only one more to go to win the election. Hayes was trailing with only 166 votes reported. In popular votes, Tilden was leading his opponent by more than a quarter of a million, and newspapers were already exclaiming the happy news of a Democratic victory.

The story becomes muddy from here on. In the early hours of the morning after the election, Republican officials got in touch with their representatives in the three southern states that had not yet returned their tallies asking them to hold their states for Hayes. They hoped that with Republican control of the state returning boards, they would be able to turn the nineteen electoral votes involved to Hayes, giving him the necessary 185. Later that day, Republican Party chairman Zachariah Chandler audaciously announced that Hayes was actually elected.

Democrats quickly responded. Committees consisting of prominent members of the party hastened to the capitals of the three still undecided states to supervise the vote tally. Since one electoral vote in the state of Oregon was still in question, the Democratic national chairman, Abram Hewitt of New York, supported a move to have that vote declared Democratic, to force the Republicans to go behind the official returns in Oregon—primarily a Republican state—and thus establish a precedent for the Democrats to do the same in Florida, South Carolina, and Louisiana.

That there was fraud on the part of the returning boards—two out of three of which were solidly Republican—there is no question. It is also clear that there was intimidation and violence on the part of both the Democrats and the Republicans in the southern states, and whether or not there actually could be a fair election in any of them is doubtful. Republican carpetbaggers still controlled much of the Negro vote—although some Negroes were already in revolt against such control—and the stakes of office were too high not to go uncoveted. The conclusion that the contemporary historian George Ticknor Curtis arrived at, that "nearly thirty of those persons who were most active in securing the return of Republican electors in Florida, Louisiana, and South Carolina by the returning boards were afterward appointed to offices of trust and profit by the administration which was brought into power by means of their returns," is corroborated by later historians, and it suggests the extent of the prize at stake in this contest and the determination of the leaders to gain it.

By the end of the year, the results still stood in Tilden's favor, with 185 votes for the New Yorker, and 184 for Hayes. But Republicans shouted Democratic fraud and would not yield the election, while the Democrats answered as loudly "Tilden-or-fight." Committees from both the House and Senate were again sent South to investigate the situation, but still the question hung fire, for no one could suggest how to count the electoral votes in a way that would be fair and acceptable to each party, since the Senate was dominated by Republicans, the House by Democrats. The new year saw the political situation in a deadlock.

Compromise was essential—especially if government was to resume its tasks without violence. Compromise involved a quid pro quo: the Republicans wanted the presidency; the Democrats, which meant primarily the South, wanted to get rid of the last vestiges of northern Reconstruction efforts—the last Union soldiers, the last carpetbagger. But the Whig leadership among the Democratic "Redeemers" wanted more: they wanted a share for the South in the internal development of the nation, which meant essentially a transcontinental railroad built at federal expense that would connect the South to California through Texas. Other measures were sought: subsidies for improvement of the Mississippi River and for constructing levees at Galveston and New Orleans were especially desired by farmers of the lower South whose prosperity depended upon the navigability of the Mississippi River; and southerners wanted a share in policy making, which meant really the postmaster generalship—the post in the cabinet that traditionally dispensed patronage.

Thus was a bargain struck. The so-called Wormley Conference set the seal on an agreement reached earlier among party leaders to avert a Democratic filibuster aimed at preventing the electoral votes from being counted. The Democrats agreed to Hayes' election and a Republican Speaker of the House, upon condition that federal troops be withdrawn completely from the South, that southerners be given a place in Hayes' cabinet with some control over local patronage, and that southern railroads be granted subsidies. One Washington correspondent summed up the bargain thus: "It is thoroughly understood here by Southern men, that Mr. Hayes means, if he should become President, to cut adrift from the carpet-baggers, and make an alliance with respectable party leaders of Whig antecedents in the South."

Although the compromise broke down almost immediately when southern leaders in the House refused to vote for the Republican James A. Garfield as Speaker and the Republicans refused to abide by their promise to vote railroad subsidies, the election ended peacefully. Hayes was firmly ensconced in the White House without violence and without filibustering on the part of the more extreme Democrats. Later, one participant in the bargain admitted that Hayes had made up his mind long before to withdraw the troops from the South and bring northern Reconstruction in that region to an end. The Wormley Conference, however, gave southern leaders propaganda and justifications to use at home—to indicate that the South had come to the aid of its sister states by sacrificing political victory to home rule for Louisiana and South Carolina.

With the end of Reconstruction, the South did not experience the prosperity and national power for which some southerners had hoped. Alignment of southern interests with northern industrialism meant, really, exploitation of southern natural resources by northern financiers with the help of southern business leaders. Politically, the Republicans soon forgot the spirit of reconciliation that marked their initial reception of the South's display of "high public duty & honor," and turned again to waving the "bloody shirt," proclaiming that "the spirit of rebellion still lives and is liable at any moment to be again entrenched in arms." The South retreated into its solidly built Democratic fortress, and used its political power to keep southern politics solidly white. Supreme Court cases and Jim Crow laws helped politicians take advantage of the race issue to prevent reforms from changing the face of southern society and economy, and it was not until the wartime prosperity of World War II that the South was finally brought as a whole into the industrialized nation. Only then was the Negro in the South given the opportunities at one time envisioned for him by zealous northern Reconstructionists, but abandoned because of political expediency. The Compromise, by bringing an end to Reconstruction in the South, and recognizing its new political regime, as Vann Woodward has put it, "more profoundly than Constitutional amendments and wordy statutes . . . shaped the future of four million freedmen and their progeny for generations to come. It preserved one part of the fruits of the 'Second American Revolution'—the pragmatic and economic part—at the expense of the other part—the idealistic and humanitarian part."

SAMUEL JONES TILDEN   *Daniel Huntington, 1882   Oil on canvas 54 5/16 x 38 5/16 inches   Bequest of Samuel J. Tilden, The New York Public Library, Astor, Lenox and Tilden Foundations*

Samuel Jones Tilden *Democrat*

1814-1886

The Democrats had every reason for optimism in 1876. Having suffered defeat in the last four presidential elections, the White House was theirs for the taking—or so it appeared. No longer could the Republicans rest securely on their reputation as the patriotic party of Union and emancipation. Nor could they expect to win public support as they had in the three previous elections simply by identifying the Democracy with Union treachery and Confederate sympathy. For, within the scandal-ridden Republican administration lay the seeds of a Democratic offensive which they thought would easily balance out such attacks. Equally important, in nominating Samuel Jones Tilden, the Democrats had a candidate whose impeccable public reputation had already won him national acclaim and popularity.

That Grant had left the Republicans vulnerable was clear. The general's leadership had spawned corruption of spectacular proportions. Under administration patronage, graft and incompetence had become rampant in the Civil Service. Though never involved himself, the malleable Grant had presided over two scandals that ultimately implicated some of his closest advisers. As Republican involvement in the fraudulent manipulations of the Crédit Mobilier and the revenue swindles of the Whiskey Ring came to light in the early seventies, public sympathy for the Democrats rose. Finally, the Democrats found additional strength in the depression that had set in after the Panic of 1873. As a result of this disaster, Republicans were open not only to charges of corruption, but to accusations of economic incompetence as well.

Unquestionably enhancing the political advantages derived from Republican scandals and economic depression was the Democratic choice of a presidential candidate. Tilden was the symbol of clean government. With his help, New York City had freed itself from the clutches of Boss Tweed who in only a few short years had cheated the city of well over fifty-million dollars. Shortly afterward as state assemblyman, Tilden was instrumental in impeaching the judges who had consorted with Tweed. Later, as governor of New York from 1874 to 1876, he continued his crusade against corruption by breaking up the "Canal Ring" which had been liberally skimming state revenues allotted for canal maintenance. Thus, despite his intellectual bent and reserved personality, the electorate could not help but be attracted to this champion of clean government.

Tilden ribbon SMITHSONIAN INSTITUTION

Tilden was also the logical Democratic choice for other reasons. Born into a family having a long tradition of Democratic partisanship, Tilden had served his party well from his teenage years on. By the time he reached voting age, he had already become a frequent participant in party caucuses and conventions; and despite a burgeoning career as a corporation lawyer, he continued to find time for politics in the 1840s and 1850s. He won election to office only once in this period—as a state assemblyman from 1844 to 1846—but nevertheless he came to occupy a high position in party councils. Having led the "free-soil" faction during the 1850s, he again took over the leadership of the effort to reunite New York Democrats in 1860 in support of Stephen Douglas. During the Civil War, he helped establish the constitutional arguments whereby Governor Horatio Seymour was guided in his attack on Lincoln's war policies. Tilden, then, not only brought a prestigious reputation to the presidential campaign of 1876, but also a wealth of political experience and expertise.

It was this latter asset that further solidified the Democrats' already advantageous position. Although the aloof Tilden never campaigned publicly, he organized, along with his manager Abram S. Hewitt, what was to be an innovative and masterful campaign. Emphasizing the need for a clean, fiscally conservative government, Tilden founded a Literary Bureau to disseminate advertising and a Speakers' Bureau to schedule speakers throughout the country and instruct them on the approach they should take in appealing to the varying interests of each locality. Tildenites also assembled and distributed a 750-page textbook which exposed in detail the scandals and economic shortcomings of the Grant administration.

On election night, it seemed to Tilden and his supporters that their well-orchestrated efforts had brought success. Despite Republican efforts to defame his spotless reputation with epithets of "copperhead" and "railroad thief," it appeared that the Democrat had won both a popular and electoral victory.

But the Tilden victory was short-lived. As already indicated, the Republicans finally succeeded in their drawn-out fight to place Rutherford B. Hayes in the presidency. Tilden himself played no small role in bringing about his own defeat. Refusing to arouse the electorate by pleading his cause publicly, as so many of his supporters begged, he remained "cold as a damn clam" throughout the controversy and confined his fight to constitutional argument. To do otherwise, actually, would have been out of character. Although a political veteran, popular politicking had never been consistent with his reserved and intellectual approach. Thus, when the Electoral Commission completed its work in Hayes' favor, Tilden, rather than embroil himself in a public crusade, opted for a graceful retreat with the comment: "I can retire to private life with the consciousness that I shall receive from posterity the credit of having been elected to the highest position in the gift of the people without any of the cares and responsibilities of the office."

PETER COOPER   *Julian Alden Weir   Oil on canvas, 36 x 29 inches   The Union
League Club*, New York

Peter Cooper *National Independent (Greenback)*

1791-1883

While his son Peter and son-in-law Abram Hewitt were busily lending support to Samuel Tilden, the aging Peter Cooper was following quite a different political course in 1876. Disturbed over the economic hardships brought on by the depression of 1873-1876, the octogenarian inventor-industrialist aligned himself with the newly formed National Independent Party. In its call for an inflated currency and repeal of the deflationary Resumption Act of 1874, which recalled the paper money issued as currency during the late war, the party, popularly called the Greenback Party, had much appeal for Cooper. He saw in its proposals a way to raise the incomes of farmers and workers whose earnings had dropped so sharply in these depression years.

Alliance with this party, composed mostly of hard-pressed farmers seeking a solution to declining farm prices, was much in keeping with the outlook of this gentle entrepreneur. Throughout his career, Cooper never allowed his personal economic interests to overshadow his conscientious concern for the public welfare. While most prosperous businessmen viewed the Greenback cause as a threat to their financial stability, Cooper applauded it and eventually consented to becoming its presidential standard-bearer.

Certainly Cooper's public-minded view had been demonstrated before. The inventor of among other things the Tom Thumb steam engine, he accumulated the bulk of his fortune from the manufacture of glue and steel; and it was perhaps a sense of gratitude for his own good fortune that motivated him throughout his life to devote a substantial part of his time and resources to public causes. Echoing the more elaborately articulated philosophy of steel mogul Andrew Carnegie, he once commented on how the rich should view their wealth: "the individuals to whose lot these fortunes fall," he said, ". . . should never lose sight of the fact that . . . they should administer them as trustees of the people."

That Cooper lived up to his beliefs was evident in his willing involvement in the municipal affairs of New York City. It had been due largely to his efforts as a city councilman that New York organized its first professional fire and police force in the 1820s. As a member of the Free School Society during the decades of the thirties and forties, he worked actively on behalf of regulations that would make education compulsory. Finally, in serving as president of the Citizens Association of New York in the late 1860s, he played an important part in exposing the corruption of the "Tweed Ring."

Probably the greatest testimony to Cooper's public spirit was the establishment of Cooper Union. Despite the fact that many of his close friends considered his project "preposterous," the philanthropist persisted in his intention to give New York City a school that would provide free technical and cultural education for people who might otherwise not have such an opportunity. The Union did indeed fulfill Cooper's hopes, and for generations its reading rooms, lecture halls, and classrooms brought incalculable benefits to the city.

By 1876, Cooper's social conscience had led him to the belief that the times demanded something more than local reform and philanthropy. Disturbed by federal policies which, he felt, were sacrificing popular welfare to the interests of America's business and banking "oligarchy," he publicly urged congressional measures that would assist the depression-ridden laborer and farmer. In place of government subsidies to privately held railroads, he called for government ownership of the nation's rail networks. He urged further that the government provide immediate work relief for the unemployed. Most important, he advocated a departure from the tight-money policies that had been instituted earlier in the decade, and which he believed were responsible for continuing the decline in wages and farm prices. Cooper's views drew unqualified approval from the Greenbackers and it was with little deliberation that they accorded the venerable New Yorker the honor of being their first candidate for president.

As one historian has pointed out, Cooper's candidacy amounted to little more than a gesture. Accepting the nomination only because neither of the two major parties had seen fit to adopt the Greenback position on currency, Cooper was too old to campaign and his candidacy had no real impact on the election. Nevertheless, the philanthropist's action in 1876 was significant; it represented the gallant climax to a career in which social concern had so frequently been the pervasive force. It also marked the first entrance into national politics of a party specifically dedicated to the interests of farmers. From the Greenbackers grew the various farmer parties that reached their most successful expression in the Populist campaigns of the 1890s.

WINFIELD SCOTT HANCOCK   *James Reid Lambdin, 1863   Oil on canvas, 36 x 29 inches*
Chicago Historical Society

Winfield Scott Hancock *Democrat*

1824-1886

By profession, Winfield Scott Hancock was a soldier. Like other distinguished soldiers whose popularity was gained on the battlefield, his exploits gave him political potential that politicians found difficult to pass up. The son of a highly successful and influential Pennsylvania lawyer, Hancock was graduated from West Point in 1844. Having served in both the war with Mexico and the Kansas border skirmishes of the mid-1850s, he entered the Civil War with the rank of brigadier general, largely as a result of General George McClellan, who, recognizing Hancock's administrative and tactical abilities, had seen fit to recommend his advancement to Lincoln. Although he never had a separate command, Hancock won considerable distinction for his roles at Antietam, Chancellorsville, and, above all, Gettysburg, where on the second day of fighting he succeeded in turning the battle in the Union's favor. By the war's end, he, like so many other Union generals, had assumed the stature of a national hero. There were few who could equal his public popularity.

After the war, the public esteem for Hancock spread southward. As military governor of Louisiana and Texas, he earned lasting gratitude from the defeated South for his gentle policies and his conscious effort to safeguard the civil rights of white southerners in the face of Congress' seemingly vindictive mandates for the defeated region.

Because of his popularity, North and South, Democrats had seriously regarded Hancock a presidential possibility as early as 1868. Certainly he was a figure against whom the Republican "bloody shirt" could have little effect. Despite his clearly conciliatory attitude toward the South after the war, his popular image could not be destroyed, as could that of so many Democrats, by Republican accusations of Union disloyalty during the Civil War.

Hancock continued to appeal to Democrats in 1880, and his name still carried sufficient weight with the public to persuade the party that their best chances for success lay in nominating him for president. After two convention ballots, Hancock became the party's unanimous choice.

Had Hancock been endowed with as much political acumen as energy, the Democrats might have finally succeeded in breaking the Republicans' twenty-year hold on the White

"The Bird to Bet On!" Campaign poster SMITHSONIAN INSTITUTION

House. Election results were close in many states. While Republican candidate James Garfield lost some votes due to his purported willingness to undercut American labor with the importation of cheap Chinese labor, Hancock, with little political experience to guide him, left himself open to endless criticism from advocates of a protective tariff by his inept remark that the "tariff question is a local question." Further swinging the balance in Garfield's favor was Hancock's lack of a political record that made him vulnerable to the accusation that there was nothing in his background to recommend him for public office. As one Republican newspaper sardonically observed, to many the Democratic candidate was little more than "a good man weighing two-hundred and fifty pounds."

Hancock took his defeat gracefully. Awakened on the morning after the election by his wife and told of the election results, he replied: "That is all right. I can stand it." With that, he turned over and went back to sleep.

JAMES B. WEAVER *George Edward Perine Engraving 10 x 7 inches From the
print collection of the National Portrait Gallery, Washington, D.C.*

James Baird Weaver *National Greenback–Labor*
1833-1912

Essentially there were two factors which made James B. Weaver a leading figure in the agrarian political movement that arose between 1870 and 1900. As the son of farming parents who had settled in rural Iowa in 1843, he was naturally sympathetic to the successive waves of farmers' protests after the Civil War. Secondly, and perhaps more important, he was by temperament an activist. Combining an aggressively idealistic turn of mind, which inspired an early love for public debate, with a persuasive speaking ability, he possessed all the prerequisites necessary for political leadership.

Weaver's entry into politics occurred in 1856 shortly after he had established himself as a lawyer in Bloomfield, Iowa. Converted to the anti-slavery movement after reading Harriet Beecher Stowe's *Uncle Tom's Cabin* and Horace Greeley's abolitionist editorials in the New York *Tribune,* he joined the Republican Party and in doing so entered actively into its state affairs.

With the outbreak of civil war, Weaver promptly offered his military services and in 1861 received a lieutenant's commission in the Union army. Present both at the battle of Fort Donelson and Shiloh, he also served in his home state where he helped to quell anti-Unionist violence.

Returning to civilian life in 1865, Weaver found his military record a political asset for rising in Republican ranks. He was elected district attorney of the Second Iowa Judicial District in 1866 and a year later received a presidential appointment as federal assessor of internal revenue.

After 1870, however, disillusionment in the party of his youth turned Weaver, as it did many other westerners of agrarian interest, away from the Republicans. He viewed declining farm prices, high railroad rates, and, above all, the federal government's deflationary currency policies as evidence of Republican favoritism towards big business interests at the farmer's expense. Thus, after losing his fight for Congress in 1873 as well as for the gubernatorial nomination in 1875, he permanently parted company with the Republican Party—probably much to the relief of his former allies who were finding his presence within the party a source of increasing discomfort.

Quite logically, Weaver now allied himself with the newly formed Greenback Party; in 1878, he campaigned successfully for Congress as the champion of the Greenback program calling for an expanded and flexible national currency that he hoped would inflate the declining incomes of his rural constituents. Distinguished in Congress by his unceasing crusade for the Greenback program, Weaver quickly gained prestige in the new party and became a moving spirit in Greenback campaigns in other states. When the party convened in 1880 to frame its national platform and select a presidential candidate, he easily became the party's choice.

In a personally run campaign such as few candidates before him had undertaken, Weaver attacked the government as well as both major parties for their policies favoring big business. America, he claimed, had lost sight of its original democratic ideals of equal opportunity. Land grants to railroads had robbed the agrarian of his rightful share of the richest public lands in the West. The maintenance of a gold standard, though benefiting banking interests, was quickly driving the farmer to desperation, while monopolies protected industries and railroads and kept the prices of goods and services at high levels. The worker as well as the farmer, therefore, possessed no advantage with which to counteract this artificial inflation. Calling for government curbs on business and an expanded currency, Weaver sought to "re-establish in the administration of public affairs, the old time Democracy of Jefferson and Jackson, and the pure Republicanism of Abraham Lincoln and Thaddeus Stevens"—a program through which he hoped all "classes" could again share in the economic wealth of America.

Although never expecting to win, Weaver, like many other minority candidates before and since, hoped to have an impact on the election of 1880. Wishing to prevent either Republicans or Democrats from gaining an electoral majority, he planned to force concessions from the two major candidates who would have to bargain for Greenback votes in order to enjoy victory.

Weaver never accomplished this end. Yet, his candidacy did have long-range implications which ultimately determined the path that agrarian protest would take in the 1890s. Winning over 300,000 popular votes—concentrated mostly in the rural West—Weaver became one of the most powerful figures in the agrarian movement. Due largely to his leadership, the Populist Party replaced the Greenbackers in 1890-1891 as a national party dedicated to agrarian and monetary reform. Although even this new party would come to an early end and merge into the mainstream of America's two-party system, its influence would be felt long after in the programs of the major parties.

NEAL DOW   *Joseph B. Kahill   Oil on canvas, 40¼ x 30¼ inches   Portland Museum
of Art, Portland, Maine*

Neal Dow *Prohibitionist*

1804-1897

More than any single individual, Neal Dow symbolized the temperance movement during its early years. Referred to by contemporaries as the "Prophet of Prohibition," he had been the key figure in making his native Maine the first state to prohibit liquor and, in doing so, had provided Prohibitionists across the country as well as abroad with renewed inspiration in their crusade against the "Demon-Rum."

In terms of background and temperament, Dow was a natural leader for the prohibition movement. His fiery temperament would have placed him in the forefront of any cause he had chosen to undertake, but family training and social experiences dictated that his cause should be prohibition. He had been brought up a Quaker and he had been taught to avoid all indulgences, especially spirits. Equally important, he had been bred in the New England concept of social "trusteeship" which made it the responsibility of the "godly" to compel all members of the community to conform to established moral standards. Armed with what his biographer termed, the "self-righteousness of his Quaker Ancestors," Dow naturally considered it his duty to impose his belief in abstinence on those around him.

Further inspiring Dow to action on behalf of temperance were his empirically based conclusions on the effect of intemperance on a community's economic well-being. Always remembering his father's mournful remark about an acquaintance of his, "At last, poor Friend —— has drunk up his land," he never ceased to insist that behind labor inefficiency and pauperism, there lurked the "Demon-Rum." Thus, as proprietor of his family's tannery and as civic leader of Portland, Maine, he came to view prohibition as something of a cure-all for the problems of mounting poverty rolls and workers' lack of dependability.

In his early career as a temperance reformer, Dow limited his crusade to Portland, where he organized the Young Men's Total Abstinence Society and used his prestige as a civic and commercial leader to become the decisive force in awakening citizens to the dangers of alcohol. His earliest significant victory came when he convinced the city's Mechanics' Association to petition town officials to eliminate the English-seaman custom whereby the employers of Portland dispensed daily rum rations to their employees.

243

In the late 1830s, Dow's efforts became statewide. Realizing that his local crusade was not having the desired effects in Portland, he now joined others in a lecture and writing campaign directed at gaining a state prohibition law. In 1846, after frightening legislators with his nearly successful attempt to unseat two Portland representatives, Dow cowed the Maine legislature into passing the nation's first prohibition law.

The new law was ineffective since the penalties were too light. In the late forties, Dow embarked on a campaign to promote more stringent regulations. Having won Portland's mayorality in 1851, he used the influence of his office to promote a state bill that sought to impose harsher penalties on those engaged in illegal liquor traffic. Ultimately successful in this attempt, Dow finally realized his long-cherished goal—to make Maine the first prohibition state.

With this victory, Dow became a figure of national importance in the temperance movement. Lecturing widely in this country as well as in Britain, he spurred the "Maine-Law" movement, which eventually took hold in almost every northern state during the 1850s.

After serving as a general in the Civil War, Dow returned to the temperance crusade in 1865. At this time, he aided James Black in forming the National Temperance Society and Publishing House and continued to speak and write on behalf of the cause.

When the Prohibition Party took form in 1869, Dow would have little to do with it in the belief that a minority party could have little impact. Instead, he preferred to promote his cause politically through the Republican Party whose abolitionist founders had always looked kindly on temperance reform. By 1880, however, Dow grew more amenable to the idea of a third party as a result of the unwillingness of Maine Republicans to support further prohibition legislation. Thus, when the Prohibitionists nominated him for president he accepted, despite the fact that he was still not thoroughly convinced of the party's value.

Dow's candidacy did not further the cause of prohibition. Lacking faith in the party he represented, he remained totally inactive throughout the campaign. In doing so, his nomination became little more than a memorial to his pioneering achievements of the early 1850s.

JAMES GILLESPIE BLAINE   *George Peter Alexander Healy, 1884   Oil on canvas,*
30 x 25½ inches   The Newberry Library, Chicago

James G. Blaine *Republican*

1830-1893

In 1884, James G. Blaine was closer than ever to fulfilling his presidential aspirations. Nominated at the Republican convention on the fourth ballot, his perennial struggle for the presidential candidacy had finally born fruit.

In many respects, Blaine was well qualified to lead his party to a White House victory. A lawyer by training and a newspaper editor by profession, he possessed all the prerequisites of an effective politician. Brilliant speaking ability, combined with an unusual faculty for remembering names and an exceptionally affable nature, guaranteed him success in politics; had these been his only characteristics, America's most cherished political prize might very well have been his in 1884. There was, however, another quality which ultimately barred him from attaining the goal for which both he and his party now hoped: he could not resist the venal temptations of public office.

Having entered politics in 1858 as a representative to the Maine legislature, Blaine began his national career in the House of Representatives in 1864. Given his magnetic personality as well as his ability to shift with the prevailing political winds within his party, he quickly became a prominent congressional leader. In 1869, as a result of his masterful use of parliamentary tactics in support of the radical program of Reconstruction, he succeeded to the House Speakership.

Serving in this capacity until 1875, Blaine became one of the leading characters in the drama of graft and corruption that was to reach its climax during the second Grant administration in the exposure of railroad frauds of the Crédit Mobilier. Since he believed that railroad expansion was vital to the nation's growth, the "Plumed Knight" from Maine saw nothing wrong in sharing in "gifts" that railroads so liberally dispensed to the nation's lawmakers in return for federal subsidization of their roads. Thus, Blaine unabashedly joined in the "Great Barbecue" of the 1870s and, in doing so, accomplished his dual purpose: while he helped the nation gain its railroads, the railroads in turn helped him to accumulate what turned out to be a very sizeable fortune.

However scandalous his conduct in the House might have been, large numbers of Republi-

Blaine and Logan frog doorstop CORNELL UNIVERSITY, DOUGLAS COLLECTION

cans never faltered in their admiration for Blaine. Although public disclosure of his role in the congressional corruption of the early seventies largely prevented nominations for the presidency in both 1876 and 1880, the GOP could not resist this convivial "Ajax Telemon." In 1884, having served in the Senate from 1876 to 1881 and then briefly as Garfield's secretary of state, Blaine, always the model of party loyalty, now seemed to have more appeal than ever among delegates who had forgotten his former questionable dealings. It was with little effort that he finally gained his party's presidential endorsement.

In the campaign, however, Blaine's tarnished record during the Grant administration caught up with him. Although Republicans did their best to smear Blaine's Democratic opponent, Grover Cleveland, with stories of his indiscreet dalliance with a Buffalo widow who had borne him a child, the Democrats succeeded in blunting this attack with new evidence linking the Plumed Knight to the railroads. Thus, while Republicans rallied to the cry:

> Ma, Ma, where's my Pa?
> Gone to the White House,
> Ha! Ha! Ha!

Democrats countered with their chant:

> Blaine, Blaine, James G. Blaine
> Continental Liar from the State of Maine.

248

In addition to providing Democrats with invaluable ammunition, Blaine's congressional record also weakened his appeal within his own party. Reform-conscious Republicans who had made government corruption their primary concern left their party in 1884. Considering Blaine's public behavior far more reprehensible than Cleveland's private indiscretions, this group—known commonly as the "mugwumps"—threw their support to the Democrats. For much the same reason, the Republicans' most influential journalistic mouthpiece, the New York *Times*, also deserted the Republican cause.

Blaine's tarnished reputation was not the only factor contributing to his defeat. Equally significant was the injudicious billing accorded him by a New York rally where the Reverend Burchard introduced him as the foe of "Rum, Romanism, and Rebellion." Never bothering to refute this statement, Blaine now suffered new onslaughts of criticism casting him as an anti-Catholic. Most of the urban Irish vote, which he had assiduously courted with his sympathetic allusions to Irish nationalism and home rule and on which he had so heavily counted in the state of New York, swung to Cleveland. Further alienating voters was the lavish Republican dinner at Delmonico's where Blaine shared a repast with businessmen like the railroad mogul and speculative banker, Jay Gould, one of the most notorious dealers in political favors. Described by the newspapers as "Belshazzar's Feast," the fund-raising gala only heightened the Plumed Knight's already tainted reputation as the political servant of big business.

Nevertheless, Blaine came close to winning the presidency in 1884. In light of the small popular margin that placed New York in the Democratic electoral column, Cleveland's electoral victory might just as easily have been Blaine's, had the latter not been so clearly identified with political corruption or anti-Catholicism.

Defeat did not, however, bring an end to Blaine's political career. Still popular among most Republicans, he continued to wield influence within his party, and in 1888, he became secretary of state under Benjamin Harrison. It was in this last office that Blaine made an enduring contribution as primary architect of a vigorous foreign policy in Latin America, which was to reach full flower at the turn of the century.

BENJAMIN FRANKLIN BUTLER   *unidentified artist   Marble bas-relief,
21 inches in diameter   The Children of Mrs. Oakes Ames, granddaughter of
Benjamin Franklin Butler*

Benjamin F. Butler

National Greenback / Anti-Monopoly

1818–1893

Considered abrasive, egotistical, and incurably ambitious, Benjamin Franklin Butler was beyond question one of the most colorful and controversial figures of his times. Vilified by many for his incessant political conniving and seemingly radical views, this soldier-lawyer-politician nevertheless enjoyed a loyal cadre of followers, drawn to him largely as a result of his vigorous support for labor reform as well as his constant sympathy for the social underdog.

Butler was raised by a widowed mother who ran a boarding house in Lowell, Massachusetts. Despite his mother's hope of his becoming a minister, he decided upon law as a career and in 1840 was admitted to the Massachusetts bar. Beginning practice in Lowell, he quickly developed a reputation as one of the best, if not the most scrupulous, criminal lawyers in the state. To many of Lowell's workers, whom he so frequently defended in his early years, his ability to win seemingly impossible cases made him a hero. On the other hand, there were many who in light of his flamboyant, and what seemed to be devious, courtroom methods found him "scaly and disreputable." But whatever their personal feelings, even his severest critics respected his skill. Though they thoroughly disliked him, many Lowell mill owners ultimately joined their workers in seeking his services—largely out of fear that if they did not enlist him, their opponents would.

Throughout the 1850s, Butler, as a Democrat, played an active part in Massachusetts reform politics. Many of his fellow partisans found him crude and distrusted his sincerity, but his advocacy of the shortened workday and the secret ballot attracted a large popular following. Thus, like the Lowell mill owners, Democrats also found it advisable to tolerate his presence within their ranks. In 1850, he led in organizing the reformist coalition of Democrats and Free-Soilers that toppled the long-ascendant Whigs. Later, as a representative to the state legislature in 1853 and 1859, he argued ardently for a law limiting the hours of workers. Although his legislation died in committee, there was little doubt that it was his agitation which finally brought pressure on state factory owners to reduce their hours from fourteen to eleven.

With the outbreak of the Civil War, Butler became a national figure. Commissioned in 1861 as a general in the Massachusetts militia, he now embarked on a career which, like his legal and political endeavors, was to inspire both admiration and distaste.

Regarded initially as a hero for his single-handed success in ensuring Maryland as a Union state, the general soon achieved notoriety as the severe and allegedly corrupt military governor of New Orleans. While esteemed by northerners for his efforts to find employment for the newly freed slaves under his jurisdiction, his confiscation of southern property and harsh treatment of recalcitrant southerners earned him lasting enmity in the South. Furthermore, his famous order to treat southern women who dared to insult his soldiers as women "of the town plying [their] trade" aroused indignation in the North as well as the South. It did not help his already blackened reputation that he permitted his soldiers to indulge in uncontrolled looting of the once-proud city. Although it was unlikely that he ever shared in the spoils—he had already accumulated a sizeable fortune as a lawyer and mill owner—it was in memory of this widespread pilfering that his enemies would ever after refer to him as "Spoons Butler."

Whatever the public reaction, Butler's war record gained him a warm welcome from Radical Republicans after the war, who viewed his stringent policies while military governor as a reflection of their own attitude toward the South. Butler severed his Democratic ties and, after his election on a Republican ticket to the House of Representatives in 1866, he rapidly became a leading force in framing the radical legislation establishing military rule in the South.

Butler, however, did not rest comfortably within Republican ranks for long. By the early 1870s, he had become too radical for many Massachusetts Republicans. By now an advocate of cheap money, woman's suffrage, the income tax, and business-labor reforms, he completely violated the conservative doctrines of his adopted party. His public opposition to the cherished hopes of Boston's Brahmin Republicans to extend Civil Service in order to eliminate the spoils system angered these "genteel reformers." A concerted effort to drive Butler from Congress and the party began.

Although Massachusetts Republicans were finally successful in forcing him out of the GOP, Butler was far from finished in politics. By 1878, after a short flirtation with the Greenback Party, he was back in the Democratic fold where as the party's four-time candidate, he finally won the Massachusetts governorship in 1883.

As governor, Butler probably drew more criticism than he deserved. Alienated by his unorthodox beliefs as well as his open support of the political spoils system, many were indignant that the spoon-stealing general should be allowed to occupy the state's highest office. As a result, although his one-year administration marked a move toward improving the deplorable conditions of the state's public institutions, the staid overseers of Harvard College broke with their time-honored tradition and refused to grant Butler the honorary degree that all other governors had received.

The climax to Butler's career came in 1884. Hardly discouraged by his detractors, the resilient ex-governor now began to eye the presidency. When the Greenback and Anti-Monopoly parties asked him to be their presidential candidate in recognition of his public support for their views on currency and labor reform, Butler anxiously accepted, hoping that his minority candidacy might lead to his nomination at the Democratic convention.

Although Butler failed in gaining the Democratic endorsement, the two major parties

"YOU WILL HAVE ONE ADVANTAGE IN YOUR CANDIDATE: YOU WILL HAVE TO SPEND NO TIME IN DEFENDING HIM. HIS DOINGS HAVE BEEN KNOWN TO THE COUNTRY FOR MORE THAN A QUARTER OF A CENTURY.

HE IS YET UNHARMED, AND HAS NO OPINION TO TAKE BACK, NO POLICY TO RECANT, AND NO JUST CHARGE TO EXPLAIN FOR WHAT HE HAS DONE EITHER IN PEACE OR WAR."

BUTLER.
(THE GOOD AND BEAUTIFUL)

A PRESIDENTIAL CONFIDENCE GAME.

"FUSION" AND CONFUSION BY BUTLER.

"STRONG ENOUGH IN MORAL RECTITUDE TO STAND FOR THE RIGHTS OF THE PEOPLE "UNAWED BY POWER AND UNBOUGHT BY GAIN."

BUTLER,
(THE UNBOUGHT)

Th. Nast.

"The Self-Made Party," by Thomas Nast   LIBRARY OF CONGRESS

clearly viewed his candidacy as a potent factor in 1884. Fearing that he would take votes away from Cleveland, nervous Democrats tried to lure him out of the campaign with promises of a position in the Cleveland administration. Refusing this first overture, Butler nevertheless accepted the offer made by Republican leaders who wanted to keep him in the campaign for the same reason Democrats wanted him out. Thus, while Butler violently castigated Republicans and Democrats alike for their conservative stands on currency and labor reform, the Republicans willingly paid the bulk of his campaign expenditures.

Butler's candidacy did not have the effect for which the Republicans had hoped despite his 175,000 votes. Although most of his support came from Democrats, it was not sufficient to throw the election to Blaine.

After 1884, Butler retired from politics, and devoted the remainder of his life to private law practice and the writing of his memoirs. But, although old age increasingly removed him from the public eye, his name continued to generate controversy. When he died in 1893, the reaction was varied. Recalling his spirited support for labor and business reform, one newspaper referred to him as the "dearly beloved . . . People's Champion." On the other hand, a New Orleans writer, recalling Butler's years as military governor, described him as the "most cordially despised and hated man that ever lived." There was one point, however, on which all could agree: unquestionably Butler had been "one of the most picturesque Americans" of his day.

JOHN P. ST. JOHN   *From the photograph in the collection of the Kansas State Historical Society*

John Pierce St. John *Prohibitionist*

1833-1916

Like many other prohibitionists of his day, John P. St. John's enthusiasm for temperance rose out of childhood experience. Having witnessed his father's gradual retreat into alcoholism, he had seen at first hand the dreadful effect that intemperance could have on a family's welfare. In taking up his career as a Kansas lawyer-politician, prohibition, therefore, was always St. John's primary concern and a cause for which he fought vigorously in Kansas both as state senator and as governor.

By 1884, St. John's fight for prohibition had made him a national figure in the temperance movement. As governor of Kansas from 1879 to 1883, he had succeeded in making Kansas the first state to outlaw liquor by constitutional amendment. As a result, he was now the hero of the hour and the major source of inspiration for Prohibitionists who hoped to extend the Kansas success over a broader national front.

It was natural, then, that the Prohibition Party should want the "lion-hearted" Kansas governor for their presidential candidate in 1884. Having recently disaffiliated himself from the Republican Party when it failed to adopt a pro-temperance position at its national convention, St. John increased his attractiveness as a potential candidate. His total commitment to the temperance cause was now complete and his final nomination but a formality. Embarking on the first truly active presidential campaign in the party's history, St. John and his supporters concentrated their efforts in the states with the heaviest electoral count. In doing so, they "sought to make the party a force that should be felt."

And, indeed, the Prohibitionists did make themselves felt. Concerned over St. John's mounting popularity, particularly in the key state of New York, certain Republican leaders went so far as to offer the temperance candidate a bribe for stepping out of the race.

It was, however, the final popular results which clearly demonstrated that St. John was a decisive force in 1884. Receiving the greatest national popular vote ever given to a Prohibitionist, St. John proved to be one of several key factors in bringing about Blaine's defeat. Since the votes of New York alone would have tipped the electoral scales in the Republican's favor, St. John's vote of 25,016 in that state—largely drawn from Republican ranks—took enough votes away from Blaine to win the state for Cleveland.

St. John ribbon KANSAS STATE HISTORICAL SOCIETY

Many other factors, of course, contributed to Blaine's defeat in this colorful election. For many Republicans of the time, however, St. John was the major villain. While one party newspaper branded him a "Judas Iscariot" for his political handiwork, Republican faithfuls in over one-hundred towns burned him in effigy. Still others accused the Republican-turned-Prohibitionist of staying in the race simply because the Democrats had bribed him to do so. Finally, in his own state, the Republican legislature expressed its bitterness toward the former governor by changing the name of St. John County.

Despite the recriminations of his former allies, St. John could take comfort in the fact that his limited success in 1884 had given new impetus to the Prohibition movement. While inspiring Prohibitionists in many states to become more politically active, the two major parties for a time at least began to regard the temperance-minded segments of the electorate a bit more seriously. Certainly, this was apparent on the state level. Whereas Frances Willard had suffered the humiliation of having her prohibition resolution trampled in the sawdust of the Republican national convention in 1884, local leaders from both parties were now more amenable to including at least moderate temperance planks in their state platforms. Remembering St. John's effect on Blaine, they came to realize the wisdom of accommodating themselves, if only occasionally, to Prohibition interests.

BELVA ANN LOCKWOOD   *Nellie Mathes Horne, 1913   Oil on canvas, 69¾ x 40 inches*
From the Collection of the National Portrait Gallery
Gift of the Committee on Tribute to Mrs. Belva Ann Lockwood   NPG.66.61

Belva Ann Bennett Lockwood *Equal Rights*
1830-1917

Writing to California suffragette and labor organizer, Marietta Stow, in the early 1880s, Belva Ann Lockwood observed that despite the legal disenfranchisement of women, there were no laws prohibiting women from seeking elected office. "Why not nominate women for important places?" Mrs. Lockwood asked. "Is not Victoria Empress of India? Have we not among our countrywomen persons of as much talent and ability? Is not history full of precedents of women rulers?"

With these words, Mrs. Lockwood unwittingly opened the way to becoming the second woman to run for president. Inspired by her correspondent's observations, Mrs. Stow banded with other suffragettes in her state to organize the National Equal Rights Party and, in 1884, was chairman of the San Francisco convention where party delegates unanimously nominated Mrs. Lockwood as their first candidate for president.

It was fitting that Mrs. Lockwood should become the standard-bearer of this short-lived party whose raison d'être lay in its demand for political and economic equality for women. Exposed in her youth to the feminist ferment that swept her native New York during the 1840s and 1850s, she had been drawn to the burgeoning woman's rights movement largely from personal experience. The daughter of moderately prosperous farming parents, who had educated her beyond the norm for most girls of her day, she had encountered frequent discrimination in her career as a teacher and lawyer. As a result, she had long been an active force in the feminist crusade and by 1884 had attracted national attention in efforts to improve the status of women.

The initial inspiration for Mrs. Lockwood's first major endeavor on behalf of feminism lay in her early experience as a teacher in New York before the Civil War. Incensed by the fact that she was able to command only half the salary of her male counterparts, the spirited teacher undertook to alleviate similar injustices after the Civil War. In 1866 she settled in Washington, D.C., where she became the primary force in persuading Congress to pass the 1872 bill guaranteeing female government employees equal pay for equal work.

In embarking on a legal career in the early 1870s, Mrs. Lockwood again felt the need for

Belva Ann Lockwood autograph card   SMITHSONIAN INSTITUTION

reform. Admitted to a District of Columbia law school only after a kindly vice-chancellor, despite faculty hostility, had consented to tutor her privately, she found that her hard-won law degree meant little to the male members of her profession. She was barred from practice in the Court of Claims and the United States Supreme Court, but her most humiliating rebuff was received from a judge in 1873, who, denying her the right to practice in Maryland, roundly lectured her on the impropriety of her effort to practice law. "Women are not needed in the courts," he told her. "Their place is in the home to wait upon their husbands, to bring up the children, to cook the meals, make beds, polish pans and dust furniture."

Mrs. Lockwood was not convinced. Immediately, she undertook what was to be her most formidable achievement on behalf of female equality. Drafting a bill which would permit women to practice before the United States Supreme Court, she worked toward its congressional passage for three years. Finally in 1879, Congress succumbed, and within two months she appropriately became the first woman to be admitted to practice before the nation's highest tribunal.

Clearly a fighter, Mrs. Lockwood regarded her candidacy in 1884 enthusiastically. One of the few members of the National Woman's Suffrage Association to support Victoria Woodhull in 1872, she viewed her presidential campaign as a means of publicizing the feminist cause. Strange to say, leading suffragettes like Susan B. Anthony and Elizabeth Cady Stanton disavowed Mrs. Lockwood's political efforts; instead, they cast their support for Blaine, hoping to achieve their goals within the two-party system. Undeterred, the White House aspirant led her party in a vigorous campaign.

It was clear, however, that America was not ready for a female candidate. In Pennsylvania, supporters claimed that indignant pollsters had thrown all Lockwood ballots into a wastebasket, and in the final count Mrs. Lockwood could claim only 4,149 of the more than ten-million votes cast. Like the Maryland judge, the male electorate remained unconvinced that woman's proper place was not still in the home.

Although she ran for president again in 1888 and continued to participate in woman's rights movements, most of Mrs. Lockwood's career after 1884 was devoted to law and the peace movement. In addition to drafting suffrage amendments for three states and the law that gave women equal property rights in the District of Columbia, she found time to attend three international peace conferences where she presented papers on disarmament and the establishment of an "International Peace Bureau." Most significantly, she finally achieved respectability within the legal profession. While her early courtroom appearances had been the occasion for derisive sneers, her poised and adept courtroom skills eventually made Mrs. Lockwood the object of admiration and respect among professional contemporaries.

STEPHEN GROVER CLEVELAND   *Eastman Johnson, 1884   Oil on artist's board,*
22¾ x 18¾ inches   From the Collection of the National Portrait Gallery,
Gift of Francis G. Cleveland   NPG.71.58

Grover Cleveland *Democrat*

1837-1908

As the White House incumbent, Grover Cleveland was the natural presidential choice of the Democrats in 1888. He had wrested the presidency from the Republicans in 1884, and Democrats were not about to jeopardize their future by deserting the man who had led them to their first presidential victory since before the Civil War. So, it was with little effort that Cleveland again received the presidential nomination of his party.

In many respects, Cleveland seemed a winner in 1888. Educated by his minister father in the lofty idealism of his New England heritage, he had entered public life equipped with a keen sense of ethics and the belief that elected office was a public trust and not a vehicle for personal self-aggrandizement. In an age of government corruption and business frauds, his principled nature presented a refreshing relief to voters who had become accustomed to the morally indifferent politician who so often prevailed during the Gilded Age. Although his Republican detractors in 1884 were able to capitalize on the moral indiscretion that sullied his private life, they could not deny his incorruptibility as a public servant.

Cleveland had joined the Democratic Party in Buffalo, New York, as a struggling young lawyer. After the Civil War, his reputation as the symbol of clean government grew rapidly. Elected sheriff of Erie County, New York, in 1870, he vigorously rooted out the graft within the local prison administration and at the same time compelled the lax deputies in his office to carry out their duties to the letter.

Further testimony to Cleveland's incorruptible character lay in his record as mayor of Buffalo from 1880 to 1882. Popularly referred to as the "Veto Mayor," he consistently thwarted the City Council who had long been accustomed to awarding city contracts to those businesses promising the fattest bribes.

Elected to the New York governorship in 1882 on the basis of his impeccable reputation, Cleveland transferred his fight against corruption to the state level. In addition to removing many appointive offices from the much-abused patronage rolls, he vetoed innumerable public and private bills from which legislators had hoped to profit personally.

Four years in the White House did not disturb Cleveland's reputation for sound leader-

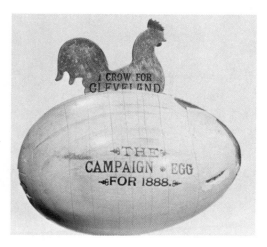

Cleveland campaign egg CORNELL UNIVERSITY, DOUGLAS COLLECTION

ship. Although he had disappointed Civil Service reformers with his ultimate surrender to the office-seeking spoilsmen of his party, he brought new efficiency to the executive branch and corrected several of the abusive practices permitted under previous administrations. In addition to reorganizing the naval department where wasteful policies were the rule rather than the exception, he succeeded in curbing the fraudulent practices whereby western lands were alloted to private speculators and railroads gained control of acreage intended for homesteaders. He intervened to bring to an end the flagrant encroachment by western cattlemen on lands reserved for the Indians. Still later, he used his influence to win passage of the Dawes Act which finally permitted Indians to become citizens. With his approval Congress also approved the Interstate Commerce Act of 1887, which represented the first federal attempt to regulate railroad rates.

Despite his sound record of reform and the prestige he enjoyed as incumbent, Cleveland was vulnerable in 1888. By approving a treaty with Britain granting fishing concessions to Canada, he alienated those Anglophobic Irish-Americans who had supported him in 1884. More important, however, were the tariff reductions which had passed Congress under his sponsorship in the last months of his administration. In this act, the rabidly protectionist Republicans found the winning issue. Equipped with a campaign fund derived from industry that far exceeded the Democrats, they cast their pro-tariff candidate, Benjamin Harrison, as the true agent of American prosperity. Claiming that a reduced tariff would spark widespread employee wage cuts, they inundated voters with literature accusing Cleveland of ruining American industry.

Had the Democrats been well organized, they might have countered these attacks and blunted their effect on the electorate. But Cleveland had imprudently left the campaign in the hands of William Barnum and Calvin Brice whose industrial interests dampened their enthusiasm for framing a campaign in defense of Cleveland's low tariff policy. Moreover, while Harrison campaigned vigorously, making eloquent pleas on his own behalf, Cleveland very conscientiously—but unwisely—remained in Washington to oversee the affairs of his administration.

Further weakening Cleveland's candidacy was his failure to unite Democratic factions in New York by endorsing incumbent Governor David B. Hill. Consequently, while the Republicans put forth a united and heavily financed effort in the ever-decisive Empire State, the Democrats remained too seriously fragmented over the question of Hill's reputation as a political spoilsman to mount a well-organized campaign on behalf of their presidential candidate. As a result, Cleveland lost the state that would have given him victory.

Cleveland took his defeat philosophically, observing that defeat had its "personal compensations." He later commented on the impact of his stand on tariff policies: "I don't regret it. It is better to be defeated battling for an honest principle than to win by a cowardly subterfuge. . . . We were defeated, it is true, but the principles of tariff reform will surely win in the end." Could he have looked into the future, Cleveland would have found still greater comfort in the knowledge that he would again lead the Democrats to victory in 1892.

Cleveland ribbon SMITHSONIAN INSTITUTION

BENJAMIN HARRISON   *Adolph Weinman   Bronze bust, 28¼ inches in height*
Indianapolis Museum of Art   Gift of the Harrison Memorial Association

Benjamin Harrison *Republican*

1833-1901

In 1892, Benjamin Harrison did not inspire the well-organized and enthusiastic party support that had brought him victory in 1888. Some Republicans would have preferred the aging political veteran, James G. Blaine, while others were already committed to the rapidly ascending William McKinley; but neither of these efforts came to fruition in 1892 and the Republicans once again—though halfheartedly—placed their presidential hopes in Harrison's hands.

By virtue of his birth, Harrison had been destined for a career in politics. The son of a two-term Whig congressman from Indiana, William Scott Harrison, he could claim direct descent from President William Henry Harrison who had been his grandfather, as well as the earlier Benjamin Harrison, signer of the Declaration of Independence and patrician governor of the state of Virginia. Thus, politics had been a part of Harrison's inheritance. Although his belief that "each man should stand on his own merit" made him reticent in capitalizing publicly on his distinguished forebearers, his heritage endowed him with the conviction that he had been destined for political leadership. Combining a distinguished legal career with politics, he had, like so many northerners brought up in the Whig tradition, joined the Republican Party in the mid-1850s. By 1860, he had become a prominent spokesman in the local affairs of his adopted party.

After serving one elected term as city attorney of Indianapolis, Harrison interrupted his budding career to serve in the Union army where he eventually attained the rank of general. Once he returned to civilian life, his fame as a lawyer and later as a powerful figure in national Republican politics spread.

With his brilliant defense of General Alvin P. Hovey against Civil War copperhead Lambdin P. Milligan, who claimed damages from the general for his role in the latter's arbitrary wartime arrest, Harrison's popularity continued to increase. In 1876, he won the Republican nomination for governor of Indiana. Ironically, however, the grandson of the original "Log-Cabin" president lost, in great measure, because of the way in which his opponent derided his reputation as a cold and aloof "kidglove" patrician.

Harrison's political fortunes, nevertheless, continued to rise. Appointed by President

Benjamin Harrison glass hat CORNELL UNIVERSITY, DOUGLAS COLLECTION

Rutherford B. Hayes to the Mississippi River Commission in 1879, he played a leading role in the election of Garfield in 1880 and a year later won election to the United States Senate, where he was made chairman of the important Committee on Territories.

By now, Harrison was prime presidential material. A powerful influence in his party, a former general and the grandson of a president, he had, in addition, become one of the Republicans' most eloquent spokesmen. It was not surprising, then, that in 1888 he won his party's presidential endorsement and eventually the popular election.

Facing Cleveland again in 1892, however, the Hoosier's political weaknesses surfaced. Although he thrived on politics, Harrison consistently remained coolly indifferent to the feelings and wishes of other politicians within his party, and while this tendency had not been detrimental to his fortunes previously, in 1892 it contributed in large part to his political failure. Unwilling to assume the role of unifying the party, he never tried to mollify those Republicans who were irritated by his efforts to curb party patronage in the making of federal appointments. As a result, the party lacked the enthusiastic unity so necessary in ensuring a presidential victory.

Equally significant, Harrison also lost ground with the voters. Having kept his promise to raise the tariff, many Americans who had voted for him in 1888 now attributed rising consumer prices to the rise in tariff rates. Workers, who formerly had feared that Cleveland's low tariff policies would depress wages, were no longer as convinced of the wisdom of Harrison's tariff revisions in light of the wage cuts suffered by Andrew Carnegie's steelworkers in Pennsylvania, despite the high tariff that shielded American steel from foreign competition. Worst of all for Harrison, the man who had implemented these cuts, Henry Clay Frick, was one of the president's closest friends and most ardent supporters.

Another source of Harrison's weakened popularity lay in the Sherman Silver Purchase Act which had doubled the amount of silver-backed currency purchased by the Treasury. Meant as a salve to "silver" Republican congressmen who had reluctantly voted for the increased tariff, the bill satisfied no one and alienated many. For the silverites, it did not go far enough in expanding currency, while fiscally conservative Republicans considered it the beginning of financial disaster. In 1892, Harrison lost significant support among both these factions.

In facing defeat, Harrison's reaction was not much different from Cleveland's in 1888. Grieved over the loss of his wife who had died during the campaign, he contemplated his political losses with mixed emotions. While fearing the national effect of Cleveland's promised tariff reduction, he nevertheless felt a sense of relief: "For me there is no sting in [defeat]. Indeed after the heavy blow the death of my wife dealt me, I do not think I could have stood the strain a reelection would have brought."

James B. Weaver campaign poster LIBRARY OF CONGRESS

James Baird Weaver *Populist*

1833-1912

Toward the end of the 1880s, agrarian problems worsened. While farm prices plummeted to all-time lows, government continued to ignore the cries increasingly emanating from the nation's rural regions for cheap money and government control of big business.

The Greenback Party withered away as a result of its fusion with Democrats in many states, but a new political force loomed on the horizon in the form of the Farmers' Alliance. Initially organized in the West and the South for the purpose of establishing marketing and manufacturing cooperatives, the new group became increasingly political. In 1890, after experiencing some political successes on the state level, members began to think in terms of forming a national party with representatives of American labor.

Early in 1892, a convention of Alliance men and labor leaders met in St. Louis to plan their first presidential campaign. Calling themselves the Populists, they framed a platform denouncing the deflationary currency policy of the government which, they believed, was destroying the "multitude" to satisfy the greed of the "millionaire." Farsighted in many ways, they further called for a graduated income tax to take the pressure off of property taxes that hit them hard as landowners; direct election of senators to bring government closer to the will of the people; regulation of work hours for laboring groups; and government ownership of railroads and the telegraph to maintain equitable rates for farm shipments.

Involved in the new party from its inception, James B. Weaver predictably became the Populists' first presidential candidate. Nationally known and already well initiated into the ways of presidential campaigning, he appeared as the wisest choice for the novice party that nominated him at its Omaha convention in July 1892.

In taking up the Populist banner, Weaver repeated the beliefs he had defined in 1880, but in stronger terms. Declaiming that this was a country "no longer . . . governed by the people," but rather by a business oligarchy of "Federal monopolies," he compared the economic situation in America to the class suppression that had sparked the French Revolution.

In contrast to 1880, great numbers of people now listened sympathetically. The violent Homestead Strike that had resulted from Frick's wage cuts, as well as the worsening farm

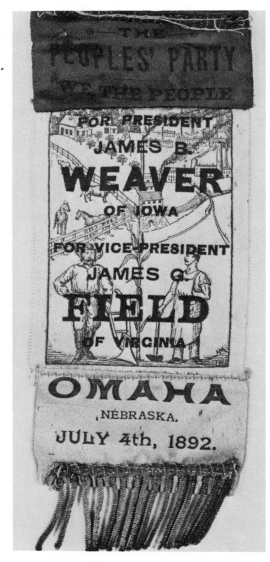

James B. Weaver ribbon   CORNELL UNIVERSITY, DOUGLAS COLLECTION

situation, won Populist converts throughout the nation. Although Weaver encountered open hostility in the South where Populist alliance with blacks inspired a violent outbreak of Negrophobia and voter intimidation—in Georgia, for instance, his wife became a "walking omelet"—he received one of the highest votes ever given to a minority candidate in the history of American elections.

Just as Weaver led the Populist movement to its peak as an independent party, he also contributed to its downfall. A believer in political fusion, he had always been willing to ally himself to like-thinking factions of the two major parties. In the 1880s, he had successfully run for Congress as a Greenback–Democrat. And in 1896, despite the strong Populist showing in the elections of 1894, he argued for alliance with the Democrats who had nominated silverite William Jennings Bryan. Following his advice, the Populists not only lost their momentum, but their issues and identity as a reform party as well, and although they continued as an organization for more than a decade, the unified and enthusiastic spirit of the early years vanished.

Many of the reform measures that Weaver and his supporters proposed in 1892, however, did not die. Incorporated to a large extent into the platforms of both major parties who had been jolted by the Populist ground swell, many of them became a reality after 1900.

Silver and a Full Dinner Pail 1896

OFTEN REGARDED AS ONE OF THE MOST HEATED OF PRESIDENTIAL CONTESTS, THE ELECTION of 1896 owed its character largely to the economic frustrations experienced by large numbers of Americans in the first half of the nineties. Not since the Civil War had so many felt the need for such drastic reorientation of their national life. The United States had rarely experienced, and certainly never so dramatically, such a deep sense of social division and alienation as that which surfaced in the midst of this decade's economic disasters.

Farmers most clearly felt alienated and frustrated during this period. Hardly sharing in the spirit of the "gay nineties," the farmer increasingly came to believe that his welfare was being sacrificed to the interests of industrial America. Raised in the Jeffersonian belief that he was both the economic and social mainstay of American life, the farmer now found himself moving toward a subsistence level of life, and even lower. He was caught between declining farm prices—wheat had fallen from the post-Civil War high of $1.50 to 49 cents a bushel by 1894, and cotton from 15 to 7 cents a pound—and the stable but high prices of manufactured goods as well as climbing interest and railroad rates. Unable to realize even a subsistence income, the once-independent farmer now angrily viewed himself as the much-abused whipping boy of government-protected business. Summing up this situation and the impulse to protest that it fostered, reformer Washington Gladden in 1890 declared: "The American Farmer is steadily losing ground. His burdens are heavier every year and his gains are more meager; he is beginning to fear that he may be sinking into servile conditions. He has waited long for the redress of his grievances: he proposes to wait no longer."

Agrarian discontent resulted from more than just declining income. The farmer also found himself helpless against what he considered the impossible demands placed on him by American business. Having no choice but to pay the monopolistic rates demanded by railroads, an Iowa farmer paid a higher price to ship his crop to Chicago than to a European port. Due to the protective tariffs, the prices of manufactured goods were kept at artificially high levels. An American-made reaper cost less in Europe than it did in Kansas. Finally, in mortgaging his lands to meet the exigencies of a depressed income, the farmer often faced interest charges that ranged as high as twenty percent. In short, however small his financial resources became, the farmer found little sympathy or help from America's commercial community in obtaining the goods and services he so vitally needed.

Joining the farmer in economic hardships and social frustrations were large segments of the urban labor force. While 1891 and 1892 had witnessed many strikes and signs of labor unrest, the Panic of 1893 marked a sharp rise in suffering and discontent among workers. In 1894, the estimate of unemployed labor rose to three million. In Chicago alone, the number of jobless rose to 100,000. Wage cuts were often imposed on those who retained their job simply as a means of maintaining corporate profits. As a result, labor unrest became commonplace after 1893. In 1894, strikes involved more workers than ever before and over twice as many as in any of the four preceding years. In Cleveland, union workers raced through the city's manufacturing section damaging property and driving out strikebreakers. Chicago's Pullman strike paralyzed the nation's rail networks, set the whole nation on edge for weeks, and gave rise to fears of anarchy and revolution.

Full dinner pail, metal lantern CORNELL UNIVERSITY, DOUGLAS COLLECTION

Aggravating the hardships and disillusion of the nineties was the feeling among the hard pressed that the leaders of American business were immune to the economic reverses of the times. While farmers and workers languished, they could read of the magnificent summer homes being built at Newport, Rhode Island, by prosperous entrepreneurs of the period. Cornelius Vanderbilt's "cottage" at Newport, built between 1893 and 1895, cost an estimated three-million dollars, while his brother William's Marble House ran in the area of two-million dollars. Or they could peruse newspapers for accounts of how great business magnates and their wives entertained each other with ten- and twenty-course dinners and then danced until dawn in rooms banked with the most elaborate of floral decorations. Thus, to the heavily mortgaged farmer and urban unemployed, it seemed that the promise of American life had become the exclusive preserve of the nation's commercial and industrial leadership.

For most of the discontented, the blame for the sufferings being experienced by the common man could largely be attributed to the indifference of national government. The nineties increasingly witnessed the complaint that government was protecting big business at the expense of the common man. Certainly, this was the theme of Harry Demarest Lloyd's *Wealth vs. Commonwealth,* published in 1894, in which the reformer argued ardently for government policies that would benefit more than just a few. Reflecting a similar outlook in *Traveller from Altruria,* William Dean Howells in the same year demonstrated his disillusionment with American institutions in his depiction of a socialistic paradise in which government ownership and controls protected the common welfare against selfish interests. Still more vocal was the newly formed Populist Party whose agrarian supporters decried government's subservience to the wishes of railroad and banking leaders and advocated federal reforms which they hoped would alleviate the hardships of the farmers and workers.

That the government under President Cleveland had not protected the farmer and worker during the crises of the nineties seemed obvious to the rising numbers of protestors. Under his Democratic leadership, the high tariff remained in force; the money supply was further curtailed with the repeal of the Sherman Silver Purchase Act; and in answer to the paralyzing Pullman strike of 1894, federal troops had disbanded the workers who were protesting management's wage cuts. Rather than consider the pleas of Coxey's army of unemployed who had marched to Washington seeking government jobs, the authorities had placed the group's leaders in jail for trampling on the Capitol's lawn.

In the midst of this turmoil and bitterness, the election of 1896 got underway.

WILLIAM JENNINGS BRYAN *Irving Ramsay Wiles, 1917 Oil on canvas,*
59¼ x 39½ inches Department of State, Washington, D.C.

William Jennings Bryan *Democrat/Populist*

1860-1925

As delegate from Nebraska to the Democratic convention of 1896, William Jennings Bryan had worked for many months previously to muster party support for his presidential candidacy. Not taken seriously by the leaders of the Democratic Party, only the most discerning could have foreseen the dramatic turn of events that was to make the "Boy Orator of the Platte" the party's presidential standard-bearer.

The convention, however, was poised for an upset. The financial panic of 1893 and the subsequent protests of hard-pressed agrarians and urban workers against a business-oriented federal administration had brought delegates to Chicago who were in no mood to accept the dictates of the party's conservative leadership.

That this was the case was certainly clear in the actions of the convention's platform committee. With Bryan as one of its key members, it broke all political precedent by flatly repudiating Cleveland's administration. Critical of the president's issuance of government bonds in peacetime and his interference in the Pullman strike of 1894, the committee completed its betrayal of the Democratic Party's titular leader on the money issue. It supported the return to silver coinage and a bimetallist standard and condemned, at least implicitly, Cleveland's important role in returning to a currency based exclusively on gold.

Here was a situation made to order for the ambitious Bryan.

A product of the agrarian Midwest, Bryan had long defended the farmer's interests. He shared the farmer's belief that the gold standard was the cause of deflated farm prices and agrarian indebtedness, and he vigorously criticized the federal government's adherence to a gold-backed currency.

The platform written, Bryan was in a position that would have been the envy of any presidential hopeful. As one of the most vocal silverites on the platform committee, he found little trouble in becoming the appointed spokesman to defend the silver plank before the convention. Possessing oratorical powers that were to make him legendary, he now had the opportunity to place himself in the limelight and spark the ground swell that could win him the nomination.

William Jennings Bryan pennant   CORNELL UNIVERSITY, DOUGLAS COLLECTION

And spark it, Bryan did. Giving America one of the most dramatic scenes in convention history, he mesmerized his audience with his evangelistic attack on the "gold bugs." America, he proclaimed, had sacrificed the welfare of the common man to the selfish wishes of financiers. Playing masterfully on the delegates' sense of frustration, and taking full advantage of the enthusiasm he inspired, Bryan dramatically climaxed his words with the now-classic warning to the gold interests: "You shall not press upon the brow of labor this crown of thorns, you shall not crucify mankind on a cross of gold."

As the sermon ended, it was clear to all present that the dark horse from Nebraska was now a front-runner for the nomination. If the convention had selected its nominee then, some say Bryan would have won by acclamation. In describing the melee that followed in Bryan's wake, one observer commented: "I could understand the scenes of the French Revolution then, I could understand Mirabeau. . . ." For Bryan had transformed the "chaotic" and "individualistic" delegates into a body, "mono-maniacally" focused on him. Here, indeed, was the leader the delegates were seeking, and here was the "miracle" for which the Nebraskan had long hoped.

Selected ultimately on the fifth ballot, Bryan now carried his cause to the people. Just as his rhetoric had determined the course of the convention, it now, in large degree, transformed the nature of the national campaign. Embarking on an unprecedented whistle-stop tour of the nation, Bryan continued to focus on the silver issue; and, in fiery tones, he appealed to the hard-pressed farmers and workers with accusations that the corporate interests were destroying economic opportunity for the common man.

As Bryan's popularity rose, so also did the fears of the Republican Party. Having nominated William McKinley on a platform that opposed silver coinage, the Grand Old Party had hoped for an easy victory—and quite reasonably so in light of the popular disenchantment with the present Democratic administration. But with Bryan as their opponent, there was obviously a need for more than just the normal campaign. Although they had intended to ignore the question of currency, McKinley's supporters now found they had to deal with it.

While Bryan introduced the country to a stump campaign, the Republicans, under the inspiration of Mark Hanna, embarked upon a campaign that was to exceed all others in cost and organization. Barraging the American electorate with all forms of literature, Hanna and his cohorts consumed a campaign chest of over 3.5 million dollars in their efforts to convince the public of the wisdom of a gold standard.

In the end, superior Republican organization and resources won out. But in a certain sense, Bryan had attained victory also. For while articulating the cause of silver, the importance of which he most certainly overrated, he was also giving eloquent voice to the need for reorientation of a national government that had for too long given free rein to the nation's corporate interests. Reflecting the feelings particularly of farmers, his campaign for silver symbolized the very real need to control industrial and commercial interests whose unchecked power had enabled them to ignore public interest. In this sense then, the Bryan of 1896 was really a harbinger of the many reforms that were to take place during the Progressive period of the early 1900s. Although many historians have come to believe that Bryan's crusade resulted from a reactionary desire to return America to the mythical time in the past when agrarian interests presumably held sway, his campaign did result in an awareness on the part of many thoughtful Americans of the need for government to adjust its functions and policies to the popular needs of an industrial society.

Bryan 16-to-1 clock   CORNELL UNIVERSITY, DOUGLAS COLLECTION

JOHN MC AULEY PALMER   *Aaron E. Darling, 1869   Oil on canvas, 44 x 34 inches*
Illinois State Capitol Collection, Springfield

John McAuley Palmer *National Democrat*

1817-1900

With the nomination of Bryan in 1896 and the acceptance by the Democrats of a platform repudiating the Cleveland administration, the once ascendant "gold" Democrats found themselves without a candidate. For some of these conservative representatives of American business interests, Bryan's candidacy simply meant temporary retirement from the political arena. Though loyal to the party, they could not bring themselves to take up the cause of the "Great Commoner." Many followed the example of the long-time activist, David B. Hill, who summarized his political abstinence with the famous quip: "I am still a Democrat—very still."

Some of the "Bourbon" dissidents, however, could not sit idly by while Bryan stormed the country with his silver heresies. While not attracting any of the more prominent party regulars, 884 of these splintered activists convened in Indianapolis several weeks after Bryan's nomination to form a party that would truly represent the views of "right-thinking" Democrats who sincerely believed that Bryan Democrats were "bolters."

Calling themselves the National Democrats, the rump convention drew up a platform deploring the "grave departures from Democratic principles" that had occurred in Chicago and staunchly defending Cleveland's gold policy. As their candidate and chief spokesman they selected former Illinois governor and then United States senator, John M. Palmer.

In light of his political career, which began in 1840 when he campaigned for Martin Van Buren, Palmer seems, indeed, an appropriate choice. If anything, he was a true political maverick. Having deserted the Democrats in the 1850s to help form the Republican Party in Illinois, he joined the Liberal Republicans of 1872 in opposing the reelection of President Grant; and, finally, attracted to Tilden's reform record, he returned to the Democratic fold to support the New Yorker's presidential candidacy in 1876.

Always placing personal belief above party loyalty, Palmer took fierce pride in the fact that he had never been the "slave of any party." In 1896, then, this man of principle was little concerned that his candidacy might threaten the party solidarity which the Democrats so sorely needed to win against William McKinley.

In fact, it was this very solidarity that Palmer intended to break. Never expecting to win himself, his major hope lay in attracting enough Democratic votes to ensure McKinley's victory. With the tacit endorsement of Cleveland, the seventy-nine-year-old candidate visited most major cities east of the Mississippi in his effort to alert the public to the dangers of Bryan's beliefs.

In the end, Palmer's efforts had little impact. McKinley's well-organized and convincing campaign would have sufficed for a Republican victory. But despite his negligible effect on the final outcome, Palmer and his fellow bolters were manifestations of a trend which was to set 1896 uniquely apart from most other elections of the period.

The Democrats were not the only party to be affected by the silver issue; both the Republican and Prohibition parties also experienced division on this question. Thus, the "silver" Republicans, led by Henry Teller of Colorado, ultimately shifted their support to Bryan; and in response to their party's failure to adopt a silver plank, the "broad gauge" Prohibitionists also followed suit by forming the independent National Party with Nebraskan Charles E. Bentley as their presidential candidate.

Considering Palmer, then, in relation to these other party splits, the candidacy of the "gold" Democrat clearly indicates the political havoc that the silver issue had generated. Palmer symbolized the deep sense of conviction in 1896 which submerged traditional loyalties to party and for the first time since the Civil War gave precedence to a real political issue.

Bryan campaign poster   LIBRARY OF CONGRESS

William Jennings Bryan *Democrat*

1860-1925

Despite his defeat in 1896, William Jennings Bryan remained a powerful influence in the Democratic Party. Still the spokesman for silver, he was convinced that currency would again be the issue in 1900 and that he would be the Democrats' choice on a platform emphasizing bimetallism.

Bryan, however, was only partially correct. His lecturing and appearances before state legislatures on behalf of antitrust legislation had kept him in the public eye, and therefore he was unquestionably the strongest presidential hopeful in his party. Aware of this, the Democrats saw no alternative but to honor him with renomination. Silver, on the other hand, was only indirectly an issue. The years between 1896 and 1900 had spawned new political questions. With the end of the Spanish–American War in 1898, the United States, through a treaty with Spain, had become an imperialistic nation, extending her power in the Caribbean and Pacific. The heated debate that waged over American policy in its newly acquired domains, especially in the Philippines where the natives resented American rule as much as they had Spanish, stimulated larger questions about American foreign policy. Also overshadowing the silver issue was the problem of rapidly proliferating business trusts which by 1900 had come to dominate almost every major American industry.

Thus, although a silver plank at Bryan's insistence found expression in the Democratic platform, the party opposition to President McKinley's imperialistic policies in the Philippines assumed "paramount" importance. To a lesser degree, the Democratic Party also emphasized the issue of trusts and accused the Republican administration of sanctioning their organization to the detriment of small business.

Wisely, Bryan accepted this shift in emphasis and so overcame the factionalism in the party that had characterized his candidacy in 1896. Although his receptivity to this change resulted, in part, from his ability to shift with prevailing political winds, he nevertheless shared in his party's convictions. The democratic idealism that had stimulated his silver crusade convinced Bryan that it was wrong to deny self-rule to another people. Although he had publicly supported the Spanish–American War out of sympathy for the down-trodden Cubans and had

Bryan pin   CORNELL UNIVERSITY, DOUGLAS COLLECTION

served in the American army in 1898, he flatly opposed annexation of the Philippines because of the opposition of the population to American rule. "God himself . . .", he proclaimed in 1900, "never made a race of people so low in the scales of civilization or intelligence that it welcomes a foreign master."

Just as annexation denied political rights to the Philippines, the trusts, in Bryan's view, stripped Americans of their economic rights. Open competition, he believed, had given way to a powerful industrial "plutocracy" whose ascendance in the marketplace was rapidly displacing the small competitor and placing the consumer as well as the worker at its mercy.

Although these were the questions that Bryan emphasized throughout the campaign, the silver issue came back to haunt him. Emphasizing "the full dinner pail," the Republicans with the aid of McKinley's presidential running-mate Theodore Roosevelt and his "inexhaustible vocabulary of vilification" again cast Bryan and his bimetallist ideas as the symbol of national financial disaster. Prominent anti-imperialist Republicans reluctantly supported McKinley out of their fear of Bryan's monetary position. And even prominent Democrats were distrustful of the silver champion of 1896. Grover Cleveland, for example, despite his distaste for McKinley's foreign policy, gave his vote to the Republican, declaring: "It is a choice between evils and I am going to shut my eyes, hold my nose, vote, go home and disinfect myself."

More significant, however, independent voters agreed with these party regulars. Satisfied with increased prosperity, they readily sympathized with the economic conservatism of the Republican Party. In contrast, Bryan's continuous attacks on McKinley's imperialism were too abstract to arouse popular support. While voters might have found merit in the Democrat's eloquent invectives against trusts, they remained coolly indifferent to his attacks on Republican foreign policy. As one Bryan supporter put it, "American people could not be aroused by any wrongs done to people across the sea"; or as one Midwestern farmer philosophically observed, "Well I guess we can stand it [imperialism] so long as hogs are 20 cents a hundred."

ALTON B. PARKER   *Princess Lwoff-Parlaghy*   *Crayon on paper, 31½ x 25½ inches*
Cortland County Historical Society, Inc., Cortland, New York

Alton B. Parker *Democrat*

1852-1926

Considered one of America's dullest elections, the contest of 1904 lacked the two ingredients that might have saved it from lethargy. The issues that had been aired in 1896 and 1900 were dead, and as yet, no new political questions had appeared capable of arousing the electorate. With policies toward our Pacific territories firmly established, the debate over imperialism had lost its momentum. A gold standard was now an accepted fact of life, and in light of Theodore Roosevelt's growing reputation as a "trust-buster," Democrats could hardly expect to generate controversy by accusing their opponent of being the friend of monopoly.

Along with this dearth of issues, the behavior of the two major candidates also added to the political sluggishness of 1904. Following the precedent set by his predecessors, Republican-incumbent Roosevelt, whose vigorous speeches had added so much color and force to the election of 1900, refrained from active campaigning. Similarly, Democratic hopeful Alton B. Parker, for the most part, pursued a strategy of silence. Thus, the bitter clashes that had characterized the two previous presidential elections were practically nonexistent, and it was not until the very end that the campaign took on any semblance of a real contest.

Unknown nationally, Alton B. Parker won the presidential nomination largely due to the resurgence of monetary conservatives within the Democratic Party, who, after Bryan's defeats in 1896 and 1900, were able to recapture control of the party machinery. Under the leadership of the New York boss, David B. Hill, the again-powerful gold Democrats went in search of a candidate who would represent their views on currency while at the same time placating the Bryan factions.

Aside from his relative political obscurity, Parker met these qualifications. The son of a farmer from rural New York and a lawyer by profession, he had been involved in New York's Democratic politics since the early 1870s, and in 1877 was elected surrogate of Ulster County. After supporting Cleveland in 1884, he became chairman of the Democratic state committee and as such managed Hill's gubernatorial campaign so effectively that he succeeded in winning election for his party's entire state ticket.

Rewarded for his services with an appointment to the state Supreme Court in 1885 and to the state's Court of Appeals four years later, Parker eventually was elected by popular vote chief justice of the appeals court. While serving in these judicial capacities, he won a considerable state reputation for his favorable rulings on the rights of labor and antitrust legislation, most notable of which were his decisions upholding the closed union shop and the New York statute limiting the hours of bakery workers.

In addition to his liberal, pro-labor judicial record, which undoubtedly appealed to the Bryan faction's prejudices against big business, Parker's primary asset in 1904 lay in the fact that he had alienated no one in his party. Although a gold Democrat himself, he had faithfully supported Bryan in 1896 and 1900. Therefore, unlike Hill and so many other monetary conservatives, he was immune to the Bryanites' accusations of party disloyalty.

Further strengthening Parker's chances at the Democratic convention were his equivocal views on the question of southern disenfranchisement of the blacks. While never overtly approving southern policies, he nevertheless appealed to southern Democrats with his criticism

Alton Parker pin SMITHSONIAN INSTITUTION

of the Fourteenth Amendment and its power to restrict state actions in the field of civil rights.

Finally, the only other alternative to Parker in 1904, William Randolph Hearst, pushed indecisive Democrats closer to the conservatives' choice. Despite his well-publicized advocacy of the eight-hour day and government ownership of railroads, even old Bryan supporters shied away from the newspaper titan as a result of his well-known disregard in private life of middle-class morality.

Thus, although he never openly courted nomination, Parker soon became the party favorite. After a short flurry of criticism from Bryan and others over the failure of the platform committee to include a bimetallist plank, Hill led the convention to the overwhelming endorsement of his candidate on the first ballot.

For the most part, Parker presented an unexciting image to the public. Though not a reluctant candidate, he lacked the "feverish ambition" that might have given vitality to his campaign. Certainly, he could not match the "magnetic quality" that rendered Theodore Roosevelt so appealing. Worse still, he hardly campaigned. It was not until the last weeks of the election that he mounted an aggressive attack against his Republican opponent whom he then accused of catering to trusts in return for campaign funds.

Despite this last-minute effort, Parker's cause was hopeless. Without a real issue to excite the popular imagination, he suffered an overwhelming defeat such as had not visited any presidential candidate since Henry Clay in 1832.

THOMAS EDWARD WATSON *Edward S. Siebert, 1920* *Oil on canvas, 46 x 36 inches* *State of Georgia*

Thomas E. Watson *Populist*

1856-1922

In 1896, Georgian agrarian, Tom Watson, retired from the political arena where his fiery rhetoric and personality had made him a formidable figure and, carrying away with him "a heavier heart" than "any soldier of the Southern Confederacy carried away from Appomattox," he retreated to the peaceful environs of rural "Hickory Hill." A leader in the southern farmers' movement in the early nineties, he had only reluctantly consented to become Bryan's Populist running-mate in 1896. Southern Populists had been engaged in a bitter fight with the monolithic Democratic Party for years in an effort to break their control over southern economic and political life. To be asked now to cooperate with the enemy represented "a shameless bargain," and it became particularly shameful when Bryan refused to repudiate his conservative Democratic running-mate, Arthur Sewall, a wealthy Maine banker. Watson nevertheless campaigned for the Populist ticket in the hope that his doing so might save Populism from the emasculating clutches of the more conservative Democratic Party.

Ultimately unsuccessful in his efforts to swing votes to Bryan's Populist ticket, Watson felt dejected and humiliated. "If ever a poor devil," he later wrote, "had been outlawed and vilified and persecuted and misrepresented and howled down and mobbed and threatened until he was well nigh mad, I was he." And so for the next eight years, he lived in a self-imposed political limbo.

A product of the rural Georgia "squirarchy" that had been impoverished by the Civil War, Watson had been bred in the South's romantic agrarian tradition. Unlike the New South proponents of the late seventies and eighties who saw industrial development as the solution to their region's economic problems, he consistently believed that the South's best interests lay in revitalizing the region's rural tradition. In 1882, in the face of the mounting New South agitation, he mused: "The Past! No wonder it is seemingly better. There lie our brightest and purest hopes, our best endeavours. . . ."

Not surprisingly, then, in the midst of a prospering law career, Watson identified himself with Georgia's agrarian reform movement that, developing during the 1880s, represented an emotion-laden response to the ever-worsening rural conditions of his native Georgia. By

301

1890, with the aid of his gift for rustic metaphor and his evangelistic platform style, he had become the leading figure in the Georgia farmers' revolt against big business and its growing domination of American life.

Having already demonstrated his agrarian sympathies as a state legislator in the early eighties, Watson continued his defense of Georgia's farm interests throughout the decade. The constant foe of New South politicians who in his view were sacrificing rural interests for the sake of promoting industrial enterprise, he vocally opposed the granting of legislative favors to big business. But the action that finally placed him in the forefront of his cause and won him the lasting support of the recently formed Farmers' Alliance, was his leadership in the successful farmers' boycott that ultimately forced the "jute-bagging" trust to reduce its exorbitant rates to farmers.

Elected to Congress in 1890 with the enthusiastic support of local Alliance men, Watson soon declared himself a member of the newly formed Populist Party. As the new party's House leader, he proposed bills relating to almost every Populist reform. At the same time, he founded the *People's Party Paper* and in 1892 published *The People's Party Campaign Book* in which he forcefully attacked the alliance between business and government.

Between 1892 and 1896, however, Watson suffered bitter political setbacks. The victim of two of the most fraudulent and bloody election contests ever fought in local politics, he failed in both his attempts to regain his seat in Congress. In light of these two defeats, the election of 1896 became the last straw. Humiliated once again, he declared his retirement from politics.

Watson enjoyed an active life at Hickory Hill. He busied himself with a thriving law practice, and turned to the writing of history, completing a biography of Thomas Jefferson, whose theories of agrarian democracy he had always revered, a two-volume *Story of France,* and a study of Napoleon with whose upward struggles against poverty and class persecution he could easily identify.

In 1904, Watson, along with other Populists, felt a new sense of confidence. With the gold factions again in control of the Democratic Party, the Populists now hoped to lure the silver Democrats, including Bryan, away from their party and into the Populist camp. Thus, after winning the Populist presidential nomination that year, Watson enthusiastically stumped the country, and in doing so, provided the election with what little color it had. As one contemporary observer put it: "[Watson] is entertaining; he does funny things with language, laughs himself and gives hilarity to the crowd."

But although voters enjoyed his colorful rhetoric in which he referred to Roosevelt and Parker as "two drinks from the same jug," Watson did not win their support. Following the advice of Bryan, that "every vote for Watson is a vote for Roosevelt," silver Democrats for the most part remained loyal to Parker.

After 1904, Watson's public career took a strange and drastic turn. With racial prejudice as his keynote, he, like some other southern Populists before him, turned against the blacks, whom he had formerly considered as allies of poor white farmers in their fight against white conservatives. He now saw them as the nemesis of his cause. Feeling that white voters had remained faithful to the party of white supremacy out of fear that the success of Populism would bring more political power to blacks, he applied his energies to the cause of black disenfranchisement. In doing so, Watson helped to spur the bitter outbursts of racism that were to lead to the bloody Atlanta riots of 1906 and the ultimate rebirth in 1915 of the Ku Klux Klan.

Expanding on his crusade of bigotry after 1910, Watson turned his invectives against Catholics and Jews. When a Jew, Leo Frank, was imprisoned for murder, it was his flaming rhetoric of hate that unleashed the mob that was ultimately responsible for Frank's lynching.

Although he remained in the dying Populist Party long enough to be its token presidential candidate in 1908, Watson returned to the Democratic Party in 1910. Still maintaining a popular following, he became an influential power in the organization and in 1920 was overwhelmingly elected to the Senate where he finished out his colorful career as the articulate opponent of the League of Nations and what he considered to be the growing militarism of American foreign policy.

To explain Watson's flight from liberalism into policies of bigotry and racism would probably demand the vocabulary of a psychiatrist. But it is important to point out, as Richard Hofstadter and others have already, the conservatism in some aspects of the Populist movement. As an agrarian, representing the poor farmer of the South, Watson sought measures and panaceas that would help men of his class. When the southern Democratic machine cast its whole mechanism against such a splinter group as the Populists, fearing it as a divisive force in the solid Democratic white front, the Populists lost their hold in that region. They became identified with blacks and, therefore, subject to the prejudices of the southern farmer whom they were attempting to help. Either consciously or unconsciously, Watson, by articulating traditional racist concepts was appealing for reacceptance into the Democratic Party, where he could serve the farmer against the restraints of big business. In the last analysis, his campaigns represented the rural resentment of the financial power of the North and Northeast. He could see no further than the farm or farmer, and it was this narrowness of vision and purpose that contributed to his loss of power and his defeat.

"Miss Democracy's Valentine," by Clifford Berryman LIBRARY OF CONGRESS

William Jennings Bryan *Democrat*

1860-1925

After the debacle of 1904, William Jennings Bryan again emerged as the Democrats' most likely presidential candidate. Due in part to the fact that there again was no one to equal the Nebraskan's national stature, his nomination also resulted from his diligence as a party worker. In the years between 1904 and 1908, Bryan had earned the gratitude of many Democrats through his constant willingness to aid the local candidates of various states in their campaigns for office.

While he mended his political fences, Bryan also kept himself before the public as the vocal critic of Theodore Roosevelt's second administration. Through his newspaper *The Commoner* and in speeches throughout the country, he criticized Republican progressivism for failure to arrive at a well-formulated program. And although he applauded Roosevelt for his antitrust policies and increasingly vigorous stand on railroad regulation, Bryan nevertheless accused the progressive Republicans of taking only halfway measures. When a reporter asked him how he felt about Roosevelt's appropriation of his ideas in the area of business and labor reforms, he replied: "He didn't take all my clothes. I doubt whether what he did get fit him very well."

By the time the Democrats convened in 1908, Bryan was the front-runner. Despite minor efforts of the more conservative party elements who shared Woodrow Wilson's desire to "knock [the Nebraskan] once and for all into a cocked hat," he won his third nomination for the presidency.

In the course of this last campaign, in which he faced Roosevelt's hand-picked successor, William Howard Taft, Bryan achieved respectability. Roosevelt's progressivism had significantly decreased the popular tendency to view Bryan as the prophet of economic doom. Silver was forgotten, and, as the Republican *Nation* observed, "People really can't work themselves up into a fright . . . any more. . . . How can they be expected to despise in Bryan what they have applauded in Roosevelt?" Even Bryan's old arch-enemy, Grover Cleveland, for the first time did not seriously object to the Nebraskan's candidacy.

Taking full advantage of his new-found respectability, Bryan focused his campaign on the

Bryan ribbon   SMITHSONIAN INSTITUTION

argument that Republican reform had not gone far enough. With an eye to the labor vote that he had failed to attract in his previous campaigns, he emphasized the need for legislation that would curb the use of antitrust laws in disbanding organized strikes. Further hoping to tarnish the GOP's seemingly impeccable reputation as the foe of industrial monopolies, he accused the Republicans of being incapable of extensive antitrust actions in view of the party's traditional alliance with big business.

Ironically, Bryan's third failure to win the presidency resulted in large degree from the popular acceptance of his views. With so many of his ideas already implemented, he now seemed politically passé. Unlike 1896, his positions no longer electrified his audiences, nor did they inspire the spontaneity that had characterized his political rise. As one biographer has pointed out, he had "outworn his novelty."

Also conspiring against Bryan was his close association with Governor Charles Haskell of Oklahoma, the treasurer of the Democratic Party. Given the latter's fraudulent dealings with the Standard Oil Trust, Taft campaigners were able to rally support by questioning the sincerity of Bryan's promises for more stringent antitrust regulations. Bryan's failure to lure eastern labor, to whom Republicans still represented the party of prosperity, also contributed to his defeat, despite the Democratic stand on the rights of labor.

Bryan never again became a candidate for office, but he still continued to play an influential role in the affairs of his party. In 1912, he helped turn the Democratic convention to Woodrow Wilson, when he very characteristically announced his refusal to vote for Champ Clark, on the grounds that Clark was the favorite of the party's business factions. In return for his support, Wilson appointed Bryan secretary of state; however, as Wilson pushed America toward active involvement in World War I, Bryan's pacifist beliefs forced his resignation.

A religious fundamentalist all his life, Bryan made his last public appearance as prosecutor in the famous Scopes trial of 1925. Arguing that evolution stood in contradiction of God's word as presented in the Book of Genesis, he defended the Tennessee law prohibiting the teaching of Darwinism. Exhausted by the drawn-out legal proceedings, he died five days after the trial ended.

Unfortunately Bryan's last act, in defense of a theology that had for the most part become an anachronism in the light of twentieth-century scientific progress, overshadowed the very substantial accomplishments of his career. Forgetting his role in the earlier reform movement, many people came to view the "Great Commoner" as a rather ludicrous reactionary, unable to accept the realities of modern technology. Nevertheless, the fact remains that Bryan's perceptions of the social and economic problems of his day in large degree led America toward the political adjustments that had become so necessary in the face of the nation's industrial development.

Progressives All 1912

IN 1909, AFTER TWO ALMOST COMPLETE TERMS AS PRESIDENT, THEODORE ROOSEVELT turned the reins of government over to his hand-picked successor, William Howard Taft, and sailed to Europe and Africa for another kind of big-game hunting. Fifteen months later, he returned to the United States, having shot nine lions, five elephants, thirteen rhinoceroses, and seven hippopotamuses with the help of three gunsmen who were far better marksmen. He returned to find the Republican Party divided, the program of reform he had begun clogged by the obstructions of Old Guard Conservatives, and liberals in the party bitter at the failure of their program. Fifteen months later, President William Howard Taft and former President Roosevelt were not on speaking terms; in the press and in private letters, they were bitterly critical of each other's behavior.

What had happened to Republican progressivism, so auspiciously begun at the turn of the century by Theodore Roosevelt, the crusader for righteousness in politics as well as in national policy? And what had happened between such good friends as Taft and Roosevelt to create disagreement and the later insurgency that prompted Roosevelt and his liberal followers —faithful Republicans all, who regarded bolting as a form of treason—to stalk out of the Republican convention in 1912 to the cries of "robber" and "thief" and launch, two months later, the Bull Moose or Progressive Party?

To a large extent what happened to the progressive Republican program was the fault of both Taft and Roosevelt. Taft was essentially a conservative. Straightforward, honest, and dedicated to duty, he found himself caught between his own predilections and what he knew was expected of him by Roosevelt. He was not a political animal, nor did he possess skill of leadership, and what Roosevelt would have finessed, he handled straight-on—and clumsily.

Roosevelt was the opposite of Taft in many ways. His progressivism was as much a result of energy as it was of belief, perhaps even more so. He believed especially—and this belief was also a matter of temperament—that the president could do anything not forbidden by law. He also believed in his own righteousness and acted always in the light of that belief. Essentially a man of action, he vigorously and unhesitatingly asserted executive leadership; thus inspiring loyalty to himself more than to his policies, and influencing men not by the force of intellect but of personality. As a result, Roosevelt when president overlooked the necessity to create within the Republican Party a staff devoted only to progressive reforms and capable of maintaining such a program in the face of administrative changeover.

Moreover, Roosevelt's "theatrics" interfered with his long-range effectiveness. He could dramatize progressivism and seemingly radical reforms, and make them appear respectable. Sometimes, however, his dramatizations obscured the core issues, while the necessity to make reform respectable frequently led him into compromises. Thus, he pleased no one: his reforms which smacked of radicalism alienated the conservatives and even the moderates within the Republican Party, despite his attempts to win them over by not taking strong action after he had shouted strong words. His failure to follow through cost him the support of independent liberals and reformers who believed he did not go far enough. On the one hand, he denounced "malefactors of great wealth," but he also denounced the muckrakers who were busily exposing such malefactors. He demanded a square deal for labor, but he was scathing in his descriptions of labor reformers, whom he believed were socialists intent on taking the country down the road to anarchy. Roosevelt avoided controversial issues—and it might have been better if Taft had, too, for these were essentially the causes of the falling-out between Taft and Roosevelt and the formation of insurgent Republicanism devoted exclusively to progressive reform.

Tariff reform was of primary significance in 1910; even the Republican Platform Committee of 1908 clearly recognized it as such, and in its platform promised to revise the tariff schedules. There was pressing need for lowering tariff rates, given the rising costs of living and the increasing number of trusts growing strong on the basis of the artificial protection accorded to American industry. Taft, when inaugurated, called for a new tariff that would afford merely a protection equal to the difference between the cost of production at home and abroad; but something happened to the tariff bill on the way from the House, where it originated, to the Senate, where special interests were actively at work to change the schedules. Of the 846 changes made in the bill in the Senate, 600 of them were upward. As the humorous columnist "Mr. Dooley" explained to his patient friend, Mr. Hennessy:

"Th' Republican Party has been thru to its promises. Look at th' free list if ye don't believe it. Practically iverything nicessary to existence comes in free. Here it is. Curling stones, teeth, sea moss, newspapers, nux vomica, Pulu, canary bird seed, divvy-divvy, spunk, hog bristles, marshmallows, silk worm eggs, stilts, skeletons, and leeches. Th' new tariff bill puts these familyar commodyties within th' reach iv all."

Under the leadership of Robert LaFollette, the progressive senator from Wisconsin, the opponents of the tariff waged one of the most stirring, but ineffectual, debates in American political history. They attacked the schedules one by one analyzing the connection between each item and the burgeoning trusts. Failing in the Senate, they urged Taft to veto the bill, but Taft, vacillating and at first undecided, refused, and later declared the Payne-Aldrich tariff "the best tariff bill the Republican Party has ever passed."

One of the bitterest causes for division between the former president and the incumbent in 1908-1909 was the question of "Uncle Joe" Cannon's eligibility for the Speakership of the House—a question of little importance now, but one that then seemed significant. Cannon represented the most orthodox Republicans, a spokesman for special interests, and a symbol of all that progressive Republicanism opposed. Roosevelt had hedged on Cannon, publicly denouncing him while privately reassuring him of his faithfulness and friendship; Taft could not perform thus. "There is no use trying to be William Howard Taft with Roosevelt's ways," he wrote, ". . . our ways are different." Taft did not interfere with the fight for the Speakership, and so lost the loyalty of the liberal Republicans; but the fight against Joe Cannon weakened Cannon's strength and, in turn, weakened the strength of the president who did not oppose him.

Taft's position on conservation and the fact that one of his appointees seemed to be permitting Guggenheim mining interests to obtain reserved coal lands in Alaska—an exaggerated accusation—did not help his standing with progressives in his party either, since under Roosevelt conservation had loomed large in the progressive reform program. The estrangement between the two former friends was sharpened by the fact that in this controversy their own appointees and loyal followers were involved.

Taft's "rule of reason" as applied to trusts, finally, accentuated the intraparty differences. Despite the fact that it was during Taft's administration that the Standard Oil Trust and the Tobacco Trust were dissolved under the Sherman Antitrust Act, the quick reorganization of these trusts into new companies with the same set of officers proved to liberals that business organizations of this size constituted a threat to economic freedom. Taft's rule of reason—that a trust ought to be judged in terms of whether or not its restraint on trade was "reasonable" or "undue"—obviously did not operate effectively. Liberals who feared the gaining strength of the business monopoly that was rapidly changing the face of American industry turned against Taft's sincere reform efforts.

There is no question that Taft's administration did introduce some important liberal reforms like the Mann-Elkins Act of 1910 regulating railroad rates, the establishment of a federal Children's Bureau, the division of the Department of Commerce and Labor into two separate departments, the expansion of the merit system in the Civil Service, and the proposal to the states of the Sixteenth and Seventeenth Amendments to the Constitution authorizing the laying of an income tax and the direct election of senators. These, however, were insufficient to the group calling themselves "Insurgents," and they were insufficient to the returned Roosevelt, who believed that Taft was a traitor to the progressive cause and was leading the Republicans down the road to defeat; in the midterm election of 1910 the Democrats had gained an impressive majority in the House and had much narrowed the Republican majority in the Senate.

The crisis between Taft and Roosevelt came to a head at the Chicago Coliseum in 1912. The enthusiasm that filled the hall emanated solely from Roosevelt's Bull Moose supporters and rivaled the older Populist conventioneering in religious fervor. The rolling phrases of Roosevelt that "We stand at Armageddon and we battle for the Lord" gave the proceedings the tone of a religious revival, while the lusty singing to the tune of "Onward Christian Soldiers" of the ditty "We will follow Roosevelt" left no doubt as to where the bulk of the convention was committed. But the Old Guard triumphed—Roosevelt, in fact, did what he could to see that Taft was renominated—and by preordained plan, the Roosevelt faction marched out of the Coliseum, returning two months later to launch their own party and their own candidate.

The Bull Moose Progressive, trusting in what they called the "New Nationalism," was clearly a reform party, but what they were reforming is something of a question. Although the issue was clearly the trusts, Roosevelt did not call for trust busting. Rather, making a "confession of faith" at the convention, he called for retention of the Sherman Antitrust Act, a document now as precious to Americans as their Declaration of Independence, and asked that it be made more effective where applied. The Commission enforcing the act, he believed, had to be strengthened; the basic solution to the problem of the trusts was not "trustbusting" but federal regulation, a program easily accepted by Roosevelt's political advisers who were also his financial backers, George W. Perkins of J. P. Morgan Company and Frank A. Munsey, owner of the *New York Press.*

The Democratic Party suffered no such division as did the Republicans. Eager for victory after so many years out of office, the delegates to the convention found it easy to rally around Woodrow Wilson and his brand of Democratic progressivism—although only after forty-six ballots! In the Northeast, urban reformers looked to Wilson to effect on the national stage the kind of changes he had begun to institute at Princeton University when president, and in the state of New Jersey when governor. In the South and West, where farmers at firsthand witnessed the way in which control of their region as well as the nation was passing into the hands of the industrial classes, the movement towards progressivism within the Democratic Party was enthusiastically received. Farmers were immediately and intimately affected by the rising costs of the goods they needed in order to survive as farmers—like jute bags, machinery, oil, and oil products; they experienced directly the oppression of high railroad rates and discriminatory warehouse and railroad practices; and in their search for credit they found themselves helplessly outmaneuvered by a national bank system that seemed to further the interests of business groups and prevent a free flow of credit to rural areas. Thus, the promise of the Wilsonians to effect change in these matters brought quick response.

If progressivism had its origins in the West, it traveled quickly southward, for the South had been prepared for reform by the various farmer movements that had culminated in Populism. In many states, southern Populist leaders had forced out of the party conservative Bourbons and reoriented the Democratic Party toward more radical measures. They were ready for Wilson, then; and in Texas and Tennessee, as well as along the eastern coast of the deep South, they looked to him for help in their attempt to wrest government from the control of conservatives for more democratic ends. Wilson especially appealed to the educated and professional groups in the South, who responded to the Jeffersonian flavor of the politician–scholar's carefully reasoned "New Freedom" philosophy.

Wilson had worked out his political and economic ideas long before he campaigned for the presidency in 1912. As an academic political scientist, he had been indoctrinated in political theory and historical political practices; as a southerner, he had absorbed Jeffersonian ideals concerning free enterprise and economic individualism. What he would have the government do—and this was the substance of New Freedom political philosophy—was to remove all obstacles from the operation of the free market and make laissez-faire a practicable and just principle of government. He felt that government should avoid extending privileges and favors to any group or special interest. The tariff would have to be revised to eliminate all features in it which granted special privileges to particular industries. The national banks would have to be regulated so that they would distribute their favors equitably; a new code of business would have to be promulgated that would restore competition while preventing corporations from misusing the power already acquired by them as a result of their size. And all this would have to be carried out without conferring on government any more power than necessary; in fact, power would have to be decentralized and government would have to be taken out of business as well as out of all class and occupational enterprises.

While Wilson emphasized a mythical age of the past when all economic activity regulated itself in a kind of natural balance of supply and demand, Theodore Roosevelt—and his New Nationalism—emphasized the present and the future, where concentration of power was seen as inevitable and, indeed, necessary for efficient and scientific progress. Therefore, government must take into account such inevitabilities and plan accordingly: business, farm, and labor consolidations should be encouraged; government should balance benefits bestowed on these by granting similar benefits to those in society who were underprivileged or unfortunately affected by the consolidating processes; and government should act as a mediator balancing and directing the various interests for the good of all.

That Wilson's philosophical program was bound to fail did not enter the thinking of the many Americans who swarmed to his banner in 1912. There was something appealing about his fantasy of returning to a Jeffersonian past. When, however, after taking office, he came back to reality in the practical realization that government had to act strongly if it was to act at all with respect to the great concentrations of economic power that existed at the time, most Americans went along with him. That he ended up with a program that bespoke the validity of Roosevelt's New Nationalism rather than his own New Freedom suggests a great deal about the times as well as about the viability of progressive politics. What it suggests is that by 1912 American democracy had reached the point where expansion of democratic opportunity was regarded by at least two of the three major candidates as absolutely necessary for its survival. The fact that two progressives were battling for the presidency in 1912 suggests how far progressivism and reform had permeated the consciousness of the American people, forming and formulating the temper of the time. The contest was merely over means to an end already agreed upon by the numerous submerged groups in American life who were now seeking to be recognized and to have their needs met.

WILLIAM HOWARD TAFT *Robert Lee MacCameron, 1909 Oil on canvas,*
39½ x 31⅞ inches From the Collection of the National Portrait Gallery
Gift of Robert F. MacCameron and his sister, Miss Marguerite MacCameron NPG.65.10

William Howard Taft *Republican*

1857-1930

William Howard Taft was, during the course of his career, a practicing lawyer, assistant prosecuting attorney, collector of Internal Revenue, judge of the Superior Court of Ohio, solicitor-
general of the United States, judge of the Sixth Federal Circuit Court of Appeals, president of
the Philippine Islands Commission, secretary of war, president of the United States, professor of law at Yale, and, finally, chief justice of the Supreme Court; "always in public service,
generally in public office, and only once before he came to the White House, did he face an
election."

Taft was a man who believed in a "government of laws, not of men." Although his greatest ambition was a seat on the Supreme Court—hopefully the chief justiceship—it was a long
time coming, for loyalty to an ambitious family and a strong reluctance to leave a job un-
finished decreed otherwise. Twice while he was in the Philippines, President Theodore Roosevelt offered him a seat on the Court, which Taft refused because he felt his work in the Islands
was not complete. Then, in 1903, came Roosevelt's offer of a cabinet post—secretary of war.
After much consultation with his family, Taft accepted.

Roosevelt and Taft were said to make "an excellent team." Their personalities—one,
conservative and disciplined, the other, impetuous and unrestrained—complemented each other.
In accepting the post, Taft became the administration's "trouble-shooter" during four crowded
years. "I am overwhelmed with work. Philippine matters, Panama Canal matters, army matters, the disaster at San Francisco. . . ." These years were marked by a marvelous efficiency, and
Taft rose so highly in Roosevelt's estimation that when the president left Washington for a
vacation, he in effect gave over the governing of the nation to his secretary of war, for everything would be all right with Taft "sitting on the lid." During all this time, he carried out
Roosevelt's policies to the letter, seldom—and never publicly—disagreeing with them. By
1906, Roosevelt knew that the "continuation of his policies" depended upon a "successor who
agreed with them," and there was little question that Taft was the man. But Roosevelt was
fair with his friends. Knowing that Taft much preferred the judiciary to politics, the president
left the final decision to Taft: the Supreme Court or the presidency. "Make it the chief justice-

ship," said Mr. Taft. "Make it the presidency," said Mrs. Taft. In 1908, William Howard Taft succeeded Theodore Roosevelt as president of the United States.

Taft had a particularly difficult time adjusting to the new life. The president he had worked with so well was gone. The decisions now had to be made by William Howard Taft. "My dear Theodore," began Taft's last letter before Roosevelt sailed for Africa. "If I followed my impulse, I should still say, 'My dear Mr. President,' I cannot overcome the habit. When I am addressed as 'Mr. President,' I turn to see whether you are not at my elbow." Taft, a man of private thoughts, also said to Roosevelt, a man of public words, "I have not the facility for educating the public as you . . . so I fear that a large part of the public will feel as if I had fallen away from your ideals; but you know me better and will understand that I am still working away on the same old plan. . . ." It was an eloquent and poignant confession. It would have been easier for both if Roosevelt had remembered it in the conflict to come. Never again would it be possible for Taft to turn to "My dear Theodore" for advice and guidance.

Tariff had been the kiss of death to many a president from Thomas Jefferson to Grover Cleveland. Roosevelt, a consummate politician, avoided the issue, but Taft fell right into it. The Republican platform of 1908 promised only a "revision" in the tariff schedules; whether downward or upward, it did not specify. Taft declared himself: "I am not a high-tariff man; I am a low-tariff man." And the battle was joined. The resulting Payne-Aldrich Act was heartily disliked by everyone except Taft. By defending and praising the bill, he "reaped the unpopularity which the act itself received." The bitterness of the insurgent Republicans began with Payne-Aldrich; it reached its peak in the affair of Gifford Pinchot and Richard A. Ballinger.

The principals in the Pinchot–Ballinger drama were the president of the United States; his secretary of the interior, Richard Achilles Ballinger; a suspicious government employee, Louis R. Glavis; a "passionately zealous conservationist" and Roosevelt appointee, Gifford Pinchot. One other principal was not seen. He was in Africa, but many of the strong words and wild accusations that were thrown about were directed at him.

The affair began in *Collier's Weekly* in an editorial proclaiming "the Cunninghams and Guggenheims are reaching out" for the Alaskan coal deposits estimated at more than 3.5 million dollars. Louis R. Glavis, chief of the Field Division of the Department of the Interior, published in the next issue an article headlined by such extreme captions as "The Whitewashing of Ballinger" and "Are the Guggenheims in charge of the Department of the Interior?" Ballinger was called "tricky, furtive and menacing" in later issues, while Glavis was praised for saving "natural resources estimated at perhaps three times the amount of our entire national debt."

The charges were inaccurate and exaggerated. Ballinger handled the crisis clumsily and "permitted delays fatal to his reputation and damaging to the Taft administration." Taft, however, decided that "if I were to turn Ballinger out, in view of his innocence and in view of the conspiracy against him, I should be a white-livered skunk." Instead, Glavis was reluctantly dismissed and Pinchot soon followed. The matter had now gone beyond the issue of corruption in government and centered instead on one of the most vital parts of Roosevelt's program—conservation. Roosevelt attempted to be fair: "[I] am not yet sure whether Taft could . . . have followed any course save the one he did." The former president, however, was uncertain, and the current president—the man who believed in a "government of laws, not of men"—was discovering his predecessor had made some serious mistakes.

Although few realized it, then or now, Taft accomplished much during his administration. It was a record that, if he had been more of a political animal, he should have pointed out proudly to the electorate. With his Tariff Board, he began the first scientific study of tariff rates; as an active "trust-buster," more investigations were begun in his four years than in Roosevelt's seven; he pushed through Congress a reciprocal trade agreement with Canada, which would mean "relatively free trade" between the two countries, only to see it founder in that British dominion. Above all, Taft considered the most important question facing his administration "that of economy in expenditures and sufficiency of revenue." Roosevelt left a

William Howard Taft pin   CORNELL UNIVERSITY, DOUGLAS COLLECTION

deficit of 59 million dollars. By July 1910, between the Payne-Aldrich Tariff and new economy, there was a surplus of 13 million dollars. Previously, the budget estimates of each federal department were sent directly to Congress, with no check on them for extravagance. Now, by executive order, all estimates were first sent to Taft. As a result, the budget for 1911 was 42.8 million dollars lower than the budget for 1910.

Roosevelt returned from Africa in time for the 1910 congressional campaign at the behest of the troubled Republicans. While urging the election of a Republican House, however, Roosevelt sounded the call for his New Nationalism and, at the same time, conferred with the vocal opponents of the president, the insurgent groups. Taft was hurt and angered by his friend's new radicalism, but after the congressional defeat in November, the two settled down into seemingly cordial relations. Then came the antitrust action against the United States Steel Corporation.

The bill included among its specifications one which was unknown to Taft until after it was published. It charged that the trust's monopolistic strength was increased during the Panic of 1907 by the company's "deceiving and misleading" Roosevelt, when it was granted permis-

"Bill-a-Gain," Taft bust   CORNELL UNIVERSITY, DOUGLAS COLLECTION

sion to take over the Tennessee Coal, Iron and Railroad Company. This hit Roosevelt in his most sensitive spot—his ego—and it was a mortal blow to chances of reconciliation.

The convention of 1912 opened with Roosevelt and the Progressives vs. Taft and the Old Guard. Roosevelt entered Convention Hall in Chicago with 281 delegate votes from the primary states he had won. Taft, however, gained his more considerable strength from the states where the delegates were chosen by convention method. Roosevelt lost the battle for declaring the Taft delegates illegally elected, and also for the temporary chairmanship of the convention; in doing so, he lost the war.

The campaign was a disastrous one for the Republicans. Labor, tariff, trusts, all turned against them. Vice-President Sherman died during the campaign, and the sudden substitution of President Nicholas Murray Butler of Columbia University confused the voters. In the final balloting, Taft carried only Utah and Vermont. Within a few days, however, people began praising him—partly a very American reaction to a good loser, partly a human one in looking back on the "good old days." The crowds along Pennsylvania Avenue on the day of Wilson's inauguration cheered almost as loudly for the ex-president as for the present one, and the *New York Times* published a friendly and discerning editorial which said: "President Taft has been the victim of too much Roosevelt."

Taft, however, was not to join the ranks of retired presidents. He first joined the faculty of Yale as professor of law. Then, in 1920, President Harding named him Chief Justice of the Supreme Court—a court with an enormous backlog of cases. In the ten years he sat on the bench, Taft proved his unusual abilities as administrator and coordinator, for when he retired, the Court business was practically current. The dismal years 1908 to 1912 faded like a bad dream, and these last ten years were probably the happiest of his life.

THEODORE ROOSEVELT *Adrian Lamb, 1967, after the 1908 Phillip de Laszlo*
Oil on canvas, 50 x 40 inches From the Collection of the National Portrait Gallery,
Washington, D.C. NPG.68.28

Theodore Roosevelt *Progressive*

1858-1919

"Politics," sneered the men of the best clubs, cultivated ways, and social pretensions, "politics is a cheap affair run by saloonkeepers and horsecar conductors and shunned by gentlemen." If so, answered Theodore Roosevelt, "it merely meant that the people I knew did not belong to the governing class, and that the other people did." Without hesitation, then, and without apology, Roosevelt burst into the spittoon-filled world of politics to join the Jake Hess Republican Club, because "a young man of my bringing-up and convictions could join only the Republican party."

Roosevelt's upbringing and convictions were derived from a socially prominent and moderately wealthy New York family, who, while opposing political reform, was very active in civic affairs and philanthropies. His father, whom he adored, gave to his son "great love and patience . . . sympathy and consideration . . . combined [with an] insistence on discipline." Roosevelt's early years were considerably restricted by a weak body wracked with asthma and by poor vision, but under the direction of Theodore Roosevelt, Sr., the young boy began a program of activity and body-building which never stopped. Action was his god; doing, his goal. "Get action, do things; be sane," he said, sounding his first battle call, "don't fritter away your time; create, act, take a place wherever you are and be somebody: get action."

Roosevelt boxed with professionals; rode the Bad Lands with cowboys; defied Jay Gould, J. P. Morgan, political machines, and a pope; wrote a biography of Thomas Hart Benton in four months; started Admiral George Dewey and his squadron on their journey to Manila, disregarding his superior's orders; charged up a hill in Cuba and was recommended for the Medal of Honor—which he never received; terrorized the New York City police department; "stole" a country and built a canal; negotiated a settlement in the Russo-Japanese War and won the Nobel Prize for Peace; and at the age of fifty-six and in poor health demanded a war and a regiment from Woodrow Wilson.

"This country needs a war," Roosevelt once wrote to Henry Cabot Lodge. A war was necessary for two reasons: because "every foot of American soil, including the nearest islands in both the Pacific and Atlantic, should be in the hands of independent American states," and

Teddy and the bear vase   CORNELL UNIVERSITY, DOUGLAS COLLECTION

because expansion "was a sign and proof of greatness in the expanding nation." The battleship *Maine* sank, and a happy jingoist, now called Colonel Roosevelt, began the formation of a company composed in large part of the men he admired most: the cowboys, those men who had in them "real power of joy in battle," and who reveled "in the toil, the pain, and the danger." This "splendid little war," as John Hay called it, did not last long. But out of it came an image of Roosevelt that the American people have never relinquished: the image of the gallant soldier leading his company in the San Juan charge. "Are you afraid to stand up when I am on horseback," he shouted, and killed a Spaniard with his own hand "like a Jack rabbit." The American people overlooked his unaccountable pride in his own heavy losses, and his disgust with "a public sentiment which screamed with anguish over the loss of a couple of thousand men"; and it never heard the final indignity: "Look at those damned Spanish dead." He returned home to become governor of New York.

In his years as governor, the colonel developed a somewhat more liberal policy toward labor. During the Pullman strike of 1894, Roosevelt had carelessly indicated that he would "like to see a mob handled by the regulars, or by good State-Guards, not overscrupulous about blood-shed." Now, he was beginning to see that concessions to labor had to be made; some, he was forced to admit, even deserved to be made. The New York laborer's problem, he believed, resulted not from too few laws, but from "the lack of proper means of enforcing them." With this in view, he appointed a commission whose board included—to the delight of the unions— ten representatives of labor. But Roosevelt was not consistent in his labor policies, sometimes approving labor-reform measures and other times vetoing them. His lack of consistency and his temperamental behavior made him such a problem to the New York Republican machine controlled by Senator Thomas Collier Platt that, over his own protests, he was "kicked upstairs" to become William McKinley's running mate in 1900. Within a year, he was president.

Roosevelt's attitude toward the presidency was colored by his assumption that government involved men, not laws—or more honestly, one man—Theodore Roosevelt. When once asked how he knew justice had been done, he answered: "Because I did it."

Conservation was the one issue on which the president made no compromises or concessions. In 1905, he transferred the Forest Reserves to a branch of the Department of Agriculture —the Forest Service—and gave tremendous power to its head, Gifford Pinchot. The Forest Service could use money received from sale of its lands or products for administration of other reserves and creation of new ones and could arrest anyone violating its regulation. "While we could still say nothing but 'Please' to private forest owners," Pinchot said, "on the national Forest Reserve we could say, and we did say, 'Do this,' and 'Don't do that' . . . . From that time on it was fight, fight, fight."

In 1907, Senator C. W. Fulton of Oregon—who like "Uncle Joe" Cannon stood "not one cent for scenery"—added to the appropriations bill for the Department of Agriculture and its subordinate agencies, a clause forbidding the creation of further forest reserves within the states of Colorado, Idaho, Montana, Oregon, Washington, and Wyoming. Responding to this "sullen threat to the American future," Pinchot mounted an ingenious counterattack. During the ten days given to the president to either sign or veto the bill, the forestry office force worked "straight through . . . thirty-six and even forty-eight hours on end" to gather the material necessary for authorization as National Forests all the remaining suitable lands in those six states—twenty-one new reserves, sixteen million acres. "The opponents of the forest service turned hand springs in their wrath," Roosevelt wrote gleefully six years later.

The agitation for a canal across the Central American isthmus reached a peak in 1902 over the dispute between the proposed routes through Nicaragua or Panama, which was then governed by Colombia. The eruption of Mt. Momotombo in Nicaragua while the Senate debated the bill resulted in the choice of the Panama site—a choice warmly approved by the president. But the Hay-Herrán Treaty was unsatisfactory to the Colombian government and people. Granting $40 million to the New Panama Canal Company, but only $10 million plus $250,000 annually to Colombia, the treaty, they believed, cheated them of deserved income. The establishment of a five-kilometer-wide zone across the isthmus that would be controlled perpetually by the United States compromised Colombian sovereignty. Roosevelt was furious at the Colombian objections: "I do not think that the Bogota lot of jack rabbits should be allowed permanently to bar one of the future highways of civilization," he declared. But while he debated the suggestion of actively fomenting a revolt, the Panamians took the matter out of his hands entirely by going ahead on their own. "I did not lift my finger to incite the revolutionists," Roosevelt later wrote in his *Autobiography*, "I simply ceased to stamp out the different revolutionary fuses that were already burning." Shortly thereafter, another treaty was signed

Theodore Roosevelt ribbon   CORNELL UNIVERSITY, DOUGLAS COLLECTION

with the new Republic, virtually making Panama a United States protectorate. Throughout the affair, the president was driven by "my belief . . . that there should be the immediate establishment of easy and speedy communication by sea between the Atlantic and the Pacific. . . . If we had sat supine, this would doubtless have meant that France would have interfered . . . and the gravest international complications might have ensued." What Roosevelt left, then, was not only a great canal, but a heritage of ill will toward the United States that has never been wiped out. "I took the canal zone and let Congress debate," he said later, on one of the many occasions when he felt compelled to defend his action, "and while the debate goes on the canal does also."

After finishing his second term in the presidency, Roosevelt retired, handing over the reins of government to his hand-picked successor, William Howard Taft. He was only fifty when he declared that he now only wished to be a private citizen. Off he sped to the jungles of Africa

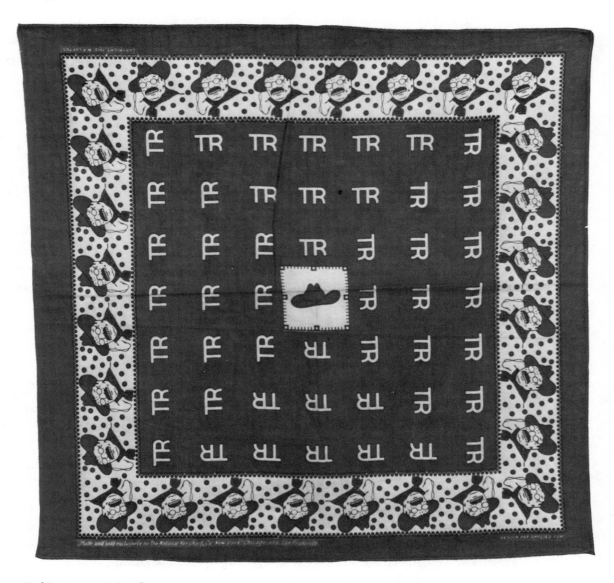

Teddy Roosevelt bandanna   CORNELL UNIVERSITY, DOUGLAS COLLECTION

327

on a trip sponsored by the Smithsonian Institution. But he had not really given up politics. By 1910, President Taft observed "that if you were to remove Roosevelt's skull now, you would find written on his brain '1912'." When Roosevelt returned to find progressive Republicanism seemingly shattered by Taft's conservatism, he went to the convention believing that he held a mandate from the people to resuscitate progressivism; indeed, he had won all but two of the state primaries in which he was entered. When Taft was nominated, then, the colonel stalked out of the convention, crying "Thou Shalt Not Steal," and the Bull Moose Progressives were born.

The third-party movement was doomed before it had begun. Of the seven governors who had begged TR to fight Taft in the Republican convention, only two joined the new Progressives. "They have not the heart for a fight," Roosevelt said bitterly, "and the minute they were up against deeds instead of words, they quit forthwith." Moreover, Roosevelt was persuaded by George Perkins, one of J. P. Morgan's partners, to delete a plank from the platform calling for the strengthening of the Sherman Antitrust Act, an action which alienated some Progressives who believed Perkins was thereby protecting his own interests in the United States Steel Corporation and International Harvester Company. Finally, rather than welcome the southern Negro to the Progressive cause, Roosevelt held to his belief "that by appealing to the best white men in the South, the men of justice and of vision as well as of strength and of leadership, and by frankly putting the movement in their hands from the outset we shall create a situation by which the colored men of the South will ultimately get justice. . . ." Northern Negroes swallowed hard, but most stayed; a small number, however, did abandon the Progressive movement. The Democrats launched the final blow. Roosevelt and his followers had hoped for the nomination of Champ Clark of Missouri, but instead they found themselves confronting Woodrow Wilson, the "strongest nominee" the Democrats could have produced, and also a declared progressive. Insisting that there was now no necessity for a third-party, Chase Osborn of Michigan, one of the two governors who had remained in the Bull Moose camp, urged Roosevelt not to run. But Roosevelt could not be deterred, for he truly believed that his New Nationalism offered a program of necessary reform for the American people.

The returns confirmed Roosevelt's fears: Wilson won with 435 electoral votes, but less than a majority in popular votes. The Bull Moose Party, however, was not entirely forgotten. Within four years, Wilson and the Democrats wrote into law the majority of the Progressive planks.

Roosevelt retired to lecture, write, and travel. One of his most agonizing adventures occurred the year before the outbreak of World War I, while in Brazil on a lecture tour. Deciding excitedly to explore the River of Doubt, an uncharted stream, he encountered disaster after disaster: two men were killed; boats, food, and equipment were lost; Kermit Roosevelt, TR's second son, and TR himself nearly lost their lives. The colonel was stricken by malaria and dysentery and ran a fever of 105 degrees—each morning the party expected to find him dead. Two months later and fifty-seven pounds lighter, he walked out of the jungle, completing a major exploration—the mapping of a river which the Brazilian government named after him.

This thoroughly unique man died still battling—although this time it was the League of Nations. For weeks afterward, the tributes continued to pour forth. "Like all Americans," wrote Newton Baker to General John J. Pershing, "I had a sympathy for his irresistible energy and courage. . . . In practically every field of human endeavor he has made his mark. . . ."

EUGENE VICTOR DEBS   *Louis Mayer, 1919   Bronze, 24 inches in height*
From the Collection of the National Portrait Gallery   NPG.68.36

Eugene Victor Debs *Socialist*

1855-1926

The reform enthusiasm that permeated the battle for the presidency among three progressives in 1912 spilled over in other political directions as well, bringing briefly to the forefront of American politics a minor party and minor candidate who had been straining for recognition since 1900. In 1912, Eugene Victor Debs, candidate of the Socialist Party, polled 900,672 votes out of approximately fifteen million cast, the highest vote received by Socialists up to that time. As a result of his campaign, eighteen new Socialist legislators obtained state or municipal offices while many smaller posts in communities throughout the country, from road inspector to sheriff, were also filled by Socialists.

Of course, 1912 was a year of political ferment and unrest. Americans were seeking answers to the many changes that had taken place in all areas of life—on the farm, in the factory, in business, and in the professions. Still seeking "the promise of American life," as Herbert Croly had titled his influential book, they listened attentively to all messages promising either reform, readjustment, or reconciliation. Perplexed by the contradictions between great wealth and great poverty, and between the material success and spiritual failure of the American dream, they were quite convinced that some kind of reform was required. Some six percent of them hoped to find this in the Socialist utopia and cooperative commonwealth so glowingly pictured by Debs.

Eugene Victor Debs came from a background of French liberalism and democratic idealism that found itself baffled by midwestern and frontier realities. His father had come from the Alsace region of France to Terre Haute, Indiana, to escape class barriers and the reactionary politics that eventuated in the great libertarian uprisings of 1848. Debs' name bespoke his father's iconoclasm and political sentiments, taken as it was from the two radical writers his father revered and who continued to exert an influence on their American namesake—Eugene Sue and Victor Hugo. Debs knew almost by heart Hugo's *Les Miserables,* a fictional portrayal of poverty that did not seem far different from the poverty and ugliness of the rough western cities and towns sprouting up under the shadow of the railroad in the post-Civil War decades.

Debs also found support for his position as social activist in American protest writings.

Largely self-educated, his intensive reading was in American history, where revolutionary figures like Thomas Paine and Patrick Henry provided him with rhetorical inspiration for his reforming efforts. He lived at a time when such giants of reform as Wendell Phillips, Robert Ingersoll, and Susan B. Anthony were striding up and down the country, from lecture platform to lecture platform, calling for radical reform of American society. He attended their lectures and absorbed their message, and he also absorbed the rhythms of their speech and oratorical tricks that entered into the development of his own oratory.

Moreover, Debs' experiences provided the reality needed to flesh out the philosophy and rhetoric that structured his behavior. The Civil War had left men crippled and widows and orphans beggared; two severe depressions marked by large-scale unemployment, starvation, and severe distress left impressions that were later to turn into convictions. He had seen the general bleakness of life in ugly frontier communities which were still bust and boom, where mud and animals competed with children in the streets, and where poverty and tawdry wealth existed side by side in accidental democracy. All these alerted him to the ills of the new industrialism. Finally, his experiences as an officer of the Brotherhood of Locomotive Firemen, which involved him in riding the railroads and caring for the insurance of workers fatally injured because of unsafe roads and equipment, educated him to "the hardships of the rail in snow, sleet and hail, of the ceaseless danger that lurks along the iron highway, the uncertainty of employment, scant wages and altogether trying lot of the working-man, so that from my very boyhood I was made to feel the wrongs of labor. . . ."

Thus it was that this gentle, humanitarian, and affectionate man, who drew to himself all sorts of people in all walks of life simply on the strength of his personality, turned to the life of a labor organizer and leader rather than to politics or business. He could have become a successful businessman or politician—even president of the United States, if he had looked straight ahead at the main chance and turned neither to the right or left. He tried business, but it was too confining; and a session as representative in the Indiana state legislature convinced him that politics involved compromise of a nature contrary to his idealism. Given his sentimentalities and social ideals, his role had to become that of an agitator, a crusader after justice. After participating in a series of confrontations between labor and management, most of which resulted in labor's defeat, he finally found a cause and a philosophy that served him well in this role for the rest of his life—socialism.

Socialism in America had its origins in Marxist theory, brought to this country especially by German scholarly immigrants like Victor Berger, who introduced Debs to a modification of Marx's lessons in the writings of Karl Kautsky. Debs accepted the rhetoric of socialism, adapted it to the American situation, clothed it in the oratory of the radical tradition, and thus brought it squarely into the mainstream of the American reform movement.

From 1900 to 1912, and again in 1920, Debs was the candidate of the Social Democrats, who later called themselves the Socialist Party. Satisfied with "immediate demands," Debs' socialism differed from that of more radical theorists who warred against compromise. Debs participated little in party organization or in theoretical definitions; instead, he tried to rise

Eugene V. Debs ribbon   CORNELL UNIVERSITY, DOUGLAS COLLECTION

above the factional splintering that constantly plagued the party's theorists, and which ultimately seriously damaged its effectiveness, and concentrated instead on his single message—the necessity to change the system. Once the environment was changed, men would change. "The civilization reared upon this old foundation is crumbling," he wrote. "Under the benign sway [of love and labor in alliance] the world can be made better and brighter." Distrusting violence, he urged the worker to turn to the ballot in order to improve his lot, and he never swayed from his belief in peaceful and orderly revolution.

In 1912 Debs found himself confronted by the western "Wobblies" of the IWW (International Workers of the World), who favored sabotage or syndicalism, and rejected political agitation as the road to social change. He also opposed the more conservative wing of the party who preferred "evolution" to "revolution" and who succeeded in having adopted a compromise platform that called for progressive reforms but, according to Debs, did not adequately represent the workers' revolutionary needs. Fearing that the reform promised by both Democratic and Progressive parties would dampen enthusiasm for socialism, especially the watered-down version his party was offering, he decided to begin his campaign early, and to wage it strenuously. Speaking five and six times a day for sixty-eight consecutive days, he criss-crossed the country, addressing enormous crowds in towns and cities, parks and public halls, receiving wild ovations wherever he went, and all the time preaching the cooperative commonwealth. As one observer said, "The raging of Debs' fire is superbly specutacular." Eighteen-thousand Philadelphians, two-thousand Oklahomans, five-thousand citizens of Indianapolis—the pattern was the same throughout the East, Midwest and Far West, and Debs' message was the same. He impugned the sincerity of the major parties promising reform, denying that either of them could adequately reconstruct the existing system. And everywhere he went, he spoke of the need to elevate the laboring man and bring equality and justice to the land.

The votes do not tell the whole story, for although the center of the Socialist strength remained where it had originated—in the Midwest—the strength of the party in Idaho, Kansas, Nebraska, Montana, Nevada, North Dakota, and Oregon weakened the appeal of Theodore Roosevelt and gave those states to the Democrats. Moreover, if all the people who voted for Debs in California, Minnesota, Pennsylvania, and Washington had instead cast their ballot for Woodrow Wilson, then those states would not have gone Progressive. In other words, the Socialist Party under Debs' inspired leadership cut into traditional voting patterns and in specific areas seriously affected by the voting results.

The election returns indicated quite clearly that the Socialists were a force in American politics. Given time, funds, and the kind of organization they demonstrated in 1912, they could well have become an even more effective force; but international politics sparked by an assassin's bullet at Sarajevo brought World War I and with it the virtual demise of socialism.

CHARLES EVANS HUGHES *Phillip de Laszlo, 1921 Oil on canvas, 35 x 27½ inches*
Chauncey Lockhart Waddell, New York

Charles Evans Hughes *Republican*

1862-1948

A jurist by profession, Charles Evans Hughes much preferred the courtroom to the political arena. Despite himself, however, politics did become an important part of his life. For while he "deemed it presumptuous" to seek elected office on his own initiative, his sense of public duty frequently compelled him to surrender to the pleas of politicians urging him to run for office. Moreover, once enveloped in the political fray, he proved himself quite capable of dealing with the realities of campaigns and elected office. So, as his supporters moved the Republican convention of 1916 toward Hughes' nomination, the reticent New Yorker calmly resigned himself to the campaign trail which was now to deny him the quiet western vacation that he had so hoped to enjoy in the summer of 1916.

Precocious as a child—he learned to read when he was three—Hughes grew up under the tutelage of his minister father whose mealtime counselings provided his son with a "regular diet of moralizing." Combining an exceptional intelligence with an acute sense of moral responsibility, it was inevitable that he should eventually take a part in the reform politics of his day.

Beginning his career as a lawyer in 1884, Hughes' reputation for thorough research and well-reasoned briefs won him wide acclaim, and by 1887 he had become a partner in one of New York City's most prestigious law firms. Though "modestly" involved in Republican politics throughout the first twenty years of his career, he had flatly shunned the idea of political office until 1905, when his life took a significant turn. As counsel for the commission set up to investigate the "Gas Trust" in New York City, he succeeded in exposing the inflated valuations and overcapitalization by which the Consolidated Gas Company justified its exorbitant rates to New Yorkers. Shortly afterward, he lent his services to still another commission, established to investigate New York's three largest life insurance companies; it was in this capacity that Hughes gained a national reputation. Uncovering malpractices that ranged everywhere from legislative bribery to the misinvestment of policyholders' funds, he helped to pioneer state regulation of this hitherto uncontrolled industry.

Like it or not, in the eyes of New York Republicans who were anxiously searching for an appealing gubernatorial candidate, Hughes was now prime political timber. In 1906 after some prodding from Theodore Roosevelt, he mounted his first successful campaign for governor.

While serving in this office, Hughes continued his reform efforts and, after two terms, had established a record that became the envy of his fellow progressives in other states. Following through his investigation of the New York gas utility, he succeeded in procuring a law establishing two new state utility commissions. In addition to framing a series of laws intended to control state banking practices, he was responsible for placing new legal curbs on the use of child labor. Finally, responding to the growing drive to control tuberculosis, he made New York one of the pioneers in the fight against this disease which had become the nation's number one cause of death.

In 1910, Hughes finally found some relief from politics. Appointed by President Taft to the Supreme Court, he spent the next six years at the work he loved best. Though he had had no previous bench experience, he drew considerable praise from other members of the Court for his skilled presentations of the majority opinion extending federal jurisdiction over railroad rates.

In 1916, Republicans were looking for a candidate who could close the divisions left by Roosevelt's Bull Moose split in 1912. As convention time drew near, Hughes seemed to be the only man capable of effecting this unity. Considered a presidential possibility as early as 1914, his record as governor and Supreme Court justice held great appeal for the progressive factions, while more conservative Republicans regarded his brand of progessivism as moderate and therefore relatively safe. Thus, after the first balloting, the perennial non-candidate gained convention strength and on the third vote became the party's unanimous choice.

Reluctant though he was, Hughes entered his campaign with energy. Focusing on the growing possibility of direct American involvement in World War I, he attacked his opponent Woodrow Wilson for his failure to prepare for war as well as for his reluctance to take stronger action against German encroachments on American neutrality. "We have outlived the time," he declared in one campaign speech, "when Americans can go up and down the earth boasting of a free government and of the unparalleled resources of America and win respect for that declaration." Thus, while Democrats incessantly repeated the slogan "he kept us out of war," and presented Wilson as the peace candidate, Hughes tried to alert voters to the need for "military preparedness."

Despite his efforts, Hughes failed. Although he captured the East, the growing pacifism and desire for neutrality among westerners kept the West in Wilson's camp. Further weakening the Republican's strength was Wilson's record in the area of labor reform. Having supported child-labor legislation and the workmen's compensation act, the White House incumbent further solidified his labor support with his last-minute support of the Adamson Act, giving railroad workers the eight-hour day. Still another factor in Hughes' defeat was the women's campaign train which toured the country on his behalf. Composed mostly of wealthy Republican women hoping to get the female vote in those western states that had already granted the franchise to women, this group of campaigners largely alienated the voters to whom they had hoped to appeal. Regarding them for the most part as "voteless moneybags" the enfranchised women of the West felt only disdain for their carefully preened sisters from the East.

Of even greater importance, however, was Hughes' failure to placate California's temperamental progressive leader, Hiram Johnson, who still remained alienated from the Republican Party. Personally popular in his own state, which Hughes vitally needed to win an electoral majority, Johnson and his following felt slighted when the Republican candidate failed to acknowledge the California leader during his tour of the state. Hughes' oversight was the result of conservative Republican efforts to keep Johnson alienated from the national party, but it unfortunately served to discourage the still-influential California progressives from actively supporting the Republican choice.

After what his biographer has called a "defeat without bitterness," Hughes gladly returned to the private practice of law. With American entry into World War I, however, he again found himself in public life as the chairman of New York's Draft Appeals Board and later as Wilson's legal investigator into purported mismanagement on the part of the army's aircraft administrator. With the end of the war, he became a leading partisan on behalf of American membership in the League of Nations. Appointed secretary of state under Harding, Hughes continued to promote international cooperation by sponsoring the disarmament conferences of the 1920s, and by serving as a member of the Court of International Justice.

In 1930, Hughes returned to the Supreme Court as chief justice. Here, he was the spokesman for the many decisions that struck down much of Franklin Roosevelt's early New Deal program. Although some accused him of being a moribund laissez-faire conservative, the root of Hughes' objections lay in what he considered to be the arbitrary nature of this revolutionary regulatory legislation. Once the New Deal reformulated its programs in more carefully defined terms, he was able to lead his Court toward approving the New Deal's constitutionality.

When he retired from public life in 1941, Hughes left the Court as one of the most respected jurists of his times. Even Roosevelt, who had so roundly criticized the Hughes Court for its "horse-and-buggy" decisions, recognized the "splendid service" Hughes had performed in guiding the Court through some of its most trying years.

JAMES MIDDLETON COX   *Douglas Chandor, 1948   Oil on canvas, 39½ x 31½ inches*
The Cox family

James Middleton Cox *Democrat*

1870-1957

As the Democratic candidate in 1920, James M. Cox experienced what he described as "the worst drubbing" in the history of presidential elections. In the popular vote, he lost by one of the widest margins ever tallied by a candidate for the highest office of the land. Even more disheartening were the results in the electoral college where the Democrats captured only the traditionally Democratic "solid South."

However total the defeat, the statistical results could hardly be taken as an indication of Cox's possible fitness as a president. Dynamic and vigorous, he had proved himself both a skilled journalist and a capable politician, and by the time he was in his mid-forties his reputation extended well beyond his native Ohio.

A farm boy, Cox had risen rapidly in his chosen profession. He began his career on the staff of his brother-in-law's small-town newspaper, but he soon moved on to the Cincinnati *Enquirer* largely as a result of his talent for sensing what would be an exclusive story. After serving as the *Enquirer's* railroad editor and political reporter, the aggressive young journalist finally struck out on his own and, in 1898, he bought the Dayton *News*. Cox's "hard-hitting" style breathed new life into this languishing newspaper, and by the early 1900s, he had succeeded in making it, along with the Springfield *Press-Republican* which he acquired in 1903, one of the most popular papers of the region.

Not satisfied with his local renown as a journalist, Cox now tried his hand at politics and in 1908 overwhelmingly won election to the House of Representatives. After serving two relatively uneventful terms in the House, he successfully ran for the Ohio governorship as a progressive Democrat, and it was in this office that he acquired the national prominence that was to lead to the 1920 presidential nomination.

A disciple of Wisconsin's reforming governor Robert LaFollette, whom he frequently praised in his campaigns, Cox proved himself an amazingly effective executive. In the face of legislative hostility, he managed the passage of over fifty major reform bills during his three terms. In addition to a workman's compensation and widow's pension law, he was responsible for upgrading Ohio's rural school system as well as for laws more strictly regulating

James M. Cox and Franklin D. Roosevelt campaign poster   SMITHSONIAN INSTITUTION

state banking practices. Still further testimony to Cox's executive abilities lay in his successful drive to outlaw child labor and provide Ohioans with the initiative and referendum.

Cox, however, was not one to rest contentedly on past political victories. As one contemporary observed of him: "When he goes fishing, he wants to catch all the fish in the creek; when he goes hunting he never quits until he has the legal limit. . . ." Thus, in 1920, he was more than a little amenable to the possibility of a presidential candidacy. Although he faced formidable competition from Woodrow Wilson's two cabinet members, William McAdoo and Attorney General A. Mitchell Palmer, the Ohioan's skillful manager persevered in the knowledge that at the convention the Wilsonian forces would be split between these two men. Finally, on the forty-fourth ballot with only McAdoo and Cox still in the running, Cox was declared the Democratic choice.

Unfortunately for Cox, 1920 was not a Democratic year. The Wilson administration had alienated many Americans. While the business world objected to the increasing stringency of the president's banking and trust legislation, workers blamed Democrats for the depression that had followed in the wake of industry's postwar adjustment to peacetime production. Tired of war and the austerity measures necessitated by military mobilization, many Americans had grown weary of Wilson's idealistic pleas for American membership in the League of Nations. The prospect of involvement in new international disputes, which Article X of the League Charter seemed to promise, had little appeal for an electorate who now wanted nothing more than to relax its vigilant posture in world affairs.

Thus, as Wilson's progressive heir and a defender of the League, Cox faced insurmountable obstacles in his campaign against Republican Warren G. Harding. Calling for senatorial approval of the League, he succeeded in attracting only small numbers of international idealists, while Harding's equivocating generalities on the issue not only provided salve for anti-Leaguers, but also appealed to the League's more moderate supporters. Similarly, on domestic questions, Cox's pleas for more effective federal action in the fields of social welfare and labor met with popular indifference and ennui. Contrary to the Democrats' belief that the country was "predominantly and decisively progressive," reform-weary voters much preferred the affable Harding, who emphasized "normalcy" and talked glowingly of "cultivat[ing] friendliness and neighborliness."

Thus, Cox's defeat marked the end of a political era. Progressive democracy and international idealism, though not dead, at least for the moment lay dormant, while business took over "as usual." Taking his cue from the electorate's decision, Cox retired from politics and devoted the remainder of his life to the management of his newspapers.

EUGENE V. DEBS   *Campaign poster   National Museum of History and Technology,*
Smithsonian Institution

Eugene Victor Debs *Socialist*

1855-1926

In 1920, Americans faced the unusual situation of being presented with a convict in the Atlanta, Georgia, prison as a presidential candidate. Convict No. 9653 was Eugene Victor Debs, who had been imprisoned a year earlier for sedition under the wartime Espionage Act. Sentenced for ten years for a speech presented in Canton, Ohio, opposing the country's entrance into the war and the repressive policy of the government against dissenters, Debs was unanimously and enthusiastically endorsed for the fifth time by the Socialist Party as "the embodiment of all the militant working class spirit . . . [as] a challenge to all who stand for repression." Amidst jubilant shouts of "we want Debs," the Socialists danced around the convention-hall floor and piled red roses high in front of their candidate's portrait. Bitterly divided between radicals and conservatives, the party found itself united on a single and happy goal—support for "the Lincoln of the Wabash," their beloved leader who had risked all—family, health, life itself —to offer himself as a symbol of protest against the injustice abroad in the land. Through conviction and imprisonment, Debs believed he could aid his party and his country best. Only that way could he dramatize the plight of the nation's victims: "while there is a lower class, I am in it," he had told the silent court during his trial; "while there is a criminal element I am of it, while there is a soul in prison, I am not free."

Debs had not been the Socialist Party's candidate in 1916. Tired from sixteen years of strenuous exertion to advance the cause, and disheartened by factional strife within the party, he had presumably retired from the political lists, leaving the presidential campaign to Allan Benson, a newspaperman and Socialist organizer, and the vice-presidential candidate, George Kirkpatrick, also a newspaperman. In 1916, the party platform concentrated its attention primarily on non-intervention in the European war, which had brought, they believed, European Socialists to ruin. But Benson, despite his writing skills and experience, was not a Debs, and the campaign of 1916 lacked the excitement and vitality that the party leader had been able to instill in his listeners and party members. Although the Socialists still were capable of mustering good-sized crowds to their rallies, they were fighting an unpopular fight; most Americans were inoculated with the virus of "100 percent Americanism" and, therefore, easily accepted

Wilson's and Charles Evans Hughes' accusation that the Socialists were enemies of the nation.

Debs did not rest as much as he had hoped during the 1916 campaign, for he had been nominated for Congress against his wishes by his Indiana friends, and soon found himself campaigning for the cause with all his old energy and enthusiasm. Even more strongly than Benson, he attacked the Wilson program that he believed was inexorably leading the country toward intervention.

Despite Debs' efforts in Indiana and the party's unceasing activity on the national front, the Socialists' campaign in 1916 was a disappointing failure, with Benson's votes—only 585,113—falling far below Debs' in 1912. Debs failed in his bid for Congress, while the party, now that unity was no longer required, tried to maintain itself in an atmosphere quickly marked by hostility and repression. With the United States' declaration of war, some Socialists accepted Wilson's justification for intervention. They opposed the more radical members of the party who insisted on pacifism, arguing that the Socialists' anti-war position lost them the respect and, therefore, the potential support of their fellow citizens. By being "peculiarly un-American," William R. Gaylord of Wisconsin insisted, the Socialists were crystallizing "needlessly the ignorant and vicious anti-Socialist prejudices" and giving "reckless occasion for those rantings by the capitalist press which will most effectively close the public mind . . . to the effective and constructive socialist propaganda—if nothing worse."

The "worse" that Gaylord foresaw as a possibility was quick to come, as the nation entered into a period of enormous repression and prejudice. Super-patriots drummed up support for the war and insisted upon uniformity in belief and behavior; disagreement was answered by lynchings, riots, and special legislation of the Justice Department against sedition and treason, both of which were equated with dissent. With the Russian revolutions of 1917, the mass hysteria increased, as unthoughtful and anxious Americans closed ranks against anyone who advocated a different—or foreign—ideology. Socialism, then, as the Detroit *Journal* succinctly put it, was "Bolshevism with a shave."

Debs could not condone the war, for his entire mature life had been devoted to pacifism; neither could he condone the unjust repression of civil rights, and he was ready to go to prison to defend his beliefs. His sacrifice was one that many responded to with sympathy and enormous affection. To the Socialists, he represented the best in their cause. Moreover, he represented their one hope of bringing unity again to a party wracked by strife and bitter factionalism, for the Russian Revolution had not left the Socialists unaffected. Members divided in their feelings about communist Russia, a division that increased once it became apparent that "the age-long dream of a reign of reason and justice" was not to be realized so quickly. The right-wing Socialists did not approve the Soviet state at all. "The Bolshevists do not favor representative government," Victor Berger, one of their oldest spokesmen, claimed; "they preach 'direct action' and the 'dictatorship of the proletariat'."

Debs was more tolerant of the Russian revolutionary forces: "From the crown of my head to the soles of my feet I am a Bolshevik, and proud of it," he had jubilantly announced upon entering prison. Later, however, he became disenchanted with the Russian experiment and condemned the murder of the Czar and his family and the unnecessary bloodshed and violence practiced by the communists. Yet, he still hoped that Russia would eventually establish the utopian community he so much longed for. He realized that Soviet communism would never meet American needs, nor could it coexist with the ideas of freedom and individualism that constituted American ideology. But his major concern was to unite the party, overlooking the divisive issue of communism. He believed he could do this, since, having lost his rights of citizenship, he was now, as he said, "a citizen of the world." For the sake of party harmony, then, he agreed to become once again a candidate, even if his campaign had to be waged from a jail cell.

The party platform in 1920 called for trade and diplomatic relations with Russia, cancellation of war debts, an international democratic parliament instead of the proposed League of Nations, freedom of speech and the press, release of political prisoners, and limitations imposed on courts and government in cases of civil liberties, along with the usual socialistic demand for nationalization of industry. The Socialists disengaged themselves from the violence and bloodshed in Russia and opposed American communist efforts to take over the party.

Against overwhelming odds, Debs' party carried on their fight for the presidency. His campaigning was restricted to issuing the 500 words a week he was permitted. The party had no money, and war and repression had weakened its organizational structure while blackening its reputation with many of the electorate. Debs received 919,799 votes, 3.55 percent of the total cast. The radical Far West no longer supported him as it had through all his previous campaigns, but now the East and Midwest responded. Much of this vote, however, indicated repudiation of Wilson more than conversion to Socialist ideals, and many Socialists realized this. Although they could congratulate themselves on receiving nearly a million votes for a candidate who was in prison, those who were clear-sighted knew that they were losing ground. "The relatively big vote was the last flicker of the dying candle," Morris Hillquit reminisced, "and did not deceive the Socialists."

One good result came from Debs out of the election. President Harding, personally a kind and gentle man and not as inflexibly committed to principle as was Wilson, ordered Debs' release from prison on Christmas Day, 1921. Debs was old and in poor health when he returned to Terre Haute, but he carried with him the love of his fellow prisoners and knowledge of prison conditions. Much of his remaining life was spent working for prison reform as well as acting as the Grand Old Man of his party. Maintaining sympathy with the Russian people, he continued to deplore the excesses of bolshevism in Russia and communism at home, tried to maintain a united party, and heal the wounds of factionalism. In 1924, he persuaded the party to endorse the candidacy of the Progressive, Robert LaFollette, thus marking the weakness of the Socialists. His death in 1926 after a long illness symbolized the slow decline of the party he had so well represented for a quarter of a century.

JOHN WILLIAM DAVIS   *Phillip de Laszlo, 1920   Oil on canvas, 44 x 27 inches*
Julia Davis Healy, Princeton

John William Davis *Democrat*

1873-1955

In the early months of 1924, John W. Davis appeared to be no more than a very remote possibility in the race for the Democratic presidential nomination. Although well known for his many services to the Wilson administration, the humorless and sedate New York lawyer, in comparison to William McAdoo and New York Governor Alfred E. Smith, inspired little enthusiasm among Democrats. Even Davis himself found the idea of his candidacy rather absurd; and, when political friends from his native West Virginia took it upon themselves to lay the groundwork for his nomination, he felt obliged to "protest" against their activities. Despite his objections, however, the Davis supporters stubbornly persevered and in what turned out to be "the longest, wildest, most turbulent" political convention in history, finally emerged the victors.

Although not previously in the political forefront, Davis was not an unknown in the Democratic Party before 1924. Disregarding the adamant opposition of his lawyer father who had become soured on politics as a result of his two terms in Congress during the scandal-ridden Grant administration, he combined political service with law practice throughout much of his adult life. While making a name for himself as both a corporate and labor lawyer in West Virginia, he also found time to serve as Democratic chairman of his county and in 1898—much to the chagrin of his father—became a representative to the state legislature where he served for one term.

In terms of political ideology, Davis found his inspiration in the ideal of the Jeffersonian tradition. Adhering to the belief that "the best government is that which governs least," he believed that a government's primary responsibility lay in safeguarding equal rights and opportunities for all. Further reflective of Jeffersonian thought, he distrusted the centralization of power and saw "local self-government" as the "indispensable" mainstay of individual liberty.

Despite his faith in the wisdom of political decentralization, Davis was not opposed to innovation in the use of federal authority. Insofar as new federal regulation served to protect the public welfare and popular equality against privileged interests, he favored the extension of centralized powers. After his election to the House of Representatives in 1910, Davis

349

identified himself increasingly with the Progressive movement and in 1913 became instrumental in framing the final draft of the Clayton Antitrust Act which in addition to expanding government control over business monopoly, largely exempted labor unions from antitrust proceedings. Still later, as Woodrow Wilson's solicitor general from 1913 to 1918, he demonstrated his progressive sympathies in his able defense of the Adamson Act for the eight-hour day, the Federal Reserve Act, and the newly instituted Income Tax.

In 1920, after serving two years as Wilson's envoy to the Court of St. James, Davis temporarily retired from politics and government service to private law practice in New York, where his clientele included Standard Oil and the Morgan Guaranty Trust—an odd enough relationship given his opposition to monopoly and privilege. Though Davis was content with his "pleasant" and "profitable" new employment, his old political allies from his days as a West Virginia politician were not. So, by June of 1924 Davis became by their urgings a contender for presidential nomination, and while he remained relatively aloof from the movement on his behalf, events drew him ever closer to Democratic endorsement.

The root of Davis' ultimate success lay in the weaknesses of the Democrats' front-running hopefuls. For while McAdoo could claim support from over half the delegates to the Democratic convention, his tacit acceptance of support from the Ku Klux Klan alienated many and prevented him from winning the required two-thirds of the convention vote. Al Smith's Irish-Catholic origins and his "wet" position on the question of prohibition, largely repelled delegates from the nation's more rural states—particularly in the South—where anti-Catholic feeling and "dry" sentiment prevailed. As the convention continued in bitter deadlock, delegates began to look to Davis as a compromise. After twenty-one days and a record-setting one hundred and two ballots, McAdoo and Smith, finally recognizing the hopelessness of their situations, threw their delegate support to Davis.

As his party's new standard-bearer, Davis acquitted himself well; however, as in 1920, the political odds ran overwhelmingly against the Democrats. Enjoying the fruits of an undreamed-of national prosperity, the American public approved the economic policies of Republican–incumbent Calvin Coolidge and his financial cabinet adviser, Andrew Mellon. As a result, voters were hardly sympathetic to Davis' attacks on the high tariff or Republican indifference to the rights of labor. Prosperity also deafened the electorate to Davis' indictment of Republican corruption that had reached its climax in the public airing of the Teapot Dome scandal of 1923. Americans generally refused to identify the puritanical Coolidge, who had been in the presidency only since Harding's death in 1923, with the series of scandals that came to light after 1922. Without the support of a united Democratic Party, which was still recovering from the political wounds left by the drawn-out convention battle, Davis found it even more crushing to realize that the Republicans were ignoring him almost entirely; instead, they concentrated their public attacks on the more threatening third-party candidate, Progressive Robert LaFollette. In doing so, the Republicans succeeded in making Davis the forgotten man. Toward the end of the campaign, Davis reflected on his anomalous position, complaining: "If scandals break out in the government, the way to treat them is—silence. If petted industries make ex-

John W. Davis ribbon CORNELL UNIVERSITY, DOUGLAS COLLECTION

tortionate profits under an extortionate tariff, the answer is—silence. . . . The Republican campaign is a vast, pervading and mysterious silence. . . ."

After 1924, Davis returned to his law practice in New York. With the exception of his public repudiation in 1936 of Franklin Roosevelt, who, in Davis' eyes was carrying federal power beyond its proper bounds, the former Democratic candidate for the most part remained aloof from national politics.

351

ROBERT M. LA FOLLETTE   *Jo Davidson, 1923   Bronze, 22 inches in height*
LaFollette Senior High School, Madison, Wisconsin   Gift of Bronson LaFollette

Robert M. LaFollette *Progressive*

1855-1925

As the decade of the twenties progressed, growing numbers of Americans came to believe that the nation was well on its way to becoming an economic paradise. As never before, industries were expanding, and with this growth employment opportunities seemed to abound. If poverty and unemployment still persisted, these were, in the eyes of many, only ephemeral problems that would soon disappear in the wake of an ever-mounting prosperity.

Certainly this vision of boundless wealth had some basis. For members of the urban middle class, the twenties assumed the aspect of a golden age. The suburban dream house, the car, the country club, now seemed more accessible than ever. And if these and other accouterments of the "good life" were not attainable immediately, they most certainly would become so in the near future.

Politically, the economic upswing which set in after 1921 had a significant impact. To many Americans, further regulation of business as well as more protective labor legislation appeared unnecessary. Business and banking leadership was guiding the nation toward undreamed-of wealth. Would not new government controls only hamper prosperity?

For some Americans, however, the prosperity of the twenties was little more than an illusion. With the end of World War I, the farmer faced the problem of overproduction and declining farm prices in what was essentially an inflationary economy. By 1922, the farmer's purchasing power in terms of non-agricultural goods was only sixty percent of what it had been in 1919. Though not as badly off, the urban worker also failed to reap the full benefits of the boom prosperity. While industrial wages began to rise after 1922, they hardly kept pace with the rising cost of living. More disturbing, labor organizations, through which workers might have realized greater material gains, lost considerable ground as a result of a postwar revival in anti-union sentiment and court decisions enabling industrial management to gain legal injunctions against striking unions.

Thus, while the burgeoning economy of the twenties convinced many Americans that progressivism had become an outmoded ideology, there were nevertheless segments of American society who continued to feel the need for reform on behalf of the nation's laboring and farming interests. By the election of 1924, a national movement was afoot to restore progressivism to its former prominence in American politics.

Founded under the title of Conference for Progressive Political Action (CPPA), this new alliance of labor, farmers, and Socialists grew out of the Non-Partisan Leagues and Farmer-Labor parties that for the past several years had been agitating for reforms on the state level. Intending to act merely as a supportive arm for progressive-minded candidates of the two major parties, the CPPA's liberal organizers had hoped to back the presidential nomination of the Wilsonian progressive, William McAdoo. However, in the light of the California Democrat's well-publicized legal association with Edward Doheny, who had been implicated in the Teapot Dome oil scandals of the early twenties, the resurging Progressives felt that they now had little alternative but to run their own presidential candidate.

In settling on Robert M. LaFollette as their nominee, the CPPA could have hardly made a more appropriate choice. Reared in an environment of rural poverty and intellectually nourished on the writings of Henry George, the Wisconsin Republican had been a long-time champion of laboring and farming interests. Always the opponent of big business and its influence in government, he had devoted his entire political career—which he began within a year of his graduation from law school—to making government more responsive to the needs of the "common man." As governor of Wisconsin from 1900 to 1905, he inspired reforms that were to make his state a pioneering model of progressive government. His dynamic state administration not only made Wisconsin one of the first states to introduce the direct primary; it also saw the passage of some of the most comprehensive banking and insurance regulations, a workman's compensation law, and legislation establishing a commission to regulate state railroads.

Beyond an impeccable progressive record that he continued to enhance during his subsequent three terms as a United States senator, LaFollette had still another important qualification that made him the best choice for the Progressives' uphill struggle against the era's political conservatism. Known to contemporaries as "Fighting Bob," he possessed an electric quality that seemed to sweep all before him. As one devotee observed:

Unfortunately for romance, LaFollette was caught young and civilized. What a pirate or highwayman, what a redhanded ripper and raider, might not this barrel of wildcats have made! What a swashbuckling Dumas hero! But alas! He is civilized!

Despite ill-health, the pugnacious LaFollette took up the Progressive's new banner with great élan. Attacking the Coolidge administration for its deplorable neglect of the welfare of the farming and laboring population, he called for laws that would finally free union strikers from the ever-stifling court injunctions. He argued for federal programs that would boost the farmer's declining incomes as well as reduce freight rates on agricultural goods. Most extreme of all, he advocated government ownership of railroads.

Probably the best general explanation for LaFollette's defeat lay in the fact that voting Americans on the whole saw no need for further economic reforms in an age of growing pros-

"Not Easily Mesmerized," by Clifford Berryman LIBRARY OF CONGRESS

perity. Important, however, was the Republican strategy which cast LaFollette and his movement as the tools of "Bolshevism." Certainly this struck a responsive chord among voters who during the "Red Scare" of 1919 and 1920 had been panicked by the thought that the communist revolution in Russia might spread to America. When Republicans attacked LaFollette for his socialistic views on government ownership, voters began to see the Wisconsin Progressive as Karl Marx reincarnated.

Also contributing to LaFollette's failure were the obstacles that Democratic and Republican local officials frequently threw in the path of his campaigning. Countless times, Progressive rallies were dispersed for "disturbing the peace." Farmers and workers were clearly intimidated into not voting for LaFollette: while in many factories signs were posted stating that if Coolidge lost, workers need not report to work, rural banks warned farmers that they could not expect extensions on their loans unless the Republicans won.

Though his defeat was personally disheartening, there was one fact in which LaFollette could take comfort: as a third-party candidate, he could claim one of the highest tallies in American history—4,822,856 popular votes.

355

ALFRED E. SMITH   *Douglas Volk   Oil on canvas, 49 x 37 inches*
New York State Office of General Services, Albany

Alfred E. Smith *Democrat*

1873 - 1944

In 1928, the Democrats' greatest hope lay in avoiding the catastrophic bitterness and infighting that had characterized their national convention four years earlier and which had done so much to alienate an already Republican-oriented voting population. In an effort to present a harmonious image, they lost little time in settling on Alfred E. Smith as their presidential standard-bearer.

Nominated by his party on the first ballot, Al Smith in many respects had the makings of a formidable candidate. A persuasive speaker of the first order, he was doubtlessly one of the most personable public figures of his day—one writer described him as "the man that everyone feels that he knows well." Smith was also an exceptionally skillful politician, capable of commanding party loyalty while at the same time pursuing an independent course. His greatest strength, however, lay in his record as a reformer.

Serving in the state assembly of New York from 1903 to 1915, Smith had first realized the need for reform of deplorable industrial labor conditions when he investigated the Triangle Shirtwaist factory fire of 1911 in which nearly one-hundred and fifty workers had died. Elected Democratic assembly leader in 1911, he helped spearhead innumerable laws to improve working conditions as well as provide security for the factory laborer. As governor from 1918 to 1920, and later from 1922 to 1928, he reorganized his state's confusing labyrinth of administrative agencies and expanded New York's state-park system; he encouraged the development of some of the nation's first low-rent housing projects and an extended program of state aid to public education. By 1928, his record in welfare and reform legislation made Smith the very symbol of what Walter Lippman so glowingly referred to as the nation's "most enlightened government."

Smith, however, faced serious obstacles in 1928. To many voters who still cherished visions of a homogeneous Protestant Anglo-Saxon America, basically rural in its orientation, this congenial "Happy Warrior" from New York appeared not suited to occupy the nation's highest office. The product of New York's immigrant melting pot, Smith epitomized all the urban forces that they feared were rapidly leading American astray. He represented fearful

Al Smith sheet-music cover   SMITHSONIAN INSTITUTION

social change that they could neither comprehend nor accept. As an Irish-Catholic who had risen from poverty to public prominence through New York's Tammany Hall, he symbolized for many Americans elements in American life that they believed to be corrosive: the corrupt urban machine, the supposed Catholic threat to the nation's time-honored tradition of church-and-state separation, and the immigrant population that posed a challenge to the nation's Anglo-Saxon Protestant heritage.

As Smith's campaign progressed, the fear created by his social, religious, and political origins became one of the major focal points of the election. Labeled by opponents as a tool of the pope, the Democrat faced an endless barrage of anti-Catholic propaganda. Conjuring up visions of a president taking orders from the papacy, one Protestant minister warned his flock that "If you vote for Al Smith, you're voting against Christ and you'll all be damned." Just one night after Smith had addressed a somewhat hostile audience in the Oklahoma City auditorium on the subject of religious toleration, popular evangelist Dr. John Roach Stratton, filling the same auditorium, enraptured his audience with his fiery diatribe on "Al Smith and the Forces of Hell."

Smith's Tammany connections also undermined his presidential chances in 1928. Since the days of Boss Tweed, Tammany Hall was identified with crime and corruption. Though personally honest and conscientious in his political dealings, the Happy Warrior's political alliances inspired his opponents to new heights in the art of political smear. While some of his detractors whispered it about that he had already purchased a site for a papal mansion on the shores of the Potomac, others predicted that the advent of Smith's administration would see "harlots" dancing on the "White House lawn."

Al Smith donkey pin   CORNELL UNIVERSITY, DOUGLAS COLLECTION

Al Smith Toby mug CORNELL UNIVERSITY, DOUGLAS COLLECTION

Ironically, in a nation where the self-made image was so frequently a source of political strength, Smith's lowly origins were also the inspiration for sneering derision. How could this "Bowery Tough," or for that matter his unassuming wife who was also the product of New York's immigrant community, possibly possess the dignity and refinement required of the nation's first family?

Bigotry and snobbery, however, do not provide a complete explanation of what turned out to be a resounding defeat for Al Smith. Any Democrat in 1928 would have been at a severe disadvantage in light of the unparalleled prosperity that Americans had enjoyed during the decade's first two Republican administrations. Despite the fact that Coolidge and Harding exerted only a negligible effect on the economy, the public could not help but feel that it was the Republicans who, indeed, held the key to the nation's economic well-being. It was inevitable, then, that the GOP candidate Herbert Hoover should maintain the political upper hand throughout the campaign. To a nation that had experienced a 40 percent rise in national income during the last eight years, the slogan "Hoover and happiness or Smith and soup houses" had unlimited appeal. Try as he might to acquaint voters with the need to alleviate rural poverty and the continuing wage lag in many industries, Smith could not dispel the legend of the Republican's "golden touch."

In spite of his defeat, Smith did, however, have an impact on the political future of his nation. For while repelling many, his urban-ethnic background in combination with his record of liberal reform, drew new forces to the Democratic fold. In unprecedented numbers, the ethnic laboring populations of the cities cast their vote for the Smith ticket and in doing so laid the groundwork that was to transform the Democratic party four years later into a coalition of liberal-urban interests.

Paradoxically, Smith did not play a significant role in the final realization of this new political alignment. Largely pushed aside by the emergence of Franklin D. Roosevelt in 1932, whom four years earlier he had helped become governor of New York, Smith gradually retreated into the background. Losing touch with the liberal movement within his party, he ultimately came to feel alienated by the more extreme features of Roosevelt's New Deal legislation and ended his political career as a vocal critic of the party to which he had devoted so much of his life.

NORMAN THOMAS *Joy Buba, 1951 Cast stone, 16¼ inches From the Collection of the National Portrait Gallery NPG.71.56.79*

Norman Thomas *Socialist*

1884-1969

In 1928, Socialist Norman Thomas embarked on what was to be the first of six presidential campaigns. In doing so, he began his career as the nation's leading spokesman for socialism in the twentieth century—a career that in retrospect played no small part in effecting significant reforms in modern American life.

The son and grandson of a minister, Thomas developed his socialist ideas only gradually. Having decided on the ministry shortly after being graduated from Princeton in 1905, he first felt the need for far-reaching social and economic reform largely as a result of his experience as a settlement worker in New York City. Here, he saw at firsthand the squalid tenement and working conditions endured by so many members of the city's immigrant labor force. Still more influential in molding his reformist outlook was his assignment to the East Harlem Presbyterian Church soon after being graduated from the Union Theological Seminary in 1911. Already well acquainted with the reform doctrines of Christian socialism which had been articulated by such prominent Protestant theologians as Walter Rauschenbush, his daily confrontation with the economic sufferings of members of his impoverished parish convinced him still more of the need for a drastic reorientation in American life and institutions. Although he was not yet quite certain of what the nature of these changes should be, he was obviously searching for answers when he inquired in 1915:

What is our democracy worth? How shall we apply it to our social, industrial and political problems? Are we preparing well for a national safety in peace or war when so many of our workers cannot even under favorable conditions make the proper living wage?

With American entry into World War I, Thomas finally cast his lot with socialism. Convinced that war and Christianity were "incompatible," he was inevitably attracted to the Socialists who were agitating against Wilson's war efforts. In 1918, believing that the war was "only the most horrible and dramatic of the many evil fruits of our present organized system of exploitation . . . which exalts competition instead of cooperation," he committed himself to the Socialist Party.

Given his talents as a writer and his "commanding presence" as a public speaker—even the cynical H. L. Mencken referred to his speeches as a "rare and exhilarating experience"—Thomas rose rapidly within his adopted party. He served as editor of two socialist publications, *The Nation* and *The New York Leader,* and became co-director of the League for Industrial Democracy which had been established to aid labor in its efforts to unionize.

In serving as the Socialist presidential standard-bearer in every election from 1928 through 1948, Thomas fully realized that he faced a "rather indifferent or even hostile" electorate who generally considered socialism the antithesis of American ideals. Nevertheless, hoping that his words and those of his supporters might generate sympathy for his cause, he consistently approached his candidacies with enthusiasm. In 1928, while Hoover Republicans talked glowingly of a "chicken in every pot," the Socialist tried to make voters aware that despite prosperity, many Americans were still not sharing in the nation's plenitude. Pointing out that the Republican high-tariff policies were operating to the disadvantage of farmers and consumers, he also decried the fact that over four-million workers were still unemployed.

Although it would be difficult to quantify the exact impact of his views on American social development, the fact remains that many of Thomas' solutions to the problems he enumerated in 1928, as well as in later elections, have in great measure been incorporated in current legislation. Old-age pensions, public works projects, public employment agencies, unemployment insurance, the five-day week—these represent only a few of the Socialist reforms that have found their way into the mainstream of American life. Although Thomas never saw the advent of his "cooperative commonwealth," in which he envisioned a society based on common ownership of social facilities and industrial machinery, his candidacies at least served as a means of popularizing reforms which at the outset seemed alien to American ideology.

Thomas' presidential campaigns represented but a fraction of his contribution to the cause of economic, political, and social equality. As "the conscience of the American people...," Thomas successfully defended in the 1930s the right of free speech and congregation against public officials who in their fear of organized labor sought to limit the civil liberties of unionists by arbitrarily applying martial law and municipal ordinances against union activities. During the New Deal period, Thomas attempted to acquaint government officials with the plight of southern sharecroppers who were being ignored by Roosevelt's agricultural program. During World War II, he applied much of his energy to defending the rights of West Coast Japanese-Americans whom the government had placed in concentration camps in fear of sabotage. Finally, in the midst of the red scare of the late forties and early fifties, no one was more active than Thomas in attempting to curb the excesses of the campaign directed at America's political left.

Thomas, then, was not simply the elder statesman of American socialism. First and foremost a humanitarian, he consistently served as the "voice" of the oppressed and underprivileged. One radio commentator aptly summarized his life, observing that "So long as [Thomas] is alive and capable of standing before a public forum, those who are alienated and excluded are not entirely mute. One man articulate in the service of so many. It is beyond Socialism, beyond political system and beyond economic doctrine."

Democracy Confronts Depression 1932

THE EMERGENCY THAT EXISTED IN 1932 HAD NO PARALLEL IN AMERICAN SOCIAL AND economic history. Depressions of varying depth had occurred time and again from colonial times on, frequently with disastrous consequences for individuals caught up in them; but seldom had the nation as a whole experienced the enormous sense of catastrophe and pessimism about the future—not only of the economy, but of the whole American system—that was experienced in 1932. It was obvious that something, or someone, was at fault, and that the promise of American life was a mere mirage when one out of four wage earners was unemployed; when nearly one farmer out of four had lost his farm; when bread lines were growing longer and longer, while hundreds were housed in "Hoovervilles" and riding freight cars in a desperate search for work; and when thousands of others were perilously close to the brink of disaster.

The decade of the twenties had been years of relative prosperity. What economic difficulties existed lay beneath the surface of American life, slowly eating away at the facade of gaiety and good times that characterized the decade. If some Americans were not eating adequately, or were badly clothed or housed, or jobless for part of the year, most Americans were unaware of their plight, or heedless of it. Stocks rose as did all economic indices, pointing to a healthy state of economic activity, but their dizzying heights should have made wiser minds realize the unsoundness of the corporate practices responsible for their quick rise and the speculative nature of the boom that could not withstand the effect of even a slight fall in the market. Thousands of bank failures during what was considered a prosperity decade should have pointed to basic weaknesses in the banking structure. Similarly, the imbalances in foreign exchange that rendered America the world's banker and supplier of industrial goods—while leaving Europe without funds to buy these products or repay debts incurred during World War I and after—should have illuminated the precarious nature of the international economic situation. But Americans, even those who should have known better, were more concerned with questions of prohibition, and the criminality it encouraged, with buying new cars and new homes, and speculating in Florida lands and marginal stocks. Some were simply intent upon making a living. In any case, they enjoyed the freely extended credit and ignored the warning signals, so that when the stock market crashed in October 1929, they were unprepared for the event. The "Great Crash," as John Kenneth Galbraith has called it, took five days to render the stock market a complete debacle. By the end of October, the full extent of the crisis was realized; and when the decline had run its course by mid-November, a new world was already being born.

Various explanations of the crisis were offered. Although many people could argue that the nation had lived extravagantly and that all that was needed was a stiff upper lip and a tightening of the belt, others were forced to think more seriously of the reasons for the economic collapse and its consequences. The conservatives argued that the cause of America's distress lay in the loss of European markets, and that with certain minor correctives, the free capitalistic system could be maintained and prosperity achieved again. The reformers—and these ranged from moderate to radical—argued that the free capitalism of the twenties had led to a maldistribution of income, and that prosperity could be regained only by the intervention of the government in the regulation of the economic life of the nation. Only then could the many share the national income on a more equitable basis.

The Republicans and President Herbert Hoover shared the conservative's position. Hoover, in fact, became the spokesman for economic individualism, which meant simply restriction of governmental activities in the economy. He believed that the depression was the result of a failure of confidence in the American system, and that therefore the task of government was to restore confidence in order to get the wheels of commerce moving once again. Prosperity, said Hoover, was just around the corner.

The Republican program reflected this interpretation. It based recovery on voluntary activity by producers of grains and cotton, and by industrial and labor leaders, to follow policies that were regarded as necessary for the health of the economy. But a voluntary agreement not to cut wages or to cut them only in proportion to a decline in prices could not work when there was no market for the goods produced, and, of course, there were many who were not inclined to curtail their economic activities at all if these promised economic profit. Toward the end of his administration, Hoover found it necessary to modify his position, and, in fact, began to use governmental power in a limited way to ameliorate the effects of the depression — but not enough, and it came far too late to do much good in changing his popular image.

Hoover's image was established primarily by his attitude toward poverty. It was this more than anything he said that gave the people the impression that he was a calloused leader. His refusal to meet with the Bonus Army, which in 1932 marched on Washington in the hope of persuading Congress to appropriate funds for veterans' bonuses, and his role in having them turned out of the city at the point of bayonets, struck sensitive observers as particularly cruel and inhumane. Hoover seemed to have no patience with poverty. He believed it to be the fault of the individual, not the system. And although he had supervised an enormous amount of relief work himself, especially as director of the Belgium Relief Commission after World War I, he condemned charity on the part of government, believing it ought to be a personal act rather than governmental policy. Government intervention in the individual's economic status contributed, he believed, to the weakening of the individual's character. "The function of the Federal Government," he said in his address to the Republican nominating convention in August 1932 "is to use its reserve powers and its strength for the protection of citizens and local governments by support to our institutions against forces beyond their control. It is not the function of the Government to relieve private institutions of their responsibilities to the public, or of local government to the states, or of state governments to the Federal Government."

Hoover was not immune to the suffering of his fellow citizens, but in his refusal to use the powers of government completely in order to meet the problems caused by unemployment and starvation, he could never convince Americans again to put their trust in his leadership.

Clifford Berryman cartoon LIBRARY OF CONGRESS

Roosevelt saw the depression both as a world crisis and as a result of flaws in the domestic economy; the basis of his New Deal program was to reform those flaws. What he looked for was "enlightened administration" to carry out the tasks of government, which, as he defined them, were to administer resources already at hand, reestablish foreign markets for the country's surplus productions, meet the problems of underconsumption, and adjust production to consumption, distribute wealth and products more equitably, and "adapt existing economic organizations to the service of the people." It was the task of government, said Roosevelt, to secure to man his right to live. Democracy was still a viable political system, he assured worried Americans. It was not the people who had failed, it was their leadership.

Between 1929 and 1932 as the depression deepened and suffering increased, the debate about what to do and how to do it also increased in scope. As some European nations turned to fascism and dictatorships as a solution to their economic distress, many Americans did too, in the belief that only a strong man with unlimited powers could pull the country out of the terrible morass into which it had floundered. Others turned to the Russian solution for the answer, seeing in state-owned and state-operated enterprise relief from private oppression and exploitation. Communists and Socialists advocated solutions in keeping with their ideological programs, while more simplistic thinkers, like Jacob Coxey, advocated government employment of all the unemployed on public-works projects. What they all agreed on, however, was that drastic, even revolutionary, methods were necessary to meet the demands of an unprecedented situation.

As a result, the 1932 campaign played on this single note. Questions of tariff, agriculture, industrial regulation, taxation, and the budget hardly figured in the many addresses and orations that were made to the people at mass meetings in public squares and parks and over the air waves. The results were clear from the very beginning. Hoover's position was hopeless and his gloomy warnings did not help his cause. Roosevelt's warm reassurances, his direct and straightforward appraisals of the conditions of the day, and his promises of experimental and new methods to meet these conditions—vague though they were—heartened a people despondent from seeing their neighbors rummaging in garbage cans for scraps of food or selling apples on street corners. The Hoovervilles established by the thousands of wandering Americans who crossed the country looking for work were a constant reminder to the electorate of Hoover's particularly unfortunate remark to newspapermen that "the hoboes . . . are better fed than they have ever been."

On election day, the voters flocked to the polls to register their lack of conviction in their president's assessment of the situation. More than twenty-two million votes were cast for Roosevelt to over fifteen million for Hoover, and the Democratic Party won an overwhelming majority in both houses of Congress. The New Deal was in the saddle, and would ride to victory for four more administrations. By the time it would be over, the face of American economic and social life would have been greatly modified. Never again would government refuse to participate in the economy, even though it might pretend that it was not doing so. The New Deal, moreover, wrote into law a whole series of legislation of lasting significance for American society as a whole, including the Social Security Act, the minimum wage and hour principles, insured bank deposits, and improved housing for low-income groups. The New Deal underwrote the private-enterprise system even while it helped its victims. Especially did it help restore morale and faith in democracy and in constitutional procedures at a time when masses of people would have turned to a dictatorship for security. It brought the people into a direct relationship with the national government creating a vast centralized network that has continued to increase through succeeding administrations, Democratic and Republican, whether for the good or bad. And, finally, it resulted in a tremendous concentration of power in the executive—something which those who were critical of the Rooseveltian program believed was injurious to the slow working of democracy, yet something which FDR believed was not to be feared given the frequency of American elections and the freedom of the people to pass judgment every four years upon their leaders.

369

HERBERT HOOVER   *Douglas Chandor, 1931   Oil on canvas, 45 x 38 inches*
From the Collection of the National Portrait Gallery   NPG.68.24

Herbert Hoover *Republican*

1874-1964

The Republican convention of 1932 was a dismal affair. Having no choice but to renominate Herbert Hoover, the GOP delegates might just as well have been attending a funeral. Ushered into the White House in 1928 on the wings of "Coolidge" prosperity as well as his own brilliant reputation as a businessman, administrator, and humanitarian, Hoover had become one of the most maligned figures in presidential history. Despite public unpopularity, the president still controlled the party machinery, and so, knowing full well that he had little chance of winning in November, disheartened delegates obediently gave their endorsement to the man whom so many Americans now viewed as the very symbol of national depression.

In 1928, Herbert Clark Hoover had seemed to possess all the necessary qualifications for the nation's highest office. Orphaned at age seven, the sober and industrious Iowa Quaker epitomized the Horatio Alger concept of success. He had grown up in relative poverty, worked his way through Stanford University and after receiving a bachelor of arts degree in mining and geology, embarked on a spectacular career as a mining engineer and business administrator. Eventually establishing his own mining consultant firm with branch offices through the world, by 1910 he had gained an international reputation as the infallible "doctor" on whom national governments and private companies alike relied in developing their mineral resources.

By 1920, however, Hoover had proven that he was more than just an exceptional businessman and engineer. Caught in London at the outbreak of World War I, he had embarked on the task of relieving the starving masses of war-torn Europe. American Ambassador Walter Hines Page, who had initially enlisted him in aiding over 160,000 Americans stranded in Europe in August of 1914, had drawn him into this undertaking. Hoover became the chief administrator of Belgium war relief. While serving in this capacity, he systematically raised funds from government and private sources that eventually totaled over a billion dollars, and with a fleet of some 200 ships, skillfully managed to feed the helpless inhabitants of German-occupied Belgium.

With his appointment as United States food administrator shortly after America entered the war, Hoover again demonstrated his formidable abilities as the coordinator of the nation's

Cartoon of Herbert Hoover by Rollin Kirby LIBRARY OF CONGRESS

food production and rationing programs. At the war's end, he again returned to Europe, this time to administer the much-needed food and medical relief programs for practically all of Western Europe. Still later, the indefatigable Hoover extended his work to Russia where in 1921, he contributed substantially to the alleviation of the widespread famine that had grown out of the turmoil of national revolution and postwar exhaustion.

By the early 1920s, Hoover was one of the most popular men in America. Hailed as the "savior of mankind" by Britain's Lady Astor, Americans doted on him as the "great humanitarian." While universities showered him with honorary degrees and European nations struck medals and erected statues in his honor, politicians from both parties regarded him as prime presidential material.

Although he chose to ignore these tempting offers, Hoover nevertheless did involve himself in politics. And in accepting from Harding an appointment as secretary of commerce, he opened a new phase of his career which was to add still further to his already considerable public reputation. Under Harding and later Coolidge, his administrative expertise transformed the Department of Commerce into a vast and effective network of information agencies to which

Hoover license plate SMITHSONIAN INSTITUTION

business could apply for advice on current business trends as well as ways to achieve greater commercial and industrial efficiency. As the economy skyrocketed during the twenties, Hoover, not unlike his counterpart in the Department of the Treasury, Andrew Mellon, became increasingly identified with the economic genius with which voters now credited the nation's Republican leadership. It was hardly surprising, then, that Republicans should turn to the almost charismatic Hoover in 1928 after Coolidge refused to run for president a second time.

The Republicans won in a landslide, and Hoover entered the White House as one of the most popular presidents in American history. Exhilarated by his inaugural predictions of continuing economic growth that would virtually eradicate the nation's poverty, the public could not have been more confident of the abilities of its new leader. With the advent of the Great Depression, however, the euphoric confidence soon disappeared. Despite the administrative talents that had previously served him so well, Hoover now seemed incapable of dealing with the catastrophic events facing his country in the early thirties. Moving from one explanation of the depression to another, he first accused the people of harboring illusions that they ought patriotically to ignore; he then denounced the economic collapse as being European-inspired and therefore non-American. Finally, he chastised Americans for blaming the Republicans for the depression just because they took credit for the previous prosperity—but as Republican Douglas Morrow admitted, "those who took credit for the rainfall should not complain when they are blamed for the drought."

The root of Hoover's inability to deal with the nation's economic ills lay both in his per-

373

sonality and his ideological outlook. A self-made success himself, he could not abandon his faith in the "rugged individual" and the belief that it was largely through individual and private initiative rather than the federal government that the nation's economic problems would be solved. Thus, under Hoover, federal action to curb the depression was sharply limited and, when it was taken, was slow in arriving and insufficient to the demands of the situation.

Equally important, however, in arriving at an explanation of Hoover's administrative ineffectiveness, were the limitations of his personality. Aloof and ill-at-ease in public, he was incapable of providing Americans with the confidence they so vitally needed in this era of desperate despair—a confidence that perhaps might have effected a more favorable response on the part of businessmen and farmers to his federal loan programs. Unlike his successor Franklin Roosevelt, who so skillfully enhanced the effectiveness of his New Deal programs with personal warmth and paternal optimism, the "remote" Hoover could not dispel the cynical pessimism that now pervaded the nation.

In 1932, the American people were ready for a change. Although Hoover conscientiously applied himself to the business of presidential campaigning, his opponents clearly held the trump cards. When he predicted that if Roosevelt won, "grass" [would] grow in the streets of a hundred cities," the majority of voters, already seeing evidence of economic desolation, ignored his ominous warnings and in unprecedented numbers rallied to the Democratic ticket.

JAMES R. COX   *Photograph   Courtesy of the Archives of Industrial Society,*
University of Pittsburgh Libraries

James R. Cox *Jobless*

1886-1951

In January of 1932 as the nation approached the lowest point in the Great Depression, Father James Renshaw Cox descended on the nation's capital with a contingency of 15,000 unemployed Pennsylvania workers. Expecting to stir official sympathy for the plight of labor, the Pittsburgh priest, not unlike Jacob Coxey in 1894, led his "army" jubilantly through Washington in the hope that Congress would take its cue from this spectacle of jobless marchers and initiate a national program of public works. The movement, however, was short-lived and the group disbanded after three days—with the help of Secretary of the Treasury Andrew Mellon, who in his anxiety over the presence of this unsettling element in Washington, personally contributed funds to return some 270 of the marchers to Pittsburgh.

Although largely unsuccessful in its immediate goal, the march neverthlesss gave impetus to great enthusiasm among Cox's unemployed following, some 5,000 of whom shortly convened at the Pittsburgh stadium to urge further action in the nation's war against unemployment. Out of this gathering emerged the new Jobless Party whose members promptly and quite unceremoniously proclaimed James R. Cox their candidate for president.

Son of a Pittsburgh millworker, the "outspoken" and "picturesque" Cox had always had great sympathy for the problems of workers. When the depression fell as a blight upon the country, he immediately attempted to ameliorate the many hardships experienced by his blue-collar parishioners. He lent vigorous support to striking workers in and around Pittsburgh. He took charge of a massive food-relief program through which he eventually distributed more than a half-million food baskets. And it was also under his guidance that 250 of the city's homeless unemployed finally found shelter in a cluster of deserted packing houses. Still later, he helped to provide hard-pressed workers with a community center and swimming pool.

With the announcement of Cox's candidacy, the Jobless Party movement quickly spread to other major cities where workers were naturally attracted to the new party's call for public-works projects as well as for further legislative safeguards for labor unions. As the election drew near, however, Cox became increasingly convinced of the sincerity of Franklin Roosevelt's promises to provide the nation's unemployed with work relief, and by September 1932 he was urging his followers to vote Democratic. Despite his withdrawal, a handful of his supporters nevertheless cast their votes for Pittsburgh's "Pastor of the Poor."

After his short-lived candidacy, Cox continued his relief work in Pittsburgh. In the mid-thirties, he became a member of the Pennsylvania Commission for the Unemployed, shortly after which Roosevelt appointed him to the state recovery board of the National Recovery Administration.

JACOB SECHLER COXEY   *Clinton Peters, 1916   Oil on canvas, 48 x 44 inches*
Robert R. Coxey, Charlotte, North Carolina

Jacob Sechler Coxey *Farmer–Labor*

1854-1951

In 1932, the name of Jacob S. Coxey on a presidential ballot probably did not mean too much to the newer generation of voters. Among those, however, who were living out their twilight years in the midst of economic catastrophe, mention of the seventy-six-year-old "General" from Massillon, Ohio, did, indeed, strike a response, and even if they did not vote for him—and the vast majority of them did not—Coxey's name nevertheless evoked memories of yet another time when the nation's whole economic and social structure seemed to be on the verge of collapse.

Now the candidate of the Farmer-Labor Party, Coxey had made his name during the turbulent years of the mid-1890s. A successful quarry and foundry owner, who had begun earning his living as a millworker at age fifteen, the ever-gentle and generous Ohioan, always mindful of his own labor origins, never lost his concern for the problems of workers. As labor conditions worsened in the early 1890s, his sympathy for the economic underdog which had already attracted him to the Greenback movement, now drew him to the problem of devising a method whereby industrial workers could be assured of constant employment as well as reasonably sufficient wages.

The inspiration for Coxey's ingenuous theory came upon him in 1891, while trying to maneuver his carriage over a washed-out country road. Deciding that what the nation needed most was a good system of public highways, he combined his already strong sympathy for Greenback monetary doctrine with the idea of a national public-roads project. Out of this emerged his cure-all solution for the nation's perennial problems of unemployment and depressed wages: if the government would issue 500 million dollars in currency, so the theory went, and use it to employ jobless workers in the construction of roads, it would not only alleviate unemployment, it would also force private industry to raise its wages and shorten labor hours in order to meet the exigencies of a contracted labor supply.

To promote his program, Coxey founded the Good Roads Association, through which he disseminated pamphlets and innumerable letters to editors. Although his crusade initially met with indifference, the economic disasters of 1893 which forced Coxey to lay off forty of his own workers from his sand quarries, inspired the Massillon entrepreneur to new action. In January 1894, he joined forces with "spieler and chalk talk artist" Carl Browne, whom he had met in Chicago during a public lecture tour, to organize a march of the nation's unemployed on the city of Washington in the hope that the industrial "army" would convince Congress of the wisdom of Coxey's economic theories.

So the famous "Army of the Commonweal" was born. Responding to Browne's national publicity campaign, 150 hard-pressed workers gathered in Coxey's hometown and on March 24, with Coxey in the lead riding in a phaeton drawn by a sleek "$40,000 horse," the "petition in boots" set out for Washington under a swirling banner depicting Christ.

By the time the army, which eventually numbered 450, reached its destination, Washington was on edge. Violent labor unrest was already rife in many of the nation's largest cities. For capital officials, who had been reading alarmist newspaper accounts of the army's progress through Pennsylvania and Maryland, this motley crew of workers and vagabonds smacked of revolution. Ready to take advantage of the slightest infraction, police promptly placed Coxey and Browne under arrest for "trespassing on the grass" when they inadvertently stepped onto the Capitol lawn. So ended one of the most colorful and publicized events of strife-ridden 1894.

Although he never attracted wide public attention again, Coxey continued to expound his economic programs throughout the remainder of his life. He made it his business to explain personally his economic theories to every president from McKinley to Franklin Roosevelt. In 1914, having enhanced his public-works theories with proposals of government ownership of railroads as well as a federal-loan program to farmers and small business, he unsuccessfully tried to organize another march on Washington. An incessant candidate for office—he first ran for the presidency in 1924—he realized his one political success in 1931 at which time he won election to the Massillon mayorship on a platform urging the establishment of a local public-works program.

Finally in 1932, with the nation experiencing a more severe version of the economic events of 1893–1894, Coxey as presidential candidate once again placed his economic doctrines before the nation.

Although he won only a little over 7,000 votes, Coxey doggedly continued his one-man crusade on behalf of "Coxeyism." Having paid his visit to Roosevelt in 1932, he proudly took credit for inspiring the formation of the New Deal work projects. Still going strong after World War II, the inveterate theorizer appeared before Congress in 1946 to present his newly developed plan for a "double faced" international currency which he claimed would "avoid future wars over debt and poverty." When he died in 1951, at age ninety-seven, he was toying with the idea of leading still another march on Washington in an effort to promote his economic theories that had now expanded into the field of foreign exchange.

ALFRED MOSSMAN LANDON *John Doctoroff, 1936 Oil on canvas,*
30 x 25 inches Alfred M. Landon, Topeka, Kansas

Alfred M. Landon *Republican*

1887–

Newspaper magnate, William Randolph Hearst, called him "marvelous" and, to most Republicans in 1936 anxiously searching for a presidential candidate capable of defeating the incumbent Franklin D. Roosevelt, Alfred M. Landon was just that. Genial and down-to-earth, moderately progressive, and fiscally conservative, the two-term governor of Kansas seemed to be a politician who offered something for everyone. On the one hand, his "just-folks" manner made him a man with whom the average voter could easily identify. At the same time, his progressive image which he combined with a cautious financial program seemed to increase his chances of attracting Roosevelt's more moderate supporters who despite their approval of New Deal measures had come to deplore the tremendous costs incurred by the Democrats' recovery programs. So, believing that he possessed a winning combination of political assets, the GOP optimistically placed its White House hopes for 1936 in Landon's hands.

Although a lawyer by training, Landon decided early that he preferred the more active life of an oil-field operator to the tedium of a law office. By the early 1920s, his oil ventures had earned him a sizeable fortune. A growing business, however, did not keep Landon from dabbling in politics. A supporter along with his father of Theodore Roosevelt's Bull Moose candidacy in 1912, his masterful campaign for Roosevelt won him much respect among Kansas' progressive Republicans. After serving a short stint as secretary to Republican Governor Henry Allen in 1922, he became the acknowledged leader of the state's progressive faction and in 1928 won election to the state Republican chairmanship.

Not satisfied with helping others to win office, Landon embarked on his first campaign for the governorship in 1932. For most Republican candidates, this was an unfortunate year to be running for office. With the depression approaching its lowest point, voters were in no mood to cast their lot with the party of Herbert Hoover. In spite of his party affiliation, however, the amiable Landon proved successful, and won the honor of being the only Republican in a year of Democratic landslides to win a gubernatorial contest west of the Mississippi.

Elected on the strength of his progressive reputation, Landon provided Kansas with what one historian described as "one of the most effective [administrations] in the history of the state."

Facing, like all governors in this era, the seemingly unsurmountable problems of alleviating the depressed conditions of his state, he embarked on a vigorous program of economic relief. In addition to reducing tax rates, he succeeded in instituting a moratorium on mortgage foreclosures, a state-supported plan for local relief, and a series of emergency banking laws that ultimately rescued the state's many floundering financial institutions.

To many, Landon's greatest accomplishment lay in the fact that he had implemented his recovery programs without burdening his state with a single debt. By 1936, Republicans were enthusiastically touting the governor of Kansas as the logical answer to Roosevelt and his New Deal programs which had forced the federal government into a policy of deficit spending. After all, had not Landon's administration clearly demonstrated his ability to promote economic recovery without saddling government with debts?

However hopeful some Republicans were—one poll indicated a clear-cut GOP victory—the Democrats ultimately held the upper hand in 1936. During Roosevelt's first administration, the economy had clearly improved, and for the many voters who had begun to reap the benefits of New Deal relief programs, there seemed little question that it had been Roosevelt who had rescued them from the dire conditions of the early thirties. Reflecting the prevailing sense of gratitude that so many felt toward the Democratic administration, the Republican mayor of Johnstown, Pennsylvania, pointed out to his constituents that had it not been for the work-relief programs, their city would still be mired in the depression, and he urged them to "vote solid for Franklin Roosevelt."

Further contributing to Landon's defeat were the campaigner's own weaknesses. Though poised and warm in his more personal contacts with voters, the Kansas governor was totally ineffective before large audiences. Nervous and halting, his major speeches became studies in monotony. As a result, even his appearances at solidly Republican gatherings failed to gen-

Landon and Knox decal sticker   SMITHSONIAN INSTITUTION

386

Landon metal donkey   CORNELL UNIVERSITY, DOUGLAS COLLECTION

erate enthusiasm. It was following one such rally in Maine, a state which Landon ultimately won, that the Republican candidate himself, after being told what a warm reception his speech had received, commented: ". . . it may have been warm for Maine, but it was damned cold for Kansas."*

Also obstructing Landon's candidacy were the Old Guard Republicans on whom he relied so heavily for support. While he assumed a moderately favorable position on the question of New Deal measures and largely limited his criticisms to Roosevelt's fiscal "irresponsibility," his conservative allies attacked the New Deal entirely, calling it "Un-American" and "communistic." Under their influence, toward the end of the campaign Landon himself began to succumb to similar diatribes. In one instance, he claimed that Roosevelt was "destroy[ing] the American way of life." As a result, voters became increasingly fearful that a Republican victory would signify complete repudiation of the policies that seemingly were effective in curing the depression.

But perhaps Landon himself provided the most succinct analysis of his defeat. As he reflected on the formidable popularity of his opponent shortly after the election, he remarked to a friend: "I don't think that it would have made any difference what kind of a campaign I made as far as stopping this avalanche is concerned. That is one consolation you get out of a good licking." Indeed, in the eyes of most Americans Roosevelt had become a savior, and although more effective campaign tactics might have lessened the margin of Landon's defeat—he won the electoral votes of only two states—the fact remains that in 1936 Roosevelt was invincible.

*In a letter to the authors, June 5, 1972, Governor Landon corrected this interpretation: "it was the weather I was speaking of—not the meeting."

387

EARL RUSSELL BROWDER   *Photograph, 1971   Daniel Kramer, New York*

Earl Browder *Communist*

1 8 9 1 –

By 1936, Earl Russell Browder had become the most significant figure in the American Communist Party. Selected six years earlier as the party's general secretary, he had led his followers toward an increasingly "revisionist" outlook that, in effect, called for repudiation of the Marxist doctrine of proletarian revolution, and opted for a strategy of promoting gradual reform in cooperation with various non-Communist movements. Despite their separate identity as a party, in the 1930s the Communists allied themselves with many of the era's more moderate labor organizers as well as with the Farmer-Labor Party, which included progressive reformers of all stripes. And it was in the same spirit of gradualism and cooperation that Browder embarked upon his first campaign for the presidency.

Browder viewed his candidacy as a means of supporting Roosevelt, whom he considered an ally in liberal reform. While he hoped that his campaign would splinter the anti-Roosevelt opposition on the left and thereby minimize its impact, his primary goal was to alert voters to the dangers he saw in a Landon victory. Although he had little expectation of attracting voters to himself, he hoped that by directing his "main fire" against the Republicans, he might at least divert voters away from Landon and thereby insure victory for FDR.

Unlike so many members of his party who had been attracted to Communist doctrine largely as a result of the economic failures of the thirties, Browder had arrived at his political beliefs early in life under the tutelage of his father who was a teacher and a Socialist. Shortly after his fifteenth birthday he joined the Socialist Party, but gradually moved farther to the left, until around 1912 he allied himself with William Z. Foster's Syndicalist League which was directing the Socialist efforts to achieve a proletarian revolution. After serving a short prison term for his attacks on military conscription during World War I, he became a member of the American Communist Party which Foster had founded in 1919.

During the twenties, Browder became involved in a variety of Communist activities. Shortly after his abortive attempt to establish a cooperative commune near Independence, Missouri, he became managing editor of the Communist paper, *The Labor Herald*. Later, he went to Moscow as a member of the Trade Union Council, made several lengthy trips to

China where he worked with other Communists in attempting to promote a revolutionary take-over; and, finally, in 1930, after Foster retired from the party because of ill-health, took over the leadership of the party.

In carrying out his campaign objectives in 1936, Browder encountered such hostility that it hardly seems likely that he played much of a role in effecting the Roosevelt landslide. In Tampa, Florida, he found himself locked out of the hall where he was to speak; in Atlanta, officials would not let him off the train; and in Terre Haute, after suffering a pelting of eggs, he was arrested for vagrancy.

Clearly, Browder was not discouraged by his first experience in presidential politics. He ran again in 1940, but this time as the foe of Roosevelt. Claiming that the Democrat's aid to Britain was leading an unwilling America into an "imperialist war" against Germany and her temporary Communist ally, the Soviet Union, Browder hardly enjoyed an opportunity to campaign. Fearful, perhaps, that the Communist candidate might jeopardize the nation's defense and military preparations, a federal judge—presumably at the behest of the administration—imposed a court order forbidding Browder to travel within the country. His campaign efforts had for the most part to be limited to written pleas and the distribution of recorded speeches.

With the end of World War II, the American Communist Party, reflecting the growing hostility between the Soviet Union and the United States, now considered the doctrine of revisionism and cooperation with non-Communist governments party heresy. The party began to adopt a militantly revolutionary line which in essence meant that American Communists had to achieve their goals independent of the established system. Thus, in 1945, largely shunned by members of the party who disapproved of his wish to continue in the revisionist path, Browder was read out of the party and his career in Communist politics came to an abrupt end.

WILLIAM LEMKE   *Photograph by Harris & Ewing*
Robert M. Lemke, Potomac, Maryland

William Lemke *National Union*

1878-1950

By 1936, although the nation had not fully recovered from the calamities of the early thirties, it did not seem unreasonable to hope that America was on its way to full economic recovery. With its myriad of public-works projects and reform legislation, Franklin Roosevelt's New Deal had already brought significant improvement in the nation's economic life; and despite evidence of persisting hardships, most Americans confidently looked to the day when they would once again share in the growing national prosperity.

There were some, however, who did not share in the mounting optimism. Feeling that the president's policies in meeting the Great Depression's crises were not nearly as comprehensive or as immediately effective as they should be, some Americans became disenchanted with the aura of promise that had enveloped Roosevelt in the first years of his administration. Playing to this still unallayed discontent, a new national party emerged in 1936, whose organization represented the alliance of three of the era's most colorful and widely publicized dissidents.

The National Union Party was the brainchild of Father Charles E. Coughlin, whose weekly radio broadcasts berating Roosevelt alternately for his conservative and communistic tendencies had brought him a large popular following. Drawing most of its vitality from Coughlin himself, the party was soon joined by Francis E. Townsend, whose crusade for government-sponsored pensions for the aged had won him substantial popularity among the nation's retired population. Completing the triumverate was Gerald L. K. Smith, the self-appointed heir to Huey Long's "Share Our Wealth" clubs, whose members had found their answer to the depression in their deceased leader's program of a federally guaranteed income for all Americans.

Although on the surface an alliance of three equally popular movements, the party in reality belonged to Coughlin. For it was he who drew up the party's platform advocating greater agricultural relief, the establishment of a national bank as well as government pensions, and a watered-down version of Smith's guaranteed income. It was also Coughlin who, in a one-man convention, took it upon himself to bestow the party's presidential nomination on William Lemke.

The son of a prosperous North Dakota farmer and a lawyer by profession, William Lemke had originally made his political reputation as the dynamic spokesman of his home state's farming interests. Emerging in 1915 as a leader of the "Nonpartisan League" which had been established to promote various state agricultural programs within the two parties of his state, he succeeded between 1916 and 1920 in making the League the controlling influence in state Republican politics. Although he lost considerable ground after 1920 in the face of a growing Republican conservatism, he continued to play a prominent role in the agrarian politics of his state; and as the depression began to take its toll among North Dakota's farmers in the early thirties, Lemke's political fortunes again began to rise. In 1932, on the strength of his promise to promote a comprehensive program of federal relief for agriculture, his rural constituents elected him to Congress.

Lemke began his first term in the House of Representatives with great hope of ameliorating the severe economic plight in which his depression-ridden farming constituency now found themselves. Knowing that his hard-pressed district was suffering under conditions that were common throughout the nation's agricultural regions, the freshman congressman was confident that Roosevelt's New Deal administration would look favorably on his well-delineated program to relieve the farmer of his burdensome debts. In fact, after meeting with Roosevelt during the 1932 campaign, Lemke came away with the distinct impression that the Democrat fully supported his proposals and it had been on the strength of this interview, that the North Dakotan, though nominally a Republican, had decided to campaign for Roosevelt.

Lemke's optimism, however, soon died and with it his faith in the Roosevelt administration. Considering his bill enabling bankrupt farmers to scale down their debts and thereby remain on their farms too drastic a measure, Roosevelt made every effort to thwart Lemke's efforts to gain its congressional passage. In spite of the administration, Lemke succeeded in maneuvering his Bankruptcy Act through Congress, but his proposal for a federal loan program to refinance farm mortgages at reduced interest rates met with total failure as a result of presidential hostility. The embittered congressman, convinced that Roosevelt was not really concerned about the nation's farm problem, remarked, "I look upon Roosevelt as a bewildered Kerensky of a provisional government. He doesn't know from or where he's going." Thus, by 1936, Lemke was an implacable critic of the New Deal and it was not surprising that he consented to oppose Roosevelt's attempt to win a second term.

Like many minority candidates, Lemke, though not expecting to win, hoped that his candidacy would attract enough voters to convince the two major parties of the need for broader relief programs, particularly as they related to the farmer. From the start, however, his plan went awry. Though promised substantial funds by Coughlin, he found himself chronically short of money. Further, as Coughlin's speeches on behalf of the Union Party cause became increasingly bitter and revolutionary in tone—in one address he referred to Roosevelt as an "anti-God" and in another suggested that "bullets" might ultimately be necessary to save the nation from the clutches of the New Deal—voters who might have been sympathetic quickly deserted Lemke's cause. Finally, the anti-Semitic strain that had gradually crept into the rhetoric of

Coughlin and Gerald Smith, both of whom frequently blamed the nation's economic ills on a Jewish conspiracy, alienated many others who came to see Lemke as little more than a spokesman for racial and religious bigotry.

In the end, then, Lemke's effort bore little fruit. With his defeat, he returned to Congress where he was to serve almost continuously until his death in 1950.

WENDELL WILLKIE   *Malvina Hoffman, 1947   Limestone; 26 inches in height*
The Corcoran Gallery of Art, Washington, D.C.   Gift of Simon & Schuster, Inc.

Wendell Willkie *Republican*

1892-1944

A political novice and an avowed Democrat for most of his life, Wendell Willkie aroused much consternation among Republican regulars in 1940. Descending on the GOP convention with the intention of winning its presidential nomination, to many delegates he was little more than an interloper. Although party veterans found his recent conversion to Republicanism laudable, many could not help but feel that this political upstart, now in the process of winning over substantial numbers of delegates, was hardly worthy of their party's most coveted honor—an honor normally limited to the politically seasoned faithful. As one long-time Republican put it when Willkie unabashedly sought his support on the eve of the convention: "Well, Wendell, you know that back home in Indiana it's all right if the town whore joins the Church, but they don't let her lead the choir the first night."

Ultimately nominated on the sixth ballot, Willkie's 1940 candidacy climaxed one of the most singular tales in American political history. Although his personality, an amalgam of "charm . . . breathless energy and . . . unbounding faith in himself," made him likely material for the political arena in the early phase of his career, he had never found much time for politics. Following in the footsteps of his parents, both of whom were lawyers, he turned his talents to corporation law. After a short period with his father's firm in Elwood, Indiana, Willkie established himself in Akron, Ohio, where his impressive work for an Ohio utility ultimately attracted the attention of Commonwealth and Southern, one of the nation's largest utility holding companies. In 1929, Commonwealth and Southern brought him to New York as their legal counsel. Here, Willkie demonstrated his formidable abilities and within four years became the company's president.

Although relatively removed from politics throughout this early phase of his career, Willkie always maintained his identity with the reform element of the Democratic Party— during his college days he had been known as a "red-sweatered radical." Influenced by his father, who had for a time been a member of the Socialist Party, he had frequently expressed his belief in the need for increased government regulation of business as well as labor reform. In 1924, as delegate to the Democratic convention, he had given his support to Al Smith.

Wendell Willkie bumper tag   SMITHSONIAN INSTITUTION

Later, in 1932, enthusiastic over Franklin Roosevelt's promises of reform, he contributed $150 to the Democrat's campaign chest.

With the coming of the New Deal, however, Willkie's political outlook underwent a change, and by 1936 he was voicing regrets that he had ever been foolhardy enough to lend financial support to Roosevelt. In his view, the Democrats had gone too far in their efforts to legislate business and labor. Just as the nation had, at the turn of the century, faced the danger of domination by a business plutocracy, the New Deal now presented an equally foreboding prospect: "domination of the people by Big Government." In large degree, Willkie's alienation from Roosevelt grew out of his relationship with the New Deal as president of Commonwealth. Like all other major utilities, Commonwealth had suffered severely in the depression, and it was only after hard struggle that Willkie succeeded in restoring his company to a sound financial footing. With the advent of the New Deal's Tennessee Valley Authority, however, he found that his company faced a new threat quite unlike the hazard of depression. As the TVA began to lay plans for the development of governmental power projects in Tennessee as well as in four neighboring states, it was evident that Commonwealth's southern subsidiaries were now competing against a government which, in charging substantially lower rates, could unquestionably drive Commonwealth out of the region. To Willkie, this was clearly a misuse of federal power. To regulate private enterprise was one thing, but to force it out of business was quite another. Applying all the business and legal knowledge at his command, Willkie threw himself into the fight against TVA—a fight which finally ended in 1939 with the Supreme Court's decision upholding the government's right to compete against private utilities.

Out of this defeat, Willkie began to emerge as a presidential candidate. By 1939, he was one of Roosevelt's greatest critics; he became increasingly convinced that the various federal policies were not only threatening private enterprise, but also in large degree were responsible for the persisting lag in national recovery. Combining his attacks on the TVA with the accusation that many of the new federal controls on business and increased taxes had deterred the nation's businessmen from engaging in capital expansion, he harangued the Roosevelt administration for its failure to provide proper incentives for the private sectors of the nation's economy.

Attracted to his views, which he aired in magazine articles and radio appearances, numerous members of the business community—who like Willkie had come to thoroughly distrust the Democratic administration—began to take a growing interest in Willkie's political potential. By early 1940, a full-fledged campaign had been launched to make him the Republicans' next presidential candidate. With the aid of such figures as Russell Davenport, who as editor of

GOP *"Life begins in '40" pin*   CORNELL UNIVERSITY, DOUGLAS COLLECTION

Fortune made every effort to acquaint his readers with Willkie, and the young Oren Root, who early in 1940 embarked on the task of organizing a national network of Willkie clubs, the Willkie movement gained momentum. As the Republican convention approached, it was quite apparent that, like it or not, the GOP delegates would have to recognize this one-time Democratic neophyte as a serious presidential possibility.

In the end, the Republicans had little choice but to give their endorsement to Willkie. Handicapped by the absence of any other candidate whose experience and national stature might have balanced out Willkie's obvious popularity among the nation's anti-New Dealers, the GOP succumbed to the whirlwind barrage of Willkie propaganda and supporters who flooded the convention's galleries.

The nomination won, Willkie now took his cause to the people. At first, the robustly attractive and poised candidate seemed to hold much promise as a vote-getter. While castigating the Democrats for their failure to stimulate business, he made it clear that he fully approved of much of the New Deal's economic legislation and thereby reassured moderate liberals that his candidacy did not represent a complete rejection of the concept of government control.

Although his moderate position in some respects exerted a positive effect, at the same time it exposed Willkie to the accusation that he was no more than an echo. Reacting to the Republican's first major speech, one newspaperman observed: "All I got from that speech was an endorsement of the New Deal." Adding to the impression that he was simply a "me-too" candidate were his remarks on the nation's foreign policy in which he joined Roosevelt in espousing a policy of support for Britain who now stood almost alone in its struggle against German aggression. As if to applaud Roosevelt's step-up in military preparedness, he argued that America must increase its security against the day when she too might find herself drawn into the war with Hitler.

Willkie's lack of a concrete program together with the increased prosperity that had begun to skyrocket as a result of accelerated military spending also weakened his appeal; his ambiguous promises to implement a program to encourage private enterprise appeared somewhat superfluous as industry began to move toward a full-employment, wartime production. Capping these handicaps was Willkie's background and ineptitude as a campaigner. As a "Wall Street" lawyer and corporation executive, he automatically alienated many workers who could not help but identify him with the anti-union business establishment which had so frequently opposed Roosevelt's labor legislation in the thirties. Moreover, Willkie's proclivity for the casual and off-the-cuff remark cost him innumerable votes. Stopping his campaign train in Cicero, a Chicago suburb, he remarked on how happy he was to be in Chicago. After the crowd corrected him, he flippantly remarked "To Hell with Chicago" and in so doing, found his words quoted on the front pages of major newspapers throughout the nation. In another careless

Willkie elephant pin   CORNELL UNIVERSITY, DOUGLAS COLLECTION

moment in which he alluded to the Munich Pact and accused Roosevelt of selling Czechoslovakia "down the river," he exposed himself to endless criticisms of his ignorance of the realities of international politics.

With his defeat, Willkie entered into the last phase of his career. Now the leader of the Republican Party at a time when America was gradually drawing closer to war with Germany

Willkie matchfolder   CORNELL UNIVERSITY, DOUGLAS COLLECTION

and Japan, he undertook the task of rallying his party to support Roosevelt's war efforts. In 1941, he went to England as Roosevelt's unofficial emissary to determine Britain's specific needs in fighting Germany; on his return, he testified before Congress on behalf of the administration's Lend-Lease program to aid Britain. Still later, he urged his fellow partisans in Congress to support repeal of that part of the Neutrality Act which had prohibited the arming of American merchant ships. Finally, in 1944, Willkie's career came to an end. Having spent the first part of the year in an effort to recapture the Republican nomination, he collapsed in exhaustion and within a few months he died.

401

THOMAS E. DEWEY *Molly Guion* *Oil on canvas, 31½ x 41½ inches*
Thomas E. Dewey, Jr., New York

Thomas E. Dewey *Republican*

1902-1971

"How," asked Alice Roosevelt Longworth, "can you vote for a man who looks like the bridegroom on a wedding cake?" Polished, handsome, and somewhat aloof, Thomas E. Dewey could not claim personal appeal as one of his more notable political virtues. Instead, Dewey's strengths lay in an impeccable record of public service as well as organizational abilities, and it was these latter assets that won him the Republican presidential nomination in 1944.

Considering his family heritage, it was fitting that Dewey should become the GOP candidate. Not only was he the son of a lifelong Republican who had done yeoman service for his party both as a journalist and county chairman; he was also the grandson of one of the Republican Party's original founders—a fact, needless to say, widely publicized in 1944.

Dewey, however, had more than an appropriate pedigree. Hailed by one magazine as a modern-day "St. George," he first achieved national fame as a result of his highly successful efforts to curb New York City's network of organized crime. Settling in New York City after having been graduated from Columbia Law School in 1925, he shortly became an assistant to the United States attorney for southern New York. While serving in this capacity, he managed to indict Waxey Gordon, one of New York's leading underworld figures. Later, as a specially appointed counsel, he succeeded in prosecuting two more of the state's most notorious racketeers, Legs Diamond and Lucky Luciano. By 1938, his reputation as the unbeatable foe of organized crime was legendary, and it was with little effort that he won election as New York City's district attorney. With his victory, one local paper jubilantly announced: "Hoodlums Start Out As Dewey Starts In."

Continuing his crusade in this new office with much the same results, Dewey soon found himself tapped for higher offices. In 1939 after running unsuccessfully for governor, a movement began to make him the 1940 Republican presidential candidate; had it not been for Wendell Willkie's well-organized campaign, the dashing D.A. would probably have won— one early poll indicated that sixty percent of the voters favored his candidacy.

Despite his defeat in 1940, Dewey's chances for nomination were hardly dead. Elected to the New York governorship in 1942 on a moderately liberal platform, he further added to his reputation by running an efficient and economical administration. By 1944, Dewey once again was a front-running contender for the Republican nomination. After defeating Willkie in the Wisconsin primary without even campaigning, it was a foregone conclusion that the New Yorker would be the new GOP standard-bearer in its struggle to depose the hitherto invincible Roosevelt.

Based on a platform that essentially endorsed the New Deal, the Dewey campaign concentrated its attacks on the wartime inefficiency of the Democratic administration and its inability to restore the nation to a peacetime prosperity once the war was over. The New Dealers, Dewey and his followers claimed, were worn out, and it was the war and not the Democratic recovery measures of the thirties that had finally raised the nation out of economic depression. With peace near at hand, it was time to depose the party that had required a war to fulfill its economic promises.

Moreover, Dewey told his audiences the controls on free enterprise imposed by the New Deal were turning America into a corporate state in which government "would tell each of us where we could work; at what and for how much." To give credence to this statement, he suggested that the Democratic Party had been "taken over" by Communists like Earl Browder and Sidney Hillman, pro Roosevelt labor leader and chairman of the CIO's Political Action Committee whom some Republicans attempted to link with the Communist Party.

Dewey organized his campaign well. A master of political orchestration, he left nothing to chance. Under his tutelage, the Republican National Committee wrote campaign speeches for Republican governors, and in his own appearances, he made certain that all preparations were exactly as he wanted them—even the height of the speaker's rostrum and the number of cars in a motorcade did not escape his calculating eye.

To a large extent, however, Dewey's preoccupation with detail and iron control of his supporters led to his defeat. Though fascinated with his "metronomic precision," reporters could not refrain from viewing this cold and seemingly unspontaneous Republican as an automaton.

Weakened by his press image, Dewey also lost ground as a result of Hillman's fruitful efforts to keep labor in the Democratic camp. On the one hand, the labor leader reminded workers of the multitude of benefits they had derived from the New Deal; and on the other, he gave labor's support to a massive voter registration drive in factories throughout the country.

But probably the most decisive factor in Dewey's defeat was Roosevelt's image as a world leader. To voters who now saw that the problem of establishing lasting international peace was one of the major tasks facing the nation and its allies, Roosevelt seemed to be the wisest alternative in 1944, particularly in comparison to Dewey who only four years earlier had been advocating an isolationist policy.

Thus, Dewey became the fourth Republican to lose to Roosevelt.

GERALD L. K. SMITH   *Edward V. Runci, 1971   Oil on canvas, 30 x 24 inches*
Elna M. Smith Foundation, Eureka Springs, Arkansas

Gerald L. K. Smith *America First*

1898-

In 1944 the nation was locked in a global struggle of major proportions, in the midst of which it had to find time to mount and participate in a national campaign for the presidency. So united were most Americans on the meaning and necessity of the war that both major parties skirted the issue, emphasizing instead the necessity to maintain the reforms wrought by the New Deal and their hopes for a world organization that would keep the peace.

In the face of such unanimity, there remained still a hardcore of isolationists from prewar days who would not accept the facts of the war and who advocated the building of an impregnable western hemispheric-defense system as the best means to avoid entanglement in Europe's struggles. In the face of the Japanese attack, they turned to a program of concentrating American forces in the Pacific and abandoning entirely the war against the Axis in Europe. Many isolationists would have liked to forward the candidacy of General Douglas MacArthur within the Republican Party; but when the general showed himself more intent upon fulfilling his promise to return to the Philippines, they lost their force. Some of them turned their attention to a small minor party that had developed out of the America First Committee of 1940, and to its candidate Gerald L. K. Smith.

The America First Committee had been organized largely by anti-New Deal industrialists, opposed to what they considered "Rooseveltian communism" and opposed, too, to the increasing interventionism sentiment. A strange mixture of idealists, fascists, conservatives, businessmen, and demagogues, the America First Committee appealed equally to politicians like Senator Burton K. Wheeler of Montana and Representative Hamilton Fish of New York, businessmen like Robert E. Wood of Sears, Roebuck, publishers like Robert McCormick of the *Chicago Tribune,* idealists like Charles Lindbergh, and self-styled leaders of the people like Gerald Smith. Through speeches, pamphlets, and propaganda, they hoped to influence a majority of the American people to an isolationist course and to prevent Congress from modifying its neutrality legislation or adopting legislation that might jeopardize the peace. Their strength lay primarily in the Midwest, where the tradition of isolationism was strong, but it also appealed to some southern Ku Klux Klanners and followers of Father Coughlin's Christian Front throughout the country. In 1944, the remaining die-hards who had not been convinced of the necessity for war despite the attack on Pearl Harbor, converted the Committee into a party and placed its name on the national ballot. As their candidate, they selected Smith.

Smith had emerged into the national limelight on the coattails of Huey Long in the early 1930s. Long had been engaged in building up the strength of his "Share Our Wealth" movement, a scheme to rectify the existing maldistribution of wealth in the United States by taxing all incomes over a million dollars and all inheritances over five million, and using the money to furnish all Americans with allowances of five-thousand dollars, annual incomes of two thousand, pensions for the old, and college educations for the youth. Long's economic fantasy was not only the answer to every poor family's dreams—and in the 1930s there were many poor families in America—but it also became the basis for his political kingdom in Louisiana. Long hoped to make it the basis for his political authority throughout the country, and to this end, he took on Smith as the director of the "Share Our Wealth" crusade.

Smith was a minister in the Disciples of Christ Church, who had just been ousted by his wealthy parishioners in Shreveport, Louisiana, for his social and political radicalism. Born in a small town in Wisconsin, he had been nurtured on populist and rural radicalism. Besides being endowed with a handsome appearance, he possessed a magnificent voice and effective speaking manner. Using fundamentalist techniques, he could whip up audience enthusiasm with dramatic impressiveness, exhorting his listeners to "Share, share, share," and urging them to

pull down these huge piles of gold until there shall be a real job, not a little old sow-belly, black-eyed pea job but a real spending money, beefsteak and gravy, Chevrolet, Ford in the garage, new suit, Thomas Jefferson, Jesus Christ, red, white and blue job for every man.

And then, combining prayer with exhortation, he would conclude:

lift us out of this wretchedness, O Lord, out of this poverty . . . rally us under this young man [Long] who came out of the woods of north Louisiana, who leads us like a Moses out of the land of bondage into the land of milk and honey where every man is a king but no man wears a crown. Amen.

With the assassination of Long, Smith took over the movement, but was soon ousted by the politicians who captured the Long machine in Louisiana. Turning his attention to Dr. Francis E. Townsend, whose pension plan for the aged had achieved great popularity in 1934, he pursued the doctor "like a bridegroom still trying to catch up with my bride," and founded with him and Father Coughlin, a Catholic priest from Detroit who had secured a wide hearing through his radio broadcasts advocating social justice, anti-New Dealism, and anti-Semitism, the National Union Party, with Congressman William Lemke as their standard-bearer in 1936.

The triumvirate behind Lemke soon fell apart, as Coughlin became more distrustful of Smith and his tactics. Smith genuinely believed he was a man of destiny, and as the crowds responded to his wild oratory, he became convinced that there were no limits to what he could accomplish. "Religion and patriotism, keep going on that," he once remarked, it's the only way you can get them really "het up." Then, certain nerve centers in the population will begin to twitch—and the people will start fomenting, fermenting, and then a fellow like myself, someone with courage enough to capture the people, will get on the radio and have the people with him, hook, line, and sinker. I'll teach 'em how to hate. The people are beginning to trust true leadership.

In his enthusiasm for leadership, Smith announced that he would create a new nationalist movement that would "seize the government of the United States." Lemke and Townsend forthwith disowned him, while Coughlin, intent upon his own cause and reputation, ignored him; on election eve, Smith was jailed in New Orleans for using obscene language and disturbing the peace, and until 1940 he more or less dropped from public view.

The war in Europe gave him his second chance. As most of the "Keep America out of War" organizations closed shop, and either joined the war effort or remained silent, Smith got possession of their mailing lists and began systematically to write letters to the members of at least sixty-five such organizations, giving special attention to the "Mothers" groups: "Mothers of American Heroes," "American Mothers Against Communism," and "True American Mothers with Outstretched Arms," among many. Forming these groups into cells, he kept them together through letters and a magazine, *The Cross and The Flag,* and made them the base of a party devoted to America First. Among the party's policies were included the necessity to "build a hoop of military steel around America after this war, which will guarantee protection from invasion and make it unnecessary to wage future wars of aggression"; "food before whiskey"; ". . . stop giving the poor man's taxes to save the British Empire"; "money for our servicemen before milk for Hottentots"; and opposition to labor movements that were not in the "hands of patriotic American leadership."

Whatever Smith's claim, his following in the 1944 election amounted to only 1,780 votes cast primarily in Texas and Michigan. In 1948 he changed his party's name to the Christian Nationalist Crusade, and again received a small number of votes from the few die-hards who were caught by his evangelical fervor. Still hopeful in 1956, the Smith group called themselves the Christian Nationalist Party, and not only received even fewer votes—only eight popular votes from California—but seemingly disappeared from the political scene. His magazine continued to be published and continued to carry anti-Semitic, anti-Negro, right-wing materials. In 1966, he had built and dedicated a giant statue of Christ on the top of Magnetic Mountain at Eureka Springs, Arkansas, and an amphitheatre next to it for the staging of a Passion play.

Pollsters Confounded 1948

COLUMNISTS AND POLLSTERS WERE AMONG THE MOST BEWILDERED AMERICANS ON THE morning of November 3, 1948, when the people of the United States woke up to the news that Harry S. Truman had won another term in the White House. On its front page, *The Washington Post* advertised a banquet for the president, during which "political reporters and editors, including our own, along with pollsters, radio commentators and columnists" would be served "breast of tough old crow en glace." If Truman came, he would eat "turkey."

Thomas E. Dewey, Truman's Republican opponent, was also bewildered at the strange turn of events. "I am as much surprised as you are," he told reporters crowding into his office the day after election. "I have read your stories. We were all wrong together."

One of the few public officials who was not surprised at the election results was Truman himself, who never doubted, publicly at least, his eventual victory. Speaking at Madison Square Garden, at the rally traditionally marking the end of the Democratic campaign, he told his audience a story of his consultation with the White House physician. "I told him," Truman reported, "that I kept having this feeling that wherever I go there's somebody following behind me. The White House physician told me not to worry. He said, 'You keep right on your way. There's one place where that fellow's not going to follow you and that's into the White House.' "

In 1948 the electorate had hardly recovered from wartime stringencies and dislocations. World War II had come to an end in a holocaust of atomic explosions that marked the arrival of a new age for mankind. With the introduction of nuclear energy and the possibilities of universal annihilation through deadly atomic weapons, man's international behavior had to undergo change. The old diplomatic reliance on international law was obsolete. Whatever institutions World War II had already affected—imperialism, territorial mandates, international treaties—the coming of the atomic bomb changed even more. The fear of new and more terrible war was heightened by the descent of the Iron Curtain, which separated not only the peoples of the East and the West, but specifically the troops of Stalin from the troops of the Western world. The Truman Doctrine and Marshall Plan were intended to prevent Communist expansion into Western Europe and to aid in the reconstruction of the war-torn nations of that region; but still chaos threatened and the fear of another war hung heavily over the American electorate during the months that saw the presidential campaign underway.

The fear of war gave rise to, and paralleled, a fear of Communist infiltration of government. This fear was melodramatically symbolized by the testimony of Whittaker Chambers before the House Un-American Activities Committee, the consequent accusation of Alger Hiss, and the disclosures of alleged sabotage by trusted civil servants.

Fear of communism was actually an aspect of an even larger anxiety experienced by many Americans who were coming to be called "conservatives" because of their anti-New Deal posture and their criticism of increasing governmental controls over American economic life. Adopting as their bible Friedrich von Hayek's scholarly *The Road to Serfdom,* a treatise that equated New Deal liberalism with Nazism in terms of their ideas of national economic planning, the conservatives bent all their efforts to rid the country of its New Deal legacy and turn it back to the happy utopia of nineteenth-century unregulated capitalism. The social reform efforts of liberals, and their seeming willingness to tolerate communism, created a strong conservative, anti-Communist movement that inextricably associated in conservative minds domestic problems with foreign affairs, so that no issue—whether it was the rash of "unpatriotic" strikes among railroad workers, automobile workers, or coal miners, or food shortages, rising prices, black-market trading, or farm policy—was free of a Communist interpretation. It was all very well, said Nebraska's conservative Senator Kenneth Wherry, "to win a war with socialist New Dealers and Bolsheviks having a love feast, but what follows then?"

What followed then was a gradual stiffening of national policy towards Russia, which by 1948 divided Americans into various camps, but the Democrats especially into two: those who approved of Truman's "containment" policies on the question of feared Communist expansionism in Western Europe, and those who like Henry A. Wallace, believed sincerely that the Soviet Union was a peaceful power and that the Truman policy towards that country constituted warmongering. "The danger of war," said Wallace in the New York City speech that marked his break with the Truman administration, "is much less from Communism than it is from imperialism."

The bitterness experienced by Americans as a result of the fear of communism was sharpened by anxieties over postwar economic and social readjustments. Inflationary prices took the place of wartime price controls as Americans, yearning for goods and appliances and luxuries after four long years of war and many more years of deprivation, went on a spending spree. Race riots and lynchings followed the loud demands of Negroes for civil rights and equal treatment in housing, employment, and public facilities, and Jews were again being threatened by new organizations modeled on the Ku Klux Klan. Tensions in the Palestine region added to Jewish–American complaints against the administration which seemed slow to act in helping the nation built out of the sweat and blood of European Jewry from achieving independence. "All the advances which minorities made during the New Deal and the war seem to be in question," editorialized the *Cleveland Plain Dealer*. "And what is the longtime trend? Who knows?"

"Had enough?" the Republicans asked the country in 1946—and the American people answered affirmatively by electing the first Republican Congress since 1930. The Eightieth Congress, which during the 1948 election became the butt of Truman's devastating humor, contained 51 Republicans and 45 Democrats in the Senate, and 246 Republicans and 188 Democrats in the House. The results of this midterm election suggested to pollsters, newspapermen, and political observers everywhere that the Republicans would enjoy certain victory in 1948. Especially important as portents of the coming Democratic defeat was the seeming trend towards Republicanism among Negroes, who, losing faith in the Democratic administration of Truman, identified him with the southern Democrats who were slow to give them their rights. They blamed Truman for the failure of the federal government to establish a permanent Fair

413

Employment Practices Commission and to outlaw lynching, and they were ready by 1946 to test their luck with a change of party.

Truman's clash with organized labor during the railroad strike also alienated many liberal voters, who saw in his threat to draft striking workers intimidation and lack of concern for civil liberties. They were not attracted either by his "get-tough" policy towards the Soviet Union, and therefore turned to Henry Wallace to fulfill their desire for peace and social justice.

Southern Democrats, resentful of their decline in power within Truman's party, feared that their rural and agrarian interests were taking second place in governmental policy to urban industrial needs. Bitter, too, at the 1947 report of Truman's Committee on Civil Rights, which advocated government action in several civil rights areas, they began to organize a revolt in the hope of forcing party leaders to take a more conservative position. They turned to Strom Thurmond, governor of South Carolina, for leadership, and thus further contributed to the weakening of Truman's Democratic coalition of party regulars, southern conservatives, urban liberals, Negroes, and ethnic minorities. Again, it seemed as if a Republican victory was inevitable.

The disintegration of Truman's support was reflected in the efforts of the Americans for Democratic Action (ADA), a group of liberal "independent" voters who most frequently voted Democratic, to recruit General Dwight D. Eisenhower as a candidate for the presidency. They hoped he would "stir the popular enthusiasm which will sweep progressive candidates across the country into Congress," while defeating "both the forces of vested reaction and the Communist-dominated third party [the Progressives]." Eisenhower, however, steadfastly refused to state a party affiliation or to accept a nomination for the presidency, and eventually the field narrowed down to the candidates endorsed by the several parties during the spring and summer of 1948: Henry Wallace (Progressive), Harry S. Truman (Democratic), Thomas E. Dewey (Republican), and Strom Thurmond (Dixiecrat).

With the Democrats so divided, how was victory possible? The requirements of the election moved Truman toward the left and toward, therefore, satisfying the large and needy groups in the country. Deciding to minimize the differences between the Democrats and liberals and to make a pitch for the Negro, Progressive, and labor vote, the Truman group based its campaign on issues that would reassure these disaffected Democrats while not too harshly alienating southerners, whom they depended upon to vote according to party tradition, whatever their disagreement with policy. As a result, Truman refused to bargain with the Republicans on any compromise relating to labor legislation. His veto of the Taft-Hartley bill earlier had "paid big political dividends," as Clark Clifford, Truman's special counsel, reminded him; therefore, on "all the *domestic* issues—the rising cost of living, housing and rent control, tax revision, conservation, and civil rights—" the president did not hedge. Instead, by presenting these issues directly to a special session of the Eightieth Congress the summer of the election year, knowing that they would be voted down or not considered at all because of time limitations, Truman proved himself the friend of the downtrodden and oppressed—the group to whom his Fair Deal campaign and programs were addressed.

414

Dewey pennant   CORNELL UNIVERSITY, DOUGLAS COLLECTION

As for foreign policy, the Democrats rested their case for containment and the Marshall Plan on the good sense of the majority of Americans, whom World War II had convinced of the necessity for international commitments and responsibilities. They were inadvertently helped by the Russians, when the Communists staged a coup in Czechoslovakia in February 1948, overturning a liberal regime. The Soviet blockade of Berlin in June further proved the inefficacy of Wallace's peace position, and most Americans responded positively to Truman's organization of an airlift for the blockaded city. And in May, Truman, after much consultation and in the face of conflicting advice, decided that the establishment and recognition by the United States of the State of Israel was in America's national interest—a step widely welcomed by American Jewish leaders as well as liberals everywhere who believed that some help had to be tendered to the remnant of Jews who had survived Hitler's holocaust and now hoped to fulfill the Messianic promise.

So far had Americans come in internationalism, in fact, that the Republican platform on foreign policy did not drastically differ from the Democrats', except in intensity and extent. The Republicans endorsed the United Nations and the containment policy, although it compromised, as the Democratic platform did not, on a reciprocal trade program and said nothing about aid to Israel. The Democrats went further, asking for larger appropriations for the Marshall Plan and United States support of international control of atomic energy.

On domestic programs, the Democrats were more forceful in their expression of civil rights' aims and policies and in their demands for labor—the repeal of the Taft-Hartley Act and an increase in minimum wage and social-security benefits. But even on these questions, the Republicans were willing to concede somewhat, recognizing that whatever their personal feelings, these measures were permanent reforms and had to be retained.

From Labor Day to election day, Truman stumped the country giving the Eightieth Congress "hell" and defending the New Deal and his extension of it from its critics. Interpreting the New Deal as beneficial to the interests of the great majority of the American people, Truman hit hard at the Republican-dominated Congress that threatened its continuation.

Dewey, believing that victory was his tended to avoid issues and conducted what the Republicans termed a "high level" campaign. Seeking unity, he spoke in generalities that could not be refuted. He promised "the biggest, untangling, unsnarling, weeding and pruning operation in our history" once he became president, and reiterated what came to be the Republican keynote—the belief that "our future and the peace of the world are staked on how united the people of America are." His well-organized campaign train smoothly made its way across the country, but Dewey's efficiency was not impressive, nor were his careful preparations and discreet avoidances. Whatever admiration he aroused was lackluster and even newsmen aboard his "Victory Special" found themselves bored and without colorful material to offer their readers. "I kept reading about that Dewey fellow," reported one ordinary voter from Ohio, "and the more I read the more he reminded me of one of those slick ads trying to get money out of my pocket. Now Harry Truman, running around and yipping and falling all over his feet—I had the feeling he could understand the kind of fixes I get into. . . ."

Truman was more fun to watch and listen to. He introduced his family in folksy midwestern manner; he mimicked Dewey's "mealy-mouth unity speeches" and he hit hard at the Republican candidate's strategy. His liberal posture, moreover, which partook of the plain sincerity of his nature, took the steam out of the Wallace program, while more sober southerners began to have second thoughts about abandoning the Democratic organization that had served them so well for all these past decades. Thus, overlooked by the pollsters and the political quizmasters, the southerners and progressives began moving back into the Democratic fold. Dewey's self-confidence led him to ignore what the people wanted to hear—an explanation of the troublesome issues of the time and a promise to relieve them of some of their difficulties—and propelled the independents into Truman's camp.

It took time for Dewey to concede the election, even though the results from the first ballot returns pointed to a Truman victory; but it was not until ten-thirty on the morning of the day after election that he finally admitted his error and his defeat. He had waged his campaign mistakenly on the basis of the pollsters' predictions and had lost.

Truman, however, was not elected by a majority of the American people, testifying to the fact of a still-divided electorate. He received only 49.5 percent of the popular vote—and, interestingly enough, the total popular vote was less in 1948 than in previous presidential tallies, although the population had increased by fifteen million during the past eight years. Angus Campbell, of the Survey Research Center, regarding the "extraordinary low turnout" as 1948's most striking feature, referred to it as "the prototype of the low-stimulus presidential election."

Even so, Truman achieved an astonishing victory. The Democrats captured both houses of Congress and five new governerships, while Truman himself emerged as a plucky and bold fighter representative of the best of grass-roots America. Truman accomplished his surprising victory, however, not only through his aggressive and steadfast campaign, but also because he had taken advantage of the strength of the Democratic Party that still remained from the days of Franklin D. Roosevelt. The strategy devised to exploit that strength—a revival of the socio-economic issues of the New Deal and an appeal to the same groups that had supported that program—was as important as Truman's personal symbolization of those issues.

Truman emerged from the 1948 election as the friend of the common man—the farmer, Negro, worker; he promised to protect their hard-earned gains and to increase them; and he identified himself with their aspirations for a better life. "I talked about voting for Dewey all summer," one Iowa farmer confessed, "but when voting time came I just couldn't do it. I remembered . . . all the good things that have come to me under the Democrats." Urbanites also remembered. "I own a nice home," one Bostonian suburbanite explained: "I have a new car and am much better off than my parents were. Why change?"

All these groups looked to Truman to reinstate and continue FDR's New Deal policies. Thus, Truman's victory represented a continuation of political commitments made during the 1930s. "Truman benefited and Dewey suffered," Richard Kirkendall claims, "from the party realignment that had taken place then." So well had FDR wrought a Democratic coalition during the thirties, that in 1948 its strength emerged to save the election for his successor. The greatest strength of the New Deal had lain in its approach to domestic problems, in its emphasis on the use of national power to deal with the nation's social and economic problems. Truman, by promising vigorously and aggressively to maintain this approach, not only retained the government for the Democrats for another four years, but instituted New Deal policy permanently in the life of the country. After him, no future candidate—Republican or Democrat—could afford to ignore it.

Harry S. Truman and Thomas Dewey *Photograph* NATIONAL ARCHIVES

Thomas E. Dewey *Republican*

1902-1971

Despite his 1944 defeat, Thomas E. Dewey continued to maintain his prestige within the Republican Party. Running again for the New York governorship in 1946, he began his second term with an unprecedented landslide victory and in so doing demonstrated to his fellow partisans that he had not lost his ability to win votes. As the election of 1948 drew near, the New Yorker again showed promise of becoming a presidential candidate.

This time, however, nomination was not so simple a matter as it had been in 1944. With several strong candidates in the field—Ohio Senator Robert Taft and former Minnesota Governor Harold Stassen—Dewey found it considerably more difficult to muster delegates behind him. Nevertheless, his popularity in the public polls along with his superior ability to organize his supporters ultimately knocked out his opponents and on the third ballot, his nomination became unanimous.

Again running on a liberal platform which took issue with the Democrats more on how they did things rather than on what they did, Dewey was certain—as were most Americans—that the White House would finally be his. The off-year elections of 1946, in which Republicans after eighteen years finally regained control of both houses of Congress, had already indicated a national swing away from the Democratic Party. By 1948, divisions within the Democratic ranks over foreign policy and civil rights had deepened to the point where they were now in the throes of outright revolt. Thus, the New York Republican found himself in the happy position of facing a severely fragmented opposition.

Given this propitious situation, Dewey settled on a low-risk strategy. Fearing that he might jeopardize his advantage in an issue-oriented campaign, he confined himself to generalities. Despite Truman's persistent efforts to draw him into debate on specific issues, he remained confidently aloof and instead talked glowingly of such things as the "future" and the fact that it most certainly lay ahead.

As in his previous campaign, Dewey assiduously looked to details. When it was decided that Mrs. Dewey's favorite hat did not lend itself to the photographer's lens, husband and wife settled on a compromise; she would wear the hat in small towns where news photographers were not present, but in the larger cities she would wear something else.

As Truman so happily pointed out the day after election, Dewey's optimism proved to be unfounded. Both farmers and labor had been alienated by the Republican Congress. Considering the GOP–inspired Taft-Hartley Act of 1947—with its stipulations banning the closed shop and secondary boycotts—a betrayal of the nation's laboring interests, workers continued to identify themselves with the party of the New Deal. Similarly, farmers plagued by crop surpluses blamed the Republicans for Congress' failure to renew government authority to expand federal crop-storage facilities. As a result, farmers had no choice but to dispose of their surpluses at deplorably low prices; when Truman accused the Republican Congress of sticking "a

Dewey and Warren pin SMITHSONIAN INSTITUTION

pitchfork in the farmer's back," many in the nation's rural population, overlooking the fact that the indifference of the Democratic administration had also played a part in creating this situation, listened and agreed.

Surprisingly, Dewey also suffered from indiscretion. In one uncharacteristic moment of carelessness, when the engineer on his campaign special nearly injured local bystanders in his attempt to back up the train, he impatiently remarked that perhaps the engineer "should be shot at sunrise." Seizing upon the remark, newsmen in the entourage wired their papers who promptly publicized the Republican's thoughtless departure from his otherwise cautious rhetoric. Worse still, Truman could not resist taunting Dewey with metaphorical allusions to another Republican statesman: the Republican nominee, he remarked, "objects to having

420

engineers back up. He doesn't mention that under the great engineer Hoover, we backed up into the worst depression in history."

With his defeat, Dewey returned to Albany, New York, to complete his term as governor and, in 1950, reelection to still another term. Now the elder statesman of his party, he continued to play a leading role in Republican national affairs. Largely due to his influence, Dwight Eisenhower became the GOP candidate in 1952. It was also Dewey who urged that the general accept Richard Nixon as his running mate. In doing so, he opened the way for Nixon's presidential candidacy in 1960 and 1968. On Dewey's death in 1971, *The Washington Post,* pointing out that it would be unfair to view him as simply a defeated presidential candidate, hailed Dewey as a "valuable public servant" whose presence in American politics had "made a considerable difference in the political history of his times."

HENRY A. WALLACE   *Grant Wood, 1940   Crayon, 24 x 20 inches   Pioneer Hi-bred International Inc., Des Moines*

Henry A. Wallace *Progressive*

1888-1965

Spurred on by the struggle to stem Communist influence in Western Europe following World War II, the United States embarked on a "get tough" foreign policy toward the Soviet Union. As President Truman later explained, "The ideals and traditions of our nation demanded that . . . we put the world on notice that it would be our policy to support the cause of freedom wherever it was threatened." The Truman Doctrine, which provided military and economic aid to Greece and Turkey, both debilitated by guerilla warfare; and the Marshall Plan, a program of economic assistance to war-torn Europe, constituted a broad policy of containment of Russian expansion to the areas in Eastern Europe already negotiated by treaty.

While majority opinion supported the administration, many groups in the nation viewed the firm policy toward Russia with misgivings. Progressives, pacifists, religious leaders, scientists, and isolationists argued that the United States was committing itself in areas in which historically it had little interest, and that such a policy might lead to a direct clash with the Soviet Union. In the presidential election of 1948, this opposition found expression in the candidacy of Henry Agard Wallace, former philosopher of the New Deal, secretary of agriculture and vice-president under Franklin Roosevelt, and Truman's secretary of commerce.

Born in Iowa, Wallace was raised close to the soil and the men who worked it. His family was long distinguished in agriculture; his grandfather, the first Henry Wallace, was a member of President Theodore Roosevelt's Country Life Commission and the founder and editor of *Wallace's Farmer,* an influential agricultural journal. "Uncle Henry" to half of Iowa, he was the "idol of prairie men throughout the West." Henry Cantwell Wallace, his father, had been secretary of agriculture under Harding and Coolidge.

At an early age, young Henry had committed himself to "unleashing the productive capacities of nature, machines, and men." Before he was graduated from Iowa State College, he was already widely known for developing a hybrid corn seed that significantly improved corn production throughout the Middle West. To distribute the seed, Wallace organized the Pioneer Hi-Bred Corn Company and became its president and general manager. Continuing family tradition, he took over editorship of *Wallace's Farmer,* using it as a sounding board for agricultural problems and grievances.

Embittered by Herbert Hoover's opposition to price-fixing legislation which he believed would have greatly aided farmers severely hit by the depression, Wallace bolted the Republican Party in 1928 to support Alfred E. Smith. He worked eagerly in 1932 for the election of Franklin D. Roosevelt, because of his promise of progressive social and economic reforms; for this, he was rewarded with the office of secretary of agriculture.

Wallace quickly became a significant symbol of the reform spirit of the New Deal. Believing that America needed economic and social "rebalancing," he advocated a comprehensive program of government regulation of the economy. Although he acknowledged that there was "something wooden and inhuman about the government interfering . . . with the details of our private and business lives," he asserted, "we are committed to getting the farmer, the laborer, and the industrialist such share of the national income as will put each in a balanced relationship with the other." Supervising the controversial Agricultural Adjustment Administration, which raised farm prices by the systematic destruction of surplus produce, he helped introduce the new principle of government subsidization to create a better social order. In

Henry A. Wallace button   SMITHSONIAN INSTITUTION

1940 Wallace became vice-president, but largely because of his avowed support of an active alliance with the Soviet Union, he was replaced on the Democratic ticket in 1944 and named instead secretary of commerce.

Wallace's political philosophy evolved from a fervid and ingrained Christian morality that expressed itself in sincere concern for the "common man, the forgotten man." Much of his thinking focused on the effects of American foreign policy on this segment of the world population. He considered peace essential to improving man's lot on earth; too much was wasted, the cost of war was too dear in terms of raw materials, manpower, and time. The maintenance of peace through "economic collaboration" was, he believed, the only feasible goal of American foreign policy. During World War II he had been a spokesman of the country's idealistic war aims, and after the war he remained a strong proponent of international cooperation and understanding.

As the new American policy of "containment" became formalized after World War II, Wallace openly protested what he considered to be the "war-breeding" attitude of the administration toward the Soviet Union. In September 1946, in a speech at Madison Square Garden in New York—at the very time when Secretary of State James F. Byrnes was meeting with the Soviet foreign minister in Paris—Wallace charged that the United States was not trying to meet the Russians halfway and argued that Truman's "get tough" policy would inevitably result in atomic war. Reaction to his speech was volcanic, and Wallace was dismissed within a week.

After his abrupt removal from office, Wallace continued his "fight for peace." Accepting the position of editor for the *New Republic,* he elaborated in that magazine on his opposition to President Truman and his policies. In 1947, he made a highly publicized tour of Western Europe during which he accused the administration of launching the United States on a "wild and mad nightmare" of ruthless imperialism. Again and again, he expounded the thesis that "no powerful idea—and Communism is a powerful idea—can be countered by a gun, however powerful that gun may be."

Although the idea of forming a third party had been proposed to Wallace for some time, he consistently expressed his intention of working within the Democratic Party until the end of 1947. His final decision to bolt came only after he decided that if both parties stood for war and depression, "the people must have a new party of liberty and peace. The people must have a choice." Finally, on December 29, 1947, he announced his candidacy for the presidency, declaring "I have fought and shall continue to fight programs which give guns to people when they want plows. . . . We have assembled a Gideon's army—small in number, powerful in conviction, ready for action. . . . By God's grace, the people's peace will usher in the century of the common man."

The Progressive Citizens of America, formed by a consolidation of liberals and Communists, had been backing Wallace's candidacy for some time, and it was this group which became the basis for the new Progressive Party. Composed of a disparate collection of young people, blacks, pacifists, liberals, and Communists, and only a few professional politicians, the party met in convention in Philadelphia in July and formally nominated Wallace for the presidency. Glen Taylor, singing cowboy and Democratic senator from Idaho, was selected as his running mate. Chanting:

> One, two, three, four,
> We don't want another war,

the Progressive Party proceeded to formulate a platform that condemned the Truman Doctrine and the Marshall Plan, proposed the destruction of atomic-bomb stockpiles, and criticized rearmament and the defense build up.

425

Wallace, labeled the "Pied Piper of the Politburo," seemed likely to weaken Truman's chances for election. He was reported to be popular in the Far West and in urban areas, and it was estimated that he would poll at least five-million votes. Although he campaigned strenuously, logging over 55,000 miles and visiting nearly every state in the Union, his candidacy was, however, sapped of much of its strength virtually from the beginning.

Wallace spent a good deal of time in the South where his stress on civil rights evoked violent reactions, including numerous drenchings with rotten eggs and tomatoes. Foreign policy was, however, the crux of his campaign; and on this issue, he was hurt by his close identification with the Communists. Seemingly innocent of political realities, Wallace had accepted Communist support simply because he believed that Communists were as anxious as he was for peace: "Anyone who will work for peace is okay with me," he once told a reporter. As the Communists gained effective control of the Progressive Party, however, Wallace's non-Communist support dropped away. American labor and the Americans for Democratic Action refused to support the Iowan because they believed his election would play directly into the hands of the Soviet Union. Events in the USSR during the campaign also hurt Wallace's candidacy: a coup ousting the liberal regime in Czechoslovakia and the blockade of West Berlin greatly heightened American resentment of communism, turning the electorate soundly against Wallace and his party.

Harry Truman, by conducting a campaign designed to minimize the Wallace movement, also cut deeply into Wallace's potential support. Moving toward the left, Truman portrayed himself as the true friend of the "common man" and as the champion of their better interests, thereby stealing much of Wallace's thunder.

Wallace's final tally came as a surprise to him and to political experts. He earned slightly more than a million votes and did not meaningfully influence the outcome of the election. The people he had called on to "stand up and be counted" had failed to materialize. His domestic program of reform, however, entered into Truman's Fair Deal campaign and program.

Soon after the election, Wallace left the Progressive Party, maintaining an independent political attitude for the rest of his life. Returning to his farm and agricultural studies, he resumed his early experiments in genetics until his death in 1965.

STROM THURMOND   *Louis Lupas, 1959-60   Pastel and wash, 24 x 18½ inches*
Senator Strom Thurmond

Strom Thurmond *States' Rights Democrat*

1 9 0 2 –

Acting upon the long-standing grievances of the nation's black community—much to the dismay of many southern Democrats—early in 1948 President Truman presented Congress with a set of civil-rights proposals such as had not been seen since the days of Radical Reconstruction. In addition to urging the elimination of the poll tax in those states where it still persisted and the enactment of a federal anti-lynching law, he asked Congress to prohibit racial discrimination in employment. Some white southerners reacted to this projected legislation immediately. Meeting in Florida shortly after the president had made his wishes known, southern Democratic governors warned that if the president did not "cease attacks on white supremacy," he would face a "full-fledged revolt" among his white southern supporters.

Bitter though they were, the dissident southerners nevertheless did not carry out their threat immediately. Confident that they could thwart Truman's proposals by applying pressure within the party, they were willing to confine their show of disapproval to party councils. One southern politician, for example, reserved an entire table at a Jefferson–Jackson banquet and, making sure that it remained vacant, thus dramatized what might happen to southern support if Truman were allowed to have his way. However, when northern liberals finally succeeded at the Democratic convention in gaining a platform endorsement of Truman's policies, some southern delegates now found their position within Democratic ranks untenable. As soon as the roll-call vote on the civil-rights plank reached completion, thirty-five delegates from Mississippi and Alabama demonstrated their disapproval by walking out of the convention.

With this act, the States' Rights Democratic Party was born. Calling a convention in Birmingham, Alabama, just days after the Democratic convention in Philadelphia, the southern bolters now undertook the business of drawing up a platform and nominating their own candidate for president. Denouncing Truman's program as a blatant violation of the right of states to determine their own racial policies, they defended southern segregation as the main cornerstone of "peace and order" in their region. So saying, they entrusted their presidential fortunes to Strom Thurmond, governor of South Carolina.

The son of a South Carolina lawyer, Thurmond began his adult life as a rural schoolteacher.

By the age of twenty-five, he had become superintendent of schools for his home county of Edgefield. Not satisfied, however, with confining himself to education, he began to study law under the tutelage of his father and in 1930 was admitted to the state bar. Two years later, Thurmond ran a successful campaign for the state senate, where he served for six years. Here, he distinguished himself as the advocate of an extended rural-electrification program as well as various bills to improve the state's educational system. In 1938, he received appointment to a circuit judgeship, which he left in 1941 to undertake army service. After winning many decorations, he was discharged with the rank of lieutenant colonel.

In 1946, Thurmond campaigned for the South Carolina governorship on a platform advocating soldier bonuses and a twenty-five percent pay increase for teachers. Ultimately

States' Rights lapel button for Strom Thurmond's campaign   CORNELL UNIVERSITY, DOUGLAS COLLECTION

successful, he gave South Carolina what in many respects was one of its most active and progressive administrations. He sponsored plans to "streamline" the state's administrative branches; kept his promise to raise teachers' salaries; helped to institute a variety of programs improving the state's vocational and adult-education facilities; and supported legislation to create new health standards for factories and a system of state-farm markets.

As the States' Rights standard-bearer, Thurmond threw himself vigorously into the campaign in the hope that his strong showing in the South would destroy what seemed already to be the slender chance of a Truman victory. Confining his campaign to the southern states, the "Dixiecrat" tried to rally voters with arguments that the passage of federal civil-rights legislation would strip states of their "integrity." Agreeing with his vice-presidential running-mate's allegation that Truman's scheme for equal-employment opportunity had been "hatched in the brains of Communists," he likened the enactment of such a proposal to the coming of a "federal gestapo."

In the end, Thurmond succeeded in winning four states—Alabama, Louisiana, Mississippi, and South Carolina. However disenchanted they may have been with Truman's civil-rights policies, most Southerners could not bring themselves to break with the party that had dominated politics in their region since the Civil War, and which under Roosevelt had brought so many economic benefits. Many important southern politicians, although sympathetic with the Dixiecrats, were unwilling to jeopardize their long-standing influence within national Democratic councils by aligning themselves with a maverick faction.

After the campaign, Thurmond returned to South Carolina to complete his term as governor. In 1954, he won election to the United States Senate where he became a member of the Armed Services Committee. Continuing to adhere to the doctrine of States' Rights, he took a leading role in drawing up the Declaration of Constitutional Principles of 1956, commonly known as the Southern Manifesto, which in essence denied the right of the federal government to regulate states' racial policies. Finally, in 1964, sixteen years after his first bolt from the party, Thurmond, responding to a resurgence of Republican conservatism, severed his connections with the Democratic Party completely and joined the Republicans.

Time for a Change 1952

IT IS IRONIC THAT THE VERY FORCES THAT RETAINED HARRY TRUMAN IN THE WHITE House for another four years after 1948 were the same that propelled the Republicans into it in 1952. The change that the American people voted for in 1952 was a change in party rather than in policy or program. The Republicans won because they promised to do what the Democrats had done, but do it better; they would maintain the prosperity of the Truman administration, the "social gains" of the New Deal–Fair Deal program, the foreign policy of the United Nations, Marshall Plan, Point 4, and containment. But social legislation would be administered more efficiently and honestly, without danger of subversion from Communists and corrupt politicians; and the containment policy would be extended to Asia and strengthened by more explicit threats of retaliation and serious consequences to Communist acts of aggression in the Far East. The Republicans also won because they presented their candidates as Truman had presented himself in 1948—as representative middle-class Americans desiring and achieving the goals sought by the man-on-the-street, open, simple and righteous goals like a home of one's own, security for one's family, advancement for oneself and one's country.

Why did Americans want a change of personnel in 1952? What made the housewife in Harrisburg, Pennsylvania, believe that with the election of General Dwight Eisenhower and Richard Nixon "America has come home"? What had happened in the four intervening years between Truman's surprise election of 1948 and Eisenhower's landslide of 1952, to make Americans feel that somehow the nation had departed from its tried and traditional paths to undertake critical measures that threatened social revolution at home and international conflict abroad, tasks of such immense complexity that they threatened to engulf the whole population in disaster?

The Republican campaign formula tells the story—K_1C_2 was the phrase invented by Senator Karl Mundt, co-chairman of the Republicans' Speakers' Bureau, to denote the issues that the party should dwell on during its campaign—the Korean War and charges of corruption and communism in government.

Mink coats and deep freezes were the symbols in 1952 of governmental corruption. As news of such gifts to Democratic officials or presidential advisers were sensationally presented, the sense of corruption in government was paralleled by the feeling that this was simply one phase of a general immorality that had permeated the country as a whole and was bent on destroying its soul. "How do we deal with those who, under the guise of friendship, accept favors which offend the spirit of the law but do not violate its letter?" asked Senator J. William Fulbright of Arkansas. "What of the men outside government who suborn those inside it?" When Senator Estes Kefauver of Tennessee opened his investigations into crime and law enforcement agencies, the questions asked by Fulbright were again pertinent. Kefauver pointed up not just the illegal conduct of some Americans, but the unethical behavior of the whole community as reflected in teen-age sex clubs, corruption of college basketball teams, dismissal of ninety West Point cadets for cheating in examinations, and numerous other incidents of burglary, drug addiction, sex attacks, and even murder among young, middle-class children.

Corruption was tied to fear of communism in that both were seen as contradicting the

American myth of national purity. Even before Truman's election in 1948, the specter of communist infiltration of government had raised its head, but the Republican candidate had not taken advantage of the issue. Truman dismissed Whittaker Chambers' disclosures as a "red herring," and when Alger Hiss, accused by Chambers of passing on "numerous secrets [and] confidential and restricted" documents to the Russians, underwent trial for perjury in 1949, Truman's cabinet officials, notably Secretary of State Dean Acheson, stood by him and refused to take a stand on his innocence or guilt. The fact that Alger Hiss was defended by university professors, New Deal liberals, and ivy-league college graduates added to the sense of corruption among the nation's elite, and contributed to the ever-present jealousy of the intellectual which three years later was to react against the intellectual candidate of the Democrats. To many Americans, the educated community was obviously "soft" on communism, and it was this theme that Senator Joseph McCarthy of Wisconsin played over and over again between 1950 and 1952 to create the feeling that a great Communist conspiracy had influenced American domestic life as well as foreign policy, and that this conspiracy was the direct result of the Democrats' retention of national power for almost twenty years.

Two events of enormous significance for the world increased Americans' belief in the existence of a great Communist conspiracy. In May 1949, the Chinese Communist armies led by Mao Tse-tung defeated Chiang Kai-shek's Nationalist government to take over the governing of their much-troubled country; the news hit the United States in August, when Secretary of State Dean Acheson issued a "White Paper" in which he defended American policy in the Far East, blamed Chiang Kai-shek's corrupt and inefficient government for the fall of China, and explained the revolution in China as the "product of internal Chinese forces, forces which this country tried to influence but could not." A month and a half after Acheson's White Paper came the news of an atomic explosion in the USSR indicating quite clearly that the Soviet scientists had mastered the techniques of creating an atomic bomb and that the United States was no longer secure behind its atomic stockpile. The later revelation that Dr. Klaus Fuchs, a British atomic scientist, had been passing scientific secrets to the Russians from 1943 to 1947 which had been "of the highest value to a potential enemy" and without doubt had contributed to the Russian mastery of the secrets of atomic-bomb production, added fuel to the conviction that the Democratic administrations, since the days of Roosevelt, had been not only "soft" on communism, but careless in protecting the nation's safety. "How much more are we going to have to take?", rhetorically demanded Senator Homer Capehart of Indiana. "Fuchs and Acheson and Hiss and hydrogen bombs threatening outside and New Dealism eating away the vitals of the nation. In the name of Heaven, is this the best America can do?"

But there was more to come to add to Americans' discouragement and loss of faith in the Democrats. On June 24, 1950, North Korean armies invaded the Republic of South Korea, separated arbitrarily by the 38th parallel. Both governments claimed to be speaking for a united Korea, but it was Syngman Rhee's South Korean Republic that had received the recognition of the General Assembly of the United Nations. The UN Security Council, under Truman's prompting, acted quickly. Taking advantage of the USSR's absence from the Council, because of its five-month boycott protesting the refusal of the Council to replace the Nationalist Chinese delegation with representatives from Red China, the Security Council in relatively short time approved the United States resolution accusing North Korea of "armed attack" and demanding that both sides cease fire, with a withdrawal of North Korean troops behind the 38th parallel. Broadly interpreting the United Nations resolution, Truman acted by ordering military support to South Korea and sending the Seventh Fleet into waters surrounding the island of Formosa, to contain as well as protect the Nationalist Chinese established there.

Truman's decision to go to the aid of the Koreans with the support of the United Nations was enthusiastically welcomed at first by Americans of both major parties. Even the conservative Taft wing of the Republican Party approved the president's step to "uphold the hands of the United Nations and the free peoples of the world," as Senator William Knowland of California, a respected Taft follower, put it. Truman, Knowland added, "should have the overwhelming support of all Americans regardless of their party affiliation." For once, Truman made the "right decision" said the head of a Republican county organization in Iowa, while other commentators lauded the president's "magnificent courage" and "statesmanship."

The popular reaction was also at first sympathetic to Truman's "police action" in Korea; but as the war continued, through terrible moments of defeat, retreat, bloody casualties, and mounting American deaths, enthusiasm for a war in an exotic "hell hole" under situations so terribly different from accustomed battlefields waned. The entrance of the Chinese Communist armies on the side of North Korea rendered a grim situation even grimmer; and even though the United Nations forces were able to push the invading armies back across the 38th parallel by 1951, the war reached a stalemate that distressed those Americans who expected quick victories and who, like General MacArthur, believed that limited warfare was simply the "appeasement of Communists." MacArthur took issue with the Truman administration's decision to limit the war in fear that a full-scale conflict would invite full-scale Chinese and Soviet participation. To MacArthur such a limitation could only result in "prolonged indecision"; in war, said MacArthur, "there is no substitute for victory."

Differences in policy, and MacArthur's unwillingness to subordinate his ideas to his civilian commander-in-chief's, led to Truman's dismissal of the "Old Soldier" with consequent public reaction. Explaining that MacArthur's program would "involve us in the wrong war, at the wrong place, at the wrong time, and with the wrong enemy," General Omar Bradley along with other administration officials speaking at the hearings of the Joint Chiefs of Staff managed to turn opinion away from MacArthur and to support of the Truman position; but nevertheless the MacArthur incident added one more argument to the Republican claim that the Democrats were leading the country into disaster.

Economically, the country experienced a prosperity as a result of the Korean conflict, a prosperity already begun, it should be added, by the Truman program involving the increase and expansion of Social Security benefits, the tightening of price supports for farmers, expanded programs for soil conservation, flood control, rural electrification, and public power, as well as increased military expenditures abroad. The success of the Marshall Plan and containment policies in Europe and the signing of NATO treaties in March 1949, had guaranteed Western Europe economic and political security, while at home social gains in integration of the armed forces, and the breaking down of racial barriers in other areas, constituted a social revolution of significant proportions.

But the irritations against the Democrats were stronger than the satisfactions with what the party had accomplished. The Democratic candidate, Adlai Stevenson, governor of Illinois and grandson of President Cleveland's vice-president in 1893, met these irritations with wit and intelligence, but the American people were not open to wit or intellect during these days of confusion, frustration, and changing social values. They understood when Eisenhower commented that it would be "very, very fine if one could command new and amusing language, witticisms to bring you a chuckle," but admitted that he had "no intention of trying to do so" since "the subjects of which we are speaking these days . . . are not those that seem to me to be amusing." Working-class Americans were tired of ivy-league college administrators like Dean Acheson who made issues seem even more confusing by talking about the need for restraint, patience, "discipline," and the establishment of a "defensive perimeter" of the United States in the Pacific. They reacted against the intellectual Democratic candidate, associating such "egg-heads," as did the novelist Louis Bromfield, with "muddled economics, Socialism, Communism, crookedness and psychopathic instability." Intellectuals were "feminine," conceited "prigs," frequently professors, but in any case, not red-blooded, true Americans. Eisenhower, on the other hand, emphasized his lack of "education," apologized whenever he found it necessary to use large words, reminded his audiences of his military heroism. "I've been shot at by real artillerists," he claimed, dismissing the Democratic attacks; and he insisted that "the issue always and at bottom is spiritual." The Eisenhower image of being a plain and simple man of the people—a midwesterner from Abilene, Kansas, with all the simple virtues associated with this most representative of American cities—was heightened by the image that developed around his vice-presidential nominee, Richard Nixon, who, after a television speech defending himself and family against accusations of living off a "slush fund," became the image of the everyday American on the rise upward, worried as was the everyday American, about the purchase of a home, his children, his dog, his country. The combination was unbeatable. The Republican ticket won in a landslide, with more than six million votes over the Democrats, and was the first Republican ticket since 1928 to break the Solid South.

Intellectuals and professionals who were dismayed at the results believed, as did a professor at the University of Utah, that Stevenson's defeat meant that a "whole era is ended, is totally repudiated, a whole era of brains and literacy and exciting thinking." Perhaps so. But the gains of the previous eras were not ended or repudiated. Although Eisenhower tried to play down the role of the government in domestic affairs, and although his cabinet was composed of "eight millionaires and a plumber," as the *New Republic* characterized its members, the social and economic gains made by the New Deal–Fair Deal could not be repudiated. Neither the cutting of foreign aid nor the attempts to cut military spending could alter the pressures for still more economic and social benefits that persisted into the Eisenhower administrations. Nor could the effects on many of Eisenhower's advisers of having worked earlier in a New Deal–Fair Deal atmosphere be easily erased. The Eisenhower "Equilibrium" represented a practical adaptation of conservative policy to existing situations, a kind of flexibility that rendered it less than conservative, less than liberal, but one largely satisfactory to a majority of the people.

ADLAI E. STEVENSON   *Trafford P. Klots, 1953   Oil on canvas, 45⅛ x 30 inches*
From the Collection of the National Portrait Gallery, Washington, D.C.   Gift of
Mrs. Marshall Field and Mrs. Elizabeth Ives   NPG.67.33

Adlai E. Stevenson *Democrat*

1900-1965

Like many other presidential candidates before him, Adlai E. Stevenson did not seek the nomination of the Democratic Party in 1952. But unlike most, he quite candidly admitted it; "I would not seek your nomination for the Presidency," he told the assembled convention in Chicago, "because the burdens of that office stagger the imagination. Its potential for good or evil now and in the years of our lives smothers exultation and converts vanity to prayer." That he did not seek the office, however, and, in fact, turned it down when it was thrice offered to him by outgoing President Truman, did not mean that he valued it less: rather, he insisted, "it is that I revere the office of the Presidency of the United States."

Stevenson's reluctance to accept the draft of his party, and his modesty concerning his qualifications for it, were typical of the man and his attitude toward life and politics. Skeptical about the platitudes in which most men find comfort, questioning judgments that many take for granted, and meditative over decisions involving complexity and subtlety where most would see only simple questions and clearcut answers, Stevenson at times presented the appearance of a Hamlet in politics—a man "sicklied o'er with the pale cast of thought." Yet, he was as capable of firm action and crucial decision making as the strongest executive, and those who thought him indecisive misjudged the quality of the man's mind. For Stevenson was essentially an intellectual in politics, rather than a professional politician. Called an "egghead"—to which he answered *"Via ovum cranium difficilis est"* (the way of the egghead is hard)—he endowed that word with distinguished meaning. Like no other public figure before him, except perhaps Lincoln, with whom he closely identified, he saw refinements and shades of meaning in every situation and worried and debated with himself over possible alternatives. Like Lincoln, too, he covered his doubts with witticisms and anecdotes, and clothed in humor his anxieties and tendencies to look at all sides of a question. Above all, he was tortured by the necessity to speak honestly to the American people, to approach the electorate with reason in just expectation that his overtures would be met with reason, and to speak intelligently on the assumption that people could meet his intelligence with understanding. He never abandoned his trust in the basic capacity of the people to act wisely if they were shown the way. "Judgment and decision," he said,

depend on information and understanding. In matters of public policy, candidates then have the greatest responsibility of all to inform truthfully, so that the people will understand and will have the tools of good judgment and wise decision. One can argue, indeed, that all candidates claiming the people's confidence have even a higher mission; honestly to help man to know . . . what he ought to believe; to know what he ought to desire; to know what he ought to do.

Adlai Stevenson's sense of public service was derived from a family background in which such activity was emphasized. His grandfather, for whom he was named, was a prosperous Illinois gentleman–farmer who after two terms in the House of Representatives, and one term as assistant postmaster-general, became Grover Cleveland's vice-president in 1893. Continuing to offer himself for office, he ran with William Jennings Bryan in 1900 and for the governorship of Illinois in 1908, at the age of 73. Stevenson's maternal grandfather was Jesse W. Fell, the first newspaper publisher and lawyer in Bloomington, Illinois, and friend and backer of Abraham Lincoln. Adlai's father was also involved in newspaper publishing and politics, being at one time assistant business manager of Hearst's *Los Angeles Examiner,* and secretary of state of Illinois in 1914. Young Stevenson grew up, then, in a well-to-do, highly respected, politically inclined family, into whose home and lives came and went many national notables whose friendships and influence were to play a large role in the young man's life and career.

After an undistinguished student record at Choate and Princeton, Stevenson received a law degree from Northwestern University and settled down in Chicago to practice law and participate in public affairs, notably the Chicago Council on Foreign Relations. His first government post in Washington was as special counsel to the Agricultural Adjustment Administration that was being organized in 1933 by Secretary of Agriculture Henry A. Wallace. He served briefly with the Federal Alcohol Control Commission before returning to Chicago, but by 1941 he was off for the capital again to become legal counsel to Frank Knox, President Franklin D. Roosevelt's secretary of the navy. Later, he was assigned by Roosevelt to head a mission to Italy, and in 1945 he became public-relations man for the American delegation to the United Nations Conference at San Francisco. He remained with the delegation when it traveled to London for preparatory meetings, and later, at Lake Success, New York, he acted as senior adviser to the United States Delegation to the General Assembly. In all of these roles, he met and made friends with numerous politicians, diplomats, and public officials; he also discovered that he enjoyed public life and had a talent for it, as well as an obligation.

Thus, he was receptive to the overtures made to him in 1947 by Jacob M. Arvey, the boss of the Democratic Party in Illinois, to become the party's nominee for either the governorship or the Senate. When Paul Douglas was made the senatorial candidate, Stevenson was rewarded with the gubernatorial nomination at a time when it was clearly a Republican year for Illinois. To the surprise of political pros, in his state as well as in the nation, Stevenson not only won, but by a plurality of over 500,000 votes, more than those received in the state by Harry S. Truman or Douglas. It was an election that propelled him almost immediately into the 1952 presidential election.

Some have said that in 1952 Stevenson was the right man at the wrong time; others have countered that actually he did appear at the right time, because what the nation required, even if it refused to accept him, was a spokesman for reason and intelligence when both had seemingly fled the country. However one felt, there was no question that Stevenson brought an elevation and intellectual breadth to the art of politics that was sorely needed in 1952, and that, as Alden Whitman has said, "election to office was not the measure of his stature."

The 1950s were marked by fear and anxiety as well as prosperity. The phenomenon called McCarthyism had entered government, the schools, the press—even the army—creating

Stevenson cigarettes   CORNELL UNIVERSITY, DOUGLAS COLLECTION

an atmosphere of anti-intellectualism and distrust under the guise of an anti-Communist crusade. McCarthyism was not the only issue, however, in 1952. That year saw a more vocal demand on the part of blacks for desegregation of school facilities in line with the Supreme Court decisions to that effect; on the part of labor, for repeal of the detested Taft-Hartley Act; on the part of the people, for eliminating corruption from government and—what was perhaps of the greatest significance—for bringing an end to the Korean War. In addition, the prosperity of the previous years had to be maintained and bipartisanship in foreign affairs relating to Europe continued.

Stevenson's program encompassed all these points; the Republicans reiterated three slogans that summed up their sense of the campaign issues: "the mess in Washington"; "time for a change"; and "bring the boys home from Korea." Inflation, the exposure of favoritism and unethical practices among government officials, and the frustrating deadlock in Korea—but primarily the prestigious image of a hitherto nonpolitical general, Dwight D. Eisenhower, who had the reputation for getting things done—militated against Stevenson and the Democrats. There was no question that in 1952 the people were seeking a change from almost twenty years of Democratic politics, and all of Stevenson's literacy and wit could not divert them from what

Stevenson and Sparkman pin   CORNELL UNIVERSITY, DOUGLAS COLLECTION

was almost an instinctive response to all that General Eisenhower as a person promised. And when in late October, Eisenhower made the dramatic announcement that "I shall go to Korea," the consequences were clear to all political observers.

Eisenhower won by over 6.5 million votes, taking 39 states to Stevenson's nine. Stevenson's loyal supporters wept when their candidate conceded the election; and many Americans who had voted for Eisenhower felt compelled to write to the rejected candidate to explain why they had deserted him and to apologize for their action—so great was Stevenson's impact on the American conscience. But as Stevenson humorously admitted, "you really can't beat a household commodity—the catsup bottle on the kitchen table." Against the familiar figure of Eisenhower, he hardly had a chance. But, "I am content," he said to a party rally at the end of the campaign. "I have said what I meant and meant what I have said. No man can do more and you are entitled to no less."

ERIC HASS   *Photograph, 1960   Eric Hass, New York*

Eric Hass *Socialist-Labor*

1905-

At the present time—1972—Eric Hass is librarian for the Trinity Parish of the Episcopal Church in New York City and a free-lance writer of gardening and conservation articles. He professes no formal political affiliation. From 1952 to 1964, however, Hass was the presidential candidate of the Socialist Labor Party (SLP) which, officially organized in 1874 and reorganized in its modern form in 1890, is the oldest socialist political group in the United States.

Born in Lincoln, Nebraska, of German and Danish immigrant parents, Hass traveled throughout the country selling advertising until 1928 when he joined the Socialist Labor Party in Detroit. That year the Kellogg–Briand pact, ultimately ratified by sixty-three nations including each of the major powers, was signed. This international agreement theoretically "outlawed" war as an instrument of national policy and called for the settlement of all international disputes by peaceful means. Shortly after its ratification, Hass saw for the first time army bombers flying in formation. To him, this evidence of America's rearmament was indicative of the "hypocrisy" of mere pledges of abstention from war.

Hearing speeches attacking "war-breeding capitalism," made by Verne L. Reynolds, the SLP candidate for president in 1928, Hass became convinced that true world peace was not possible in a competitive society. "The nature of the international struggle for markets compels the government, responsive to the material interests of the capitalist class, to adopt aggressive policies that threaten the use of force," he later explained. War, poverty, and other social ills could be eliminated only by destroying the capitalist system and replacing it with an "industrial democracy"—a government completely in the hands of the workers.

After joining the SLP, Hass became a national organizer and in 1938 was elected to the post of editor to the party's official journal, *The Weekly People.* Besides being the party's candidate for president four times, he was candidate in 1936 for United States senator from Oregon. He ran for mayor of New York City five times, and for governor of New York three times.

As a presidential contender, Hass campaigned actively, traveling extensively throughout the country, and delivering three to four speeches a day before television and live audiences.

447

Yet he ran without any real hope of winning, and many Americans knew little of his candidacy. Often asked why he continued the race when success was so remote, he replied, "While I do not expect to win I do expect—*I am certain*—that sooner or later the principles I stand for, the principles of the Socialist-Labor Party, will be supported overwhelmingly." The campaign for the presidency was for Hass, as for many minor-party candidates, an important vehicle for presenting party ideology to the American public.

Stevenson campaign poster DIVISION OF POLITICAL HISTORY, SMITHSONIAN INSTITUTION
NATIONAL MUSEUM OF HISTORY AND TECHNOLOGY

Adlai E. Stevenson *Democrat*

1900-1965

In 1956 Adlai E. Stevenson was no longer a reluctant candidate. For four years as "titular head" of the party, he had led the Democrats in active opposition to Republican policies. Between the election of 1952 and January 1953, he completed his work as governor of Illinois, his most notable achievement being prison reform growing out of the Menard prison episode. During the previous campaign, Stevenson had been called to the Illinois prison to deal with a rebellious riot of the prisoners who were pressing for reform of the intolerable conditions that made Menard, in Stevenson's words, a "hell-hole." At the risk of his life, Stevenson had entered the prison yard and spoken reasonably to the prisoners, promising to listen to their complaints if they would relinquish their weapons. In the remaining weeks of his term, he attempted to fulfill his promise by improving the food, shop conditions, and prison staff while providing vocational and rehabilitation facilities.

Once having retired from the governorship, Stevenson was not to remain "an unemployed politician" for long. The 1952 campaign had revealed his stature as a public speaker and spokesman for liberal causes both at home and abroad, and the next four years were spent in traveling "around the edges of the Communist empire through Asia, the Middle East and Western Europe" talking, as he said to his Harvard audience, to

the Emperor of Japan, the Queen of England, the Pope, and to all the kings, presidents, and prime ministers along my route. And I also talked to countless diplomats, journalists, students, soldiers, peasants, porters, and multitudes of new and warm-hearted friends. Everywhere I encountered an eagerness to talk and a candor of expression . . . that touched and astonished me—and has heavily taxed my discretion. And often the hospitality made me wonder if my hosts were confused and thought I had been elected President in 1952.

Upon his return, the one question that came to concern him most was McCarthyism, to which he believed the Republican administration had succumbed. Deciding that the nation ought not to be governed by "promise, postponement and slander," he insisted that "the Bill of Rights is besieged, ancient liberties infringed, reckless words uttered, vigilante groups are formed, suspicion, mistrust and fear stalk the land, and political partisanship raises strange and ugly heads, the security of secret files is violated, and the specter of a political police emerges." The president, Stevenson believed, had failed in his appointed role, and persuaded by a "group of political plungers," Eisenhower had "taken McCarthyism away from McCarthy." "What an end," he exclaimed, "to the great crusade!"

During these years of waiting, Stevenson also took upon himself the role of defining democracy and its challenges. As "a great believer in national humility, modesty, self-examination and self-criticism," he deplored attempts to attack academic freedom or nonconformity, and he also deprecated those who would submit cowardly to slanders about the nation. "If we but lift our heads for a moment above this storm of criticism, of abuse, doubt, and 'un-American activities,' and survey the past fifty years," he asserted, "I think you will say with me 'Hooray for America!' " The nation's greatness had been accomplished by "putting government to the service of the people," by those who "led a revolt of the American conscience," by the "bloodless revolution" created by "child labor laws, wage and hour laws, antitrust acts, banking regulation, rural electrification, soil conservation, Social Security, unemployment compensation, the graduated income tax, inheritance taxes." But too many people, he believed, "still dwell in wretched slums or on worn-out land. . . . Our schools and hospitals are overcrowded; so are our mental institutions and our prisons. Too many of our cities are wasting away from neglect . . . and . . . more than one of every ten citizens still does not enjoy fully equal opportunities."

Turning his attention away from domestic problems, Stevenson surveyed the world scene, decried isolationism, emphasized the necessity for cooperation and sought to "help others help themselves, to help make independence and democracy work, to share the burdens of the less fortunate, to raise the tide a little all around the world, lifting all of the boats with it, just as we have done here at home."

Having accomplished such great tasks, America need not fear communism or national suicide. Asking rhetorically, "What's the matter with us anyhow?", he answered that "ignorance and fear" were the most "subversive" forces of all: "If America ever loses confidence in herself," he insisted, "she will retain the confidence of no one, and she will lose her chance to be free, because the fearful are never free."

In the midterm election of 1954, Stevenson campaigned hard for Democratic candidates, and on election day, his party gained two seats in the Senate, nineteen seats in the House, nine governors, and a host of state offices. There was no question that some of this success was due to Stevenson's hard-hitting campaign that made him a front-runner for the nomination in 1956. A seasoned politician by this time, he determined to announce his candidacy and run in the primaries against other Democratic contenders like Senator Estes Kefauver of Tennessee and Governor Averill Harriman of New York. He clung to a moderate position, even in the face of minority demands for more extreme action, and rejected the easy answers—and perhaps in some cases the right ones—because of his sensitivity to the complexity of implementing policy to achieve ends that would be good for all concerned. So in the segregation issue, he bravely told a Negro audience that he thought using the army and navy to enforce integration would be a "great mistake." "We must proceed gradually, not upsetting habits or traditions that are older than the Republic." Some black leaders called him "a phony," but he was undeterred in his insistence on frankness. Winning, he said, was not "the first objective of any political race" and he had "an allergy for holiday promises."

Stevenson lost the primary elections in New Hampshire and Minnesota, but after these upsets, a succession of victories in Florida, Oregon, and California brought him to the convention as the overwhelming favorite of the Democratic Party. Although in 1956 the Democrats were disunited—especially on the Civil Rights issue—and many were not sure of Stevenson as a potential winner, he won the nomination easily on the first ballot. Stevenson's campaign was

Stevenson pin   CORNELL UNIVERSITY, DOUGLAS COLLECTION

far more aggressive now than it had been four years previously. Centering primarily on domestic policy and a program for New America, Stevenson also, as the campaign went on, began to discuss questions of peace in the Middle East, the necessity for arms parity between the Arabs and Israelis, and chiefly the military draft and hydrogen-bomb testing. Fighting an Eisenhower recovering from a heart attack and therefore even more entrenched in the people's sympathies, and a Republican platform that rested its case on the president's personality and record, Stevenson's campaign was uphill all the way. More and more his program swung to the left in domestic policy as he sought programs for the old, the farmers, and laboring men. Asking the American people to accept "the challenge of history," he invited them to consider all the avenues available for securing peace in the world, and especially in the Middle East, where Israel and Egypt were already engaged in battle. But the American people chose to ignore his plea, and soon after it was made, they again elected Eisenhower to the presidency.

Stevenson's philosophical acceptance of defeat was characteristic. "There are things more precious than political victory," he told his supporters; "there is the right to political contest."

453

Optimistic that America would go forward, he assured them that though they had lost a battle, their cause would prevail.

Stevenson's role in American public service was not over, however. He wrote extensively, lectured widely, traveled throughout the world studying peoples and nations. When Senator John F. Kennedy of Massachusetts scored a triumphant victory in West Virginia's presidential primary in 1960, Stevenson withdrew his candidacy; and when Kennedy was nominated on the first ballot, Stevenson supported the party's choice. Kennedy's election meant that some useful governmental post could be given to Stevenson so that his services would not be lost to the nation. Many wanted to see him made secretary of state, but Kennedy instead offered him the ambassadorship to the United Nations with full cabinet membership and a role in all aspects of foreign policy planning, including a seat in the National Security Council. Here in the world assembly, Stevenson came face to face with even more difficult problems, but here, too, he found his true métier, where all his intelligence, wit, and personality could be taken advantage of for an end in which he firmly believed: world peace. He died in the course of attempting to fulfill that end.

RICHARD M. NIXON   *Bernard Safran, 1960   Oil on panel, 24 x 17¾ inches*
TIME, The Weekly Newsmagazine

Richard M. Nixon *Republican*

1913 –

In 1960, after eight years in office, the Republicans were still a divided party. The unity that they had hoped to achieve through General Dwight D. Eisenhower was merely nominal, for although Eisenhower was still one of the most popular Americans of the century, he frequently acted as if he was not a Republican at all, and the party was unable to point to him as the embodiment of either its program or philosophy. Nelson Rockefeller and Barry Goldwater represented the two extreme poles of Republican thinking, and the nomination of middle-of-the-road Richard M. Nixon as the party's presidential candidate reflected the split between the liberals and conservatives within the Republican fold. Nixon, taking advantage of his vice-presidential position in President Eisenhower's administration, presented himself as a candidate with Eisenhower's neutrality and flexible enough in his political ideas to please both wings of the party. As one member of the Republican platform committee told author Theodore H. White, "in this party you have to run as hard as possible to stay in the same place; getting them to approve what Eisenhower has already done is an achievement in itself."

If anyone could get Republican Old Guard approval for a platform that would please the liberals or moderates in the party, it was Richard Nixon. Throughout his career as a lawyer in California and service in the navy during World War II, he had always risen to the opportunities that presented themselves and to the responsibilities. He has always, wrote Robert Coughlan in *Life,* "shown the capacity to grow." Born in California into a family of Quakers whose roots went deep into American history, his was the typical history of the self-made man. As he wrote, "I sold gas and delivered groceries and met a lot of people. I think this was invaluable as a start on a public career." From public high school to Whittier College and then to Duke University's law school, he worked hard to excel in all that he undertook, becoming president of the student body at college and law school. Even in the navy, in which he entered as a lieutenant (j.g.) and emerged as a lieutenant commander, he continued the pattern of assiduous attention to details and a careful eye to the opportunities and responsibilities presented by the situation.

Almost immediately after he was mustered out of the navy, Nixon entered politics, receiving the Republican nomination for Congress from the Twelfth District of California in 1946. Early in his political career, he found the issue that was to carry him into the vice-presidency and into the public eye as a possible presidential contender: communism. To a great extent, he won election to Congress on the charge that a vote for his Democratic opponent, who was supported by the CIO Political Action Committee, was a vote for "Communist principles." During his two terms as congressman from California, Nixon's energies were devoted to the House Committee on Un-American Activities. According to *Life,* it was "Nixon's stubborn persistence [that] brought about the now-famous confrontation" between Alger Hiss and Whittaker Chambers which eventually led to Hiss' conviction for perjury. Nixon also co-authored the Mundt-Nixon bill on Communist control, parts of which were later incorporated into the McCarran Internal Security Act. His election to the Senate in 1952 was helped by his charge that the Democratic administration had lost in the Far East as a result of being soft on communism, and when his opponent Helen Gahagan Douglas defended the administration, she inevitably was branded as being sympathetic to communism. It did not help her reputation that she had voted to cut off the funds for the House Committee on Un-American Activities of which Nixon was the leading member.

Thus in 1952, Nixon seemed a good vice-president for General Eisenhower on a Republican platform that continued to give concentrated attention to the Truman administration's seeming inattentiveness to the Communist threat, both at home and abroad. Nixon's record in the Senate also made him attractive to both wings of the Republican Party. In domestic issues, he had voted conservatively, supporting the Taft-Hartley Act, overriding President Truman's veto of the McCarran immigration bill, and supporting legislation giving control of the tidelands oil to the states. Usually, he opposed Truman's Fair Deal measures, voting against the Brannan Plan for direct subsidies to farmers. Internationally, however, Nixon was a strong supporter of bipartisan foreign policy and military and economic assistance to American allies. Almost eliminated from the campaign by the Democratic accusation that he had improperly accepted an $18,000 special fund raised by California businessmen, his decision to face the people on television and radio, accompanied by his family and dog; and his promise to "campaign up and down America until we drive the crooks and communists and those who defend them out of Washington" brought him the sympathy of many, while Eisenhower, convinced of his sincerity, retained him as his running mate. The incident pointed out to him the effectiveness of television as a campaign instrument.

During his two terms as vice-president, Nixon identified almost completely with Eisenhower's "modern Republicanism." Traveling widely as the president's representative to the Middle East, the Far East, Central America, Austria, Africa, and Latin America, he became convinced of the necessity for "adequate programs of mutual security and foreign aid, a strong national defense, and reciprocal trade." On domestic policy, he remained conservative, emphasizing the necessity of going to government only as "a last resort." On civil rights, although he spoke of the necessity to go forward, he was ambivalent, as was Eisenhower, who did not throw his presidential weight behind the Supreme Court civil-rights decisions of 1954 or take a strong stand in support of the release of Martin Luther King when he was jailed for demanding service in an Atlanta, Georgia, restaurant.

Richard Nixon pin SMITHSONIAN INSTITUTION   *John F. Kennedy pin* SMITHSONIAN INSTITUTION

Campaign events played an influential role in determining the outcome of the 1960 election. Nixon's television debates with John F. Kennedy gave the electorate an opportunity to judge Kennedy as no other exposure could have done, and they found his youth and energy appealing, as well as his command of the domestic situation. On the other hand, Nixon was considered to be overly concerned with "image." Because he was determined to "convey three basic impressions to the television audience—knowledge in depth of the subjects discussed, sincerity, and confidence"—he appeared self-conscious. If the debates didn't decide the election, as some pollsters believed, then his hesitancy on civil rights was not helpful. His silence on the Martin Luther King incident cost him many Negro votes—whereas Kennedy's spontaneous call to Mrs. King and his promise to help in getting her husband released from prison found a response in the great majorities given to him from Negro wards, North and South, which undoubtedly helped him win. Similarly, with the rest of the domestic program, Nixon accepted a liberal platform, but tried to make it acceptable to conservatives. In the attempt not to be controversial, his speeches contained many generalities; and in the desire to run his own campaign, he shunned the advice and support of the more experienced politicians in his party.

By 1960, then, Nixon had pretty well revealed his policies and capacities. Marvin Weisbord has written that "he was the inevitable result of a party which for 50 years had been running in two directions at once and couldn't break the habit." The fact that he almost won the election in 1960 suggests, however, that there were elements of strength still left in the GOP that drew voters to the man who seemed to represent them most clearly, but also that there were serious weaknesses. One of the real problems facing Nixon in 1960 was that the Republicans had no program of their own that invited the attention of the electorate; Eisenhower's "me-too-ism," as Adai Stevenson had characterized the general's election policies, had permitted the electorate to respond to his personal charms without worrying about the question of his program.

They were concerned with Nixon's program, however, and when the vice-president referred to his eight years of on-the-job training, Kennedy baited him on the point. Claiming his own "direct succession" from Wilson, Franklin D. Roosevelt, and Truman, Kennedy pointed out repeatedly that "Mr. Nixon . . . stands in direct succession to McKinley, to Coolidge, to Hoover, to Landon, to Dewey"—losers all, he implied, whose administrations had no significance and conveyed no message to the twentieth century. Theodore H. White commented that the Nixon campaign had "neither philosophy nor structure to it, no whole picture either of the man or of the future he offered." Thus, when Kennedy offered a future of new frontiers, the appeal was obvious.

In the final count, Kennedy received only one-tenth of one percent more votes than had Nixon—a plurality of less than 120,000 votes—with 303 electoral votes to Nixon's 219. Nixon won more states, however, and in the South, he ran better than had Eisenhower in 1956. Kennedy's Catholicism may have had an impact on the voting; only 64.55 percent of the eligible voters cast their ballot for the presidency, with many Democrats either staying away from the polls or ignoring the presidential contest, because, it is believed, they could not bring themselves to vote either Republican or Catholic, and so remained silent.

The campaign taught the Republicans and Nixon a great lesson. Campaign techniques had obviously changed, as this election clearly revealed. No previous candidate had visited so many states, in such short a time, as had Nixon. Flight by jet aircraft gave candidates opportunities to be seen in person all over the nation. Television exposed them to a larger public and frequently revealed them for whatever they were: TV highlighted emptiness and gave strength to programs that were intrinsically strong. Thus, the Republican Party had to find policies that would appeal to the people's needs if they were to look forward to future successes. In 1964 Barry Goldwater could not, but by the time 1968 rolled around, Nixon had found both a program and an image and was able to propel himself into the office he had been seeking so energetically in 1960.

BARRY M. GOLDWATER   *Charles L. MacNelly, 1971—Oil on canvas, 42 x 34 inches*
Mrs. Barry Goldwater

Barry M. Goldwater *Republican*

1902-

By the 1950s, the success and popularity of New Deal liberalism, by now thoroughly integrated into the fabric of the nation's life, had convinced many Republicans of the untenability of their party's traditional conservatism. Believing that they could no longer oppose the nation's liberal trends and remain viable as a national party, in increasing numbers they gravitated to a moderately liberal position. Certainly, this trend had been evident since 1940 when Republican standard-bearers Wendell Willkie, Thomas E. Dewey, and Dwight D. Eisenhower took issue with their Democratic opponents on the implementation of federal policies rather than on the wisdom of the policies themselves.

Nevertheless, the Republican Party continued to harbor significant numbers of conservatives, who, although willing to support the moderate wing of their party, still wished for a return to more traditional policy. When Barry Goldwater, campaigning on a conservative platform, began his quest for the 1964 presidential nomination, the "Old Guard" segments of the Republican Party, who looked back to a time when federal government did not play such an important role in the nation's domestic affairs, took on new life. In one of the most well-mechanized, grass-roots efforts ever organized in the history of American politics, the conservatives and their new-found spokesman gradually gained in strength, and despite Goldwater's low returns in most of the presidential primaries, they came to the Republican convention confident that the nomination would go to their candidate. Although the days before the convention saw a last-minute effort on the part of GOP liberals to head off the Goldwater movement, the latter held its ground and on the first ballot succeeded in making Barry Goldwater the Republican presidential nominee.

Raised in Phoenix, Arizona, Goldwater's early life gave little suggestion that he was destined for national prominence as a politician and presidential aspirant. After attending the University of Arizona for one year, he entered his family's department-store business and within ten years had become its president. Always an avid sportsman, he found much time in these early years for rugged outdoor activities. In the 1930s, he became one of the first white men to navigate the Colorado River rapids in the Grand Canyon.

463

After serving as a pilot during World War II, Goldwater returned to Phoenix and became involved in politics. Elected to the Phoenix City Council in 1949, he soon became prominent in the Republican circles of his state. In 1952, after managing his party's successful bid for the Arizona governorship, he won his own campaign for the United States Senate.

As a senator, Goldwater gave evidence of his conservative leanings from the beginning. A frequent opponent of increased government spending, he favored the reduction of foreign aid and quite often opposed the expansion of federal spending in domestic matters such as aid to education, soil-conservation subsidies, and profits-tax relief for small business. Goldwater

Barry M. Goldwater pin SMITHSONIAN INSTITUTION

supported revision of the Taft-Hartley Act which would have given states the primary responsibility for settling labor-management disputes. He was also known in these years to have suggested that states should be allowed to "outlaw collective bargaining if they so wished."

Goldwater was an ardent believer in the American system of free enterprise and individual initiative, and he was convinced that world communism presented the greatest threat to the United States. In 1954, he joined the minority of senators who opposed the censure of Senator Joseph McCarthy whose recent investigations of Communist influences in the government had raised heated controversy. He also became an ardent advocate of military spending in the belief that American preparedness and willingness to apply force would prevent the spread of communism. In the early 1960s, he favored an American invasion of Cuba to put an end to the dictatorship of Fidel Castro. Similarly, as the question of Vietnam arose, he advocated the use of "tactical" nuclear weapons in protecting South Vietnam against a Communist invasion.

Senator Goldwater possessed many advantages as a candidate for his party's nomination. Disarmingly affable—even his opponents could not resist what one commentator described as his "easy, breezy, aw-shucks, western manner"—he had earned the gratitude of innumerable party leaders as a result of his constant willingness to lend active support to local GOP candidates throughout the country. As early as 1961, conservative Republicans had begun to mobilize their forces on his behalf, and by mid-1964, having captured control of their party at the precinct level, they claimed support—in some cases pledged and in others favorable—from over 600 of the delegates to the Republican convention. Despite desperate attempts by liberals such as Governor Nelson Rockefeller of New York and Governor William Scranton of Pennsylvania, Goldwater's candidacy was assured.

From the beginning, Goldwater's chances of defeating incumbent Lyndon B. Johnson were weak. Opening his campaign with the statement that "extremism in the cause of liberty is no vice," the Republican immediately aroused fears among voters who saw in this statement a reflection of the candidate's aggressive position on foreign policy. In light of his advocacy of nuclear weapons and his frequent expression of the necessity for military interference in Vietnam, the possibility of Goldwater in the White House aroused visions of a nuclear holocaust— a vision which the Democrats lost no time in dramatizing in their advertising campaign.

Contrary to his supporters' belief that there were large numbers of silent Americans who already sympathized with their political views, Goldwater's conservative image on domestic matters also proved an obstacle. When he voiced his disapproval of Social Security and suggested that its compulsory nature represented a violation of individual freedom, he found himself labeled a reactionary. Although Goldwater showed considerable strength in the South largely as a result of his opposition to federal civil-rights legislation—five of the six states he won were located in the South—local Republican candidates were fearful that identification with the GOP candidate would alienate moderate voters in their state and generally refrained from supporting him. Even many traditionally Republican newspapers endorsed Lyndon B. Johnson.

Although defeated, Goldwater did not retire from politics after 1964. Continuing to serve as the spokesman for conservatism, he spent considerable time lecturing throughout the country. In 1968, he was reelected to the United States Senate.

HUBERT H. HUMPHREY   *Robert Templeton, 1970-1971   Oil on canvas,*
38 x 27⅞ inches   Senator Hubert Humphrey, Washington, D.C.

Hubert H. Humphrey   *Democrat*

1911-

On March 31, 1968, President Lyndon B. Johnson, after fifty-two months and ten days in the White House, addressed the nation on television to announce his plan to de-escalate the war in Vietnam. The speech ended with a summary of American achievements in southeast Asia, despite the devastating war, and the expression of his belief that Communist expansion in that area of the world had been halted. In the last five minutes, however, the speech changed its tone. Stressing the necessity for unity and deploring the partisan divisions that he believed were creating disharmony in the nation, the president announced to a shocked nation that he would not seek nor accept the nomination of the Democratic Party for another term as chief executive of the United States. Johnson's surprise announcement propelled into the campaign for the presidency his vice-president, Hubert H. Humphrey, former reform mayor of Minneapolis, fighting congressman, and liberal senator from Minnesota.

What forced such a self-denial from a president who up to a few weeks before was a certain candidate for reelection? Johnson's domestic program had been spectacularly successful. More than forty education bills had been passed during his administration; the first clean-air bill had been approved, and under his program of conservation more land had been returned to the public domain than had been removed; parks had been planted within and near large cities, and legislation establishing health centers and Medicare had been passed to provide the poor and the old with better medical facilities. Housing and urban renewal legislation provided more employment and better living conditions for urban dwellers. Perhaps the most spectacular achievement of Johnson's administration, however, was the passage of the Civil Rights acts of 1964 and 1965, which seemed to answer all the demands of the black community for equal opportunity and real freedom.

Yet, despite these achievements, 1965 to 1967 had been years of unrest in the United States. Nineteen sixty-five had witnessed the violent upheaval in the Watts district of Los Angeles; 1966 had been marked by more race riots than had ever before troubled American cities in one year; and underprivileged and working-class groups in American society found themselves even more discontented under the inflationary spiral unleashed not only by the high military expenditures, but also by the costs of Johnson's "Great Society" legislation itself.

The prosperity of the Great Society had also, ironically, given rise to other pressing problems. Drugs loomed larger than ever as a social problem that demanded attention, and racial and urban discontent gave birth to the question of "law and order" in the cities. All of these became issues in the subsequent presidential campaign, but, above all, it was the Vietnam war that was most responsible for forcing Johnson and the Democrats out of office and bringing into the White House Richard M. Nixon and the Republican Party.

The Vietnam situation had developed gradually since the day in 1954 when John Foster Dulles, Eisenhower's secretary of state, decided to extend American aid to the southern government of Vietnam in the civil war that followed the French defeat by the Vietnamese at Dienbienphu. From 300 military advisers, the American commitment grew to 600 in 1961 when John F. Kennedy assumed the presidency, and from 1961 on, in the face of what appeared to be guerrilla terrorism, American participation in South Vietnam's defense escalated. By February 1965, a program of bombing North Vietnamese military installations was undertaken, and finally, on June 8, 1965, American ground troops were sent to fight in Vietnam.

The Democratic Party was sorely divided on the war question in 1968. Early that year, Eugene McCarthy, Humphrey's fellow senator from Minnesota, undertook an antiwar campaign that continued to gain momentum and strength, reaching its crest in April in the Wisconsin primary. Robert F. Kennedy, a younger brother of the former president, after some hesitation because he did not wish his candidacy to be construed as representing personal hostility between him and the president, also began organizing a campaign on an antiwar program, and gained surprising victories in the Indiana and Nebraska primaries. He was celebrating victory over McCarthy in California when an assassin's bullets cut his life short in Los Angeles on the night of June first. Hubert Humphrey, however, remained quiet about the war, primarily because of his loyalty to the administration—a factor that had entered into Johnson's decision to tap him for the vice-presidency in 1964. Although privately he kept repeating his opposition to the escalation of the war whenever the opportunity presented itself, publicly he expressed no criticism of the war. Humphrey's continued refusal to repudiate Johnson and Johnson's policies during the campaign intimately linked his image with that of the president, who more than anyone had come to symbolize for the American people a hated war policy. Even when Humphrey would have liked to establish his own position on the Vietnam situation shortly before the Democratic convention was scheduled to open in August, he had been asked, presumably by the president, to desist since there was an "imminent breakthrough in the Paris [peace] negotiations" that would be threatened if the vice-president spoke out at that time against the war.

Before the war issue had arisen to impugn Humphrey's liberalism, the former senator from Minnesota had enjoyed a reputation of deep commitment to liberal causes. During the 1948 Democratic national convention, when he was mayor of Minneapolis and candidate for the Senate, Humphrey had sponsored and obtained the strongest civil-rights plank in the party's history. In the Senate, Humphrey's Food for Peace program benefited the farmers who had surpluses, but it was of even greater benefit to the hundred-million people in eighty-five countries who ultimately shared in the nation's largesse. As early as 1949, he had advocated and fought for a program that would provide health insurance for the elderly; in 1965 such a program was passed as Medicare. As chairman of the Senate Committee on Disarmament, Humphrey advocated a nuclear test-ban treaty between the United States and the Soviet Union, which was finally signed by the two nations in 1963. As Majority Whip during John F. Kennedy's administration, the Minnesota senator was so closely identified with policy decisions characterizing New Frontier legislation that *The New York Times* was impelled to comment, "Without Humphrey, the liberal contingent in the Senate would be fragmented and impotent." Finally, as floor leader at the time of the passage of the Civil-Rights bill of 1964, Humphrey was responsible for the strategy that saw that bill through debate and passage; to do so, he had enlisted the support of Republican leader Senator Everett Dirksen of Illinois, who ultimately received much of the public credit for the bill's success. But President Johnson wrote on Humphrey's presentation copy of the printed bill "To Hubert Humphrey, without whom it coudn't have happened."

Humphrey seemed to be the logical Democratic nominee, appealing as he did to the various elements that since the New Deal had constituted the Democratic coalition: the workers in the factories, the professionals, the old and sick, the young and idealistic, blacks and middle-class whites, who desired greater equality and justice in the United States. He also commanded the support of organized labor, most of the Democratic governors and mayors, and the party bosses. He did not secure absolute support in the South, which was anxious about his domestic liberalism, but he hoped that traditional voting habits would hold here, despite the segregation issue raised by George Wallace and the American Independence Party and despite the inroads of the Republican Party in a formerly solid Democratic electorate.

Why, then, did Humphrey lose the election in 1968—a most tragic and bitter election year? The bitterness of the antiwar crusade was partly responsible, especially as it became involved with a youth movement of sizable proportions designed to change the structure of American politics, and as it manifested itself in the events of the Democratic convention meeting in Chicago in August of that year.

The youth movement was the work of Eugene McCarthy, who came to the convention in Chicago hoping to influence the Democrats to repudiate Johnson's war policy. He had been followed by his "youngsters," who had disregarded his urgings to remain at home, and by "Yippies," or members of the Youth International Party, by poor-people demonstrators from the Southern Christian Leadership Conference, and by members of the National Mobilization Committee to End the War in Vietnam. These groups milled outside the convention hall, each group seeking something different but all immediately suspected by the Chicago police and the Illinois National Guard because of their numbers. It took very little to ignite the fuse that would lead to riot and bloodshed—just a crowd growing restless under the impact of a rumor that the convention had voted for a resolution defending the Johnson position on Vietnam, and a fearful officer of the Guard armed with tear-gas grenades. The violence that followed set off continuous although sporadic riots that horrified Americans as they viewed on television the happenings in the Windy City.

The worst was yet to come, however. McCarthy supporters, most of whom lacked roots in the political system, confronted in the convention a political professionalism for which they were unprepared. Johnson as president had been able to decide the constitution of the credentials committee and the organization of the convention, and Humphrey as his heir-apparent was the recipient of Johnson's expert control of the party apparatus. Thus, despite McCarthy's favorable showing in the primaries—in which Humphrey did not participate—Humphrey received the nomination, greatly embittering McCarthy's following. These youthful workers for McCarthy retired to the fifteenth floor of the Hilton Hotel after Humphrey's nomination to rest and console each other. Suddenly, without any seeming provocation, they found themselves confronting the Chicago police, who clubbed and dragged them out of the building. McCarthy was able to rescue his battered crew, but Humphrey, unfortunately asleep and not awakened by his aides, did not intervene in the brutal event; nor later, did he make any protest about what had occurred. His silence was considered to be corroboration of his earlier refusal to take an independent position on Vietnam. McCarthy refused to support the man who seemed to condone brutality—until it was too late in the election for his support to be effective—and so did many of McCarthy's supporters. After Chicago, Humphrey's candidacy, already tainted with the blood of Vietnam, became even more intimately associated with the bloodbath of the Windy City. "I was a victim of the convention," he said later, "as much as a man getting the Hong Kong flu . . . it's difficult to take on the Republicans and fight a guerrilla war in your own party at the same time. Chicago was a catastrophe."

Despite Chicago and Vietnam, the election was a close one. The Republican candidate, Richard M. Nixon, campaigning on the theme of "law and order" and speaking to what he termed "the forgotten American," received 31,783,783 votes or 43.4 percent of the total, to Humphrey's 31,271,839 votes, or 42.7 percent. If Nixon's and Wallace's combined vote are considered indicative of a repudiation of Johnson's administration, then it can be said that it was also a rejection of his Vietnam policy, although there is no question that racial hatreds and the disorder of the cities also entered into the ultimate decision. Despite the fact that neither Humphrey nor Nixon had presented clear-cut programs for dealing with the war situation, the war underlay the mood in which Americans went to the polls. Many former Democrats who had supported McCarthy's peace movement did not vote at all, thereby depriving Humphrey of much-needed votes. In casting their ballots for Nixon, the "silent majority," especially grouped in the Midwest and West, was responding to the candidate who promised restraint in domestic as well as foreign programs in reaction to a strong executive whose domestic reforms threatened the status quo and whose foreign policy led to unwanted war.

There is no question, however, in the light of the close returns and the divisive issues, that the nation in 1968 was still divided, still restless and unsatisfied. Although Humphrey lost because a portion of the nation seemed to have lost confidence in the Democrats, neither had the Republicans fully gained that confidence. Especially, both parties had lost the confidence of the "kids," the youth who entered politics in the McCarthy campaign and raised questions that had seldom been raised before. Two years after the election, Humphrey came to believe that the questions raised by the nation's youth were the best thing that had emerged from the campaign. The kids, he said, "blew the whistle on our use of power as the main instrument in our international affairs. Raising the question they did on the whole concept of power politics in international relations . . . they questioned our values in America and the role of the country into the world, and now it's seared into our flesh."

GEORGE WALLACE *Campaign Poster, 1968 The Smithsonian Institution's National Museum of History and Technology, Division of Political History, Washington, D.C.*

George Wallace *American Independent*
1919–

In 1968 a small-town boy from Clio, Alabama, entered the presidential lists as a knight-errant for southern and northern white Americans who feared the changes in race relationships promised by the Civil Rights acts of 1964 and 1965. George Wallace was the son of an unsuccessful southern farmer, who worked his way out of the world of poverty and cotton crops through the time-honored American way of politics. From senior-class president and foremost debater in his class, Wallace moved on to law courses at the University of Alabama, paying his way by boxing professionally—he had won the state's Golden Glove bantam-weight boxing championship in 1936—and received his law degree in 1942. Enlisting in the Air Force almost immediately, he became a flight engineer on a B-29 assigned to the 20th Air Force in the Pacific. After many aerial combat missions over Japan, he was honorably discharged in December 1945 with the rank of flight sergeant and a ten-percent "nervous disability" allowance. From war service to politics was a direct course. In 1946, he was assistant attorney general for Alabama, and the next year, he was elected to the Alabama legislature as a delegate. From then on, politics became his life. "George," one fellow Alabaman observed, "can out-politick any man all day long. When I'm through politicking I like to go home, I like my likker, I like my woman. George just goes on politicking right through the day."

In the state legislature, Wallace successfully sponsored many measures designed to bring industry to the state and increase the state's industrial labor potential. An anti-lottery bill introduced by him was considered to have thwarted the activities of racketeers in Alabama, while his Highway Responsibility Law and his Natural Gas District Act gave aid to municipalities in supplying necessary services. He also led the fight for more hospitals and old-age pensions, and he filibustered against a bill that would have increased the state's sales tax.

It was an impressive record for a young man. In 1953, Wallace was elected judge of the Third Judicial Circuit, where for six years he was known as the "Fighting Judge," because of his defiance of the United States Civil Rights Commission. He had found his issue—one which would propel him into the governorship of his home state and put him in the national limelight as a presidential candidate running on the race issue.

473

Wallace held clear-cut views of race and made no attempt to disguise them. As a southerner holding fast to tradition, he quite firmly believed that segregation of the races was best for both groups of people if each wished to preserve the values of his own race. In his opinion, blacks developed a particular life pattern in which whites should not interfere; nor should whites permit Negroes to interfere with their way of life, with the so-called "Anglo-Saxon tradition." Wallace denied that he was a "hater"; as a southern reporter told Theodore H. White, Wallace "doesn't hate Negroes. He's a segregationist, not a lyncher." What Wallace seemed to dislike more were the "intellectual morons" who, he believed, influenced national policy and acted against nature in attempting to integrate the races.

On the question of segregation, then, Wallace was like "a one-man army at war with the Federal Government," as the *Saturday Evening Post* put it in 1963 while commenting on Wallace's campaign for the governorship of Alabama. On that platform and stressing at the same time economy in government, Wallace was elected governor of Alabama. In his inaugural speech, he again shouted defiance at the federal government: "I draw the line in the dust and toss the gauntlet before the feet of tyranny," he proclaimed to his audience. When the test actually came, he personally attempted to prevent two Negro students from registering at the University of Alabama despite the fact that they were accompanied by federal officers. Only after President Kennedy had signed an order federalizing the Alabama National Guard and ordered units to the campus to carry out federal law did the governor step aside and allow the students to register.

Similar tactics were used to discourage integration of the public schools in Alabama—from sending state troopers to prevent the opening of schools under such conditions to closing the schools entirely. Once more President Kennedy had to federalize the Alabama National Guard to enforce federal authority against the obstructionist tactics of the state's governor. But each act of Wallace or Kennedy brought Wallace further and further into the national scene. Obviously, Wallace had hit a still-exposed nerve in the American system, one that could arouse sharp emotions and reactions. Overnight, he became a popular public speaker, visiting colleges and universities in the North, exposing himself to rocks and violence, but also exposing his message. Three Democratic primaries in 1964 scored him astonishingly high percentages, but that year Wallace permitted Barry Goldwater to take over the segregationist cause for him; in 1968, however, he was ready to campaign himself.

Enormously successful in presenting the American Independence Party to the American people in the different states, Wallace really reached the peak of his popularity after the assassination of presidential-candidate Robert F. Kennedy. The violence of the Chicago convention turned many more in his direction, especially on the issue of law and order. "Law and Wallace" read the placards which greeted the candidate wherever he went to speak; "George, Protect our Home"; "Have Our Schools Been Sold to the Government?"; others read, "Wallace—Friend of the Working Man" and "Give America Back to the People, Vote Wallace." As the working classes responded more and more to Wallace, they turned with greater violence on those who opposed him: on the youth who carried McCarthy signs for peace, on, in Wallace's own words, the "nigger-loving homosexual," "Jew bastards," "Communists with beards," and "bureaucrats in Washington." At Cicero, Illinois, and in Boston, Massachusetts, violence broke out between hecklers and the crowd of supporters. Nevertheless, wherever he went, in the industrial towns of Michigan or the south side of Milwaukee, Wallace's message was short and simple: the government had sold out the people; their homes, their schools, their jobs were threatened; they could not walk the streets of their cities in the evening—their very lives were in danger. Wallace claimed that he alone could change the situation and, if elected, assure the people of their freedom to determine things for themselves.

In the early fall, Wallace seemed to be on the ascendancy; by October, he had reached his peak and his popularity began suddenly to take a drastic downward turn as Humphrey's campaign took on greater eloquence. Preaching "Trust" to George Wallace's "Distrust," Humphrey tried to appeal to the consciences of the workingmen who had once waved Wallace banners. "Let's lay it on the line," Humphrey said to the automobile workers in Detroit, "George Wallace's pitch is racism. If you want to feel damn mean and ornery, find some other way to do it, but don't sacrifice your country. George Wallace has been engaged in union-busting whenever he's had the chance . . . and any union man who votes for him is not a good union man."

Wallace's greatest weakness as a campaigner was the single note he kept playing, the issue of race and law and order, which as he repeated it over and over began to penetrate the American consciousness with a reality that at first it didn't seem to possess. Hearing the same accusations and criticisms week after week, some working people began to disengage themselves from him. In turn, as the label of racist was applied to Wallace in the news media and by the other candidates, they began to drop him from their consideration. Organized labor, too, began to fight back, rendering more support to Humphrey and single-handedly attempting through its own organizations to get out the black vote, to print and distribute millions of leaflets and pamphlets denouncing Wallace's views and to work on election day to see that the voters got to the polls. By October, the effect on Wallace's campaign in the North was obvious. In the election, however, Wallace still managed to garner 14 percent of the national total; and the vote was not, as it has been frequently pointed out, sectional. Of the 9.9 million votes he received, 5.8 million came from the South, with the remainder coming from northern and western states and representing overwhelmingly the votes of the white workingman. This seemed to be the alienated group in American society, the group who believed that it had been overlooked by government in the distribution of favors; government welfare policies for the unemployed, economic aid for the blacks, subsidies for business and industry—but what was left for them? Their neighborhoods were feeling the effect of violence, not those of the middle-classes; their homes were being threatened by proposed changes in zoning and public housing; their lives—even their union membership which used to assure them of special privileges— were threatened by the agitation of the blacks to have a share in the pie. It was this group that responded to Wallace in 1968 as the only candidate who seemed to understand their predicament and promise a solution. Their vote was a portentous sign of the future.

ELDRIDGE CLEAVER *Poster* *41¾ x 29¼ inches* *Private collection*

Eldridge Cleaver *Peace and Freedom*

1935-

In 1968, an ex-convict and avowed revolutionary entered upon a campaign for the presidency of the United States and received 30,000 votes nationally. This was Eldridge Cleaver, the candidate of the Peace and Freedom Party, which represented a coalition of blacks and white radicals seeking a "rearrangement . . . in the system that controls the world." Black liberation was simply one measure in a program that would allow all people—white and black—to "be in control of their own destiny." Their motto: "Do your own thing, but not on my back."

By 1968, Cleaver had come a long way intellectually from the reformatory he had entered on the charge of bicycle theft while still in junior high school. From the inmates of the reform school, Cleaver had learned about peddling marijuana and soon was caught "with a shopping bag full of love." Sent to Soledad Prison in California in 1954, he completed his high school studies and read widely and eagerly, especially the works of revolutionary writers from Thomas Paine and Voltaire to Bakunin and Karl Marx. Reading sharpened his insights as well as confirmed his obvious intellectual bent. Philosophical analysis of the human condition inevitably followed, as the young man tried to make sense out of the confusion of his experiences. He discovered, he reported, that other people were confused too, that "out there beyond the horizon of my own ignorance" unanimity did not exist; rather, "the whole U.S.A. was in chaos of disagreement over segregation/integration" and other values. Determining to be truly free, to reject what he could not accept, he became "an extreme iconoclast"; by negating all the values that society seemed to hold dear—"marriage, love, God, patriotism, the Constitution, the founding fathers, law, concepts of right-wrong-good-evil, all forms of ritualized and conventional behavior"—he focused all his rejections on a single "insurrectionary act"—rape. Released from prison, he put his new philosophy into practice, "delighted . . . that I was defying and trampling upon the white man's law, upon his system of values, and that I was defiling his women." Inevitably, a return to prison followed after eleven months of freedom, and he was sentenced to a two-to-fourteen years for assault with intent to kill. It was this second long stay in prison that turned him to writing and rethinking his values, and sent him out into the world again as a black revolutionary leader.

Cleaver's prison education began at the time when discontented blacks became impatient with the slowness and seeming limitations of the Civil Rights Acts of 1964 and 1965 to effect the kind of changes in their life and environment that were so glaringly needed. They rose in violent protest against the ghetto environment and urban slum conditions in which they were forced to play out their lives. Watts in Los Angeles was the first scene of riot—Cleaver's boyhood home, actually—and from then on, race riots wracked American cities throughout 1966. News of the revolution in Watts easily penetrated the prison gates, confirming Cleaver's own sense of being involved in a larger struggle for freedom; but first he had to come to grips with himself as a "human, civilized" being. The Black Muslims, a religious movement that preached Negro separation, provided the structure and philosophy through which personal discipline was achieved and a direction given to his life. Cleaver's greatest admiration was for Malcolm X, the black Muslim leader who toward the end of his life had come to believe that separatism was not the answer for the black, but, instead, political and racial awareness. After Malcolm X's assassination, Cleaver, too, split with the Muslims. "I have, so to speak, washed my hands in the blood of the martyr, Malcolm X, whose retreat from the precipice of madness created new room for others to turn around in," he wrote, "and I am now caught up in that tiny space, attempting a maneuver of my own."

Late in 1966, Cleaver won his parole after nine years in prison on the guarantee of a writing position with the magazine *Ramparts*. While writing for the periodical, he helped organize Black House in San Francisco, a social and cultural center for young blacks and others interested in black culture. There, he met Huey P. Newton and Bobby Seale, the co-founders of the Black Panthers, whose "revolutionary courage" Cleaver came to admire, especially their willingness "to lay down [their] life in defense of the rights of [their] people." The Black Panthers started out as a black self-defense organization that supervised the activities of police in the slums of Oakland, across the bay from San Francisco, as they came into contact with Negroes. Armed with guns and law books, the Black Panthers would attempt to maintain order among their own people while preventing the police from acting hastily or illegally. Violence, of course, inevitably broke out between Panthers and the police, who became irritated at the surveillance of a self-appointed constabulary. It was during one of these confrontations on the day after the assassination of the black-leader Martin Luther King that a seventeen-year-old Panther, Bobby Hutton, was killed and Cleaver was wounded. Released on a writ of habeas corpus on the judge's contention that Cleaver had been jailed not because he had failed to rehabilitate himself adequately, but because of his "undue eloquence in pursuing political goals which were offensive to many of his contemporaries," Cleaver was free to lecture and campaign for the presidency of the United States. During these speeches, he rejected separation of the races as the solution to the black's problems, and instead claimed that black liberation would come with "the removal of artificial restraint blocking . . . access to all the benefits of the economic, political, and social systems"; in this cause, all people were involved.

Cleaver's release was overruled by a higher court decision, and the presidential candidate was ordered to return to prison on November 27, 1968. Instead, insisting that he could not "relate to spending the next four years in the penitentiary, not with madmen with supreme power in their hands," he fled the country. Whether or not Cleaver will return to the United States in 1972 as he has planned, however, remains a question for the future.

Selected Bibliography

GENERAL

Beard, Charles A. *The American Party Battle*. New York, 1928.

Binkley, Wilfred E. *American Political Parties: Their Natural History*. New York, 1962.

Bowers, C. J. *The Party Battles of the Jackson Period*. Boston, 1922.

Current Biography Yearbook. New York, 1941-1968.

Dictionary of American Biography. Vols. 1-10. Edited by Allen Johnson. New York, 1927.

History of American Presidential Elections 1789-1968. 4 vols. Edited by Arthur M. Schlesinger, Jr., New York, 1971.

Kent, Frank R. *The Democratic Party: A History*. New York, 1928.

Lorant, Stefan. *The Glorious Burden*. New York, 1968.

Mayer, George. *The Republican Party, 1854-1964*. New York, 1964.

Nichols, Roy F. *The Invention of the American Political Parties*. New York, 1967.

Rhodes, James Ford. *History of the United States from the Compromise of 1850*. Chicago, 1966.

Roseboom, Eugene H. *A History of Presidential Elections*. New York, 1957.

Schachner, Nathan. *The Founding Fathers*. New York, 1954.

Seitz, Don C. *The "Also Rans", Great Men Who Missed Making the Presidential Goal*. New York, 1928.

Stone, Irving. *They Also Ran, The Story of the Men Who Were Defeated for the Presidency*. Garden City, 1966.

Weisbord, Marvin R. *Campaigning for President*. Washington, D.C., 1964.

Williamson, Chilton. *American Suffrage from Property to Democracy, 1760 to 1860*. Princeton, 1960.

CAMPAIGNS

1789-1792

Borden, Morton. *Parties and Politics in the Early Republic, 1789-1815*. London, 1967.

Chambers, William Nisbet. *Political Parties in a New Nation, The American Experience, 1776-1809*. New York, 1963.

Koch, Adrienne. *Power, Morals and the Founding Fathers*. Ithaca, 1961.

Miller, John C. *The Federalist Era 1789-1801*. New York and Evanston, 1960.

Nichols, Roy F. *The Invention of the American Political Parties.* New York, 1967.

Rossiter, Clinton. *Alexander Hamilton and the Constitution.* New York, 1964.

1800

Adams, Henry. *History of the United States of America During the Administrations Of Jefferson and Madison.* Edited by Ernest Samuels. Chicago, 1967.

Chambers, William Nisbet. *Political Parties in a New Nation, The American Experience, 1776-1809.* New York, 1963.

Chinard, Gilbert. *Honest John Adams.* Boston, 1933.

Cunningham, Noble E. Jr. *The Making of the American Party System 1789-1809.* Englewood Cliffs, New Jersey, 1965.

Kurtz, Stephen G. *The Presidency of John Adams, The Collapse of Federalism, 1795-1800.* Philadelphia, 1957.

Lodge, Henry C. *Alexander Hamilton.* Vol. 3. 1917; reprinted New York, 1969.

Miller, John C. *The Federalist Era, 1789-1801.* New York and Evanston, 1960.

Morison, Samuel E. *Harrison Gray Otis, 1765-1848, The Urbane Federalist.* Boston, 1969.

Smith, Page. *John Adams.* 2 vols. Garden City, 1962.

1820

Adams, John Quincy. *The Diary of John Quincy Adams, 1794-1845.* Edited by Allan Nevins. New York, 1929.

Dangerfield, George. *The Awakening of American Nationlism, 1815-1828.* New York, 1965.

Hammond, Bray. *Banks and Politics in America.* Princeton, 1957.

Livermore, Shaw Jr. *The Twilight of Federalism: The Disintegration of the Federalist Party, 1815-1830.* Princeton, 1962.

Walters, Raymond Jr. *The Virginia Dynasty.* New York, 1965.

Ammon, Harry. "James Monroe and The Era of Good Feelings," *Virginia Magazine of History and Biography,* vol. 66, no. 4 (October 1958), pp. 387-398.

Preyer, Norris W. "Southern Support of the Tariff of 1816: A Reappraisal," *Journal of Southern History,* vol. 25 (August 1959), pp. 306-322.

1824

Bemis, Samuel Flagg. *John Quincy Adams and the Union.* New York, 1965.

Dangerfield, George. *The Awakening of American Nationalism, 1815-1828.* New York, 1965.

Livermore, Shaw Jr. *The Twilight of Federalism: The Disintegration of the Federalist Party, 1815-1830.* Princeton, 1962.

Schlesinger, Arthur M., Jr. *The Age of Jackson.* Boston, 1953.

Van Deusen, Glyndon G. *The Jacksonian Era, 1828-1848.* New York, 1959.

Brown, Richard H. "The Missouri Crisis, Slavery, and the Politics of Jacksonianism," *South Atlantic Quarterly,* vol. 65 (Winter 1966), pp. 55-72.

Chase, James Staton. "Jacksonian Democracy and the Rise of the Nominating Convention," *Mid-America,* vol. 45 (October 1963), pp. 229-249.

McCormick, Richard P. "New Perspectives on Jacksonian Politics," *American Historical Review,* vol. 65 (January 1960), pp. 288-301.

Wallace, Michael. "Changing Concepts of Party in the United States: New York, 1815-1828," *American Historical Review,* vol. 74 (December 1968), pp. 453-491.

1840

Bassett, John Spencer. *The Life of Andrew Jackson.* Hamden, Connecticut, 1967.

Bowers, Claude G. *The Party Battles of the Jackson Period.* Boston and New York, 1922.

Curtis, George T. *The Life of James Buchanan.* 2 vols. New York, 1883.

Curtis, James C. *The Fox at Bay: Martin Van Buren and the Presidency, 1837-1841.* Lexington, Kentucky, 1970.

Gunderson, Robert G. *The Log Cabin Campaign.* Lexington, Kentucky, 1957.

Lynch, Denis T. *An Epoch and A Man: Martin Van Buren and His Times.* New York, 1929.

Miller, Nathan. *The Enterprise of a Free People.* Ithaca, 1962.

Nichols, Roy F. *The Invention of the American Political Parties.* New York, 1967.

Norton, A. B. *The Great Revolution of 1840. Reminiscences of the Log Cabin and Hard Cider Campaign.* Mount Vernon, n.d., and Dallas, Texas, 1888.

Poage, George Rawlings. *Henry Clay and the Whig Party.* Chapel Hill, 1936.

Remini, Robert B. *Martin Van Buren and the Making of the Democratic Party.* New York, 1959.

Schlesinger, Arthur M., Jr. *The Age of Jackson.* Boston, 1953.

Silbey, Joel H. *The Transformation of American Politics, 1840-1860.* Englewood Cliffs, New Jersey, 1967.

Sumner, W. G. *Andrew Jackson.* Boston, 1890.

Van Deusen, Glyndon G. *The Jacksonian Era, 1828-1848.* New York and Evanston, 1959.

1860

Crenshaw, Ollinger. *The Slave States in the Presidential Election of 1860.* Baltimore, 1945.

Fite, Emerson David. *The Presidential Campaign of 1860.* New York, 1911.

Halstead, Murat. *Three Against Lincoln; Murat Halstead Reports the Caucuses of 1860.* Edited by W. B. Hesseltine. Baton Rouge, 1960.

Klein, Philip S. *President James Buchanan.* University Park, Pennsylvania, 1962.

Luthin, R. H. *The Real Abraham Lincoln.* Englewood Cliffs, New Jersey, 1960.

Milton, George F. *The Eve of Conflict.* New York, 1969.

Nevins, Allan. *Ordeal of the Union: A House Dividing, 1852-1857.* Vol. 2. New York, 1947.

Nevins, Allan. *The Emergence of Lincoln.* Vol. 2. New York, 1950.

A Political Textbook for 1860. 1886; reprinted New York, 1969.

Rhodes, James Ford. *History of the United States From the Compromise of 1850.* Edited by Allan Nevins. Chicago, 1966.

Silbey, Joel H. *The Transformation of American Politics, 1840-1860.* Englewood Cliffs, New Jersey, 1967.

The Union in Crisis, 1850-1877. Edited by Robert W. Johannsen. New York, 1965.

1876

Barnard, Harry. *Rutherford B. Hayes and His America.* Indianapolis, 1954.

Haworth, P. L. *The Hayes-Tilden Disputed Presidential Election of 1876.* Cleveland, 1906; reprinted 1966.

Woodward, C. Vann. *Reunion and Reaction, The Compromise of 1877 and The End of Reconstruction.* Boston, 1956.

Koenig, Louis W. "The Election That Got Away," *American Heritage,* vol. 11, no. 6 (October 1960).

1896

Leech, Margaret. *In the Days of McKinley.* New York, 1959.

Weisbord, Marvin. *Campaigning for President.* Washington, 1964.

Whicher, George. *William Jennings Bryan and the Election of 1896.* Boston, 1953.

1912

Croly, Herbert. *The Promise of American Life.* New York, 1912.

Goldman, Eric F. *Rendezvous with Destiny.* New York, 1952.

Hofstadter, Richard. *The Age of Reform.* New York, 1955.

Kelly, Frank K. *The Fight for the White House, The Story of 1912.* New York, 1961.

Link, Arthur S. *Wilson, The Road to the White House.* Princeton, 1947.

Link, Arthur S. *Woodrow Wilson and the Progressive Era.* New York, 1951.

Mowry, G. E. *The Era of Theodore Roosevelt.* New York, 1958.

Mowry, G. E. *Theodore Roosevelt and the Progressive Movement.* Madison, Wisconsin, 1946.

Roosevelt, Theodore. *The New Nationalism.* New York, 1910.

Wilson, Woodrow. *The New Freedom,* New York, 1913.

1932

Bernstein, Irving. *The Lean Years.* Boston, 1960.

Galbraith, J. K. *The Great Crash.* Boston, 1955.

Leuchtenburg, W. E. *Franklin Roosevelt and the New Deal.* New York, 1963.

Mitchell, Broadus. *Depression Decade.* New York, 1947.

Schlesinger, Arthur M. Jr. *The Age of Roosevelt,* Vol. 1. Boston, 1957.

Warren, H. G. *Herbert Hoover and The Great Depression.* New York, 1959.

Wector, Dixon. *The Age of the Great Depression.* New York, 1948.

1948

Goldman, Eric F. *The Crucial Decade—And After: America, 1945-1960.* New York, 1961.

Kirkendall, Richard. "The Presidential Election of 1948," *The American Scene.* Edited by R. D. Marcus and D. Burner. Vol. 2, pp. 400-427.

Shogan, Robert. "1948 Election," *American Heritage,* vol. 19, no. 4 (June 1968), pp. 24-31, 104-111.

1952

Eisenhower as President. Edited by Dean Albertson. New York, 1963.

Goldman, Eric F. *The Crucial Decade—And After: America, 1945-1960.* New York 1961.

Rovere, Richard. "Eisenhower Over The Shoulder," *The American Scholar,* vol. 31, no. 2 (Spring 1962).

CANDIDATES

JOHN ADAMS

Chinard, Gilbert. *Honest John Adams.* Boston, 1933.

Dauer, Manning J. *The Adams Federalists.* Baltimore, 1953.

The Johns Adams Papers. Edited by Frank Donovan. New York, 1965.

Smith, Page. *John Adams.* Vol. 2, 1784-1826. Garden City, 1962.

JOHN QUINCY ADAMS

Bemis, Samuel Flagg. *John Quincy Adams and the Foundations of American Foreign Policy.* New York, 1949.

Bemis, Samuel Flagg. *John Quincy Adams and the Union.* New York, 1956.

The Selected Writings of John and John Quincy Adams. Edited by Adrienne Koch and William Peden. New York, 1946.

JOHN BELL

Bartlett, D. W. *Presidential Candidates: Sketches of Prominent Candidates for the Presidency in 1860.* New York, 1859.

Crenshaw, Ollinger. *The Slave States in the Presidential Election of 1860.* Baltimore, 1945.

Nevins, Allan. *The Emergence of Lincoln: Douglas, Buchanan, and Party Chaos 1857-1859,* vol. 1. New York, 1950.

Parks, Joseph Howard. *John Bell of Tennessee.* Baton Rouge, 1950.

Caldwell, Joshua W. "John Bell of Tennessee," *American Historical Review,* vol. 4, 1899.

Richardson, Charles F. "The Constitutional Union Party of 1860," *Yale Review,* vol. 3, 1894.

JAMES G. BIRNEY

Birney, William. *James G. Birney and His Times.* New York, 1890.

Fladeland, Betty. *James Gillespie Birney: Slaveholder to Abolitionist.* Ithaca, New York, 1955.

Ford, Worthington Chauncey. *The Campaign of 1844.* Worcester, Massachusetts, 1909.

JAMES BLACK

Black, James. *Brief History of Prohibition and of the Prohibition Reform Party.* New York, 1880.

Cherrington, E. H. *The Evolution of Prohibition in the United States.* Westerville, Ohio, 1920.

Colvin, D. Leigh. *Prohibition in the United States.* New York, 1926.

JAMES G. BLAINE

Nevins, Allan. *Grover Cleveland: A Study in Courage.* New York, 1964.

Rosenburg, Marvin. "The Dirtiest Election," *American Heritage,* vol. 13, no. 5 (August 1962).

JOHN CABELL BRECKINRIDGE

Crenshaw, Ollinger. *The Slave States in the Presidential Election of 1860.* Baltimore, 1945.

Eaton, Clement. *A History of the Old South.* New York, 1966.

Hess, Stephen. *America's Political Dynasties: From Adams to Kennedy.* Garden City, 1966.

Stillwell, Lucille. *John Cabell Breckinridge: Born to be a Statesman.* Caldwell, Idaho, 1936.

EARL BROWDER

Browder, Earl. "The Most Peculiar Compaign," *The Campaign Speeches of Earl Browder.* New York, 1940.

Gitlow, Benjamin. *The Whole of Their Lives.* New York, 1948.

Shannon, David. *The Decline of American Communism.* New York, 1959.

Stein, Harry. "Marx's Disenchanted Salesman," *American Heritage,* December 1971.

WILLIAM JENNINGS BRYAN

Coletta, Paolo. *William Jennings Bryan.* Lincoln, Nebraska, 1964.

Glad, Paul. *The Trumpet Soundeth: William Jennings Bryan and His Democracy, 1896-1912.* Lincoln, Nebraska, 1960.

Koenig, Louis W. *Bryan: A Political Biography of William Jennings Bryan.* New York, 1971.

Whicher, George. *William Jennings Bryan and the Election of 1896.* Boston, 1953.

AARON BURR

Parmet, Herbert S. and Marie B. Hecht. *Aaron Burr, Portrait of an Ambitious Man.* New York, 1967.

Schachner, Nathan. *Aaron Burr, A Biography.* New York, 1937.

BENJAMIN F. BUTLER

Nash, Howard P. *Stormy Petrel: The Life and Times of Benjamin F. Butler, 1818-1893.* Teaneck, New Jersey, 1969.

West, Richard. *Lincoln's Scapegoat General: The Life of Benjamin F. Butler, 1818-1893.* Boston, 1965.

LEWIS CASS

McLaughlin, Andrew C. *Lewis Cass.* American Statesmen Series. Boston, 1891.

Nichols, Roy F. *The Invention of the American Political Parties.* New York, 1967.

Smith, Theodore Clarke. *The Liberty and Free Soil Parties in the Northwest.* New York, 1897; reprinted 1967.

Woodford, Frank B. *Lewis Cass, The Last Jeffersonian.* New Brunswick, New Jersey, 1950.

HENRY CLAY

Eaton, Clement. *Henry Clay and the Art of American Politics.* Boston, 1957.

Poage, George Rawlings. *Henry Clay and the Whig Party.* Chapel Hill, 1936.

Van Duesen, Glyndon G. *The Life of Henry Clay.* Boston, 1937.

ELDRIDGE CLEAVER

Cleaver, Eldridge. *Soul on Ice.* New York, 1968.

Cleaver, Eldridge. *Eldridge Cleaver: Post-prison Writings and Speeches.* Edited by Robert Scheer. New York, 1969.

Swados, Harvey. "Eldridge Cleaver: Old Con, Black Panther, Brilliant Writer and Quintessential American," *The New York Times Magazine,* September 7, 1969.

Thompson, Cordell S. "Mrs. Eldridge Cleaver Returns to U.S. to Give State of Revolution Message," *Jet,* December 2, 1971.

GROVER CLEVELAND

Nevins, Allan. *Grover Cleveland: A Study in Courage.* New York, 1964.

DeWITT CLINTON

Bobbé, Dorothie. *DeWitt Clinton.* Port Washington, Long Island, 1962.

Brant, Irving. *James Madison, Commander in Chief 1812-1836.* Indianapolis and New York, 1961.

GEORGE CLINTON

Ellis, David M., et al. *A History of New York State.* Ithaca, New York, 1967.

Spaulding, Ernest Wilder. *His Excellency George Clinton: Critic of the Constitution.* New York, 1938.

PETER COOPER

Nevins, Allan. *Abram S. Hewitt: With Some Account of Peter Cooper.* New York, 1935.

Rossiter, Raymond. *Peter Cooper.* Boston, 1901.

Lyon, Peter. "The Honest Man," *American Heritage,* vol. 10, no. 2 (February 1959).

JAMES M. COX

Cox, James M. *Journey Through My Years.* New York, 1946.

Egbert, Howard. "Cox, Democratic Candidate," *Review of Reviews,* vol. 62, August 1920.

JAMES R. COX

Conway, Raymond. *St. Mary's Church on 46th Street.* Westminster, Maryland, 1950.

Christian Century. Vol. 49, February 17, 1932.

Pittsburgh Post-Gazette. March 20, 1951.

JACOB S. COXEY

Nye, Russell B. *A Baker's Dozen: Thirteen Unusual Americans.* East Lansing, 1956.

WILLIAM HARRIS CRAWFORD

Bemis, Samuel Flagg. *John Quincy Adams and The Union.* New York, 1965.

Green, Philip Jackson. *The Public Life of William Harris Crawford, 1807-1825.* Chicago, 1938.

Wiltse, Charles M. *John C. Calhoun, Nationlist, 1782-1828.* New York, 1944.

JOHN W. DAVIS

Post, Melville Davisson. "John W. Davis," *Review of Reviews,* August 1924.

"John W. Davis," *Current Opinion,* vol. 77, no. 3 (September 1924).

"Can John W. Davis Reunite the Democratic Party?" *The Literary Digest,* vol. 82, no. 3 (July 19, 1924).

EUGENE V. DEBS

Debs, Eugene V. *Writings and Speeches.* Edited by Arthur M. Schlesinger, Jr., New York, 1948.

Ginger, Ray. *The Bending Cross: A Biography of Eugene V. Debs.* New Brunswick, New Jersey, 1949.

Karsner, David. *Debs: His Authorized Life and Letters.* New York, 1919.

Morgan, H. Wayne. *Eugene V. Debs: Socialist for President.* Syracuse, 1962.

Shannon, David A. *The Socialist Party of America: A History.* New York, 1955.

THOMAS E. DEWEY

Goldman, Eric F. *The Crucial Decade—And After: America, 1945-1960.* New York 1961.

Moley, Raymond. *Masters of Politics.* New York, 1949.

Shogan, Robert. "1948 Election," *American Heritage,* vol. 19, no. 4 (June 1968).

"Thomas Edmund Dewey." Editorial in *The Washington Post,* March 18, 1971.

STEPHEN A. DOUGLAS

Bartlett, D. W. *Presidential Candidates: Sketches of Prominent Candidates for the Presidency in 1860.* New York, 1959.

Capers, Gerald M. *Stephen A. Douglas, Defender of the Union.* Boston, 1959.

Eaton, Clement. *A History of the Old South.* New York, 1966.

Milton, George Fort. *The Eve of Conflict: Stephen A. Douglas and the Needless War.* Boston and New York, 1934.

Nevins, Allan. *The Emergence of Lincoln: Douglas, Buchanan, and Party Chaos, 1857-1859,* vol. 1. New York, 1950.

Pease, Theodore Calvin. *The Story of Illinois.* Chicago, 1925; reprinted 1967.

The Union in Crisis, 1850-1877. Edited by Robert W. Johannsen. New York, 1965.

Johannsen, Robert W. "Stephen A. Douglas and the South," *Journal of Southern History,* vol. 33, February 1967.

NEAL DOW

Byrne, Frank L. *Prophet of Prohibition: Neal Dow and His Crusade.* Madison, Wisconsin, 1961.

Dow, Neal. *The Reminiscences of Neal Dow.* Portland, Maine, 1898.

MILLARD FILLMORE

Barre, W. L. *The Life and Public Services of Millard Fillmore.* Buffalo, 1856.

Griffis, William Elliot. *Millard Fillmore.* Ithaca, New York, 1915.

Rayback, Robert J. *Millard Fillmore.* Buffalo, 1959.

Billington, Ray Allen. "The Know-Nothing Uproar," *American Heritage,* vol. 10, no. 2 (February 1959).

Smith, Theodore Clarke. "Parties and Slavery," *The American Nation: A History.* Edited by Albert Bushnell Hart. Vol. 18. New York, 1906.

JOHN C. FRÉMONT

Bartlett, Ruhl Jacob. *John C. Frémont and the Republican Party.* Columbus, Ohio, 1930.

Goodwin, Cardinal. *John Charles Frémont, An Explanation of His Career.* Stanford, 1930.

Nevins, Allan. *Frémont, The West's Greatest Adventurer.* New York, 1928.

BARRY M. GOLDWATER

The National Election of 1964. Edited by Milton C. Cummings. Washington, D.C., 1966.

Mohr, Charles. "Requiem for a Lightweight," *Esquire,* August 1965.

HORACE GREELEY

Hale, William H. *Horace Greeley: Voice of the People.* New York, 1950.

Van Deusen, Glyndon G. *Horace Greeley: Nineteenth-Century Crusader.* Philadelphia, 1953.

ERIC HASS

Personal communications between Eric Hass and the National Portrait Gallery, 1971.

JOHN PARKER HALE

Bartlett, D. W. *Presidential Candidates: Sketches of Prominent Candidates for the Presidency in 1860.* New York, 1859.

Sewell, Richard. *John P. Hale and the Politics of Abolition.* Cambridge, Massachusetts, 1965.

Smith, Theodore Clarke. *The Liberty and Free Soil Parties in the Northwest.* New York, 1897; reprinted, 1967.

Julian, G. W. "A Presidential Candidate of 1852," *The Century Magazine,* October 1896.

WINFIELD SCOTT HANCOCK

Clancy, Herbert J. *The Presidential Election of 1880.* Chicago, 1958.

Hancock, Almira R. *Reminiscences of Winfield Scott Hancock.* New York, 1887.

BENJAMIN HARRISON

Knoles, George H. *The Presidential Election of 1892.* Stanford, 1942.

Sievers, Harry. *Benjamin Harrison: Hoosier Warrior.* New York, 1959.

WILLIAM HENRY HARRISON

Cleaves, Freeman. *Old Tippecanoe, William Henry Harrison and His Times.* New York, 1939.
Goebel, Dorothy Burne. *William Henry Harrison—A Political Biography.* Indianapolis, 1926.

HERBERT HOOVER

Hofstadter, Richard. *The American Political Tradition and The Men Who Made It.* New York, 1948.
Irwin, Will. *Herbert Hoover: A Reminiscent Biography.* New York, 1928.
Smith, Gene. *Shattered Dream: Herbert Hoover and the Great Depression.* New York, 1970.

CHARLES EVANS HUGHES

Pusey, Merlo J. *Charles Evans Hughes.* New York, 1963.

HUBERT H. HUMPHREY

Martin, Ralph G. *A Man for All People: Hubert H. Humphrey.* New York, 1968.
Sherrill, Robert and Harry W. Ernst. *The Drugstore Liberal.* New York, 1968.
White, Theodore H. *The Making of the President, 1968.* New York, 1969.
Meryman, Richard. "Hubert Humphrey. Talks His Self-Portrait," *Life,* vol. 65, no. 13, September 27, 1968.
Wool, Robert. "Still the Man Who Loves to Talk, to Teach, to Preach," *The New York Times Biographical Edition.* October 14, 1970.

ANDREW JACKSON

Bemis, Samuel Flagg. *John Quincy Adams and the Union.* New York, 1965.
James, Marquis. *Andrew Jackson, The Border Captain.* New York, 1933.
James, Marquis. *Andrew Jackson, Portrait of a President.* New York, 1937.
Remini, Robert V. *The Election of Andrew Jackson.* New York, 1963.
Ward, John William, *Andrew Jackson—Symbol for an Age,* New York, 1962.

THOMAS JEFFERSON

Malone, Dumas. *Jefferson and the Ordeal of Liberty: Jefferson and His Time.* Vol. 3. Boston, 1962.
Peterson, Merrill. *Thomas Jefferson and the New Nation: A Biography.* New York, 1970.

RUFUS KING

Ernst, Robert. *Rufus King, American Federalist.* Chapel Hill, 1968.
Reeser, Robert E. Rufus King and the Federalist Party. Unpublished doctoral dissertation, University of California at Los Angeles, 1948.

ROBERT M. LaFOLLETTE

LaFollette, Belle Case and Fola LaFollette. *Robert M. LaFollette.* New York, 1953.
Maxwell, Robert S., ed. *LaFollette. Great Lives Observed.* Englewood Cliffs, New Jersey, 1969.
McKay, Kenneth Campbell. *The Progressive Movement of 1924.* New York, 1947.

ALFRED M. LANDON

Zornow, William. *Kansas: History of the Jayhawk State.* Norman, Oklahoma, 1957.
"The Landon Boom," *Fortune,* vol. 13, March 1936.

WILLIAM LEMKE

Blackorby, Edward C. *Prairie Rebel: The Public Life of William Lemke.* Lincoln, Nebraska, 1963.
Schlesinger, Arthur M., Jr. *The Politics of Upheaval.* Boston, 1960.
Tull, Charles J. *Father Coughlin and the New Deal.* Syracuse, 1965.

BELVA ANN LOCKWOOD

Douglas, Emily Taft. *Remember The Ladies.* New York, 1966.
Irwin, Inez H. *Angels and Amazons.* Garden City, 1933.
Kerr, Francis. "Lady's Chapeau in Ring in 1880's," *The Washington Post,* August 6, 1952.
Milstead, Nannette. "Women Owe a Lot to Belva Lockwood," *The Washington Star,* February 7, 1954.

GEORGE B. McCLELLAN

Catton, Bruce. *The Army of the Potomac: Mr. Lincoln's Army.* Garden City, 1962.
Catton, Bruce. *The Army of the Potomac: A Stillness at Appomattox.* Garden City, 1953.
Hassler, Warren W. Jr. *General George B. McClellan: Shield of the Union.* Baton Rouge, 1957.
Hendrick, Burton J. *Lincoln's War Cabinet.* Boston, 1946.
Hesseltine, William B. *Lincoln and the War Governors.* New York, 1948.
Miers, Eral Schenck. *The American Civil War.* New York, 1961.
Myers, William Starr. *A Study in Personality: General George Brinton McClellan.* New York, 1934.
Klein, Frederic S. "The War Election of 1864," *American History Illustrated,* vol. 3, no. 6 (October 1968).
MSS. The Papers of George B. McClellan. Library of Congress.

RICHARD M. NIXON

Alsop, Stewart J. O. *Nixon and Rockefeller: A Double Portrait.* Garden City, 1960.
De Toledano, Ralph. *Nixon.* New York, 1960.
Mazo, Earl, and Stephen Hess. *Nixon, A Political Portrait.* New York, 1968.
Nixon, Richard M. *Six Crises.* Garden City, 1962.
Wills, Garry. *Nixon Agonistes: The Crisis of the Self-Made Man.* Boston, 1970.

CHARLES O'CONOR

Gregory, Henry Ellsworth. "Charles O'Conor," *Great American Lawyers,* vol. 5, Philadelphia, 1908.
Browne, Irving. "Charles O'Conor," *The Green Bag,* vol. 12, no. 1 (January 1895).
Daly, Charles P. "Charles O'Conor: His Professional Life and Character," *Magazine of American History,* vol. 13, January-June 1885.

JOHN McAULEY PALMER

Palmer, George Thomas. *A Conscientious Turncoat.* New Haven, 1941.

ALTON B. PARKER

Cleveland, Grover. "Parker," *McClure's Magazine,* vol. 24, November 1904.
Creelman, James. "Alton B. Parker: A Character Sketch," *Review of Reviews,* vol. 30, October 1904.
"The Progress of the World," *Review of Reviews,* vol. 30, August 1904.

CHARLES COTESWORTH PINCKNEY

Rogers, George C. Jr. *Charleston in the Age of the Pinckneys.* Norman, Oklahoma, 1969.
Zahniser, Marvin R. *Charles Cotesworth Pinckney, Founding Father.* Chapel Hill, 1967.

THOMAS PINCKNEY

Kurtz, Stephen G. *The Presidency of John Adams, The Collapse of Federalism, 1795-1800.* Philadelphia, 1957.

Rogers, George C. *Charleston in the Age of the Pinckneys.* Norman, Oklahoma, 1969.

THEODORE ROOSEVELT

Harbaugh, William Henry. *Power and Responsibility: The Life and Times of Theodore Roosevelt.* New York, 1961.

Hofstadter, Richard. *The American Political Tradition and the Men Who Made It.* New York, 1948.

Mowrey, George E. *The Era of Theodore Roosevelt, 1900-1912.* New York and Evanston, 1958.

Roosevelt, Theodore. *The Autobiography of Theodore Roosevelt.* Edited by Wayne Andrews. New York, 1958.

JOHN P. ST. JOHN

Frederickson, Edna T. John P. St. John: Father of Constitutional Prohibition. Unpublished doctoral dissertation, University of Kansas, 1930.

WINFIELD SCOTT

Smith, Arthur D. Howden. *Old Fuss and Feathers.* New York, 1937.

HORATIO SEYMOUR

Coleman, Charles H. *The Election of 1868: The Democratic Effort to Regain Control.* New York. 1933.

Mitchell, Stewart. *Horatio Seymour of New York.* New York, 1970.

Wall, Alexander. *A Sketch of the Life of Horatio Seymour, 1810-1886.* New York, 1929.

ALFRED E. SMITH

Handlin, Oscar. *Al Smith and His America.* Boston, 1958.

Moore, Edmund. *A Catholic Runs for President.* Gloucester, Massachusetts, 1968.

Peel, Roy V. and Thomas C. Donnelly. *The 1928 Campaign: An Analysis.* New York, 1931.

GERALD L. K. SMITH

Burns, James M. *Roosevelt: The Lion and The Fox.* New York, 1956.

Williams, T. Harry. *Huey Long.* New York, 1970.

Davenport, W. "Mysterious Gerald Smith," *Colliers,* vol. 1113, pp. 14-15, March 4, 1944.

Ryan, J. F. "Twilight Years of a Kindly Old Hatesmith," *Esquire,* vol. 70, pp. 88-91, August 1968.

GERRIT SMITH

Dyer, Brainerd. *Zachary Taylor.* New York, 1946.

Frothingham, Octavius Brooks. *Gerrit Smith.* New York, 1878.

Harlow, Ralph Volney. *Gerrit Smith.* New York, 1939.

Smith, Theodore Clarke. *The Liberty and Free Soil Parties in the Northwest.* New York, 1897.

ADLAI E. STEVENSON

Brown, Stuart G. *Adlai E. Stevenson: A Short Biography.* New York, 1965.

Davis, Kenneth S. *The Politics of Honor.* New York, 1967.

Goldman, Eric. *The Crucial Decade—and After: America, 1945-1960.* New York, 1961.

Muller, Herbert. *Adlai Stevenson, A Study in Values.* New York, 1967.

Stevenson, Adlai E. *The Major Campaign Speeches of Adlai E. Stevenson.* New York, 1953.

Walton, Richard J. *The Remnants of Power.* New York, 1968.

Whitman, Alden R. *Portrait.* New York, 1965.

WILLIAM HOWARD TAFT

Pringle, Henry F. *The Life and Times of William Howard Taft.* Hamden, Connecticut, 1964.

NORMAN THOMAS

Flieschman, Harry. *Norman Thomas: A Biography.* New York, 1964.

Seidler, Murray. *Norman Thomas, Respectable Rebel.* Syracuse, 1961.

J. STROM THURMOND

Lachicotte, Alberta M. *Rebel Senator.* New York, 1966.

Lemmon, Sarah M. "The Ideology of the 'Dixiecrat' Movement," *Social Forces,* vol. 30, December 1951.

Shogan, Robert. "1948 Election," *American Heritage,* vol. 19, no. 4 (June 1968).

SAMUEL J. TILDEN

Flick, Alexander C. *Samuel Jones Tilden: A Study in Political Sagacity.* New York, 1939.

Nevins, Allan. *Abram S. Hewett, With Some Account of Peter Cooper.* New York, 1935.

MARTIN VAN BUREN

Alexander, Holmes. *The American Talleyrand.* New York, 1935.

Curtis, James C. *The Fox at Bay: Martin Van Buren and the Presidency, 1837-1841.* Lexington, Kentucky, 1970.

Gunderson, Robert Gray. *The Log Cabin Campaign.* Lexington, Kentucky, 1957.

GEORGE C. WALLACE.

White, Theodore. *The Making of the President, 1968.* New York, 1969.

Frady, Marshall. "George Wallace, The Angry Man's Candidate," *Saturday Evening Post,* June 15 and 29, 1968.

HENRY A. WALLACE

Ekirch, Arthur A. Jr. *Ideologies and Utopias: The Impact of the New Deal on American Thought.* Chicago, 1969.

Hesseltine, William B. *The Rise and Fall of Third Parties from Antimasonry to Wallace.* Washington, D.C., 1948.

Schmidt, Karl M. *Henry A. Wallace: Quixotic Crusade, 1948.* Syracuse, 1960.

Shannon, David. *The Decline of American Communism: A History of the Common Party of the United States Since 1945.* New York, 1959.

Kirkendall, Richard. "The Presidential Election of 1948," *The American Scene,* vol. 2, New York, 1971.

THOMAS E. WATSON

Woodward, C. Vann. *Tom Watson: Agrarian Rebel.* New York, 1963.

JAMES B. WEAVER

Hayes, Fred E. *James Baird Weaver.* Iowa City, 1919.

DANIEL WEBSTER

Brown, Norman D. *Daniel Webster and the Politics of Availability.* Athens, Georgia, 1969.

Current, Richard N. *Daniel Webster and the Rise of National Conservatism.* Boston, 1955.

Fuess, Claude Moore. *Daniel Webster.* 2 vols. Hamden, Connecticut, 1963.

HUGH LAWSON WHITE

Bowers, C. J. *The Party Battles of the Jackson Period.* Boston, 1922.

Gresham, L. P. *The Public Career of Hugh Lawson White.* Nashville, 1945.

Adams, John Quincy. *The Diary of John Quincy Adams.* Edited by Allan Nevins. New York, 1951.

Sumner, W. G. *Andrew Jackson as a Public Man.* American Statesman Series. Boston, 1890.

Scott, Nancy. *A Memoir of Hugh Lawson White.* Philadelphia, 1856.

WENDELL WILLKIE

Dillon, Mary E. *Wendell Willkie, 1892-1944.* New York, 1952.

Johnson, Donald Bruce. *The Republican Party and Wendell Willkie.* Urbana, 1960.

WILLIAM WIRT

Kennedy, J. P. *Memoirs of the Life of William Wirt.* 2 vols. Philadelphia, 1849.

McCarthy, Charles. "Anti-Masonic Party," *American Historical Association Report.* Washington, D.C., 1902.

VICTORIA CLAFLIN WOODHULL

Johnston, Johanna. *Mrs. Satan: The Incredible Saga of Victoria C. Woodhull.* New York, 1967.

Wallace, Irving. *Nympho and Other Maniacs.* New York, 1971.

Election Statistics for Presidential Elections, 1789-1968

Individual	Dates	Party	Electoral	Popular
Election of 1789				
George Washington	1732-1799	None	69	n/r*
John Adams	1735-1826	None	34	n/r
John Jay	1745-1829	None	9	n/r
Robert H. Harrison	1745-1790	None	6	n/r
John Rutledge	1739-1800	None	6	n/r
John Hancock	1737-1793	None	4	n/r
George Clinton	1739-1812	None	3	n/r
Samuel Huntington	1731-1796	None	2	n/r
John Milton	1740-1804	None	2	n/r
James Armstrong	1748-1828	None	1	n/r
Edward Telfair	c.1735-1807	None	1	n/r
Benjamin Lincoln	1733-1810	None	1	n/r
Not voted			12	
Election of 1792				
George Washington	1732-1799	Federalist	132	n/r
John Adams	1735-1826	Federalist	77	n/r
George Clinton	1739-1812	Anti-Federalist	50	n/r
Thomas Jefferson	1743-1826	Anti-Federalist	4	n/r
Aaron Burr	1756-1836	Anti-Federalist	1	n/r
Election of 1796				
John Adams	1735-1826	Federalist	71	n/r
Thomas Jefferson	1743-1826	Democratic-Republican	68	n/r
Thomas Pinckney	1750-1828	Federalist	59	n/r

* n/r: vote not recorded.

Individual	Dates	Party	Electoral	Popular
Aaron Burr	1756-1836	Democratic-Republican	30	n/r
Samuel Adams	1722-1803	Democratic-Republican	15	n/r
Oliver Ellsworth	1745-1807	Federalist	11	n/r
George Clinton	1739-1812	Democratic-Republican	7	n/r
John Jay	1745-1829	Federalist	5	n/r
James Iredell	1751-1799	Federalist	3	n/r
Samuel Johnston	1733-1816	Federalist	2	n/r
George Washington	1732-1799	Federalist	2	n/r
John Henry	1750-1798	Federalist	2	n/r
Charles Cotesworth Pinckney	1746-1825	Federalist	1	n/r

Election of 1800
Thomas Jefferson	1743-1826	Democratic-Republican	73	n/r
Aaron Burr	1756-1836	Democratic-Republican	73	n/r
John Adams	1735-1826	Federalist	65	n/r
Charles Cotesworth Pinckney	1746-1825	Federalist	64	n/r
John Jay	1745-1829	Federalist	1	n/r

Election of 1804
Thomas Jefferson	1743-1826	Democratic-Republican	162	n/r
Charles Cotesworth Pinckney	1746-1825	Federalist	14	n/r

Election of 1808
James Madison	1751-1836	Democratic-Republican	122	n/r
Charles Cotesworth Pinckney	1746-1825	Federalist	47	n/r
George Clinton	1739-1812	Democratic-Republican	6	n/r
Not voted			1	

Election of 1812
James Madison	1751-1836	Democratic-Republican	128	n/r
DeWitt Clinton	1769-1828	Federalist	89	n/r
Not voted			1	

Election of 1816
James Monroe	1758-1831	Democratic-Republican	183	n/r
Rufus King	1755-1827	Federalist	34	n/r
Not voted			4	

Election of 1820
James Monroe	1758-1831	Democratic-Republican	231	n/r
John Quincy Adams	1767-1848	Democratic-Republican	1	n/r

Election of 1824
John Quincy Adams	1767-1848	Democratic-Republican	84	108,740
Andrew Jackson	1767-1845	Democratic-Republican	99	153,544

Individual	Dates	Party	Electoral	Popular
William Harris Crawford	1772-1834	Democratic-Republican	41	47,136
Henry Clay	1777-1852	Democratic-Republican	37	46,618
Election of 1828				
Andrew Jackson	1767-1845	Democrat	178	647,286
John Quincy Adams	1767-1848	National Republican	83	508,064
Election of 1832				
Andrew Jackson	1767-1845	Democrat	219	687,502
Henry Clay	1777-1852	National Republican	49	530,189
John Floyd	1783-1837	Independent Democrats	11	n/r
William Wirt	1772-1834	Anti-Masonic	7	101,051
Not voted			2	
Election of 1836				
Martin Van Buren	1782-1862	Democrat	170	762,678
William Henry Harrison	1773-1841	Anti-Masonic/Whig	73	549,508
Hugh Lawson White	1773-1840	Whig	26	145,352
Daniel Webster	1782-1852	Whig	14	41,287
Willie Person Mangum	1792-1861	Independent/Whig	11	n/r
Election of 1840				
William Henry Harrison	1773-1841	Whig	234	1,275,016
Martin Van Buren	1782-1862	Democrat	60	1,129,102
James G. Birney	1792-1857	Liberty (Prohibition)	0	7,069
Election of 1844				
James Knox Polk	1795-1849	Democrat	170	1,337,243
Henry Clay	1777-1852	Whig	105	1,299,062
James G. Birney	1792-1857	Liberty (Prohibition)	0	62,300
Election of 1848				
Zachary Taylor	1784-1850	Whig	163	1,360,099
Lewis Cass	1782-1866	Democrat	127	1,220,544
Martin Van Buren	1782-1862	Free Soil (Democrat)	0	291,263
Gerrit Smith	1797-1874	National Liberty/ Liberty League	0	2,733
Election of 1852				
Franklin Pierce	1804-1869	Democrat	254	1,601,474
Winfield Scott	1786-1866	Whig	42	1,386,580
John Parker Hale	1806-1873	Free Soil (Democrat)	0	155,285
Daniel Webster	1782-1852	Whig	0	7,407
— Broome	—	American	0	2,666
George Michael Troop	1780-1856	Southern Rights	0	2,300
Gerrit Smith	1797-1874	National Liberty	0	72

Individual	Dates	Party	Electoral	Popular
Election of 1856				
James Buchanan	1791-1868	Democrat	174	1,838,169
John C. Fremont	1813-1890	Republican	114	1,341,264
Millard Fillmore	1800-1874	American (Know Nothing)/ Whig	8	874,534
Gerrit Smith	1797-1874	Land Reform	0	484
Election of 1860				
Abraham Lincoln	1809-1865	Republican	180	1,866,452
John Cabell Breckinridge	1821-1875	Southern Democrat	72	847,953
John Bell	1797-1869	Constitutional Union	39	590,631
Stephen A. Douglas	1813-1861	Democrat	12	1,375,157
Election of 1864				
Abraham Lincoln	1809-1865	Republican	212	2,213,665
George Brinton McClellan	1826-1885	Democrat	21	1,805,237
Not voted (states of the Confederacy)			81	
Election of 1868				
Ulysses S. Grant	1822-1885	Republican	214	3,012,833
Horatio Seymour	1810-1886	Democrat	80	2,703,249
Not voted (unreconstructed states of Mississippi, Texas, Virginia)			26	
Election of 1872				
Ulysses S. Grant	1822-1885	Republican	286	3,597,132
Horace Greeley	1811-1872	Democrat/Liberal Republican	66*	2,834,125
Thomas A. Hendricks	1819-1885	Independent Democrat	42†	0
B. Gratz Brown	1826-1885	Democrat	18†	0
Charles Jones Jenkins	1805-1883	Democrat	2†	0
David Davis	1815-1886	Democrat	1†	0
Charles O'Conor	1804-1884	"Straight-out" Democrat	0	29,489
James Black	1823-1893	National Prohibition	0	5,608
Victoria Claflin Woodhull	1838-1927	People's Party (Equal Rights)	0	n/r
William Slocum Groesbeck	1815-1897	Independent Liberal Republican	0	n/r
Not counted			17	
Election of 1876				
Rutherford B. Hayes	1822-1893	Republican	185	4,036,298
Samuel Jones Tilden	1814-1886	Democrat	184	4,300,590
Peter Cooper	1791-1883	National Independent (Greenback)	0	81,737

* Votes scattered after Greeley's death, which occurred before the Electoral College met.
† Received votes of Greeley electors.

Individual	Dates	Party	Electoral	Popular
Green Clay Smith	1832-1892	Prohibition	0	9,522
James B .Walker	—	American National	0	2,508

Election of 1880

Individual	Dates	Party	Electoral	Popular
James A. Garfield	1831-1881	Republican	214	4,454,416
Winfield Scott Hancock	1824-1886	Democrat	155	4,444,952
James Baird Weaver	1833-1912	Greenback-Labor	0	308,578
Neal Dow	1804-1897	Prohibition	0	10,305
John Wolcott Phelps	—	American/Anti-Masonic	0	1,045

Election of 1884

Individual	Dates	Party	Electoral	Popular
[Stephen] Grover Cleveland	1837-1908	Democrat	219	4,874,986
James G. Blaine	1830-1893	Republican	182	4,851,981
Benjamin F. Butler	1818-1893	National Greenback/ Anti-Monopoly	0	175,370
John Pierce St. John	1833-1916	Prohibition	0	150,369
Belva Ann [Bennett] Lockwood	1830-1917	Equal Rights	0	4,149
Peter Dinwiddie Wigginton	1839-1909	American	0	n/r
Samuel Clark Pomeroy	1816-1891	American Prohibition National	0	n/r

Election of 1888

Individual	Dates	Party	Electoral	Popular
Benjamin Harrison	1833-1901	Republican	233	5,444,337
[Stephen] Grover Cleveland	1837-1908	Democrat	168	5,540,309
Clinton Bowen Fisk	1828-1890	Prohibition	0	249,506
Alson Jenness Streeter	—	Union Labor	0	146,935
Robert Hall Cowdrey	—	United Labor	0	2,818
James Langon Curtis	c.1820-1903	American	0	1,600
Belva Ann Bennett Lockwood	1830-1917	Equal Rights	0	n/r
Albert E. Redstone	—	Industrial Reform	0	n/r

Election of 1892

Individual	Dates	Party	Electoral	Popular
[Stephen] Grover Cleveland	1837-1908	Democrat	277	5,556,918
Benjamin Harrison	1833-1901	Republican	145	5,176,108
James Baird Weaver	1833-1912	People's (Populist)	22	1,041,028
John Bidwell	1819-1909	Prohibition	0	264,133
Simon Wing	1827-1911	Socialist-Labor	0	21,164

Election of 1896

Individual	Dates	Party	Electoral	Popular
William McKinley	1843-1901	Republican	271	7,104,779
William Jennings Bryan	1860-1925	Democrat/People's (Populist)	176	6,502,925
John McAuley Palmer	1817-1900	National Democrat	0	133,148
Joshua Levering	1845-1935	Prohibition	0	132,007
Charles H. Matchett	1843-1919	Socialist-Labor	0	36,274
Charles Eugene Bentley	1841-1905	Nationalist	0	13,969

Individual	Dates	Party	Electoral	Popular
Election of 1900				
William McKinley	1843-1901	Republican	292	7,207,923
William Jennings Bryan	1860-1925	Democrat	155	6,358,133
John Granville Woolley	1850-1922	Prohibition	0	208,914
Eugene Victor Debs	1855-1926	Social Democrat	0	87,814
Wharton Barker	1846-1921	People's (Populist)	0	50,373
Joseph Francis Maloney	1865-?	Socialist-Labor	0	39,739
Seth Hockett Ellis	1830-1904	Union Reform	0	5,698
Jonah Fitz Randolph Leonard	1832-?	United Christian	0	5,500
Job Harriman	—	Social Democrats of the U.S.A.	0	n/r
Election of 1904				
Theodore Roosevelt	1850-1919	Republican	336	7,623,486
Alton B. Parker	1852-1926	Democrat	140	5,077,911
Eugene Victor Debs	1855-1926	Socialist	0	402,283
Silas Comfort Swallow	1839-1930	Prohibition	0	258,536
Thomas Edward Watson	1856-1922	People's (Populist)	0	117,183
Charles Hunter Corregan	1860-1946	Socialist Labor	0	31,249
Austin Holcomb	—	Continental	0	1,000
George Edwin Taylor	—	National Liberty	0	n/r
Election of 1908				
William Howard Taft	1857-1930	Republican	321	7,677,908
Willim Jennings Bryan	1860-1925	Democrat	162	6,409,104
Eugene Victor Debs	1855-1926	Socialist	0	420,793
Eugene Wilder Chafin	1852-1920	Prohibition	0	253,840
Thomas Louis Hisgen	1858-1925	Independence	0	82,872
Thomas Edward Watson	1856-1922	People's (Populist)	0	29,100
August Gillhaus	—	Socialist-Labor	0	14,021
Daniel Braxton Turney	1848-1926	United Christian	0	500
Election of 1912				
[Thomas] Woodrow Wilson	1856-1924	Democrat	435	6,293,454
Theodore Roosevelt	1850-1919	Progressive (Bull Moose)	88	4,119,538
William Howard Taft	1857-1930	Republican	8	3,484,980
Eugene Victor Debs	1855-1926	Socialist	0	900,672
Eugene Wilder Chafin	1852-1920	Prohibition	0	206,275
Arthur Elmer Reimer	1882-?	Socialist-Labor	0	28,750
Election of 1916				
[Thomas] Woodrow Wilson	1856-1924	Democrat	277	9,129,606
Charles Evans Hughes	1862-1948	Republican	254	8,538,221
Allen Louis Benson	1871-1940	Socialist	0	585,113
James Franklin Hanly	1863-1920	Prohibition	0	220,506

Individual	Dates	Party	Electoral	Popular
Theodore Roosevelt	1850-1919	Progressive	0	35,034
Arthur Elmer Reimer	1882-?	Socialist-Labor	0	13,403
William Sulzer	—	American	0	n/r

Election of 1920

Warren G. Harding	1865-1923	Republican	404	16,152,200
James M. Cox	1870-1957	Democrat	127	9,147,353
Eugene Victor Debs	1855-1926	Socialist	0	919,799
Parley Parker Christensen	1869-1954	Farmer-Labor	0	265,411
Aaron Sherman Watkins	1863-1941	Prohibition	0	189,408
James Edward Ferguson	c.1871-1944	American	0	48,000
W[illiam] W[esley] Cox	1864-1948	Socialist-Labor	0	31,715
Robert Colvin MacCauley	—	Single Tax	0	5,837

Election of 1924

[John] Calvin Coolidge	1872-1933	Republican	382	15,725,016
John W. Davis	1873-1955	Democrat	136	8,386,503
Robert M. LaFollette	1855-1925	Progressive	13	4,822,856
Herman Preston Faris	1858-1936	Prohibition	0	57,520
Frank T. Johns	1889-1928	Socialist-Labor	0	36,428
William Z. Foster	1881-1961	Worker's (Communist)	0	36,386
Gilbert Owen Nations	c.1867-1950	American	0	23,967
William J. Wallace	—	Commonwealth Land	0	1,532
John Zahnd	1878-1961	National Independent (Greenback)	0	n/r
Jacob Sechler Coxey	1854-1951	Farmer-Labor	0	n/r

Election of 1928

Herbert Hoover	1874-1964	Republican	444	21,391,381
Alfred E. Smith	1873-1944	Democrat	87	15,016,443
Norman Thomas	1884-1969	Socialist	0	267,835
William Z. Foster	1881-1961	Worker's (Communist)	0	48,770
Verne L. Reynolds	c.1884-1959	Socialist-Labor	0	21,603
William Frederick Varney	1884-1960	Prohibition	0	20,106
Frank Elbridge Webb	1869-1949	Farmer-Labor	0	6,390
John Zahnd	1878-1961	National Independent (Greenback)	0	6,390

Election of 1932

Franklin Delano Roosevelt	1882-1945	Democrat	472	22,821,857
Herbert Hoover	1874-1964	Republican	59	15,761,841
Norman Thomas	1884-1969	Socialist	0	881,951
William Z. Foster	1881-1961	Worker's (Communist)	0	102,785
William David Upshaw	1866-1952	Prohibition	0	81,869

Individual	Dates	Party	Electoral	Popular
William Hope Harvey	1851-1936	Liberty	0	53,425
Verne L. Reynolds	c.1884-1959	Socialist-Labor	0	33,276
Jacob Sechler Coxey	1854-1951	Farmer-Labor	0	7,309
John Zahnd	1878-1961	National Independent (Greenback)	0	1,645
James R. Cox	c.1886-1951	Jobless	0	740

Election of 1936

Individual	Dates	Party	Electoral	Popular
Franklin Delano Roosevelt	1882-1945	Democrat	523	27,751,597
Alfred M. Landon	1887-	Republican	8	16,679,583
William Lemke	1878-1950	National Union	0	882,479
Norman Thomas	1884-1969	Socialist	0	187,720
Earl Russell Browder	1891-	Communist	0	80,159
David Leigh Colvin	1880-1959	Prohibition/National Prohibition/Commonwealth	0	37,847
John W. Aiken	1896-1968	Socialist-Labor	0	12,728
William Dudley Pelley	—	Christian	0	1,598
John Zahnd	1878-1961	National Independent (Greenback)	0	n/r

Election of 1940

Individual	Dates	Party	Electoral	Popular
Franklin Delano Roosevelt	1882-1945	Democrat	449	27,244,160
Wendell Willkie	1892-1944	Republican	82	22,305,198
Norman Thomas	1884-1969	Socialist	0	99,557
Roger Ward Babson	1875-1967	Prohibition	0	57,812
Earl Russell Browder	1891-	Communist	0	46,251
John W. Aiken	1896-1968	Socialist-Labor	0	14,883
Alfred Knutson	—	Independent	0	545
John Zahnd	1878-1961	National Independent (Greenback)	0	n/r
Anna Milburn	—	National Greenback	0	n/r

Election of 1944

Individual	Dates	Party	Electoral	Popular
Franklin Delano Roosevelt	1882-1945	Democrat	432	25,602,504
Thomas E. Dewey	1902-1971	Republican	99	22,006,285
Norman Thomas	1884-1969	Socialist	0	80,518
Claude A. Watson	1885-	Prohibition	0	74,758
Edward A. Teichert	1904-	Socialist-Labor	0	45,336
Harry F. Byrd	1887-1966	Southern Democrats	0	7,799
Gerald L. K. Smith	1898-	America First	0	1,780
Unpledged Texas Regulars				135,439

Individual	Dates	Party	Electoral	Popular
Election of 1948				
Harry S. Truman	1884-	Democrat	304	24,105,695
Thomas E. Dewey	1902-1971	Republican	189	21,969,170
J. Strom Thurmond	1902-	States' Rights (Dixiecrats)	38	1,169,021
Henry A. Wallace	1888-	Progressive/American Labor	0	1,156,103
Norman Thomas	1884-1969	Socialist	0	139,009
Claude A. Watson	1885-	Prohibition	0	103,216
Edward A. Teichert	1904-	Socialist-Labor	0	29,272
Farrell Dobbs	1907-	Socialist Workers/Militant Workers	0	13,613
Gerald L. K. Smith	1898-	Christian Nationalist Crusade	0	n/r
John G. Scott	c.1880-1953	Greenback	0	n/r
John Maxwell	—	Vegetarian	0	n/r
Election of 1952				
Dwight D. Eisenhower	1890-1969	Republican	442	33,824,351
Adlai E. Stevenson	1900-1965	Democrat	89	27,314,987
Vincent William Halliman	1896-	Progressive/American Labor	0	132,608
Stuart Hamblen	—	Prohibition	0	72,768
Eric Hass	1905-	Socialist-Labor	0	30,376
Darlington Hoopes	1896-	Socialist	0	18,322
Douglas A. MacArthur	1880-1964	America First	0	17,205
Farrell Dobbs	1907-	Socialist Workers/Militant Workers	0	8,956
Henry B. Krajewski	—	Poor Man's Party	0	4,203
Homer Aubrey Tomlinson	c.1892-1968	Church of God Bible Party	0	n/r
Frederick C. Proehl	—	Greenback	0	n/r
Ellen L. Jensen	—	Washington Peace	0	n/r
Daniel J. Murphy	—	American Vegetarian	0	n/r
Election of 1956				
Dwight D. Eisenhower	1890-1969	Republican	457	35,582,236
Adlai E. Stevenson	1900-1965	Democrat/Liberal	74	26,028,887
Walter B. Jones	c.1889-1963	——	1	0
T. Coleman Andrews	1899-	Independent States' Rights	0	275,915
Harry F. Byrd	1887-1966	Independent	0	134,157
Eric Hass	1905-	Socialist-Labor	0	44,368
Enoch Arden Holtwick	—	Prohibition	0	41,547
William Ezra Jenner	1908-	Texas Constitution	0	30,999
Farrell Dobbs	1907-	Socialist Workers/Militant Workers	0	7,805
Darlington Hoopes	1896-	Socialist	0	2,192
Henry B. Krajewski	—	American Third Party	0	1,892

Individual	Dates	Party	Electoral	Popular
Gerald L. K. Smith	1898-	Christian National	0	n/r
Homer Aubrey Tomlinson	c.1892-1968	Theocratic	0	n/r
Herbert M. Shelton	—	American Vegetarian	0	n/r
Frederick C. Proehl	—	Greenback	0	n/r
William Langer	c.1886-1959	Pioneer	0	n/r

Election of 1960

Individual	Dates	Party	Electoral	Popular
John F. Kennedy	1917-1963	Democrat	300	34,227,096
Richard M. Nixon	1913-	Republican	223	34,107,646
Harry F. Byrd	1887-1966	Independent	15	0
Orval Faubus	1910-	States' Rights	0	214,549
Eric Hass	1905-	Socialist-Labor	0	46,478
Rutherford L. Decker	—	Prohibition	0	42,483
Farrell Dobbs	1907-	Socialist Workers	0	39,541
Charles Loten Sullivan	—	Texas Constitution	0	18,169
Joseph Bracken Lee	1899-	Conservative Party of New Jersey	0	8,708
C. Benton Coiner	—	Conservative Party of Virginia	0	3,647
Lar Daly	—	Tax Cut	0	1,767
Clennon King	—	Afro-American	0	1,485
Merritt Barton Curtis	—	Independent/Constitution	0	1,240
Symon Gould	c 1887-1963	American Vegetarian	0	n/r
Whitney Hart Slocum	—	Greenback	0	n/r
Homer Aubrey Tomlinson	c.1892-1968	Theocratic	0	n/r
Byrd Unpledged Democrats				116,248

Election of 1964

Individual	Dates	Party	Electoral	Popular
Lyndon B. Johnson	1908-	Democrat	486	43,129,484
Barry M. Goldwater	1902-	Republican	82	27,178,188
Eric Hass	1905-	Socialist-Labor	0	45,219
Clifton DeBerry	—	Socialist Workers	0	32,720
Earle Harold Munn	—	Prohibition	0	23,267
John Kaspar	—	National States' Rights	0	6,953
Joseph B. Lightburn	—	Constitution	0	5,090
Kirby James Hensley	—	Universal	0	19
Homer Aubrey Tomlinson	c.1892-1968	Theocratic	0	n/r
T. Coleman Andrews	1899-	Independent States' Rights	0	n/r
Yette Bronstein	—	Best Party	0	n/r
D. X. B. Schwartz	—	National Tax Savers	0	n/r
Louis E. Jaeckel	—	American	0	n/r

Election of 1968

Individual	Dates	Party	Electoral	Popular
Richard M. Nixon	1913-	Republican	301	31,783,783
Hubert H. Humphrey	1911-	Democrat	191	31,271,839

Individual	Dates	Party	Electoral	Popular
George C. Wallace	1919-	American Independent	46	9,899,557
Henning A. Blomen	—	Socialist-Labor	0	52,588
Dick Gregory	1932-	Various Parties	0	47,133
Fred Halstead	—	Socialist Workers	0	41,389
Eldridge Cleaver	1935-	Peace and Freedom	0	36,385
Eugene J. McCarthy	1916-	New Party	0	25,858
Earle Harold Munn	—	Prohibition	0	15,123
Charlene Mitchell	—	Communist	0	1,075

Artists

EZRA AMES   Portrait and miniature painter; born Framingham, Massachusetts, 1768; died Albany, New York, 1836. Ames began his adult life as a furniture and carriage painter. By 1890, he had begun to paint miniatures, and in 1794 he produced his first oil portrait. He gained considerable prominence after the completion in 1812 of his full-length portrait of George Clinton, governor of New York.

HENRY BENBRIDGE   Portrait painter; born probably in Philadelphia, 1743; died 1812. Benbridge learned to paint in Philadelphia under the tutelage or in the ambience of John Wollaston, but his style was fully formed after study in Italy and in England. He spent the major part of his career painting the gentry of Charleston, South Carolina.

CLIFFORD KENNETH BERRYMAN   Cartoonist; born Versailles, Kentucky, 1869; died Washington, D.C., 1949. In the late 1880s, Berryman went to work as an illustrator of trademarks for the United States Patent Office in Washington, D.C. His interest in Washington politics led him to the drawing of cartoons; in 1907, he joined the staff of *The Washington Evening Star,* where he worked until his death. Originator of the "Teddy Bear" image, he won a Pulitzer Prize in 1944 for his cartoon "But Where Is The Boat Going?" which presented the World War II "manpower mobilization muddle."

ALVAH BRADISH   Portrait painter; born Sherburne, New York, 1806; died Detroit, 1901. Bradish spent the early part of his life in western New York, particularly the Buffalo area. Later, he went to Chicago, St. Paul, and Detroit. From 1852 to 1863, he was professor of art in the University of Michigan, and for many years he was one of Detroit's most successful portrait painters.

MATHEW B. BRADY   Daguerreotypist and photographer; born Warren County, New York, circa 1823; died New York City, 1896. In 1839, Brady met the struggling portrait artist, William Page, who encouraged him to start drawing and gave him lessons in portrait painting. Around 1840, Page introduced Brady to Samuel F. B. Morse who was experimenting at that moment with the daguerreotype and had just opened a school of photography. Brady enrolled in the school and was instructed by Morse and John W. Draper. In 1844, Brady opened his first studio in New York City. The following year, he began his grand scheme of collecting portraits of all the notable individuals of his day, a project which culminated in the publication of *The Gallery of Distinguished Americans* (1850). Brady is best remembered for his photographic documentation of the Civil War.

HENRY KIRKE BROWN Sculptor and portrait painter; born Leyden, Massachusetts, 1819; died Newburgh, New York, 1886. Brown received his training in Chester Harding's studio. His original intention was to become a portrait painter; but after moving to Cincinnati in 1856, he found that he preferred sculpture as a medium. His most impressive work, the Union Square statue of Washington in New York City, was unveiled in 1856.

JOY BUBA Sculptress; born Huntington, Long Island, New York, 1904. Mrs. Buba studied sculpture in Paris, Milan, and New York where she now lives.

DOUGLAS CHANDOR Portrait painter; born Surrey, England, 1897; died Weatherford, Texas, 1953. During lulls in his World War I army service, Chandor tried his hand at portraiture. At the war's end, he studied art at the Slade School in London. In 1926, he emigrated to the United States where he became an established portraitist. Among the many famous contemporaries he painted were Franklin D. Roosevelt and Herbert Hoover.

WILLIAM BROWN COOPER Portrait painter; born Smith County, Tennessee, 1811; died Chattanooga, Tennessee, 1900. Worked in Tennessee and the Mississippi Valley (Knoxville, Natchez, and New Orleans). He used the same signature (W. B. Cooper) as his brother, Washington Bogart.

AARON CORWINE Portrait painter; born Maysville, Kentucky, 1802; died Philadelphia, 1830. After some training from an itinerant artist, Corwine went to Philadelphia where he studied under Thomas Sully. In 1820, he settled in Cincinnati where he realized great success as a portraitist. His sitters included Andrew Jackson and the Marquis de Lafayette.

AARON E. DARLING Darling is known to have worked in Springfield and Chicago, Illinois, 1865–1870.

JO DAVIDSON Sculptor; born New York City, 1883; died Tours, France, 1952. Davidson was a student of both George de Forest Brush and Hermon A. McNeil. His works include busts of George Clemenceau, Woodrow Wilson, and Walt Whitman. After World War I, he was selected to make bronze busts of the Allied leaders.

JOHN DOCTOROFF Portrait painter; born 1893; died 1970. Doctoroff studied at Cooper Union in New York City. His works include portraits of Herbert Hoover, Alfred M. Landon, and Wendell Willkie; the latter two were commissioned by the Republican Committee and served as presidential campaign portraits.

JAMES EARLE Portrait painter; born Paxton, Massachusetts, 1761; died Charleston, South Carolina, 1796. Brother of Ralph Earle, who has been called the "best portrait-painter in Connecticut" and the uncle of Ralph E. W. Earle, portraitist and protégé of Andrew Jackson. Earle received his training in London and there attained some distinction as a portrait painter. Most of his American work was done in Charleston. During his short career, many of his contemporaries ranked him with Copley, Trumbull, and West, and particularly lauded his ability to portray eyes.

CORNELIA ADELE FASSETT Portrait, figure, and miniature painter; born Owasco, New York, 1831; died Washington, D.C., 1898. Mrs. Fassett studied art in both New York and Paris. In 1875, she moved from Chicago to Washington where she painted numerous portraits of prominent Amer-

505

icans as well as group pictures of the Electoral Commission of 1877 and the Supreme Court of 1876.

MOLLY GUION   Portrait painter; born 1910. Miss Guion received her early training at the Grand Central Art School and the Art Student's League. Later, she studied portraiture under Dimitri Romanovsky and Gregory Gluckman. She is best known for her series of portraits of British officials entitled "Tradition and Pageantry in Britain."

CHESTER HARDING   Portrait painter; born Conway, New Hampshire, 1792; died Boston, Massachusetts, 1866. After a varied career as soldier, sign painter, and tavern keeper, about 1818 Harding settled as a self-schooled portrait painter in Paris, Kentucky. He rapidly developed his talent for portraiture and sold his paintings with phenomenal success. From 1823 to 1826, he was a social favorite in London, England. He returned to America in 1826 and settled in Springfield, Massachusetts. During his career, he painted more than a thousand portraits.

GEORGE PETER ALEXANDER HEALY   Portrait and historical painter; born Boston, Massachusetts, 1813; died Chicago, Illinois, 1894. Although untrained as a portrait painter, Healy opened a studio in Boston when only eighteen years old and earned enough money to go to Europe in 1834. He studied under Baron Gros in France and went on to paint many of the great Europeans of his day. He returned to America in 1844 where he painted a series of portraits of United States presidents and statesmen. Noted for his rapid execution, he painted about a hundred portraits a year. From 1867 to 1892 he lived in Paris, but spent his last years in Chicago.

MALVINA HOFFMAN   Sculptress; born New York City, 1885; died New York City, 1966. A student of Auguste Rodin, Miss Hoffman enjoyed wide critical acclaim in the United States and Europe. Among her most notable works were her 101 life-size bronze statues of the races of man commissioned by the Field Museum of Chicago.

NELLIE MATHES HORNE   Painter; born Eliot, Maine, 1870; died ?.

WILLIAM JAMES HUBARD   Silhouettist and portrait painter; born Whitchurch, Shropshire, England, 1807; died Richmond, Virginia, 1862. Exploited as a child prodigy for his ability to cut silhouettes, Hubard was brought to America by his manager in 1824. After three years, he was encouraged by Gilbert Stuart and Thomas Sully to give up silhouettes for oil painting. By 1830, he had acquired a reputation for small full-length portraits of American statesmen. From 1838 to 1841 he studied art in Europe. In the early 1850s, his interest turned to sculpture, and he opened a foundry in Richmond for casting bronzes.

DANIEL HUNTINGTON   Portrait, figure, and landscape painter; born New York City, 1816; died New York (?), 1906. After attending Yale College for a year, Huntington entered Hamilton College in Clinton, New York in 1832. Here, he met painter Charles Loring Elliott, who had come to Hamilton to solicit commissions for student's portraits. Influenced by Elliott, Huntington determined to become a painter and, in 1836, he returned to New York City where he became the student of Samuel F. B. Morse. Still later, he studied under Henry Inman. While devoting much of his time to portraiture, he also painted many works with narrative and historical themes.

HENRY INMAN   Portrait, genre, and landscape painter; born Utica, New York, 1801; died Kentucky, 1846. A pupil of John Wesley Jarvis for seven years, Inman settled in New York City where he became one of the city's most fashionable portrait painters. In 1845, he was commissioned by Congress to execute a series of historical paintings for the Capitol; while working on the first of these in Kentucky where he had gone to copy the cabin of Daniel Boone, he died.

JOHN WESLEY JARVIS   Portrait painter, miniaturist and engraver; born South Shields, England, 1780; died New York City, 1840. Brought to this country as an infant, Jarvis and his family originally settled in Philadelphia. After serving an apprenticeship with engraver Edward Savage and receiving instruction from some minor Philadelphia artists, he went to New York where he became a miniature painter and engraver. Soon, Jarvis began to paint oil portraits; by 1814, he was one of the most accomplished portrait painters in the country—a reputation he enjoyed until the 1830s. Among his best work is the series of portraits of heroes of the War of 1812 which he painted for the City of New York. In later years, Jarvis' skills began to wane. In 1834, after suffering a paralytic stroke, his career came to an end.

DAVID CLAYPOOLE JOHNSTON   Engraver, lithographer, and actor; born Philadelphia, 1799; died Dorchester, Massachusetts, 1865. Having served an apprenticeship to Francis Kearney, Philadelphia engraver, Johnston began to produce social caricatures. Although several of his subjects demanded that their pictures be removed from the windows of bookstores, his engravings were for the most part very popular. After a short career as an actor, he settled in Boston where he again took up engraving and lithography. During these years, he illustrated many books and for several years issued a series of comic sketches entitled *Scraps.* One of his last works was *The House That Jeff Built,* a graphic satire on Jefferson Davis.

EASTMAN JOHNSON   Genre and portrait painter; born Lowell, Maine, 1824; died New York City, 1906. Johnson began his career at the age of sixteen in John Bufford's lithographic shop in Boston. Disliking lithography, he took up crayon portraiture and worked with great success from 1841 to 1849 as a portraitist. After two years of studying with Emanuel Leutze in Düsseldorf, Germany, he studied for almost four years at The Hague. There he was known as the "American Rembrandt" and was offered the post of Court Painter. He returned to America in 1855, traveled throughout the South studying Negro life for his genre paintings, and settled finally in New York in 1859.

JOSEPH B. KAHILL   Portrait painter; born Alexandria, Egypt, 1882; died Portland, Maine, 1957. After studying art in Paris, Kahill made his home in Portland, Maine. In the 1930s, he was commissioned by the Maine State Museum Commission to paint portraits of several Maine governors.

ROLLIN KIRBY   Cartoonist; born Galva, Illinois, 1875; died 1952. After studying in New York, Kirby went to Paris where he studied for a time with James McNeill Whistler. In 1911, he abandoned his career as a painter to become a cartoonist. A three-time winner of the Pulitzer Prize, he enjoyed wide popularity during the twenties and thirties.

TRAFFORD P. KLOTS   Portrait and landscape painter; born Rome, Italy. Klots, the son of portrait painter Alfred Partridge Klots, received his art training in Rome, Paris, London, and New York. He now maintains a studio and home in Baltimore and in Brittany, France, and was recently awarded the Legion of Honor by the French government for his landscapes.

DANIEL KRAMER   Photo journalist; born 1932. Kramer has done work for most of the nation's major magazines. One of his most notable works is his "Photographic Essay of Bob Dylan."

ADRIAN LAMB   Portrait painter and copyist; born New York City, 1901. After four years at the Art Students' League in New York City, Lamb spent several years studying in Paris.

JAMES REID LAMBDIN   Portrait and miniature painter; born Pittsburgh, Pennsylvania, 1807; died Philadelphia, 1889. After about two years of study with Edward Miles and Thomas Sully, Lambdin returned to Pittsburgh as a portrait painter and proprietor of an art gallery and museum of natural history. In 1832, seeking more favorable prospects, he went to Kentucky. Disappointed, he spent the next few years as an itinerant portrait painter and in 1837 settled permanently in Philadelphia. Among his works are portraits of every president from John Quincy Adams to James Garfield.

PHILLIP DE LASZLO   Portrait painter; born Hungary, 1869; died, England, 1937; de Laszlo made his reputation as the painter of kings, presidents, and men of wealth. After studying painting in Budapest and Munich, he went to Paris where he attended l'Académie Julien. By age 24, his abilities as a portrait painter had won him fame. In 1912, Austrian Emperor Franz Joseph recognized his skill by according the artist an hereditary title. In his own day, critics were divided on the quality of his work. Some claimed his portraits gave "rare insight" into character, while others felt they represented "brilliant impersonations" of their subjects. Many prominent Americans sat for de Laszlo including Woodrow Wilson, Warren G. Harding, Charles Evans Hughes and Elihu Root.

LOUIS LUPAS   Portrait painter. Lupas has painted portraits of many prominent national leaders.

ROBERT MacCAMERON   Portrait and figure painter; born Chicago, 1866; died New York, 1912. MacCameron gained much of his training at the Ecole des Beaux Arts in Paris. Anxious that his work have a social influence, he painted emotionally moving pictures depicting the life of the poor. In later years, he turned to portraiture.

CHARLES MacNELLY   Portrait painter; born 1920. Publisher of the *Saturday Evening Post* from 1961-1964, MacNelly has been a professional artist since the mid-sixties, working primarily out of New York City. He has painted portraits of Omar Bradley, Jimmy Durante, and Robert Finch.

NICOLA MARSCHALL   Portrait painter; born Prussia, 1829; died Louisville, Kentucky, 1917. Designer of the Confederate "Stars and Bars" Marschall first studied art in the capitals of Europe. Emigrating to America in 1849, he settled in Marion, Alabama, where he earned his living as a teacher of art and foreign languages. During the Civil War, he served as a draughtsman in the Confederate corps of engineers.

LOUIS MAYER   Sculptor; born Milwaukee, Wisconsin, 1869; died 1969. Mayer received his training from Max Thedy in Weimar, Germany, and later studied at l'Académie Julien in Paris. He has sculpted busts of many notable Americans, including Theodore Roosevelt, Norman Thomas, and Robert LaFollette.

SAMUEL F. B. MORSE   Portrait and landscape painter, inventor; born Charlestown, Massachusetts, 1791; died New York City, 1872. While attending Yale College between 1805 and 1810, Morse's early artistic efforts attracted the approval of Washington Allston and Gilbert Stuart. In 1811, he accompanied Allston to England. Allston subsequently became his teacher in London. Returning to this country four years later, Morse established a studio in Boston. After settling in New York around 1825, Morse soon enjoyed wide prominence as a portrait painter and landscapist. One of his most formidable undertakings was his work *The House of Representatives,* completed in 1822, in which he portrayed eighty-six of the nation's lawmakers. In 1826, he helped found the National Academy of Design. Always mechanically inclined, Morse succeeded in 1836 in devising the first workable telegraph, an accomplishment which for a time overshadowed his reputation as an artist.

THOMAS NAST   Caricaturist; born Landau, Bavaria, 1840; died Guayaquil, Ecuador, 1902. Brought to New York City as a child, Nast demonstrated his love for drawing early. After study at the Academy of Design in New York, he worked for several publications. During the Civil War, he became staff artist for *Harper's Weekly* where his work as a Union propagandist earned him much praise from Lincoln. After the war, his cartoons came to wield "terrible" power. In 1868, President Grant claimed that the "pencil of Nast" had been largely responsible for his election. Similarly, in 1872, friends of Horace Greeley claimed that it was Nast's acid cartoons that led to Greeley's presidential defeat and subsequent death. Nast's last cartoon appeared in 1886, at which time he decided to try his hand at newspaper editing.

BASS OTIS   Portrait painter, engraver, and lithographer; born Bridgewater, Massachusetts, 1784; died Philadelphia, 1858. Otis received his early training in painting from a coach painter. He began his career as a portraitist in New York City in 1808. Later, he moved to Philadelphia where he became known for several of his copies of portraits of distinguished Americans. Otis' chief claim to fame lies in the fact that he made the first lithograph in America.

PRINCESS LWOFF-PARLAGHY   Portrait and still-life painter; born Hungary, 1864; died New York, 1923. Trained at the National School of Design in Hungary, Princess Lwoff-Parlaghy enjoyed great vogue as a portraitist at the turn of the century. Popular in both Europe and America, her works included portraits of Kaiser Wilhelm, Otto Von Bismarck, Andrew Carnegie, and Henry Ford.

CHARLES WILLSON PEALE   Portrait and miniature painter, naturalist, and museum founder; born Maryland, 1741; died Philadelphia, 1827. After studying under John Singleton Copley and later Benjamin West, Peale began his career as a painter and miniaturist. While serving as an officer in the Revolutionary War, he painted many portraits of fellow officers. After the war, he established a museum in Philadelphia which housed, in addition to many of his portraits, an extensive collection of animal specimens. In 1805, he helped found the Pennsylvania Academy of Fine Arts.

REMBRANDT PEALE   Portrait, miniature, and historical painter; born Bucks County, Pennsylvania, 1778; died Philadelphia, 1860. The son of Charles Willson Peale, Rembrandt Peale painted his first portrait at the age of thirteen. After attending the Royal Academy in London, he settled in Philadelphia and later moved to Baltimore where he established Peale's Museum. In 1825, he was elected president of the American Academy of Fine Arts in New York.

GEORGE EDWARD PERINE   Portrait engraver; born South Orange, New Jersey, 1837; died Brooklyn, New York, 1858.

CLINTON PETERS   No information available.

BENJAMIN FRANKLIN REINHART   Historical, genre, and portrait painter; borne Waynesburg, Pennsylvania, 1829; died Philadelphia, 1885. Having begun to paint when he was sixteen, Reinhart received his formal training at the National Academy of Design. His great ambition was to be a painter of historical themes; however, he soon found that portrait painting offered a better means of support. During the Civil War, he lived in England where he painted many portraits of the nobility. In this country, his clients included several presidents as well as many other prominent statesmen.

EDWARD V. RUNCI   No information available.

CHARLES-BALTHAZAR-JULIEN-FEVRET SAINT-MEMIN   Profilist, crayon and watercolor portraitist, landscape painter and engraver; born France, 1770; died France, 1852. Driven from France by the Revolution, Saint-Memin settled with his family in New York where he began his career as a painter. Best known for his profile portrait engravings of distinguished Americans, he is said to have been the last artist to have executed a life portrait of George Washington.

B. FRANK SAYLOR   Commercial photographer, Lancaster, Pennsylvania.

JULIAN SCOTT   Historical and portrait painter; born Johnson, Vermont, 1846; died Plainfield, New Jersey, 1901. After serving in the Civil War, Scott entered the National Academy of Design in New York and finished his studies in Paris. He worked for a while under Emanuel Leutze. One of his best known pictures, *The Rear Guard at White Oak Swamp,* hangs in the State House at Montpelier, Vermont.

EDWARD SELMAR SIEBERT   Portrait and figure painter; born Washington, D.C., 1856; died Rochester, New York, 1944. Siebert received his training from German artists, Carl Hoff and William von Diez.

GILBERT STUART   Portrait painter; born Rhode Island, 1755; died Boston, 1828. Stuart first won recognition for his work in England where he had gone to study under Benjamin West. The success of his first life portrait of Washington (1795) established him as a leading American portrait painter; in the succeeding years, he painted portraits of many of the nation's most prominent leaders. Stuart's best portraits offer great visual insight into the character of his sitters.

JANE STUART   Portrait painter; born Boston, 1812; died Newport, Rhode Island, 1888. Daughter of Gilbert Stuart, she collaborated with her father on many portraits and after his death, devoted much of her effort to reproducing many of her father's paintings, especially his portraits of Washington.

DUNCAN STYLES   Portrait and landscape painter.

THOMAS SULLY   Portrait painter; born England, 1783; died Philadelphia, 1872. Sully was hailed by many of his contemporaries as the greatest portrait painter of his day. Arriving in the United States in 1792 from England, he received some instruction in miniature painting from his brother,

Lawrence. In Boston, Gilbert Stuart allowed him to observe his painting techniques. In 1810, Sully left for further study in London under Benjamin West and the famous British portraitist, Sir Thomas Lawrence. Returning to this country in 1810, he settled in Philadelphia where in the ensuing years, he enjoyed much popularity. Called "The Lawrence of America," his portraits, especially of women and children, were noted for their "innocence and happiness."

ROBERT TEMPLETON   Portrait and landscape painter; born Red Oak, Iowa, 1927. Templeton received his training at the Kansas City Institute. He has painted several murals for the United States Army as well as portraits of many prominent Americans.

BENJAMIN TROTT   Portrait and miniature painter; born Boston, circa 1770; died Washington, D.C., 1843. Self-taught, Trott set himself up as a painter in New York City in 1791 and later moved to Philadelphia to make miniatures after the portraits of Gilbert Stuart. A friend of Stuart and Thomas Sully, he particularly distinguished himself in the painting of miniatures.

STEPHEN A. DOUGLAS VOLK   Portrait and landscape painter; born Pittsburgh, Massachusetts, 1856; died Fryeburg, Maine, 1935. Volk received his art education in Rome and Paris. After teaching in Cooper Institute for a number of years, he helped organize the Minneapolis School of Fine Arts. Among his more noted portraits were those of King Albert of Belgium and Lloyd George, both of which he painted at the end of World War I.

SAMUEL LOVETT WALDO   Portrait painter; born Windham, Connecticut, 1783; died New York City, 1861. After study in London, Waldo settled in New York City in 1809. Here, he met with moderate success as a painter and in 1826 helped found the National Academy of Design.

ADOLPH ALEXANDER WEINMAN   Sculptor; born Germany, 1870; died 1952. A student of Philip Martiny and assistant to Augustus Saint-Gaudens and Daniel C. French, Weinman was noted for the work he did for many of the nation's public buildings. In addition to executing the exterior sculpture of the New York Municipal Building, he also carved the frieze for the United States Supreme Court Room and the pediment of the National Archives.

JULIAN ALDEN WEIR   Portrait, landscape, and figure painter; born West Point, New York, 1852; died New York City, 1919. J. Alden Weir received his early training from his father, Robert Weir. Later studying in Paris, he came under the influence of Impressionists Monet and Pissarro. At the turn of the century, he identified himself with The Ten, a group of Americans who derived their styles from late nineteenth-century French painting.

IRVING RAMSAY WILES   Portrait, figure, genre, and landscape painter; born Utica, New York, 1861; died Long Island, 1948. Wiles received his training from his father, Lemuel Wiles, in New York and in Paris where he also trained under Lefebvre Carolus-Duran.

GRANT WOOD   Painter and sculptor; born Anamosa, Iowa, 1892; died Iowa City, 1942. Wood took his training at the Chicago Art Institute and the Minneapolis Handicraft School of Design. A portrayer of Iowa rural life, he drew wide acclaim for his effective characterization of rural subjects.

Photographic Credits

Photographs have been provided by owners or lending institutions or from National Portrait Gallery negatives. Specific photographic acknowledgments are as follows: Alt-Lee, Charleston, South Carolina (Thomas Pinckney); The Frick Art Reference Library, New York, New York (Charles C. Pinckney, Rufus King, and Peter Cooper); Monaco Studio, Oneida, New York (Gerrit P. Smith); John P. Adams, Dover, New Hampshire (John P. Hale); New-York Historical Society, New York (Victoria C. Woodhull); Geoffrey Clements, New York, New York (Charles Evans Hughes and Thomas E. Dewey); Ron Austin, Madison, Wisconsin (Robert M. LaFollette); Daniel Kramer, New York, New York (Earl Browder); Harris and Ewing, Washington, D.C. (William Lemke); Henry A. Wallace by permission of Associated American Artists.

★ U.S. GOVERNMENT PRINTING OFFICE : 1975 O—576-758